I0816551

SMALL BUT IMPORTANT RIOTS

SMALL but IMPORTANT RIOTS

The Cavalry Battles of Aldie, Middleburg, and Upperville

ROBERT F. O'NEILL

Potomac Books
AN IMPRINT OF THE UNIVERSITY OF NEBRASKA PRESS

An earlier version of appendix C was previously published as "Gettysburg Horses," *America's Civil War,* May 2020.

 Potomac Books is an imprint of the University of Nebraska Press.
Manufactured in the United States of America.

Library of Congress Cataloging-in-Publication Data
Names: O'Neill, Robert F., author.
Title: Small but important riots : the cavalry battles of Aldie, Middleburg, and Upperville / Robert F. O'Neill.
Other titles: Cavalry battles of Aldie, Middleburg, and Upperville. | Cavalry battles of Aldie, Middleburg, and Upperville
Description: Lincoln : Potomac Books, an imprint of the University of Nebraska Press, [2023] | Includes bibliographical references and index.
Identifiers: LCCN 2022017632
ISBN 9781640125476 (hardback)
ISBN 9781640125674 (epub)
ISBN 9781640125681 (pdf)
Subjects: LCSH: Virginia—History—Civil War, 1861–1865—Cavalry operations. | Aldie, Battle of, Va., 1863. | Middleburg, Battle of, Va., 1863. | Upperville, Battle of, Va., 1863. | United States—History—Civil War, 1861–1865—Cavalry operations. | BISAC: HISTORY / United States / Civil War Period (1850–1877)
Classification: LCC E475.5 .056 2023 | DDC 973.7/34—dc23/eng/20220822
LC record available at https://lccn.loc.gov/2022017632

Set in New Baskerville ITC Pro by Mikala R. Kolander.

Dedicated to my parents, Joan and Bob O'Neill,
and to
Horace Mewborn, Marshall Krolick, and Charlie Doutt.
Fiddler's Green is better for their presence.

CONTENTS

ILLUSTRATIONS

FIGURES

Following page 142

MAPS

PREFACE

In the years since Harold Howard first published *Aldie, Middleburg and Upperville, Small but Important Riots*, I have held the battlefields and the men who fought on those fields in mid-June 1863 close. The book you hold is new in every respect, from the first page to the last. Nearly thirty years of continuing research into the events that transpired in and around the Loudoun Valley in the critical days between June 10 and June 27 have convinced me to reconsider the judgments and conclusions I reached years ago. In this new book, I correct errors, timeworn assumptions and interpretations, and offer new explanations and conclusions.

Over the years I continued to mine repositories for diaries, letters, memoirs, and recollections, but the larger battles at Brandy Station and Gettysburg, which bookend the fights at Aldie, Middleburg and Upperville, dominated the memories of soldiers trying to describe the momentous events of June and July 1863. The advent of digitized newspaper archives has brought many new accounts to light in recent years, but no source has proved more critical to understanding the fighting in the Loudoun Valley than the contemporary military records held by the National Archives.

The editors of the Official Records had a staggering task, deciding what documents should or should not be included in the published records. They sifted countless thousands of telegrams, letters, orders, reports, and other documents, including some and excluding others. Their decisions continue to influence many of the conclusions we hold regarding the war. Over several decades, I examined many of the documents excluded from the Official Records, and read more than three hundred pension applications from men wounded in the fighting or from family members of those killed in the Loudoun Valley. In time, a new story emerged.

The story begins with Brig. Gen. Alfred Pleasonton, arguably the most polarizing officer in the Union Cavalry Corps. No officer's role in the Loudoun Valley has been more misunderstood or more misrepresented.

ACKNOWLEDGMENTS

I first wrote this story nearly thirty years ago, and twenty-five years later I set out to write the story again. Much has changed. Friends, mentors, and most importantly, my parents, have passed on. My memory of events thirty years ago has dimmed, but I hope to acknowledge most everyone who has in some way, large or small, contributed to the work you hold in your hand. My understanding of the events in the Loudoun Valley in June 1863 is better because of each of them.

I am especially grateful for the one constant in my life all these years, my wife, Teresa. She has been with me at every turn and helped me over every hurdle. As I have said in the past, she has made and continues to make sacrifices so I can chase my dreams. Her investigative skills with census and land records helped me to positively identify the property where Colonel Duffie's First Rhode Island spent the night of June 17 and where the regiment met its demise the next morning. She will always be first and foremost rather than "last but not least."

William Miller very graciously agreed to look over my manuscript. With a vast well of patience, Bill improved my writing style and offered suggestions that I was slow to appreciate. His knowledge of the war is as vast as his well of patience. He has read most every word, offered sage advice, and corrected errors. I owe him a debt I cannot repay.

Spread across the country as they are, every member of my immediate family has, over the years, contributed to seeing this project to completion, not just once but twice.

Many years ago, the late Marshall Krolick put me in contact with several folks who made everything else possible.

The late Elden "Josh" Billings had the most remarkable personal library I had ever seen at the time, and he shared his volumes freely and generously.

At times before their passing, John and Mac Divine must have felt like they had adopted me, or I had adopted them. John first introduced me to the battlefields and, like Marshall, to many of the folks listed below.

The late Harold Howard took a chance on an untried author and gave me the opportunity to write the first dedicated study of the battles at Aldie, Middleburg, and Upperville for his Virginia Civil War Battles and Leaders Series.

I found the National Archives an intimidating repository the few times I ventured through the doors while working on the first edition. In the years that followed, Mike Musick, then the dean of Civil War records, broke the code, so to speak, on what can appear to be a baffling and arcane filing system established years ago. Mike answered numerous questions and truly opened the doors of this national treasure to me. Though he has been retired now for many years, Mike still answers questions and meets me in Washington from time to time to help solve yet another riddle. My continuing research in the archives convinced me to tackle this revision and many staff members have given freely of their time and knowledge to facilitate my time there.

After retiring to Eastern North Carolina, the late Horace Mewborn spent untold hours poring through war-date local newspapers and sent me many firsthand accounts that have enhanced my work. His knowledge of Southern cavalry in the Eastern Campaigns was second to none and he shared his knowledge freely. Like John Divine, Josh Billings, and others, Horace had an incomparable library that he shared freely, encouraging me repeatedly to examine every piece of paper in his files or book on his shelf to enhance my own work.

The acknowledged authority on all things related to the Civil War in Culpeper County, Clark "Bud" Hall has opened his files for me many times. His knowledge of events, people, and places in Culpeper County is unquestioned and our time together has always been rewarding.

I first met John Hennessy in the early-1980s, when he agreed to look over my first article for publication. Like so many others, John immediately made his own research materials available to me. The acknowledged authority on the Union armies in the Eastern Theater, John improved this manuscript with his suggestions and sage advice.

I met Dave Roth, owner of *Blue & Gray Magazine*, in 1993 when he published my article on the battles in the Loudoun Valley to closely coincide with the release of my book. In the years since, we have spent many hours tramping battlefields in Virginia, Montana, and Wyoming, and relaxed in his favorite watering hole, his own Big Apple Bar. He and his wife, Karen, always welcome me to their home, when I travel between Virginia and Detroit, and I always leave in better spirits than when I arrived.

I met Robert E. L. Krick at the Richmond Battlefield Headquarters many years ago while working on another project. Bobby gave the manuscript a critical read and his wife, Julie, created all the maps for the book from my crude sketches. Robert K. Krick, invited me to his home to peruse his one-of-a-kind personal library. Though neither father nor son have much interest in "horsey-stuff," as they like to remind me, they have filled my inbox with a welcome bounty of scarce source material many times.

Andrew German is the authority on the First Pennsylvania Cavalry, but he has also reenacted cavalry for many years. Civil War cavalry manuals baffle me, and I have repeatedly turned to Andy for help. For several years, he has patiently given me a greater appreciation of how cavalry operated on the march and in battle.

Andy introduced me to Dr. Charles Plummer in Auburn, Maine. Doctor Plummer is a descendent of Lt. Ephraim Taylor, First Maine, and he provided copies of several of Taylor's letters and diary entries.

Andy also did yeoman work on my behalf, contacting several friends who graciously offered or provided images for the book, including Ken Lawrence, Richard Carlile, Kyle Stetz, and Stephen Heinstrom. Davis Brinson, county manager for Duplin County, North Carolina, allowed me to photograph and publish the image of Capt. William Houston that hangs in the Duplin County Courthouse, and Judge Louis Foy facilitated access to the Houston painting.

Dan Murphy, another cavalry reenactor, has also helped me to appreciate how cavalry functioned in 1863. He and Andy, as well as the late Tim Kerlin, have moved the horse-soldiers from tidy squares on nice clean maps to the dirty, dusty fields of 1863 and given me a much better appreciation for the life of a real trooper.

Likewise, reenactors Norm Hoerer, Bill Scott, and the late Charlie Doutt invited me to participate in a cavalry ride on the Aldie battlefield in 2019. A cavalryman I am not, but I found the experience enjoyable and educational, and I hope some small bit of what these troopers have tried to teach me has enhanced the story you are about to read.

I met the late Tommy Stokes, then the owner of Ayrshire farm in Upperville, shortly after the first edition came out. On a visit to his farm, I met his son Claiborne. Over the next several years, I discussed and debated the fight along Trappe Road with Claiborne and the late Welby Kenny many times. Their letters provide a wealth of information about the homes and farms around Trappe Road. Though now living in Mobile, Alabama, Claiborne's enthusiasm for my project has never wavered.

Many residents of the Loudoun Valley have welcomed me over the years and allowed me access to their property. Mr. and Mrs. Chet Moore, Mrs. Billie Van Pay, John Zugschwert, Rick Collette, Lucy Brown Armstrong, Anne McLeod, Harriet Condon, and Henry Plaster are just a few who have come to my aid many times.

Seeking to thwart threats to the battlefields, several local groups formed or supported the efforts of others, including the Loudoun and Fauquier Garden Club, Snickersville Turnpike Association, Mount Zion Church Preservation Association, Atoka Preservation Society, the Virginia Outdoors Foundation, and the

Mosby Heritage Area Association, to name a few. Over the years the Mosby Heritage Area Association (now the Virginia Piedmont Heritage Area), helmed at the time by the indomitable Childs Burden, has produced recorded driving tours of the battlefields, as well as signage at key points. The equally indomitable Paul Ziluca chaired the Citizen's Committee for the Historic Cavalry Battles of Aldie, Middleburg, and Upperville. In cooperation with local government officials and David Lowe of the National Park Service, the committee mapped the battlefields and established roadside pull-offs at key points to aid access and interpretation. Throughout these efforts, the late Deborah Fitts worked tirelessly to raise public awareness of the ongoing threats to these historic places and properties.

NOVA Parks now administers five parks related to the battles. Tracy Gillespie, who oversees the parks, has researched and answered every question I ever sent her over many years. She also gives tirelessly of her time to ensure tour groups have ready access to properties like Mount Zion Church and Mount Defiance. Likewise, her husband, Richard, has helped me on numerous occasions.

Local historian Wynne Saffer has created two amazing documents outlining property boundaries and identifying property owners in Loudoun and Fauquier Counties based on the 1860 census. His work proved a lifesaver as I completed this study.

Jim and Judy McLean, former proprietors of Butternut and Blue in Baltimore, have been close friends for many years. While researching his exhaustive study of the Fourteenth Brooklyn Infantry, Jim always kept his eye open for information regarding my own work. He has also mined the records at the National Archives and enhanced my work with the material he shared.

In the years since their shop closed, Jim and Judy, along with close friends Kathy Steckelberg, John and Laura Fuller, and Craig Johnson and Carolyn Kilgore, organize a yearly wine and history weekend. Their questions on an October 2019 tour of the Loudoun Valley Battlefields have enhanced this work.

Similarly, Bill Burkman introduced me to a collegial group of friends and Gettysburg licensed battlefield Guides, including the late Bob George, as well as Wayne Motts, Dean Schultz, Chris Army, Jim Hessler, Britt Isenberg, John Zervas, Francis Feyock, Steve Floyd, Andie Donahue, Susan Strumello and Janice Pietrone. With their knowledge of the campaign, their questions, and observations on several tours of the battlefields also helped to hone my interpretation of events and locations for this study.

A most gracious lady, Lee Lawrence has edited several diaries from women in the Loudoun Valley, and she kindly agreed to help me introduce these ladies to readers of this study. She and her husband have also restored a historic cabin on the Upperville battlefield.

Numerous authors, historians and friends have liberally given of their time to assist me. Jim Nolan and Arnold Blumberg have shared a wealth of material with me over the years and both read portions of my manuscript, offering insightful advice and encouragement. Many others who have shared information include the late Charles Jacobs, Bruce Liddic, and Sam Blackwell. Others include Chris Hartley, Bruce and Lynne Venter, Edward Longacre, Robert Trout, Jeff Wert, Eric Wittenberg, Keith Bohannon, Craig Swain, Bradley Forbush, Don Caughey, Richard and Carol McAdoo, Robert Moran, Charles Siegel, David Shultz, Peter O'Meara Evans, William Hupp, Cindy Intravartolo, Todd Berkoff, William Gorenfeld, William Welsh, and Larry Gertner. Those who helped on the first edition include the late Brian Pohanka, as well as Dr. James Milgram, Mrs. Robert Covington, Nancy Baird, Carol Jordan, Lewis Leigh, Eleanor McSwain, Greg White, Tom Savage, Decker Bristow, Charles Lowe, Ron Davis, Robert and Nancy Frost, Marty Bertera, and Gray and Jim Taylor.

The curators, librarians, and staff at many repositories across the country provided a wealth of assistance over the years, especially the late Dr. Richard Sommers at the United States Army Heritage and Education Center in Carlisle, Pennsylvania. I offer a well-deserved thank you to the staff at the Huntington Library in California; the staff at the Monroe Library, especially Charmaine Wawrzyniec, the Bentley Historical Library and the William Clements Library, and the State Library and Archives in Michigan; the Indiana Historical Society in Indiana and the

Western Reserve Historical Society in Ohio; the Historical Society of Pennsylvania, the Free Library of Philadelphia, the Pennsylvania State Library, and the Franklin and Marshall College Library in Lancaster, Pennsylvania. In New York, the Rochester Public Library and the Albany Institute of History and Art. In New England, the Connecticut Historical Society, the Rhode Island Historical Society, the Maine State Archives, and the Military Research Center in Natick, Massachusetts. In Texas, the staff of the Pearce Civil War Collection, Navarro College. In Virginia, the staff of the Thomas Balch Library in Leesburg; the Albert and Shirley Small Special Collections Library, the Mary Ball Washington Library, and the Northumberland County Historical Society. Additionally, the staff at the Virginia Museum of History and Culture, the Virginia State Library, and the Museum of the Confederacy. The staff of the Hargrett Rare Book and Manuscript Library, University of Georgia. In North Carolina, the staff at the Special Collections Library, Duke University, and the Southern Historical Collections, Manuscript Branch, University of North Carolina. In West Virginia, the staff at the Jefferson County Museum in Charles Town. In South Carolina, the staff at the South Caroliniana Library, University of South Carolina. In Washington DC, the staff at the Library of Congress.

Finally, my thanks to Tom Swanson and his design and editorial staff at University of Nebraska Press and Potomac Books for producing the fine product you hold.

Any mistakes herein are mine and mine alone.

ONE

A Small, Neat, Dapper, Dashing Little Fellow

Though he led the Union Cavalry Corps through the defining summer of 1863, few officers in the Union army have been more vilified or ignored than Alfred Pleasonton. Having left few personal papers from which we might draw a deeper understanding of his character and motives, we are left with his wartime reports, a few letters, and several postwar writings that often appear as nothing more than thinly veiled attempts to enhance his reputation. Rather than looking for context or truth when discussing Pleasonton, historians simply dismiss him. This book seeks a more balanced, objective interpretation.

The defining moment of Pleasonton's early years may have occurred ten years before he entered the world. In 1814, as British troops set about burning the capital, Alfred's future father, Stephen Pleasonton, then working for the State Department, saved several of the most important documents in the history of the young nation, including the Declaration of Independence and Constitution. His efforts made him a bit of a celebrity, if not a national hero. Twenty-five years later, his son, Alfred, sought an appointment to West Point. Too young to be enrolled, Alfred attended a preparatory school, where he impressed his instructors with his conduct and good study habits. He had, one instructor opined, "a mind capable of acquiring knowledge readily" and appeared "admirably suited, both mentally and physically, to succeed in the military academy." Then, on the cusp of their goal, father and son had their hopes dashed; two members of the same family could not attend the academy and Augustus, Alfred's older brother, had graduated in 1822.[1]

Hoping his influential friends remembered his service in 1814, Stephen Pleasonton sought an exception in his son's case. Several acquaintances, including Gen. Charles Gratiot, former chief engineer for the army, agreed and the secretary of war waived the prohibition. In his letter of acceptance, Alfred thanked the secretary "for the appointment" and promised, "I shall in some measure repay you by proving myself worthy of your confidence."[2]

After graduating a respectable seventh out of twenty-five in the class of 1844, Pleasonton reported to the First U.S. Dragoons as a brevet second lieutenant at Fort Atkinson, Nebraska Territory. In early 1846 he transferred to the Second U.S. Dragoons in time to accompany Gen. Zachary Taylor's army to Mexico, later receiving brevets for gallantry at Palo Alto and Resaca de la Palma. After assignments at Fort McHenry, Maryland, Carlisle Barracks, Pennsylvania, and Santa Fe, New Mexico Territory, Pleasonton sought a staff position in California. Finding the position had already been filled, he obtained a leave and immediately returned to Washington, possibly to be with his mother before she died.[3]

In 1851 First Lieutenant Pleasonton returned to New Mexico Territory, leading his company in at least one minor action against the Apaches, before returning east in 1853. Two years later, following the death of their father, Augustus Pleasonton asked the secretary of war if Alfred might be transferred to duty in the nation's capital, where he could look after his sisters. Augustus also mentioned Alfred's health as being so "precarious" as to prevent him from resuming duty in the field. When the secretary denied his request, Alfred sought a transfer to a new regiment then being organized, hoping to gain a promotion in the process. The War Department again denied his request, possibly because he had breached protocol by sending his request directly to the president.[4]

In 1855 Col. William Harney successfully petitioned for Pleasonton's promotion to captain. The following year, Pleasonton accepted a position as Harney's adjutant general. The army turned to Harney repeatedly during the 1850s, whenever an uprising or insurrection needed to be quelled by force. Harney had a reputation as a tyrannical officer, brutal and pitiless to soldiers, civilians, and enemies alike. Physically imposing, he had no qualms about brawling with his men, abusing animals, or quarreling endlessly with his superiors. At least one officer questioned his sanity. By almost any measure, Harney did not represent a positive role model or mentor, but he got things done and, in the years immediately preceding the Civil War, he mentored Captain Pleasonton.[5]

The War Department ordered Harney to Washington DC, in June 1860. Though Pleasonton had orders to rejoin the Second Dragoons in Utah, he accompanied Harney to Washington instead, possibly at the general's urging. In September Harney sought to send his protégé to Europe, to report on "the improvements introduced into" the cavalry during the Crimean War. "To no officer in the cavalry arm could such a mission be better [entrusted] than to Captain Pleasonton," Harney declared. His "long service in the Dragoons covering a period of sixteen years, in every climate of our country . . . as well as during the Mexican War and our recent Indian troubles . . . eminently entitles him to such a distinction." Harney touted his aide as "active, industrious, intelligent and efficient," but, as other officers, including George McClellan, had already made similar trips on behalf of the army, the War Department denied his request. Following the fall of Fort Sumter, and having again circumvented the chain of command, Pleasonton organized troops in Pennsylvania and Delaware. Exactly when he rejoined his own regiment remains uncertain, but in February 1862 Pleasonton, now a major, found himself commanding his regiment, redesignated the Second U.S. Cavalry, by reason of seniority.[6]

During the spring and summer of 1862, Pleasonton and his understrength regiment served as part of General McClellan's escort during the Peninsula Campaign. His close association with the army commander proved beneficial: Pleasonton received a promotion to brigadier general of volunteers in mid-July and took command of a cavalry brigade shortly thereafter. One month later, after McClellan had been ordered to abandon his failed campaign and evacuate his army by water, tempers flared over trivial affronts and minor infractions of protocol as officers sought space aboard ships for their own commands. Pleasonton had spent little time in the field as a company officer and, as a result, had little experience mediating disputes. Having been mentored by the argumentative Harney, Pleasonton proved quarrelsome and a stickler for protocol. Used to bending or breaking army procedure as he saw fit, Pleasonton now fought others who did the same and gained a reputation as a martinet in the process. Harney might have beamed with pride when one officer termed Pleasonton "tyrannical." McClellan, however, spoke of the cavalryman as "a most excellent officer," who had covered the evacuation of the army "most admirably." The young general had found another benefactor.[7]

In September, as McClellan pursued Lee into Maryland, Pleasonton, who had never led more than a company prior to the war, took command of a cavalry division of fourteen regiments in four brigades. Unlike an infantry division, in which the brigades and regiments usually fought alongside each other and within sight of their commander, Pleasonton's division never did. Thus, his position as a division commander, and later a corps commander, proved more administrative than tactical.

Still, Pleasonton saw his share of combat, including a furious skirmish near Boonsboro on September 15, in which he had his only personal clash with an enemy combatant. Few contemporary descriptions of Pleasonton have been found but one observer saw him as "a small, neat, dapper, dashing little fellow with a smart riding whip in his hand." The reporting soldier emphasized that "he always carries the same silver-mounted and stylish [crop]," rather than a heavy cavalry saber. Though he sometimes buckled on a thin, straight presentation blade, he preferred to carry what another scribe derogatorily termed a "feminine riding whip." During the skirmish at Boonsboro, while riding with the Eighth Illinois through blinding clouds of dust, Pleasonton tore a saber from the hands of an enemy trooper and continued the fight.[8]

Though he participated in other cavalry attacks during the war, several critics accused him of cowardice during the Maryland Campaign. Such accusations continue to taint his reputation, but one rings hollow. Nine months after the fact, Charles Francis Adams, Pleasonton's most virulent and oft-quoted critic, accused Pleasonton of sending "his cavalry into a hell of artillery fire" at Antietam, while he "got behind a bank and read a newspaper." In fact, Pleasonton had sheltered the entire command in a creek valley, including Adams, who later admitted he went to sleep in the safety of the valley during the "monotonous" cannonade. Two days later, however, during a fight at Shepherdstown, another trooper derisively said of Pleasonton that he "ran off and left us to our fate." Written later the same day, the immediacy of the trooper's claim is not easily dismissed.[9]

General Pleasonton's limitations as an intelligence officer also came under scrutiny during the Maryland Campaign. With little experience in the field, he never developed a skill for or an interest in intelligence gathering, even though his cavalry served as the eyes of the army. His time at army headquarters during the Peninsula Campaign, working for a man with a similar lack of interest in the vital task of collecting information, had done little to spark his interest or develop his talents. Hampered by McClellan's infamous short leash for his horse-soldiers, Pleasonton relied upon civilians, slaves, and Southern prisoners for information. Unwilling to verify the reports he received, he usually accepted them at face value and often offered wildly inaccurate conclusions.

But McClellan must also shoulder some blame, for holding his troopers on a short tether and encouraging caution over initiative. And, as he employed Allan Pinkerton to gather and assess information, the army commander may have seen no reason to demand more from his cavalry. Even in the heat of battle, McClellan limited his horsemen, generally holding them back to support artillery or deliver messages rather than protecting his army, seeking the enemy, or searching for weak points to be exploited.

Then, on October 10, Maj. Gen. James Ewell Brown "Jeb"

Stuart led eighteen hundred Southern troopers on a raid to Chambersburg, Pennsylvania. McClellan sent Pleasonton in pursuit, but over the next three days, Stuart embarrassed them, riding around the Union army for the second time in four months. As Pleasonton exhausted his horses in a futile chase, McClellan positioned other troops to block Stuart's escape routes back across the Potomac River. Stuart's audacity and predilection for doing the unexpected, combined with the failure of Union efforts to pin the Confederates against the river, bore lasting consequences for Pleasonton, as well as his former commander, George Stoneman.[10]

• • •

George Stoneman, West Point class of 1846, had spent much of his prewar career chasing Mexican bandits along the Rio Grande River in southeast Texas. No dapper cavalier, Stoneman presented an Old Testament biblical visage, suggesting a lack of humor. One observer saw him as a "lithe, severe, gristly" fellow, who struck some as a "brusque . . . hard disciplinarian" and others as a "generous-hearted, whole-souled companion." Promoted to brigadier in 1861, Stoneman served as George McClellan's chief of cavalry during the Peninsula Campaign before taking a medical leave in July 1862.[11]

After regaining his health, Stoneman returned to the army at the head of an infantry division exactly one month prior to Stuart setting out on his raid into Pennsylvania. Stoneman reached the Potomac River around October 10, deployed his troops along the north bank, and established his headquarters at Poolesville, Maryland. With thirty miles of river to guard, including several fords, Stoneman had deployed his men quickly but, as events proved, ineffectively. Three days later, Stuart eluded Pleasonton, drove Stoneman's infantry away from White's Ford on the river and led his men back into Virginia unscathed. Stuart's boldness had prevailed and the Union forces had been humiliated once again. Rumors, innuendo, and controversy began swirling and Stoneman found himself in the crosshairs.[12]

General McClellan could not fathom how Stuart had escaped. "I did not think it possible for Stuart to recross, and I believed that the capture or destruction of his entire force was perfectly certain," he explained. Thrown on the defensive, Stoneman said little. Pleasonton, however, accused Stoneman of leaving White's Ford uncovered and providing little assistance to his own valiant but exhausted troopers. Stoneman termed such accusations "ridiculous," but the damage had been done. In truth, Stoneman had left an insignificant force to guard Stuart's most likely avenue of escape. Seeking to clear his name, he asked for a court of inquiry, but after a personal meeting with McClellan, during which Stoneman must have satisfied his commander, the matter slipped from the headlines. Or so the beleaguered officer thought.[13]

Stoneman had married Mary Hardisty, a Marylander, in Baltimore in November 1861. The press had not been kind, with one editor claiming that "the church was crowded with fair rebels." In July 1862, after Stoneman took medical leave, an unfriendly editor suggested he had been removed from command for making comments deemed "traitorous in the extreme." Now, with Stuart having escaped through his lines, Elizabeth Blair Lee, a prominent member of Washington society, and a friend of Pleasonton, gossiped about a "fuss between Pleasonton and Stoneman." Hinting at rumors of a possible court-martial over the matter, Lee maliciously added, Stoneman's "wife is [a hot Baltimore Secessionist]."[14]

In the critical moments on October 13, as Stuart raced for the river, Stoneman may have been a little distracted by concern for his wife's health. Notified two weeks earlier of her illness, he had asked her family to keep him advised of her condition but regretted he could not rush home, "unless [my] wife is in danger." Gossip, such as that spread by Lee, almost certainly reached Stoneman in some form. We may never know if Pleasonton played a role in reviving the questions about Stoneman's loyalty in the wake of Stuart's escape, but Stoneman could not be blamed if he thought so. Questions regarding Stoneman's loyalty must have lingered within the politically partisan ranks of the army, even though he retained the confidence of the president. His relationship with Pleasonton never recovered.[15]

On February 5, 1863, army commander Joseph Hooker announced the formation of the Cavalry Corps, not as a stroke of genius on his part but rather the result of a bargain he struck with the president. Pleasonton must have been disappointed when Hooker, at Lincoln's request, named Stoneman to command the corps. Two months earlier, Pleasonton had submitted a detailed proposal for the formation of a cavalry corps to then-army commander Ambrose Burnside, and he now had reason to suspect Hooker had used his plan in organizing the corps. Though Stoneman had left the cavalry six months earlier, he returned at Lincoln's request. What Pleasonton knew of Lincoln's involvement in the decision is unknown, but this turn of events did not bode well for a thaw in the strained relationship between the two horse-soldiers.[16]

Just three weeks into his tenure as corps commander, Stoneman confronted his first crisis, when Southern cavalry dashed through the Union picket line at Hartwood Church. Bad weather, muddy roads, and poor communications hampered his efforts to coordinate an effective response and the Rebel raiders escaped across the Rappahannock River. The same bad weather and roads, as well as orders that initially sent him away from Hartwood Church, also precluded Pleasonton reaching the scene in time to prevent the Confederates from escaping.[17]

Though his horsemen had partially redeemed themselves on March 17 at Kelly's Ford, Hooker remained leery of his cavalry. Thus, his decision to include an elaborate cavalry expedition as a crucial component of his spring campaign is a bit mystifying. Nor did Hooker envision any small affair; Stoneman's entire corps, minus one brigade, would make the effort. As Stoneman finalized his plans, he embarrassed Pleasonton by leaving him behind due to deficiencies within his command. When he returned from the raid, Stoneman found "his rivals," namely Hooker and Pleasonton, had "been intriguing . . . to have him superseded in command of the [Cavalry] Corps."[18]

Stoneman and his troopers returned to an army in turmoil, following the humiliating defeat at Chancellorsville. Many of the exhausted men turned surly when they received orders to resume picket duty rather than resting and refitting. Several officers blamed Pleasonton as the cause of their misery, but they offered their complaints from a distance. Lt. George Custer, however, had spoken with Hooker, Stoneman, and Pleasonton in the wake of the raid. A new member of Pleasonton's staff, Custer knew Hooker and Stoneman "are very much opposed to each other," though he said nothing of the man he worked for. In a letter to a friend, Custer repeated Hooker's complaint "that Stoneman accomplished nothing" on the raid. He knew the army commander intended to make Stoneman a scapegoat, but Hooker first needed to craft a case against the cavalryman.[19]

In the aftermath of the defeat at Chancellorsville, a story took hold that Pleasonton had saved the army on the evening of May 2, in the wake of Lt. Gen. Thomas "Stonewall" Jackson's crushing flank attack. During the wee hours of May 3, correspondent William Swinton cobbled together an account of the previous days' fighting for the *New York Times.* Swinton credited Pleasonton with "turning back a dozen pieces of artillery taken from the flying [XI] corps, and planting them in a favorable position [at Hazel Grove], while he drew up his little brigade of cavalry . . . to protect the guns." After ordering the guns "to be double-shotted with canister" (words which later appeared in the campaign reports of both Pleasonton and Maj. Gen. Daniel Sickles), Pleasonton opened "a murderous fire" upon the enemy. "The successful check of the advancing foe," Swinton concluded, "is in no small degree owing to the indomitable energy of the gallant soldier [Alfred Pleasonton]." Though Swinton did not credit Pleasonton as his source, the general had made similar comments in earlier messages to Hooker.[20]

A solid element of truth runs through the story. Pleasonton had been present during the frenzied action at Hazel Grove, he had brought some artillery into action, and he had been under fire, as casualties in Lt. Joseph Martin's Sixth New York Light Artillery attest. Lieutenant Martin described the "confusion" as panic-stricken soldiers ran through his position, "overturning guns and limbers, smashing my caissons, and trampling my horse-holders under them." But the facts quickly morphed into fiction, probably spurred by Hooker. Within days, Pleasonton wrote two accounts of his own, further obscuring the facts and establishing the fictions.[21]

During a meeting with Lincoln on May 7, Hooker purportedly introduced Pleasonton to the president as the man "who saved the Army of the Potomac the other night." The following day, as Lincoln still pondered how the spring campaign had gone so terribly awry, General Stoneman and his saddle-weary troopers returned from their raid. Then, on May 10, the editors of the *New York Times* began questioning Hooker's leadership. The beleaguered commander needed a scapegoat and Stoneman had returned just in time. Dismissing him, however, would not be easy. Not only did Lincoln admire Stoneman but editors at the *Times* had just touted Stoneman's Raid as "one of the most successful military enterprises of the kind ever undertaken, in this or any other country."[22]

With his moment at hand, as the man who had saved the army, Pleasonton wrote his first report on May 11, followed by a second version a week later. Maj. Gen. Daniel Sickles supported Pleasonton, terming his leadership at Hazel Grove as "brilliant." Sickles then told Secretary of War Edwin Stanton, "I must not fail to tell you how magnificently *Pleasonton* behaved on . . . the 2nd. . . . He is the man to lead our cavalry . . . He is more than a good soldier—He is a man of ideas. Remember him."[23]

With his leadership now assailed by Hooker, Stoneman must have recognized the increasingly precarious nature of his position as commander of the Cavalry Corps. Rather than fight the tide running against him, he submitted another request for medical leave and departed from the army on May 20, 1863. He and Pleasonton had probably never been collegial, and one suspects they had not been civil to each other in months. Still, Stoneman knew the command would fall to Pleasonton as the senior officer. As a matter of protocol or courtesy, he offered to meet with Pleasonton and discuss the change of command before he departed. Pleasonton declined, writing, "I shall not be able to call at the Head Quarters of the Corps Commander today, as I have been under medical treatment and do not feel strong enough to do so after a ride in the sun this morning . . . I will be satisfied with any arrangements he makes in . . . turning over the command." The new corps commander officially announced the change two days later.[24]

Alfred Pleasonton led the Cavalry Corps for the next ten months, a period of near constant campaigning for his horse-soldiers. He saw the mounted arm through the important summer of 1863, when his men achieved parity with or surpassed their Southern counterparts on the battlefield. Most importantly, the officers he brought into the senior leadership of the corps became his legacy. All of this lay in the future, however. The days ahead brought nothing but challenges he might not have envisioned when he took command.

TWO

Rebuilding the Cavalry Corps, May 20–June 9

Alfred Pleasonton faced a daunting challenge on May 20: the Cavalry Corps—man and horse—was exhausted. George Stoneman's raid may have boosted morale within the ranks and provided a hint of what the men might accomplish in the future, but the effort had proved ruinous. At least one thousand animals had been abandoned during the raid. Others had been lost to wounds or capture. Thousands of other horses returned lame, diseased, or exhausted from overwork and lack of adequate food and care. Few, if any, of the animals captured along the route proved suitable as replacements. After a careful inspection, the corps, which had counted twelve thousand horses at the outset of the raid, now numbered just two thousand. Pleasonton needed thousands of remounts, but horses in such numbers would not arrive in days or even weeks. Advertisements had to be posted, bids placed, and contracts signed. Contractors had to locate, purchase, and transport the animals across vast distances to collection depots, where, upon examination, inspectors often rejected hundreds for a variety of reasons. Pleasonton competed against every other army in the field for horses, and every commander needed them in the thousands. As one quartermaster remarked with a hint of sarcasm, "Horses are hard to get for some reason." Rebuilding the Cavalry Corps would take time, even as the summer campaign season approached.[1]

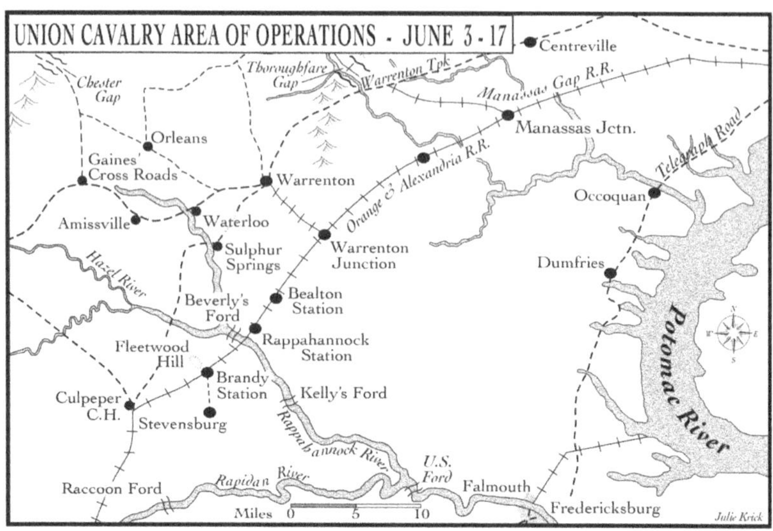

MAP 1. Union Cavalry area of operations, June 3–17. Created by Julie Krick.

Before departing on May 20, Stoneman had, to the extent possible, dispersed his cavalry to allow the horses to graze in safe pastures and to recuperate as quickly as possible. Pleasonton sought to continue Stoneman's approach, but he soon faced other demands, namely the need to protect the army, and, most especially, the Orange and Alexandria Railroad from enemy incursions. With their ranks badly depleted, the men struggled to establish picket lines of even minimal strength, even as the duty further exhausted their horses and reduced their numbers. Needing his troopers ready "for immediate duty in the field," General Hooker sought to task Maj. Gen. Julius Stahel's cavalry division, attached to Maj. Gen. Samuel Heintzelman's Department of Washington, with the onerous picket duty, while his own men and horses rested. But events in Washington conspired against him.[2]

On May 20 Heintzelman met with a reliable informant who brought word from Richmond of a planned Southern cavalry raid on the capital. Specifically, fifteen hundred horsemen wearing Union uniforms intended to "come into Washington and seize Mr. Lincoln and [Secretary of State William] Seward and [Secretary of War Edwin] Stanton." Heintzelman could not ignore the threat and immediately instituted measures to prevent such a raid. He ordered planks removed from bridges into the city and set soldiers and civilians to work enhancing the fortifications and erecting new barricades across roads into the capital. Though none of these measures directly affected Pleasonton's Cavalry Corps, another decision did. General Henry Halleck tasked Stahel with preventing the raid and protecting the city. Within days, quartermasters at the depots in Washington and Alexandria began diverting all fresh remounts to Stahel's division rather than the Cavalry Corps.[3]

By May 23 Hooker and Pleasonton began to fully appreciate the lasting effect of Stoneman's Raid. As Stahel pulled his brigades back toward Washington to refit, Pleasonton's troopers assumed responsibility for securing the Orange and Alexandria Railroad. Unsaddled recuperative time for his horses ended as the men resumed picket and patrol duty. Even as the men rolled their blankets, drew rations, and packed their saddlebags, General Halleck announced, "It is rumored that Stuart and Lee are collecting a cavalry force at Culpeper . . . probably for a raid." If true, Pleasonton, rather than Stahel, would draw the primary responsibility for preventing the raid, and Hooker instructed his corps commander to "spare no labor to place the cavalry . . . in a high state of efficiency at the earliest practicable moment." Pleasonton now found himself in a nearly impossible predicament; he could not protect the army and the railroad while resting his animals. He simply did not have enough horses. As one of his officers concluded, the need for "cavalry horses with this army has never been so severely felt as at this moment." Hooker must have recognized his own culpability in the problem now confronting him, as he had designed the plan that included Stoneman's Raid. He did not intend to make the same mistake again. When Pleasonton proposed dispersing his brigades to several locations, Hooker objected, telling him, "The main body of the cavalry must be nearer, and held well in hand . . . in case of an enemy's raid or of an advance movement, of which probably not much notice will be given."[4]

By May 27 the idea of a Southern cavalry raid had firmly taken hold within the Union army. Indeed, most anyone associated with the army kept a wary eye cast for Rebel raiders. As an engineer on the Orange and Alexandria noted in his log, "Grand Rebel Raid expected today." Intelligence reports, provided by Col. George Sharpe, head of Hooker's Bureau of Military Information, pointed to Culpeper County and when "Fighting Joe" could no longer ignore the rumors, he ordered Brig. Gen. John Buford "to drive the enemy out of his camp near Culpeper," with his understrength brigade. Luckily, Buford did not encounter the enemy. Hooker then groused to Stanton, "If Stoneman had not destroyed one-half of my serviceable cavalry force, I would pitch into [Stuart]." Frustrated, the army commander suggested employing Stahel to assist Pleasonton in an attack on Stuart or to scout the Shenandoah Valley, but Stanton refused. After all, Stanton had been named as one of the targets of the Rebel raiders. If Stahel's division is removed, Stanton told Hooker, "there will be no force in front to give notice of the enemy's raids on Alexandria or Washington." On June 2 Hooker and Pleasonton finally received a bit of good news; fresh horses began arriving in quantity. The remounts arrived none too soon, as Robert E. Lee launched his summer campaign the following day.[5]

Southern infantry began pulling out of their lines along the Rappahannock River and heading for Culpeper on June 3. The Confederates gained a day before dust trails alerted the Federals. "Rumor says the enemy are moving," Pleasonton warned Buford. On June 5 Buford advised, "I have just received information, which I consider reliable that all of the available cavalry of the Confederacy is in Culpeper County . . . My informant thinks Stuart is going to make a raid." General Halleck concurred, telling Hooker "Stuart is preparing . . . 15,000 to 20,000 men . . . for a raid." Pondering the situation overnight and temporarily shaking off his fear of losing his mounted arm, Hooker determined to strike first. "I shall send all of my cavalry against them," he told Halleck. Hooker's decision resulted in the largest cavalry clash of the war.[6]

THREE

Reorganization, June 10–11

Nearly eight thousand Union troopers, supported by two infantry brigades, crossed the Rappahannock River on the morning of June 9, precipitating the largest cavalry battle of the war. Crossing the river at two fords, four miles apart, General Pleasonton intended for his three divisions to converge near Culpeper Court House, where they expected to meet the enemy. The daring and complex plan, challenging to coordinate in a perfect situation, fell apart in the opening seconds as the first troopers across the river at Beverly Ford found themselves in a battle from the start. Throughout the day, Brig. Gen. John Buford, commanding Pleasonton's right wing, fought a stubborn, frustrating battle against Southern troopers posted on high ground and behind stone walls. Four miles downstream, at Kelly's Ford, Brig. Gen. David Gregg led the left wing, consisting of his own division and Col. Alfred Duffié's division, across the river. Meeting stiff resistance themselves, Duffié soon found himself embroiled in a fight at Stevensburg while Gregg met Jeb Stuart on the slopes of Fleetwood Hill at Brandy Station. After fourteen hours of often furious combat, during which Stuart successfully prevented the three Union columns from uniting against him, Pleasonton ordered his men to retire across the river. Reaching camp that evening, Pleasonton believed the matter of a Confederate raid had been settled, yet his assurances failed to convince Hooker.

"I am not so certain as you appear to be that the enemy will abandon his contemplated raid," Hooker told his cavalry chief.[1]

The next morning, June 10, Pleasonton sent a small detail, under a flag of truce, back across the river to recover any casualties who had been left behind. Though the Southerners treated the Yankees courteously, Stuart refused to allow them to search the fields as his men had already recovered the wounded and buried the dead. The adversaries discussed the battle, however, and, as one Union officer recalled, promised "each other more of the same when we meet again."[2]

After spending much of the day seeing his wounded, as well as Southern prisoners, placed aboard trains bound for Washington, Pleasonton turned to a more uplifting affair: inspecting and reviewing his troops. He believed his men had won a great victory and sought to allow them to celebrate their achievement. At 9 a.m. the following morning, the men formed ranks near Pleasonton's headquarters.[3]

The average trooper knew nothing of grand strategy, but every man present knew he had survived a brutal slugfest with Stuart's vaunted legions. Like their general, the proud Union troopers turned out ready to revel in their accomplishments. "Songs were sung, speeches made, toasts given & all was good cheer and hearty," a soldier in the First Maine reported. As the men paraded, Cpl. Ansel Drew, another Mainer, proudly bore the captured battle flag of the Twelfth Virginia.[4]

During the festivities, General Gregg congratulated his men for their exploits. "Your repeated bold and resolute charges . . . merit the highest commendation," he told them, "and fully establish the superiority of the sabre as a cavalry weapon when wielded by the strong hands of brave men."[5]

Inspections followed, as Pleasonton sought to determine the amount of equipment lost during the fight. Horses remained the critical need. On June 8, as the troopers moved into position near the Rappahannock River, Brig. Gen. Rufus Ingalls, Hooker's chief quartermaster, had warned a subordinate, "Cavalry horses are scarce, and in great demand." Aware of the pending offensive, Ingalls had urged his men to pull the best horses from less essential duties and send them to the cavalry. Post-battle inspections confirmed the dire need, with just one brigade needing eleven hundred horses. Within a matter of days quartermasters shipped nearly two thousand horses to the cavalry, as contracts signed in May began to be fulfilled, though the corps continued to work from a deficit for the remainder of the campaign.[6]

With the parades and inspections completed, Pleasonton had one remaining order of business. After three weeks in command, he determined to place his own stamp on the corps by abolishing General Stoneman's three divisions in favor of two strong divisions. Pleasonton gave John Buford permanent command of the First Division, counting three brigades, including the Reserve Brigade. Pleasonton then combined the Second and Third Divisions, giving David Gregg command of the new Second Division, comprising three revamped brigades.[7]

General Pleasonton wanted his men, especially his officers, to earn a reputation as fighters, a command to be counted on in the heat of battle by the other branches of the army. As he explained later in the campaign, "I am sadly in want of officers with the proper dash to command cavalry." Steady, reliable, and willing to fight, John Buford and David Gregg could be counted on in any battlefield scenario. Pleasonton now sought to build upon their dependable leadership by adding young, aggressive brigade commanders; men who would charge the gates of hell or the flaming muzzles of angry cannon when necessary but whose aggression could be tempered by the firm hand of their superiors.[8]

Col. Judson Kilpatrick's brigade had been at the very epicenter of the crucial fighting for Fleetwood Hill on June 9, when victory still lay within Pleasonton's grasp. The following day, seventy officers, from the Second and Tenth New York and First Maine presented a petition to Pleasonton requesting Kilpatrick be promoted to brigadier. At Brandy Station, Kilpatrick had, the officers declared, "displayed qualities that stamp him, at once, as one of the first officers of the Cavalry Corps." Pleasonton had his man and immediately recommended the twenty-seven-year-old Kilpatrick for promotion, the first of four young men with the "proper dash" he proposed to promote before the end of the month. Kilpatrick received his appointment to brigadier three days later.[9]

Consolidating the corps to two divisions allowed Pleasonton to rearrange and strengthen his brigades. Col. William Gamble took command of General Buford's First Brigade, replacing Col. Benjamin "Grimes" Davis, killed at Brandy Station. Col. Thomas Devin retained command the Second Brigade, and Maj. Samuel Starr now led the Reserve Brigade. In General Gregg's Second Division, Col. John Taylor took command of the First Brigade. Judson Kilpatrick soon received command of the brigade most recently led by Col. Luigi di Cesnola and Colonel Duffié. Col. John Irvin Gregg, the general's cousin, took command of the Third Brigade. The Cavalry Corps also included a brigade of four horse artillery batteries, under the overall command of Capt. John Tidball. Unlike their Confederate counterparts, the Northern troopers enjoyed no further rest, as their role in the developing campaign resumed the next day.

FOUR

Conflict and Controversy, June 10–15

The stench of battle still hung over the fields around Brandy Station as the sun broke the horizon on the morning of June 10, 1863. Many of General Stuart's men found themselves tasked with burying the dead and recovering the last of the wounded. Other victims of the previous day's battle remained above ground for months. Disposing of even a few dead horses, much less hundreds of the luckless steeds, proved a near impossible burden, and so the carcasses remained, stark silent memorials until nature consumed them. "The smell," according to one artilleryman, was "fearful." Months later a trooper gazing upon the decaying hulks noted, "The entire air was a mass of rottenness. The stench was all pervading—there was no escape from it sleeping nor waking. It was swallowed with every mouthful of food, with every drink of water." The Southern troopers, the victors on June 9, lived amid the offal and odor for nearly a week.[1]

Wherever the men gathered, they talked of "the great cavalry fight" around Brandy Station, but no parades or reviews followed the battle. Brig. Gen. Wade Hampton issued a congratulatory order, thanking his men for their "dashing gallantry." General Stuart followed with an order of his own, acknowledging his men for their tenacity and courage on the ninth. "Let the example and heroism of our lamented, fallen comrades prompt us to renewed vigilance," he urged, "and inspire us with devotion to duty." As the men pondered Stuart's words, some must have taken notice of his call for "renewed vigilance," for by then a storm of controversy had engulfed the general concerning his own lack of vigilance.[2]

By June 1863 "Jeb" Stuart was one of the more famous officers in the South. Standing a little more than six feet tall, his penetrating eyes, flowing beard, plumed hat, yellow sash, gray jacket, weighted down with yards of gold braid, and knee-high boots—all set off by his exuberant personality and flashing smile—certainly made him one of the more recognizable general officers in the Southern service. He comes down through history as a man who loved life, lived every day to the fullest, relished the life of a soldier, and reveled in the excitement of battle.[3]

• • •

Born February 6, 1833, in Patrick County, Virginia, Stuart attended Emory and Henry College for two years before seeking an appointment to West Point. Charles Collins, president of the college, recommended Stuart as a man of "irreproachable moral and social character," while Congressman Thomas Averett believed him capable of standing "with credit every test prescribed." Stuart accepted his appointment on April 8, 1850. During the summer break in 1852, Maj. Robert E. Lee assumed the duties as the academy's superintendent, and Stuart would have met Lee for the first time after returning to the academy in August. Upon being graduated by the school in June 1854, Stuart, a brevet second lieutenant, began his career in the army.[4]

Stuart's fellow officers may have first begun calling him Jeb about 1855, while he served with the First U.S. Cavalry at Fort Leavenworth, Kansas. While posted there, Stuart met and fell in love with Flora Cooke, the nineteen-year-old daughter of the humorless and dictatorial Philip St. George Cooke, lieutenant colonel of the Second Dragoons. Jeb and Flora were married at Fort Riley, Kansas, on November 14, 1855.[5]

Shortly before leaving West Point, Stuart had expressed his desire to seek the life of "a bold Dragoon," searching for "glorious war." Rather than glory, Stuart experienced the ugly abolitionist struggle to prevent the spread of slavery into the territory. Then, on July 29, 1857, a Cheyenne warrior shot him in the chest during an engagement near the Solomon River in northwestern Kansas. Left behind at a small sod fort while the main force pursued the Cheyenne, Stuart recovered quickly. Weeks later, with the remainder of the regiment still in the field and hostile Indians reported nearby, Stuart took command of the detachment and led them on a hundred-mile trek to Fort Kearny.[6]

Receiving an extended leave in March 1859, Stuart journeyed to Virginia, along with Flora and their young daughter, "Little Flora." In Washington on October 17, Stuart learned of John Brown's raid on the United States Arsenal at Harpers Ferry and immediately volunteered his services to the secretary of war. Asked to carry a message to Col. Robert E. Lee, Stuart then accompanied Lee to a meeting with the president at the White House. Charged with ending the insurrection, Lee, along with Stuart and a detachment of United States Marines, reached Harpers Ferry during the night. At 7 a.m. the next morning, Stuart carried a message to the fire-engine house where Brown and his men had taken refuge. When Brown refused to accept Lee's demands, Stuart gave a prearranged signal, and the Marines stormed the building. Jeb Stuart had just stepped into the national spotlight.[7]

Stuart credited Lee with giving him "all the prominence that was compatible with my position." The colonel "*mentioned my name first* [in his report] . . . a significant compliment to me," he told his mother. In his first moment of public glory, however, Stuart also experienced his first slight at the hands of the press. "The newspapers have erred in so many respects that to attempt to correct it is utterly futile," he complained. He found the Northern accounts especially offensive, as they "[heaped] the greatest *abuse* upon *me* for having sabered Brown," a claim he vigorously denied. Stuart also felt slighted by Virginia governor Henry Wise's decision to reward another officer, while ignoring his own actions. "I would feel exceedingly *mortified*," he groused, and "I shall certainly expect every friend I have in either house . . . to insist upon my being included" in any award or remuneration. Stuart saw the other officer as having merely obeyed his orders while he had acted voluntarily. Acclaim, Stuart learned, often came with a price.[8]

Stuart returned to Kansas as the long-simmering sectional crisis engulfed the nation. Ever more bellicose as the nation rushed to war, Stuart unequivocally declared his intention to follow Virginia. Learning of the firing on Fort Sumter, Stuart abandoned his post and headed east with his family. He submitted his resignation while en route and offered his service to the Confederacy. Initially appointed a lieutenant colonel, Stuart had gained a brigadier's star and command of a cavalry brigade by September.[9]

Dr. William Shepardson, a correspondent for the *Richmond Dispatch*, introduced Stuart to his readers shortly thereafter. Describing the new general as "very striking" and "of almost perfect [mold]," Shepardson deemed Stuart as "decisive and prompt in action" and "an admirable outpost officer," who "has never yet been caught napping." Eight months later, in June 1862, Stuart's honeymoon with the Southern press reached its zenith following his successful "Ride around McClellan." When he met with officials at the governor's mansion in Richmond a couple of days after the ride, a throng of admirers gathered outside shouting his name. Their persistence induced the general to make a brief speech, before "[leaping] into the saddle and [galloping] off amid the enthusiastic plaudits of the multitude."[10]

Eleven months later, on the eve of Lee's great gamble at Chancellorsville, Stuart provided the vital information that determined Lee's course and sent Lt. Gen. Thomas J. "Stonewall" Jackson on his famous and fateful flank march. Stuart had been resting with his staff when he learned of Jackson's wounding. Intent on resuming the battle in the morning, Lee placed Stuart in command of Jackson's corps. The cavalryman's leadership the following day at the head of an infantry corps demonstrated his mental agility under stress. Biographer Jeffry Wert believed "May 3, 1863, had been Stuart's finest day as a Confederate officer." Following the victory, Stuart believed he had earned permanent command of the corps, but Lee saw the matter otherwise.[11]

One month later, Stuart and his legions survived the desperate fight at Brandy Station. The Yankees had expected to find Stuart's cavalry posted near Culpeper Court House and had made their plans accordingly. In fact Stuart planned to begin moving his division north on the morning of June 9 and had pulled his men closer to Brandy Station to facilitate their march. The initial Union attack fell upon the brigade led by Brig. Gen. William E. "Grumble" Jones. But for the stubborn stand made by Jones and his men, Stuart's artillery might have been captured and his brigades defeated in detail. The Federals had never challenged Stuart's troopers as they did on June 9, nor had the Southerners ever been so close to such an overwhelming defeat. The smoke had hardly drifted from the field before questions, complaints, and recriminations rippled through the ranks and made headlines across the South.

Stuart had been surprised at Brandy Station, or so his critics believed. Troopers of all ranks must have debated the question of surprise around a thousand campfires. Correspondents soon caught wind of the rumors and within days the simmering discussions had erupted into a firestorm of controversy. "The fight" had "begun in a surprise but ended in victory," according to the *Richmond Sentinel*. "The latter we are accustomed to hear of Confederate soldiers; the former we trust not to hear again." Then, using the word Stuart used in his own congratulatory order, the editors added, "Vigilance, vigilance, more vigilance, is the lesson taught us by the Brandy surprise . . . Let all learn from it, from the Major General down to the picket."[12]

The editors of the *Richmond Examiner* condemned the cavalry service in general and Stuart in particular. "The more the circumstances of the late affair at Brandy Station are considered, the less pleasant they appear." Believing the troopers had been surprised on several previous occasions, including Kelly's Ford in March, the editors concluded, "Such repeated accidents can be regarded as nothing but the necessary consequence of negligence and bad management." Then, referring to the several flashy reviews Stuart had held prior to the fight, the scribes added, "If the war was a tournament, invented and supported for the pleasure of a few vain and weak-headed officers, these disasters might be dismissed. . . . But the country pays dearly for such blunders."[13]

In an error-filled commentary, a correspondent for the *Memphis Daily Appeal* attributed the near defeat "to the most humiliating of all military reverses—surprise." Residents of Richmond soon added their own thoughts to the growing tumult, with one diarist concluding, "The surprise of Stuart . . . has chilled every heart." Some troopers thought the criticism "too severe." Others reveled in the general's discomfort. Chiswell Dabney, one of Stuart's aides, defended his commanding officer, deeming the accusations "absolutely false."[14]

Just one year after Stuart had been called upon to speak to an adoring crowd in Richmond, many of those very residents now turned against him. The censure stung the general to his core, especially when the attacks proved personally painful, as when a scribe for the *Richmond Dispatch* asked if Stuart had spent too much time "rollicking, frolicking and running after girls." Flora Stuart must have seen or heard some of the comments. Seeking to reassure his wife, Stuart affirmed in one case, "The *Examiner* . . . lies from beginning to end." The general had his share of enemies, both within his ranks and across the river, leading another editor to wonder if he would not soon "make the enemy repent . . . the temerity that led them to undertake as bold and insulting a feat."[15]

FIVE

An Army on the Move, June 13–16

In a June 10 letter to President Lincoln, General Hooker proposed to move his army against Richmond. "Fighting Joe" remained convinced that General Robert E. Lee still intended to launch a raid against Washington or Maryland. Should Lee do so, Hooker planned to ignore the threat and make a "rapid advance on Richmond." Taken aback, Lincoln admonished Hooker, reminding him that "Lee's army, and not Richmond, is your . . . objective." Counseling Hooker to hold his army between Lee and Washington, Lincoln urged his general to "fight" Lee "when opportunity offers" and to "fret him and fret him." Without an alternative plan, Hooker lost vital time before finally determining on June 12 to abandon his lines near Falmouth and head north in pursuit of Lee. The move commenced at 3 a.m. the next morning.[1]

Hooker elected to move his army in two columns, with the I, III, V, and XI Corps moving along the line of the Orange and Alexandria Railroad. The II, VI, and XII Corps, along with the Reserve Artillery, would move along an interior line through Dumfries and into Fairfax County. Opting to accompany the interior column, Hooker appointed Maj. Gen. John Reynolds, commander of the I Corps, as a wing commander to oversee the troops moving along the railroad. Hooker also wished Brig. Gen.

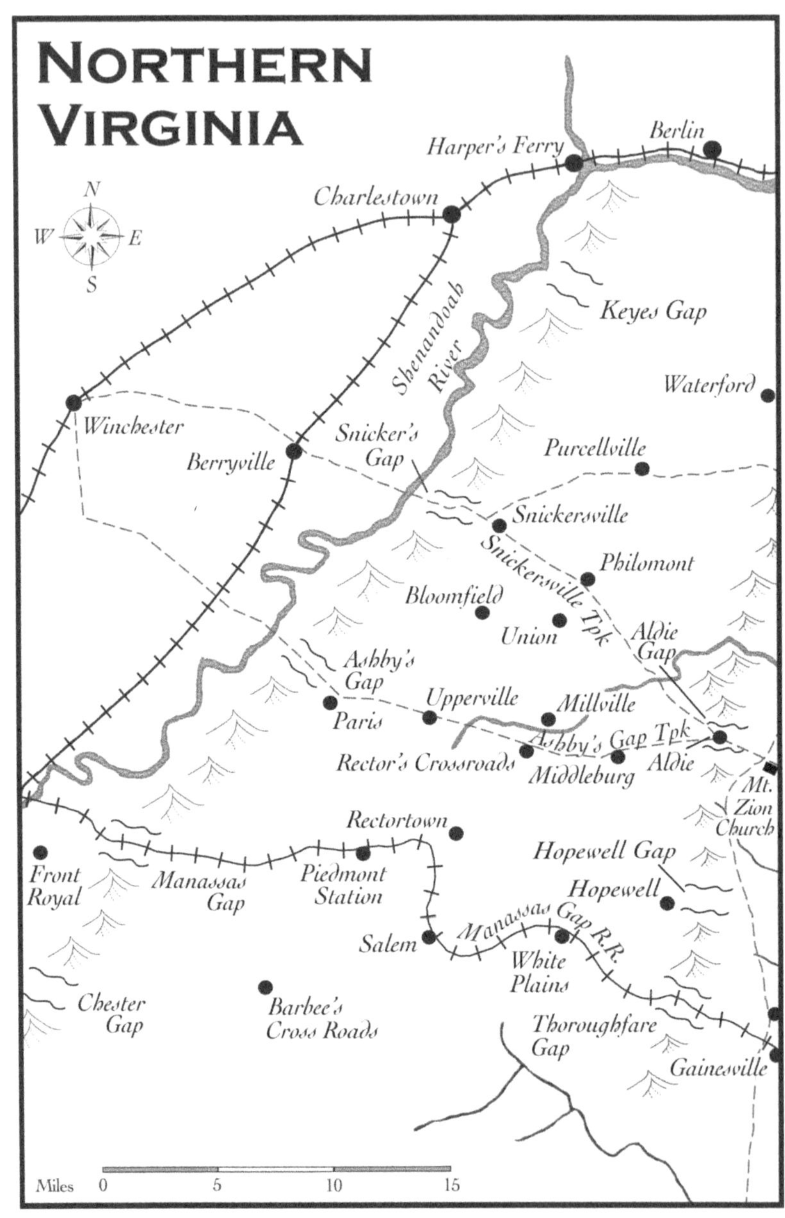

MAP 2. Northern Virginia. Created by Julie Krick.

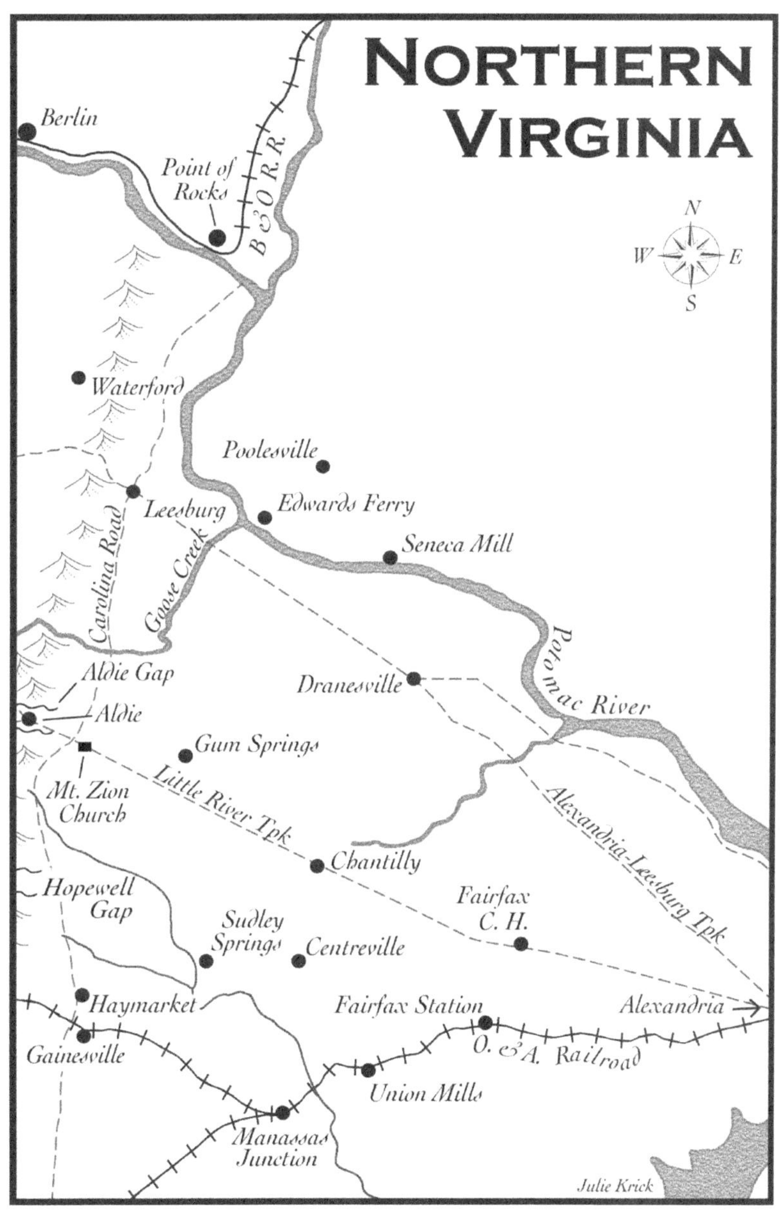

MAP 3. Northern Virginia. Created by Julie Krick.

Alfred Pleasonton's Cavalry Corps to assist Reynolds and instructed Pleasonton to report himself to Reynolds, near the railroad.[2]

Historians have long criticized Pleasonton for either not recognizing the importance of aggressively using his cavalry to locate Lee's army or for blatantly avoiding the vital task of conducting proper reconnaissance. Such claims miss an important point: Pleasonton did everything Hooker asked him to do. Hooker knew the Cavalry Corps remained badly understrength, with at least fifteen hundred men still awaiting remounts, and many other men lacking saddles, weapons, or other necessary equipment. With too many needs and too few troopers, Hooker preferred to delegate all long-range scouting missions to Maj. Gen. Julius Stahel and his cavalry division, attached to the Department of Washington. Hooker still coveted Stahel's division and still hoped to convince officials in Washington to transfer Stahel to his army.[3]

Indeed, Stahel had just sent a strong reconnaissance to the Shenandoah Valley. On June 6, 170 men from the First Michigan, accompanied by a squadron of the Second Pennsylvania, departed Fairfax Court House for Winchester. Maj. Melvin Brewer led the detachment through Warrenton to Waterloo, where the Yankees skirmished briefly with Southern pickets from Col. Thomas Munford's brigade before continuing to Chester Gap. Pushing through the gap in the early evening of June 7, the Michiganders marched through Front Royal under cover of darkness and reached Federal-held Winchester at 3 a.m., June 8. Along the way, Brewer detached Capt. Stephen Hanson and his Pennsylvanians to reconnoiter the country along the eastern edge of the Blue Ridge, including the towns of Aldie, Middleburg, and Upperville. When Hanson rejoined Brewer on June 8, with eight prisoners in tow, he reported having observed only a few guerrillas east of the mountains. In a communication of the same day, Brewer accurately placed Lt. Gen. Richard Ewell's Corps near Culpeper. And, having skirmished with enemy cavalry pickets along his entire route, Brewer reported that Stuart, "with a large force of cavalry, is between Culpeper and Front Royal." The Yankees returned to Fairfax Court House on June 12, taking a northerly route through Berryville, Snicker's Gap, and Leesburg. Major

Brewer had covered important territory during his reconnaissance. Unfortunately, he had been a couple of days too early on the way to Winchester, and, by following the old military maxim of not returning by the same route, missed Ewell's advance against Winchester on the way back.[4]

Unable to divine a logical explanation for Lee's division of his army, Hooker could not ignore a possible pincer movement against his own army, especially the western wing along the railroad. He specifically feared an attack launched through one or more mountain gaps in the Blue Ridge, including Chester and Manassas Gaps, and, most especially, Thoroughfare Gap in Bull Run Mountain. During a June 13 meeting with his corps commanders, Hooker singled out Thoroughfare Gap as his greatest concern and the point to be defended. Specifically, Hooker and Reynolds ordered Pleasonton to disperse three brigades to hold the fords along the upper Rappahannock River west of Warrenton and to block Thoroughfare Gap. In cavalry parlance, Hooker charged Pleasonton with screening or protecting his widely dispersed army from a surprise attack, rather than scouting for the enemy. Sending scouting parties through the gaps in the Blue Ridge became Pleasonton's secondary, rather than the primary, objective.[5]

On June 13, at Hooker's direction, Pleasonton sent the Reserve Brigade, from Brig. Gen. John Buford's division, to block Thoroughfare Gap and to scout the approaches to the gap. Led by Maj. Samuel Starr, the Regulars, along with the Sixth Pennsylvania, encountered numerous delays en route. Finally reaching his objective at 10 a.m., June 14, Starr established a picket line west of the gap and centered around the town of Salem. Unaware of the difficulties confronting Starr, Reynolds impatiently waited for word from the cavalry through the day on June 13. Pleasonton stayed in communication with Reynolds but could do nothing to relieve his superior's anxiety until he heard from Starr.[6]

Hooker also directed Pleasonton to secure the line of the Orange and Alexandria Railroad. The cavalry chief sent Col. John Irvin Gregg's and Col. Alfred Duffié's brigades to meet and cooperate with Reynolds near Bealeton Station. The wing commander then sent a reconnaissance from one of the brigades across the Rappahannock River; several Southern accounts mention Union cavalry forcing a crossing at Beverly Ford. Responding to the incursion, Capt. Roger Preston Chew rushed two of his guns to the crest of Fleetwood Hill, where two other Southern batteries soon joined them. As one of the gunners noted, "The Yanks did not venture very far inland . . . after they crossed to our side of the river."[7]

Pleasonton also sent Col. John Taylor's brigade, from Brig. Gen. David Gregg's division, to Warrenton, with instructions to remain "active and vigilant" and to report everything, regardless of perceived importance. Arriving late in the evening, Taylor sent a heavy force to watch the roads from the Blue Ridge, including the key intersections at Gaines Cross Roads, Orleans, and Barbee's Cross Roads, as well as several fords, including those at Sulphur Springs and Waterloo. Colonel Taylor also sent Maj. Myron Beaumont and the First New Jersey on a reconnaissance to Amissville. During the night, Beaumont sent a squadron across the Rappahannock River, drawing fire from Colonel Munford's pickets. The Northerners then encountered what they believed to be infantry pickets around Amissville. Unwilling to tangle with infantry in the dark, Beaumont retired across the Rappahannock.[8]

With most of his horse-soldiers holding ground rather than actively searching for the enemy, Pleasonton relied upon "good Union lads" or slaves fleeing bondage for his information. Unsatisfied, Reynolds told Pleasonton's troopers to rely upon their own observations rather than reports from civilians of dubious allegiance. The wing commander also tried to induce his own scouts to cross the Rappahannock River, but all refused. Frustrated, Reynolds told Hooker's adjutant, "I . . . know of no means of getting any scouts through this country."[9]

Following light, widely scattered showers during the night, searing heat returned to the region on June 14. Capt. Jonathan Hager, Fourteenth U.S. Infantry, noted, "We very soon reached the country where there had been no rain and from this morning . . . our suffering from heat, dust and want of water were indescribable." As the sun sucked the last drops of moisture from the ground, dust became every soldier's special misery for the next five days. Southerner Benjamin Jones recalled how the dust penetrated "into the clothing and accoutrements, into the eyes and lungs of man and beast, into everything." Longing for rain "to lay the soil-demon low," Jones termed a march through the impenetrable dust as "one of the severest tests of his physical endurance."[10]

Few men in the ranks knew anything of the "big picture" or the grand strategy of the developing campaign, but many, like Samuel Gilpin, Third Indiana, understood that the enemy had given Hooker the slip. "W-ha-r-e has little Robbie Lee gone," Gilpin asked sarcastically. And, like Hooker, Gilpin wondered if "it is about time for our *annual Bull Run*." Charles Smith, First Massachusetts, agreed, telling his parents, "We all think we are on the eve of a great battle . . . and the scene of the action will probably be the old Bull Run Battlefield."[11]

Should such an attack occur, Hooker and Reynolds both assumed the enemy would strike through Thoroughfare Gap and both men anxiously awaited word from Pleasonton. Unaware of the delays Major Starr had encountered during the night and his late arrival at the gap, Pleasonton had nothing to report as midday approached on June 14. When the Regulars finally reached the gap after a long night in the saddle, Starr sent Capt. William Treichel, Sixth Pennsylvania, with one squadron to scout Ashby's Gap in the Blue Ridge. A second squadron, led by Capt. Henry Hazeltine, scouted the roads to Manassas Gap. Writing after the war, Hazeltine claimed to have pushed through the gap, driven off Confederate pickets, and reached a point where he could see enemy troops forming in the valley below him and hear the Southern guns at Winchester. Upon his return, Hazeltine gave Starr a written report of his reconnaissance, which Starr then forwarded directly to Hooker.[12]

During a meeting prior to 8 a.m. on June 14, Reynolds ordered Pleasonton to relieve the last of the infantry pickets along the Rappahannock River. Pleasonton complied, sending three brigades, or elements thereof, Duffié's, Taylor's, and Col. Thomas Devin's, to secure the river between U.S. Ford and Waterloo.

Hooker expected the cavalry to hold the river fords until at least 1 a.m. the following morning, but the last of the men remained until the evening of the fifteenth. As they retired from the river, the men headed for Centreville, with orders to prepare "for vigorous service."[13]

Not until he had returned to his headquarters did Pleasonton learn of the First New Jersey's scout to Amissville during the night. At 10:00 a.m. he informed Reynolds, "My reconnaissance from Warrenton met a force of the enemy's cavalry at Amissville. The reconnaissance was a regiment—the enemy's force was much larger."[14]

During the day, Colonel Taylor's men clashed with enemy troopers who had briefly crossed the Rappahannock River, before being driven back by the First Maryland. In response to these incursions, Taylor reinforced the Marylanders with a squadron from the Third Pennsylvania. Taylor also told General Gregg that his men had seen "a column of dust about seven miles in length, moving in the direction of Luray" in the Shenandoah Valley. The Marylanders mistakenly believed the dust represented General Ewell's Corps.[15]

With Pleasonton still focused on holding the Rappahannock River fords, watching the roads from Manassas and Chester Gaps and blocking Thoroughfare Gap, one man turned his attention to Aldie Gap in Bull Run Mountain. Maj. Gen. Oliver Otis Howard, commanding the XI Corps, led Reynolds's wing of the army north along the eastern slope of Bull Run Mountain. Alone, and with little cavalry support, Howard recognized the threat of a Confederate attack launched against his corps from Aldie Gap. Ten miles north of Thoroughfare Gap, Aldie Gap (and the town of Aldie) provided Lee with another approach from the Shenandoah Valley through Bull Run Mountain. No one could fault Howard, whose corps had borne the brunt of a surprise attack six weeks earlier at Chancellorsville, for being hesitant to approach the gap without cavalry protection.

General Howard reached Centreville, about eight miles southeast of Aldie Gap, around 6:20 p.m. on June 14. He immediately queried General Stahel at Fairfax Court House, eight miles east of Centreville: "The enemy is said to [be] . . . going in a northern direction towards & beyond Front Royal. Have you any information—what gaps do you guard? Have you any force beyond Aldie & south of Aldie west of Bull Run Mountain?" Stahel's adjutant responded, telling Howard, "We have no news from Aldie . . . later than night before last when there was no enemy in that neighborhood except Mosby's guerrillas." Stahel later added, "My scouting parties which returned yesterday from Aldie, Middleburg, Salem, and that section of the country, reported no enemy in sight nor could they learn of any force in that vicinity." Still, Howard remained wary and convinced Stahel to send two hundred men from the First Michigan to picket the approaches from Aldie.[16]

General Robert E. Lee's plans and intentions continued to confound Hooker. By June 15 Hooker knew Ewell's Corps to be in the Shenandoah Valley near Winchester. He also knew Lt. Gen. A. P. Hill had, along with Stuart's cavalry, remained along the Rappahannock River. But he had lost track of Lt. Gen. James Longstreet's Corps. His fear of a pincer movement from Lee's widely dispersed army forced Hooker to keep his own army scattered as a hedge against such a threat. Having held his cavalry to largely static efforts, holding river fords, guarding mountain gaps, and screening his own infantry, Hooker had prevented his troopers from discerning Lee's motives and location. According to his youthful aide, Capt. Ulric Dahlgren, Hooker had "started this move more from information from Negroes" than from his own men and continued to rely upon outdated, and, too often, wildly inaccurate information to base his own decisions. Still, Pleasonton had urged his men to scout when possible, and reconnaissance patrols had been sent to the gaps of the Blue Ridge. Unfortunately, Pleasonton had little talent for properly interpreting the information he received. General Halleck grumbled to Hooker, "Pleasonton's telegrams to you contain all the information we have of the enemy's movements. They are very contradictory. . . . [and] very unsatisfactory."[17]

Several messages raised Halleck's ire. At nearly 1 a.m. on June 15, Pleasonton reported, "My scouts from Chester and Ashby's Gap report the rebel General Stuart, with 15,000 cavalry, at Upperville." Relying upon the local populace, Pleasonton placed Longstreet within supporting distance of Stuart "with 30,000 men." A few hours later he reversed himself, claiming his scouts had "been out as far as Middleburg [twelve miles from the Blue Ridge and] report nothing as far as the Blue Ridge." Forty-five thousand enemy troops had suddenly disappeared. In fact, Longstreet's infantry only began to depart their camps around Culpeper on the morning of June 15. The cavalry chief also placed both Hill and Ewell along the Rappahannock River, when Halleck knew Ewell to be battling Union troops around Berryville and Winchester. Pleasonton then compounded his errors by trying to divine the future and by subverting the chain of command. At 6 a.m. he told Secretary of War Edwin Stanton, "It would be well to place . . . a good force at the mouth of the Monocacy, as Stuart will attempt to cross [there]. . . . Longstreet will probably strike for Williamsport and [Hagerstown, Maryland . . . and] Stuart will strike for [Poolesville, Maryland] if he cannot cross at the mouth of the Monocacy."[18]

Pleasonton's erroneous conclusions about enemy strength along the Rappahannock River forced his men to hold their positions along the river longer than necessary. Hooker had ordered Pleasonton to begin withdrawing his pickets as early as 1 a.m. on the fifteenth, but when the cavalry chief reported two enemy corps still holding the line his own words came back to haunt him. When Maj. Gen. George Meade, commanding the V Corps at Manassas Junction, heard Pleasonton's conclusion that both Ewell and Hill remained along the river, Meade asked him to maintain his picket line beyond the 1 a.m. deadline. Pleasonton tried to have Stahel replace his men, but his ploy failed, and Reynolds told Pleasonton to leave his "pickets in Meade's front connecting with the regiments at Thoroughfare [Gap], on the railroad and Warrenton pike." Not until midafternoon would the first of his troopers begin the long, hot march to Manassas Junction.[19]

Leaving two brigades (Gamble's and Devin's) from General Buford's First Division to cover his withdrawal from the river fords, Pleasonton ordered General Gregg to withdraw his brigades at staggered intervals. Judson Kilpatrick, who had just returned to the corps and taken command of Duffié's brigade, began withdrawing at noon. Colonel Taylor, headquartered near Warrenton, and Col. John Irvin Gregg, posted along the railroad, followed at 2 p.m. Colonel Devin, serving as the "rear guard of the army," started for Manassas Junction after dark.[20]

With the Cavalry Corps now moving toward Manassas Junction, General Howard renewed his request for assistance from Stahel. Specifically, Howard asked Stahel to establish a picket line covering the roads running between Aldie and Centreville. Stahel refused, as heavy woods would leave his men isolated. Rather than maintaining a static line nearly twelve miles long, he agreed to establish a system of roving patrols along the roads. To the south, at Thoroughfare Gap, Maj. Samuel Starr kept his regiments actively patrolling the area west of the gap.[21]

As the sun cracked the horizon on June 16, "no one" at Hooker's headquarters "seemed to know what was to be done" with the army, according to Brig. Gen. Marsena Patrick, Hooker's provost marshal. Having had his plan to advance against Richmond dismissed by both Lincoln and Halleck, Hooker seemed, as Patrick observed, to have no idea as to how he should proceed, nor did he appear willing to consider his options. When Lincoln had sought his advice the previous day, Hooker repeatedly replied, "I do not know that my opinion as to the duty of this army . . . is wanted." Hooker saw Halleck as his main antagonist, telling Lincoln, "You have been long aware that I have not enjoyed" Halleck's confidence, "and I can assure you so long as this continues we may look in vain for success, especially as future operations will require our relations to be more dependent upon each other than heretofore." Hooker had challenged Lincoln to choose between his field general and his general-in-chief. But if he had hoped to see Halleck relieved, his plan failed, as Lincoln made clear hours later. "To remove all misunderstanding," Lincoln told Hooker, "I now place you in strict military relation to Halleck. . . . I shall direct him to give you orders and you to obey them." The president's directive did little to ease the growing discord between the generals.[22]

In his message to Lincoln, Hooker also sought permission to attack Lt. Gen. A. P. Hill's Corps before Hill could reach the Shenandoah Valley and rejoin Lee. Presenting his argument, Hooker made a vital point: "We can never discover the whereabouts of the enemy, or divine his intentions, so long as he fills the country with a cloud of cavalry. We must break through that to find him." Hooker had finally recognized the immediate task before him; find the enemy, even if doing so meant risking a battle while his own army remained dispersed. Lincoln had given Hooker command of the army because of his reputation as a fighter and Hooker may have seen his offer to seek battle east of the Blue Ridge as a means of convincing Lincoln to oust Halleck. When the president disagreed with his plan, Hooker quickly lost his will to fight.[23]

Rather than employing his cavalry to search for Lee, Hooker, reacting to excited reports of Rebels in Pennsylvania, sought permission to send most of Pleasonton's Corps into Maryland ahead of the army. Halleck quickly dissuaded him. General Lee's main force should be the target, Halleck counseled, "and I know of no way to ascertain [Lee's location], excepting through your cavalry, which should be kept near enough to the enemy to at least be able to tell where he is." General Halleck believed Hooker should concentrate his army at Leesburg, just south of the Potomac River, but, he reiterated, "Unless your army is kept near enough to the enemy to ascertain his movements, yours must remain in the dark or [act] on mere conjecture."[24]

Confusion, hesitation, and trepidation now engulfed Hooker's headquarters. He needed to locate the four major elements of Lee's scattered army to bring clarity. Rather than employing his cavalry to resolve his uncertainty, as Halleck had suggested, Hooker sought to sow confusion in Lee's mind by planting a false story. "Please have the newspapers announce that I am moving to the James River line," he asked Stanton. Unimpressed, Stanton warned Hooker, "The very demon of lying seems to be about these times, and generals will have to be broken for ignorance before they will take the trouble to find out the truth of reports."[25]

Having been repeatedly rebuked by his superiors, Hooker now

sought to allow them to dictate his course. But Halleck offered riddles rather than clear advice. After being told by Halleck that the Union garrison at Harpers Ferry was in danger of capture by Lee's advancing army and could expect no relief "excepting from your army," Hooker offered to march to the town the next morning. His decision, however, drew only another rebuke from Halleck. "I have given no directions for your army to move to Harper's Ferry," he told Hooker, apparently worried such a move would uncover Washington. Instead, Halleck recommended the move to Leesburg. Only when the enemy had been located would Halleck approve a move to "Harpers Ferry, or elsewhere, as circumstances might require." Still seeking clarity as to the location of the enemy, Halleck told Hooker emphatically, "I want you to push out your cavalry, to ascertain something definite about the enemy." We will not know where to move, Halleck continued, "until you can feel the enemy and ascertain his whereabouts."[26]

While Pleasonton had shown little initiative in trying to solve the mysteries that confounded Hooker, he had done everything asked of him. He still had two commanding officers, Joseph Hooker and John Reynolds, and their opinions and priorities differed from those of their commanders in Washington. While Hooker battled with his superiors, Reynolds prepared for a possible battle near Centreville. Pleasonton's decision to concentrate his corps near Manassas Junction may have violated his orders, but it also eased Reynolds's concerns as the cavalry chief deployed his troopers to block the fords along Bull Run. But Reynolds also ordered Pleasonton to continue screening his infantry by maintaining his pickets along the upper Rappahannock River and at Warrenton. Though Reynolds's decision made tactical sense, his order prevented these men from resupplying at Manassas Junction as quickly as Pleasonton would have liked.[27]

During the day, Pleasonton met with Hooker at Fairfax Station. They may have discussed plans to locate Lee, as well the demands from Hooker's superiors. They may also have discussed several logistical concerns, including dismounted men being sent back to the army without horses and horses being sent to the army without saddles and other necessary equipment. Pleasonton had asked to have grain and forage for his horses dropped at multiple points along the railroad to facilitate resupply and allow his men and animals a modicum of rest. Hooker's chief quartermaster, Rufus Ingalls, had refused. Instead, seven hundred thousand pounds of grain and forage had been unloaded at Manassas Junction. But after being delayed along the Rappahannock River, the tired men and hungry animals reached the junction only to find the food and forage gone. Several infantry corps had reached the supplies ahead of the troopers and helped themselves. Pleasonton might have prevented the theft had he remained at Manassas Junction rather than moving to Union Mills. Now, he could only order another shipment and hope it arrived before his men pulled out in the morning.[28]

The heat moderated only slightly on June 16. Marching remained a challenge of endurance as dust enveloped the men and water remained scarce. Weary though they were, the men continued to speculate as to the purpose behind their misery. Some still believed a fight to be inevitable near Bull Run, though Samuel Gilpin, ever sarcastic noted, "No more Bull Runs' for we are too sharp to stop here. Besides we have a *Hooker* now." Maj. Henry Higginson, a Boston Brahmin in the First Massachusetts, presciently concluded, "The rebel army will get into Pennsylvania . . . and finally get a severe whipping." He believed Lee's plans could "be checkmated by someone and turned into a great and final defeat." But, he noted, wryly, "we have yet to see who 'someone' is." Alfred Ryder, First Michigan, agreed. "These are action times," he told friends back home, "something is going to tell on the war before long." Throughout the Army of the Potomac, the men longed for victory and for a commander who could lead them to victory. "The rebels in arms are in deadly earnest," concluded Joseph King, Sixth Michigan. "They *must know* and be *made to feel* that there is no compromise and no rest until they have thrown down their arms," he declared.[29]

General Hooker ordered Reynolds to have his several corps moving toward Leesburg by 3 a.m., June 17. The men in the eastern column remained in camp until 3 p.m., as a means of escaping the heat. Once the men had drawn rations and ammunition and their supply wagons had been topped off, quartermasters sent all surplus material to Alexandria. "As soon as the intentions of the enemy are known I shall be able to advance with rapidity," Hooker promised Halleck. But the beleaguered army commander could only discern the intentions of the enemy, as another officer observed, by "sending out his cavalry." Yet, as events soon proved, Hooker had other plans.[30]

SIX

Stuart Moves into the Loudoun Valley, June 16–17

Learning on June 15 that the last of the Union infantry along the Rappahannock River had finally withdrawn and begun heading north, Robert E. Lee resumed his northward move. He ordered Lt. Gen. James Longstreet to abandon his campsites near Culpeper and start his men toward the Shenandoah Valley, moving through Chester Gap and Manassas Gap and concentrating at Front Royal. And, just as Alfred Pleasonton's cavalry had screened Hooker's infantry earlier in the week, Jeb Stuart's cavalry would screen Longstreet's infantry.[1]

"I was instructed," Stuart explained, "to leave a sufficient force on the Rappahannock to watch the enemy in front, and to move the main body parallel to the Blue Ridge and on Longstreet's right flank . . . through Fauquier and Loudoun Counties." A man of boundless energy, enthusiasm, and endurance, Stuart had suffered long months confined to the Rappahannock River as a wild animal endures confinement. The recent criticism cast upon Stuart by the Southern press had only added to his misery. Northern editors had also delighted in Stuart's humiliation following the battle at Brandy Station, referring to him as "Poor gasconading Jeb," but all observers expected him to soon "do something to redeem his reputation." Indeed, he longed to escape the boredom of picket duty. "I . . . feel not unlike a tiger pausing before its spring," he told his brother, adding "that spring will not be delayed much longer." Coiled up along the river, Stuart received Lee's instructions "with joy."[2]

Before ordering his men into their saddles, Stuart sought to erase any lingering doubts in their minds regarding the difficult fight at Brandy Station. "With an abiding faith in the God of battles, and a firm reliance on the sabre," he told them, "your successes will continue." Likewise, Lee sought to bolster Stuart's confidence after his recent pummeling by the press, telling him, "The dispositions made by you to meet the strong attack of the enemy [at Brandy Station] appear to have been judicious and well planned. The troops were well and skillfully managed."[3]

In compliance with Lee's orders, Stuart left the Fifteenth Virginia along the lower Rappahannock River, and Brig. Gen. Wade Hampton's brigade along the upper stretch of the river. He then sent three brigades, led by Col. Thomas Munford, Col. John Chambliss, and Brig. Gen. Beverly Robertson, moving north in two columns as an advance screen for Longstreet's infantry. Brig. Gen. William Jones's brigade followed, moving across the Hazel River, from where he could support Hampton to the south or the other brigades to the north.[4]

Colonel Thomas Munford, Second Virginia, had commanded Fitz Lee's brigade for several weeks. Hobbled by inflammatory rheumatism and recently kicked by a horse, Lee had relinquished command to Munford prior to the fight at Brandy Station. Colonel Munford's troopers stepped into their saddles at 7 a.m., June 16, crossed the upper Rappahannock River at Rock Ford, and passed through Barbee's Cross Roads, along the Lee's Manor Road, before halting for several hours at Markham, near the eastern end of Manassas Gap. The command then advanced to Summerset, a farm near the hamlet of Paris, where the men bivouacked for the night.[5]

With Rooney Lee recovering from a wound sustained at Brandy Station, Col. John Chambliss, Thirteenth Virginia, led Rooney's brigade across the Hazel River at Welford's Ford and across the Rappahannock River at Hinson's Mill Ford, north of Amissville. The brigade spent the night picketing the roads around Orleans. Likewise, General Robertson's brigade crossed the Rappahannock

River at Hinson's Mill Ford and spent the night near Salem. General Jones bivouacked his men in the narrow neck of land between the Hazel and Rappahannock Rivers, known as the Little Fork.[6]

Before departing, a North Carolina soldier told his wife, "We know nothing of Gen'l Lee's plans, but feel confident that he is making some great military movement." The Southern horsemen must have rejoiced as they finally escaped the fetid fields around Brandy Station, where, according to William McVicar, everything still looked "like desolation." Nightfall on the sixteenth found the men encamped in "the rich fields and valleys of upper Fauquier," enjoying, according to Stuart's aide, Theodore Garnett, "the fresh air of the Blue Ridge."[7]

Stuart planned to move into the Loudoun Valley in the morning. About thirty-four miles long north to south, and more than twenty miles wide, the Loudoun Valley is marked by a series of low ridges rippling between the Blue Ridge Mountains to the west and Bull Run Mountain to the east. The wide, southern end of the valley bisects the border of Loudoun and Fauquier Counties and stretches between the town of Aldie, nestled into Aldie Gap in Bull Run Mountain and the hamlet of Paris at the entrance to Ashby's Gap in the Blue Ridge. Other gaps bracket the Aldie and Ashby Gaps, and each was, in the view of one officer, "easily defended" and easily "converted into efficient military obstacles." Stuart had an intimate familiarity with the valley and the advantages of the terrain, having fought a series of sharp clashes across the region the previous autumn.[8]

The Ashby's Gap Turnpike—an improved, macadamized road—crossed the southern part of the valley from Ashby's Gap to Aldie. East of Aldie the road carried the name Little River Turnpike, after a nearby stream, and continued eastward to Alexandria. The Snickersville Turnpike, another macadamized toll road, originated in Aldie and ran northwest to Snicker's Gap in the Blue Ridge. Just east of the town and the junction of the two turnpikes, the Carolina Road followed the path of an old Indian trail between Pennsylvania and North Carolina.[9]

As the two turnpikes neared completion in the second decade

of the century, Charles Fenton Mercer, an attorney in Leesburg, envisioned a solution to a local need. By constructing a mill at Aldie Gap, Mercer could provide a service to local farmers while generating additional income for himself and his family. He soon completed a milling complex on the south side of the Little River Turnpike and a stately home across the road, which he named Aldie for his ancestral home in Scotland. A few years later he established the town of the same name just west of the Carolina Road, at the intersection of the turnpikes.[10]

The gap in Bull Run Mountain, together with the convergence of the turnpikes and the Carolina Road, made the town of Aldie militarily significant. Jeb Stuart knew, as the Federals had realized earlier in the week, that by seizing both Aldie Gap and Thoroughfare Gap to the south, he could, with a small force, deny the enemy access to both the Loudoun Valley and the Shenandoah Valley. He also knew from prior experience the difficulty of moving large bodies of troops over the smaller roads and farm lanes that crisscrossed the valley. As a Union officer explained, the secondary roads through the region were "narrow and tortuous; difficult to use at all times, and after rains almost impracticable." These smaller roads, many of which are deeply cut into the surrounding landscape and lined by stout rail or stone fences, prevented the rapid deployment of cavalry from column formations in the roads to linear formations in the fields. To prevent being surprised by the enemy while confined in the roads, commanders deployed strong flanking detachments and advance guards, a physically exhausting assignment as these men and horses traveled a much greater distance than their comrades in the roads and over much more difficult terrain. If Stuart could establish his cavalry at the eastern entrances to the Loudoun Valley, rather than the gaps in the Blue Ridge, he would have miles of defensible ground to use as he screened Lee's infantry moving along the line of the Blue Ridge.[11]

Few soldiers or travelers who passed through the Loudoun Valley failed to note the beauty of the region, as well as the productive farms and stately manor homes. Though not given to gushing hyperbole, Union colonel Charles Wainwright had an artillerist's eye for detail and nuance. The natural beauty of the region left him awestruck. When he passed through the region the previous fall, with the trees painted in a full autumn palette, "the view," Wainwright wrote, "was picture perfect . . . beautiful beyond my powers of description." A soldier from upstate New York concurred, judging the area "the finest I have yet seen in Virginia. The fields are large and well fenced, mostly with stone walls. The luxuriant pastures would delight the eyes of our valley farmers." Assessing the productivity of the farms, the soldier felt certain the farmers would not face "starvation whatever the rebel army may need." Peter Alexander, a Southern correspondent, termed the valley "a land flowing with milk and honey." A Pennsylvanian saw the "substantial and spacious" homes as proof of "intelligent farming and industrious thrift." He also marveled at the stone fences, which "intersected each other in every direction and at all angles." But while infantrymen, artillerists, and engineers gazed in wonder at the lush beauty and stately homes, cavalrymen, like Capt. William McDonald, Eleventh Virginia, understood that farmers had not erected the fences to create mesmerizing quiltlike patterns across the fields or along the roadways but rather to prevent the free movement of livestock. As such the stout walls would hinder the ability of mounted troops to rapidly traverse the fields and easily enter and exit the roads.[12]

In contrast to the lush farms and pastures of the valley, the small towns, especially Aldie, Middleburg, and Upperville, bore the scars of two years of conflict. With most of the men of fighting age serving with the army, homes had fallen into disrepair and businesses had been shuttered. A Michigander saw Aldie as "a pretty old village," though the "houses are in a dilapidated condition." Another Wolverine counted three taverns and several stores, all of them closed. One soldier thought the town "quaint," another "ordinary," while a third dismissed the village as "a miserable hamlet."[13]

Established in 1787 midway between Alexandria and Winchester, and located six miles west of Aldie, Middleburg had grown into a town of several hundred residents by 1863. A Michigander viewed the citizens as "wealthy and aristocratic," who lived in "comfortable and commodious" homes, but he dismissed them as bearing "remarkable secesh proclivities." Most Northern soldiers agreed, denouncing the town as "a secesh hole," whose residents are "secesh up to the handle." Southerners disagreed, viewing the town as "beautiful." A Pennsylvanian thought Upperville, established in 1818, nine miles west of Middleburg, "quite a smart little village," but like the residents of Middleburg, Yankees thought the people of Upperville to be "saucy" and "secesh . . . out and out."[14]

Few healthy men of fighting age remained in the valley. In the rush to war, many of the young men had joined one of the several regiments raised in the area. By 1863 most of the enslaved workers had fled the farms in a quest for freedom. Young men who sought to stay home and work the farms often found themselves conscripted into the army. The valley had escaped the destruction and trauma of a large battle, but several engagements, including First and Second Manassas and Antietam, had taken place nearby. After each, hundreds of wounded men had been left at makeshift hospitals in the valley. Cavalry clashes in the fall of 1862 sent additional men into local infirmaries, where many languished through the winter. Union cavalry patrols passing through the area delighted in capturing and paroling the invalids to prevent them from rejoining their regiments. In just one instance, a Union force paroled eight hundred convalescents from hospitals in Middleburg in September 1862. By June 1863 few healthy men remained. Yankees passing through saw only "cripples and old men."[15]

Life for the residents of the Loudoun Valley changed dramatically on December 31, 1862, when Jeb Stuart allowed his aide, John Mosby, to begin conducting guerrilla operations against the Union forces stationed along the border between Loudoun and Fairfax Counties. Mosby's success drew young soldiers into his ranks in droves, including some of the convalescents recuperating in and around Middleburg. Many of these men, deemed the "sinews of partisan warfare" by one Yankee, boarded at homes throughout the area, especially homes where young ladies resided.[16]

The continued presence of the partisans proved both a boon and a burden for the residents. The young soldiers offered protection, helped with tasks around the house or farm, and shared the spoils taken during their operations. Their loss, to death or capture, caused additional grief for families who may already have lost a father, husband, or son. Their success drew retaliatory Union expeditions bent on rooting out and destroying Mosby's command. As a matter of survival, the young soldiers fled their homes when the Yankees arrived, leaving the women to defend their property while the guerrillas looked for an opportunity to strike their enemy.

General George Meade, who made his headquarters near Aldie for several days, found the women he encountered to be ardent secessionists but also "civil and affable" when treated with respect. As the head of the household in many cases, mothers, wives, and daughters earned both respect and independence as they struggled to feed their families and maintain their homes, farms, and shops in the face of near daily confrontations with enemy soldiers. As historian Lee Lawrence explains, cultural norms generally earned "white Southern 'ladies' courtesy and respect" and allowed them "the freedom to confront hat tipping Union officers and troops and walk away unscathed," regardless of their demeanor. Enslaved women who remained on the farms often faced a harsher reality, however, and endured more brutal treatment at the hands of Federals bent on eliminating the guerrilla bands. When the enemy soldiers departed, the women "returned to their war routines: feeding and housing Confederate soldiers, sewing Rebel uniforms, turning their homes into hospitals," and seeing after the survival of their own kith and kin. "Their battlefield was the corncrib, stables, pasture, and parlor." On June 16, as Jeb Stuart and his cavalry entered the Loudoun Valley, many women, young and old, rejoiced at his arrival while remaining blissfully unaware of the struggles and horrors about to engulf them.[17]

In nearby Warrenton, Mrs. Susan Caldwell had endured the presence of Union troopers since June 13. With the Yankees expecting to be resupplied by train at Warrenton Junction, Caldwell and other residents had tolerated the soldiers as they hoped to trade fresh bread for coffee and sugar. Like the soldiers, Caldwell and the other ladies were disappointed when the trains failed to arrive. But, as she noted wryly, better to "be without sugar than be with the Yankees."[18]

Edwin and Catherine Broun owned a home and a mercantile store in Middleburg, as well as a farm nearby. A secessionist to the core, who once told a Union officer the women of the South would proudly take up the struggle if the Yankees killed all the men, Catherine maintained a diary in which she detailed her family's daily struggles to maintain their way of life. In April 1863 Yankees searching for John Mosby and his men searched the Broun's farm and seized their horses. They also set fire to their store.[19]

Mrs. Mary Eliza Powell Dulany, Ida to her family and friends, lived at Oakley Farm, just east of Upperville. With the outbreak of war her husband, Henry Grafton Dulany, had been elected a lieutenant in the Sixth Virginia Cavalry; however, an eye injury forced the dedicated young officer to resign in July 1862, lest he go blind. His difficult decision failed to bring peace or stability to his family. As a young man of fighting age, Henry found himself confronted by another hard choice: abandon his family and flee farther south or sign a parole, pledging not to bear arms against the North. Even after signing the parole, Henry constantly feared being seized by the enemy. Thus, Ida looked after her family and often ran the substantial farm alone.[20]

About twenty-four years of age in June 1863, Amanda Edmonds lived at Belle Grove, at the base of the Blue Ridge near Paris. A fiery young woman and a fierce defender of the Southern cause, Edmonds simply did not know the meaning of retreat when confronted by the soldiers she termed "Blue wretches." On the evening of June 16, as Colonel Munford's men bedded down at Summerset Farm, a picket detail marched by her home. Beaming with pride, she stood by the road and cheered as the men rode by.[21]

SEVEN

Hooker's Ruse, June 16–17

On June 16 General Hooker ordered the I, V, XI, and XII Corps to move at 3 a.m. the following morning on Leesburg, with the remainder of the army to follow later in the day. His army circular contained no instructions governing the movement of the Cavalry Corps on June 17. Still, General Pleasonton told his division commanders to have their men ready to move at the same hour, though his brief directive offered no hint of his plans or intended destination. Hooker probably issued his order prior to telling President Lincoln at 9:40 p.m. that he intended to march with "vigor and power." The president, who may have been at the War Department reviewing developments with Secretary of War Edwin Stanton and General-in-Chief Henry Halleck, received Hooker's message ten minutes later. Hooker's telegram, combined with an earlier note in which he announced his intention to march on Harpers Ferry, brought the strong rebukes from Lincoln and Halleck (previously discussed) in which Lincoln made clear that Hooker took his orders from Halleck.[1]

In response to the reproach from Lincoln and Halleck, received by Hooker at 1 a.m., Hooker's aides, Brig. Gen. Seth Williams and Maj. Gen. Daniel Butterfield, sent a flurry of messages to the infantry commanders to now move by "easy marches," in the direction of, though not to, Leesburg. During his meeting with Pleasonton earlier in the day, Hooker had agreed to allow

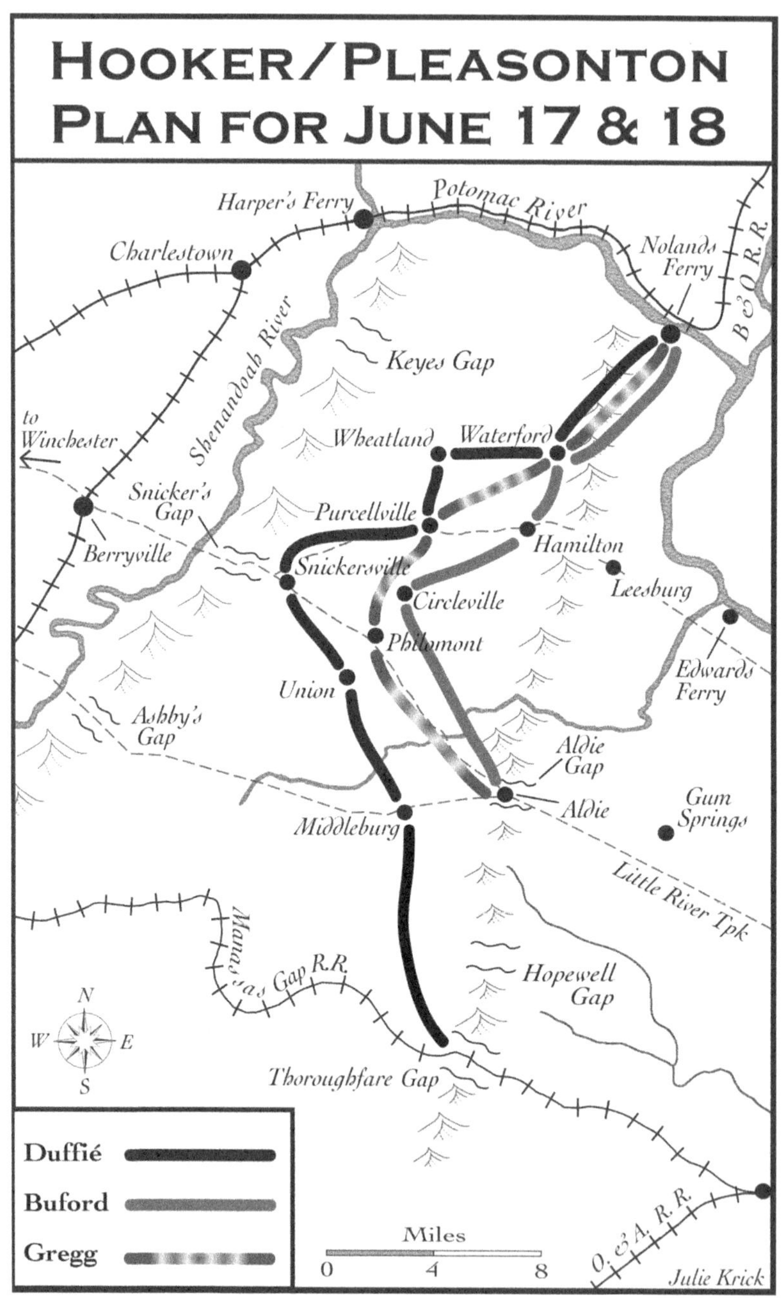

MAP 4. Hooker/Pleasonton plan for June 17 and 18. Created by Julie Krick.

Pleasonton to send most of his corps through Aldie and into the Loudoun Valley. One regiment would enter the Loudoun Valley through Thoroughfare Gap and spend the night in Middleburg, thirteen miles from Ashby's Gap and the Blue Ridge and nearly thirty miles from Winchester. The following morning, June 18, the lone regiment would "proceed [northwest] to Union; thence by way of Snickersville [east] to Purcellville," then north to Nolands Ferry on the Potomac River by way Wheatland and Waterford. At Snickersville, the scouting force would be near Snickers Gap but still nine miles from Berryville.[2]

General Buford would move two of his three brigades through Aldie (the Reserve Brigade remained near Thoroughfare Gap), and then turn north, passing through Circleville, Hamilton, and Waterford before stopping at Nolands Ferry. Though Buford would swing west of Leesburg he would not be within seventeen miles of Berryville at his most westerly point. Pleasonton directed General Gregg to take a slightly more westerly route—through Philomont, Purcellville, and Waterford—before reuniting with the other columns at Nolands Ferry. Gregg's route would also take him west of Leesburg, though still nearly twenty miles from Berryville.[3]

After Pleasonton had departed from his meeting with Hooker and after Hooker had communicated with Lincoln, Stanton, and Halleck, the army commander had a change of heart. Contrary to orders from Halleck to "push out your cavalry, to ascertain something definite about the enemy," Hooker told Pleasonton the next morning, "Verbal orders have been sent to you by Captain [Ulric] Dahlgren. . . . Instead of moving your whole command . . . put the main body of your command in the vicinity of Aldie, and push out reconnaissances toward Winchester, Berryville, and Harper's Ferry." Hooker now wanted Pleasonton to hold all but one regiment east of Bull Run Mountain between Gum Springs and Aldie. As Pleasonton later testified, Hooker wanted to "receive battle from the enemy" near Manassas, and he wanted his cavalry close at hand.[4]

Still, Hooker sought to deceive his superiors, telling his cavalry chief, "Drive in pickets, if necessary, and get us information. It is better that we should lose men than to be without knowledge of the enemy, as we now seem to be." To any prying eyes, Hooker had bowed to the will of his superiors and shifted the primary role of his cavalry from a screening force to a scouting force. But Pleasonton could not engage or locate the enemy by remaining east of Aldie. The extent of Pleasonton's complicity in Hooker's ruse is difficult to judge, based on his actions later in the day.[5]

On the march, divisions, brigades, and regiments, routinely rotated positions in a moving column from day to day, with the lead unit one day moving to the rear of the column the following day. Thus, General Gregg knew, when he received Pleasonton's orders, that Judson Kilpatrick's brigade would lead the division on June 17. As a youth, Kilpatrick envisioned a career in politics, and he saw the military as a means of gaining the fame that would allow him to realize his dream. He did well at West Point, standing seventeenth in his graduating class of forty-five. He earned a reputation as a formidable scrapper, while his gift for acting and oratory led to his selection as class valedictorian. He had also shown remarkable discipline, surviving several years without a single demerit.[6]

On May 6, 1861, the day he graduated from West Point, Judson Kilpatrick and Alice Shaler were married. The following day he bade his bride goodbye and headed for Washington. One month later, while serving as a volunteer captain in the Fifth New York Infantry, he received a leg wound in the battle at Big Bethel, near Hampton, Virginia. Recovering in New York, Kilpatrick became a darling of the press and soon garnered a commission as lieutenant colonel of the Second New York Cavalry. In December 1862 he received his colonel's eagles and command of the regiment.[7]

Colonel Kilpatrick exercised temporary command of his brigade for much of the first half of 1863. At some point, though an actual date or event cannot be established, he earned the derogatory nom de guerre "Kill-Cavalry." At West Point, his fellow cadets had termed him "Little-Kil," while his troopers referred to him, affectionately, as "Old-Kil," but he never shook the disparaging "Kill-Cavalry." Nor would he ever shake questions concerning his honesty and ethics, after being arrested and briefly imprisoned on a theft charge.[8]

Edwin Havens, Seventh Michigan, saw Kilpatrick as "one of the roughest looking specimens of rowdies you ever saw." Described as "round shouldered, homely and ungraceful" on a horse, Kilpatrick adopted a rather plain uniform and wore "one of the awfullest shaped hats you ever saw." He chewed tobacco and, according to Havens, swore "as loud and as hard as anyone." An obviously smitten woman breathlessly described his "slender, alert, springy figure, his blonde hair and whiskers, his pale, sharply cut features, his keen, cold eye, his firm, determined remorseless mouth, with its thin lips and gleaming white teeth, that one could imagine in moments of fierce excitement, clashing together like the steel teeth of a wolf-trap."[9]

Though many, including a western officer later in the war, saw him as a "vain, conceited, egotistical popinjay," most of Kilpatrick's men loved him and regretted his departure from the Army of the Potomac in 1864. Whether one liked or despised him, most everyone agreed, he would fight and Pleasonton needed commanders who would fight. On June 15, wearing a new brigadier's star on his uniform, Kilpatrick relieved Colonel Duffié and took command of the Second Brigade, Second Division, which included the First Massachusetts, Fourth New York, Sixth Ohio, First Rhode Island, and, undoubtedly at his request, his Second New York.[10]

Beyond any sentimental attachment, Kilpatrick would have appreciated the addition of his old regiment to his brigade since several of his other regiments remained badly understrength. In addition to the men awaiting remounts, a battalion of the Second New York remained on the Peninsula and a battalion of the First Massachusetts remained in South Carolina. Aside from the men on detached duty, the diminished ranks of Kilpatrick's regiments reflected the grim toll of two years of war.[11]

Capt. Ulric Dahlgren, carrying Hooker's verbal instructions to hold the main column of the cavalry east of Aldie, caught up with Pleasonton between 11 a.m. and noon, about nine miles east of Aldie. Reading Hooker's order to hold his command east of Aldie, Pleasonton had a decision to make. As he later testified, "The country between Manassas and Aldie is very wooded, and the enemy's cavalry could annoy us exceedingly—in fact it was country in which we would be taken at every disadvantage." Stopping east of the mountain gap at Aldie made no military sense, as the cavalry would only have to pass through the gap the next morning. "These facts presented themselves to my mind with such force," Pleasonton asserted, "that I sent back word to Hooker, by Dahlgren, that I considered it of such great importance . . . that I would take the responsibility of moving on through the Bull Run range." Captain Dahlgren returned to the telegraph key at Centreville at 1 p.m., informing Hooker, "Gen'l Pleasonton is between Sudley Springs and Aldie. . . . He . . . wants to push his whole command on to Aldie. I will wait here for an answer." While waiting for Hooker's reply, Dahlgren scrawled a brief entry in his memorandum book: "Pleasonton wants to push on. Dust shows our move. We should push on." Sometime after 3:30 p.m. the telegraph operator handed Hooker's reply to Dahlgren. The message read, "Written instructions are now being prepared for Gen'l Pleasonton. We shall send them from here [Fairfax Station] by an officer at 4 p.m. They cover the detention of the main body at Aldie on this [east] side. [Send a] small detachment to Leesburg. . . . The force sent to Snickers Gap to penetrate to the Valley and ascertain what is there and what has been and where gone to. Send this to Gen'l Pleasonton and return." The army commander remained defiant, authorizing only one patrol to enter the Loudoun Valley and attempt to penetrate the Blue Ridge at Snickers Gap. Shortly thereafter, as he rode west with Hooker's reply in his pocket, Dahlgren heard the rumble of cannon fire ahead. The orders he carried no longer mattered.[12]

EIGHT

Hard Work Lay Ahead, June 17

When bugles roused Col. Thomas Munford's troopers from their slumber on the morning of June 17, 1863, neither Munford nor his men could know they would achieve one of their finest days on a battlefield before nightfall. Yet, when the day ended, Munford's efforts went unnoticed at Stuart's headquarters. Eight months earlier, Munford had held Stuart's full faith and confidence, but when the general penned his report of the summer campaign, he pointedly ignored Munford's efforts at Aldie.

Born in Richmond and raised near Lynchburg, Thomas Munford attended the Virginia Military Institute, where he achieved the distinguished position of adjutant of the Corps of Cadets and earned the respect and friendship of Thomas J. Jackson, then an instructor at the institute. After graduating in 1852, Munford returned to the family farm near Lynchburg. One month after the firing on Fort Sumter, Munford, then thirty-two years old, accepted the lieutenant colonelcy of the Second Virginia Cavalry.[1]

In the still-heady days of March 1862, Stuart commended Munford's "activity, good judgment, and unceasing vigilance." Praised for his gallantry at Second Manassas by Lee, Stuart, and brigade commander Beverly Robertson, Munford received command of the brigade a month later. In October, Stuart, hoping to rid himself of the disagreeable William "Grumble" Jones, sought, unsuccessfully, to have Munford promoted to brigadier in Jones's place. "With Munford in command of that brigade," Stuart told Lee, "I shall expect hearty cooperation, zealous devotion, and indefatigable attention to his duty." Stuart also touted Munford as "a gallant soldier, a daring and skillful officer . . . thoroughly identified with his brigade as its leader." Still, some unspoken doubt compelled Stuart to mention other unnamed officers as possibly having more "ability and military genius" than Munford. Jones remained, however, and Stuart, driven by his visceral dislike of Jones, tried again in February 1863 to replace him. This time, however, Stuart preferred the younger Thomas Rosser, colonel of the Fifth Virginia. Compelled to include Munford's name as the senior officer, Stuart damned him with faint praise, stating his "career as brigade Commander, though highly meritorious in many respects, failed to give entire satisfaction, but was more satisfactory than General Jones' has been." Stuart's words lingered long after his death, and Munford ended his career an embittered colonel.[2]

On June 9, 1863, with Stuart in a bitter fight at Brandy Station, and in desperate need of every fighting man, Munford had, arguably, the worst day of his career. In temporary command of Brig. Gen. Fitz Lee's brigade, then posted near Oak Shade Church north of the battlefield, Munford received two communications alerting him to the enemy's attack across Beverly Ford. Neither dispatch stressed urgency or, as Munford argued, told him where to report with his brigade. When he finally reached the field, the fighting had nearly ended. A war of words soon ensued, with Munford blaming his delay on poorly written orders from Stuart and Fitz Lee. Stuart retaliated, claiming, "Colonel Munford's delay in coming to the field has not been satisfactorily accounted for, as the distance was not very great." After the war, Stuart's aide, Maj. Henry McClellan, sided with Munford, concluding that he "had been delayed in his march by a perplexing ambiguity in the orders which had been transmitted to him."[3]

On June 17, with Fitz Lee still unable to sit a horse, Stuart needed a competent officer to command Lee's brigade in his absence, but doubts, hard feelings, and bruised egos lingered as Stuart and Munford resumed the march in the morning. The fight at Brandy Station had done nothing to resolve Stuart's dilemma, as he came out of the fight with more questions than answers. Riding east along the turnpike from Upperville, Stuart determined to leave Munford in command.[4]

The width of the Loudoun Valley allowed Stuart to trade distance for time, as he sought to screen the Army of Northern Virginia from discovery for as long as possible. Riding east with three brigades, Stuart tasked Munford with blocking Aldie Gap and denying the Federals access to either turnpike west of the gap. Likewise, he sent Col. John Chambliss to White Plains, with orders to watch the road from Thoroughfare Gap. Stuart then held Brig. Gen. Beverly Robertson's North Carolina Brigade in reserve at Rectortown, from whence he could support either of the other two brigades. Familiar with Middleburg, as well as the local road network connecting the three brigades, Stuart established his headquarters near the center of town.[5]

Early in the morning, Stuart decided to split Munford's command; Munford would command the Second and Third Virginia and Col. Williams Wickham would command the First, Fourth, and Fifth Virginia. Tactical necessity may have driven Stuart's decision, or he may have been looking for one of the two men to prove himself ready to command a brigade on a permanent basis. Specifically, Stuart tasked Munford with blocking the vital junction of the Carolina Road and Little River Turnpike east of Aldie, as well as the Snickersville Turnpike west of town. He charged Wickham with holding the Ashby's Gap Turnpike.[6]

Williams Wickham, forty-three years old, had little military background beyond command of an antebellum militia company. Born in Richmond and educated at the University of Virginia, Wickham had practiced law and served as a judge before entering state politics in 1849. Following the outbreak of the war, Wickham's militia company entered Confederate service as Company G, Fourth Virginia Cavalry, and Wickham was soon elected as the regiment's lieutenant colonel. Sabered in a melee near Williamsburg on May 4, 1862, Wickham recovered in time to receive a promotion to colonel in August. He had been wounded a second time during the fighting in the Loudoun Valley in the fall of 1862.[7]

Following the fight at Brandy Station, Stuart may have had some reservations regarding Wickham's leadership. Learning that Union cavalry threatened the Southern position at Stevensburg, Stuart had sent Wickham's Virginians to aid the South Carolinians holding the hamlet. The Virginians arrived, unfortunately, just as the Yankees drove the Carolinians from the field. In the resulting confusion, the Carolinians fled through Wickham's ranks and scattered his command, resulting in the loss of at least forty-two men. Wickham termed his men's conduct as "disgraceful." Stuart described their retreat as a "stampede." Now, with doubts cast by that debacle hanging over his head, Wickham led his men east to Aldie, where he had been ordered to go into camp. Reaching Dover's Mill, one and a half miles west of town, Wickham sent Col. Thomas Rosser and his Fifth Virginia ahead to bivouac closer to Aldie, while the men of the First and Fourth Virginia and Capt. James Breathed's First Stuart Horse Artillery watered their horses at the mill.[8]

Turning north out of Middleburg, Colonel Munford led the Second and Third Virginia over to the Snickersville Turnpike. He had been told to picket the road junctions around Aldie and to put his men into camp nearby. He sent Lt. Abner Hatcher, Company A, Second Virginia, ahead with a picket force to seize the high ground around the town and to hold the junction of the Carolina Road and Little River Turnpike, two miles east of town at Mount Zion Baptist Church. He then sent the remainder of his men to Mountville to feed their horses and to return with corn for the remainder of the command. With three regiments and a four-gun battery posted on the Ashby's Gap Turnpike west of town, two regiments on the Snickersville Turnpike, and pickets deployed well to the east, Munford could be forgiven if he expected an easy night after a hot march along dust-choked roads. Then, about 4:30 p.m., while Munford waited for his two regiments to return from Mountville, a courier from Lieutenant Hatcher rode up on a lathered horse and delivered a startling message: Union cavalry were approaching "in considerable force." In moments, with bugles ringing in their ears, men began running for their horses, adjusting their saddles, and checking ammunition. Hard work lay ahead.[9]

NINE

The Aldie Haystack Charge, June 17

Afternoon temperatures soared into the midnineties, and rain remained elusive. Union colonel Charles Wainwright described June 17 as "Very hot" and the air "intolerable; absolutely difficult to breathe." Fearful he might suffocate in the heat, Wainwright counted nearly a thousand men along his route who had "fainted entirely away." After pleading for rain, a Northern reporter concluded, "Without it I fear for this army." Of the dust, one cavalryman complained he could not see beyond the "set of fours ahead" of him. The choking grit clung to the damp, sweaty men, and horses, covering every inch of clothing and every piece of equipment.[1]

The residents of Aldie would have first seen a dust cloud approaching from the west. Soon they would have heard a continuous rhythmic clatter of clinking metal, straining leather, iron horseshoes striking the rocky-road surface and a steady, hoarse coughing and snorting as men and animals tried to their clear throats of the killing dust. Shortly thereafter the locals would have seen faint apparitions of men riding weary horses into town. Guidons hanging limp in the still air failed to identify the men. Only when the column came to a halt, the dust had briefly settled, and officers and sergeants began barking orders would their identity have become certain; these apparitions were Virginians. Relieved, the townsfolk almost certainly rushed to bring water and share what food they had, as the men and animals shook off the dust.

Lieutenant Abner Hatcher immediately sent a detail through town to Mount Zion Church and secured the nearby intersection. Some of his men hurried to the town's blacksmith, hoping to have their horses reshod or to do the work themselves. Others sought shade, wiped the grime from their faces, and enjoyed the hospitality of the citizens. Their respite ended quickly, however, as they soon observed another dust cloud approaching from the east.[2]

The Second New York, commanded by Lt. Col. Otto Harhaus, led Brig. Gen. Judson Kilpatrick's brigade toward Aldie, with Company F riding ahead as an advance guard. Companies H and M, led by Lt. Daniel Whitaker, led the main column. Whitaker had enlisted together with his brother Edward, and both men had earned their commissions from the ranks. Daniel especially had earned Kilpatrick's respect and had served as regimental adjutant until taking temporary squadron command following Brandy Station.[3]

A trooper in Company M recalled riding alongside Lt. Augustus Martinson as the regiment approached Aldie. Martinson, a native of Denmark, had, like the Whitaker brothers, been commissioned from the ranks. As the two men talked, the Dane spoke of his premonition that he would not survive the war. Seconds later, gunshots erupted ahead of the main column, as the advance guard surprised Lieutenant Hatcher's Virginians between the Carolina Road and town. Digging in their spurs, the New Yorkers in the advance guard drew their sabers and drove the Virginians through town, scattering the townsfolk and sending the remainder of Hatcher's men racing for their horses.[4]

Col. Thomas L. Rosser had just put his men into camp for the night when he "met the pickets running in." As Hatcher's men raced past him, Rosser ordered his men of the Fifth Virginia into their saddles. As quickly as they got mounted, Rosser led a counterattack against the now surprised Federals. The chaplain of the Second New York described the "cries and yells" of Rebel cavalry in a charge as "so peculiar, so wild, shrill, feverish, [and] so ghastly," as to sound "more like horrid shrieks . . . than the utterances of living men." He thought Yankees yelled from the chest, while the Rebel yells sounded like the "shriek of a woman [or] the scream of a panther." Outnumbered and with the shrieks ringing in their ears, the New Yorkers turned and raced back into town.[5]

During the brief fracas, one of the Virginians shot Sgt. Philip Neher in the side, and another sabered him across the crown of his head, hacking out a piece of bone in the process. A few days later, while lying in a hospital bed, Neher remarked with grim humor, "I still carry the piece of skull in case of emergency." A crushing blow from a saber knocked Lt. Albert Wilson unconscious. Falling into the road, the New Yorker was cut, kicked, trampled, and left temporarily paralyzed by the horses running over him. Just as a Southerner shot one of Wilson's men in the shoulder, another Virginian sabered him across the chest. Luckily, the heavy buckle on the soldier's carbine sling absorbed the worst of the blow.[6]

With an unexpected fight on his hands, Kilpatrick quickly reformed the Second New York on the turnpike in the center of town. He had last sent his old regiment into battle at Brandy Station, and it had performed poorly, hazarding the entire brigade. Now, just eight days later, the regiment found itself in another battle. Reining his horse up in front of the lead squadron, Kilpatrick sought to inspire the troopers. "Men of Companies M and [H]," he yelled, "your conduct at Brandy Station the other day did not reflect any credit upon the regiment. You now have the opportunity to do better. I want you to charge the enemy . . . drive everything before you, and let this entire brigade see you do it." To which a trooper reportedly replied, "We'll do it, General, or bust the breechin." Lieutenant Daniel Whitaker then took his place in the column, as did Lieutenant Martinson. Whitaker had less than forty men in the two companies. Gazing at the Southern position ahead of them, the men caught their breath and pulled their hat straps under their chins as they waited for Whitaker to lead them forward.[7]

Assisting Lieutenant Hatcher's men in repulsing the Union advance guard, Colonel Rosser realized he had not encountered just a small Yankee patrol. Instead, he would have glimpsed the flags of an entire brigade moving into town. Needing time to apprise Colonel Wickham, Rosser ordered all but one squadron of his regiment to fall back toward Dover's Mill. He tasked Capt. Reuben Boston's squadron, numbering fewer than fifty men, to cover the regiment's retreat from a commanding knoll about a half-mile west of town. Rosser chose Boston's squadron because his men carried most of the rifles and carbines in the regiment. Some believed the six-foot-tall, twenty-nine-year-old Boston to be "one of the most commanding officers in appearance in the whole army." The regiment had gone into camp on the Adam farm before the fighting erupted, and Boston now deployed some of his men behind several haystacks on the eastern slope and crest of a knoll, just east of the Adam home. The men sheltered their horses in a deep ravine on the west side of the knoll. The remainder of Boston's men fell back toward the Adam house and spread out along a fence on rising ground west of the ravine. The fence enclosed the Adam home and orchard. After conversing with Rosser, Colonel Wickham ordered Capt. James Breathed to put his guns into battery along a hillcrest six hundred yards west of the Adam home. Wickham also deployed Col. James Drake's First Virginia and his own Fourth Virginia to defend the artillery and to block the Ashby's Gap Turnpike.[8]

As soon as Lieutenant Whitaker's New Yorkers cleared the west end of town, they could see Captain Boston's position to their right front. Turning off the road to the right and passing through a narrow gap in a stone wall, the men moved into an open field, where they reformed under carbine fire. Commanding his men to draw sabers, Whitaker yelled for the men to advance. With bugler John Miller relaying Whitaker's orders, the men accelerated to a canter or military gallop as they swept past the haystacks and up the slope of the knoll. Reaching the crest, they found themselves confronted by the "yawning gully," where the Virginians had sheltered their horses. Raked by murderous fire now from front and rear, some of the Yankees spurred their horses over the ditch, described as "six to twelve feet wide and at least six feet deep." Many horses refused to make the attempt, however, and threw their riders as they came to a jolting stop at the edge of the ravine.[9]

The sudden shock of the Yankees cresting the knoll scattered the Southern horses and sent them racing away from the men who had ridden them moments earlier. Lieutenant Martinson, the glum Dane, may have been the first man killed. Two other privates went down with fatal wounds in the opening moments of the fight. Another trooper fell with a penetrating gunshot to his chest and a second wound to his thigh and died hours later. Just as Lt. Jasper Raymond rode past the Virginians at the haystacks, one turned and fired at him. The bullet punched through Raymond's left ear lobe before passing through his neck. Lieutenant Whitaker survived just long enough to signal for help from the top of the knoll. Then, as he yelled for his men to "hold your ground," a bullet knocked him from the saddle; he was dead when he hit the ground. Having driven the Confederates from the eastern slope of the knoll, and with several officers down and men and horses dropping all around them, the survivors fell back below the crest along the eastern slope. Sheathing their sabers, drawing their revolvers, or unslinging their carbines, these Yankees began returning fire as quickly as they could load and pull the trigger.[10]

Watching the fighting from the edge of town, Kilpatrick saw Lieutenant Whitaker's frantic signal for help. Turning to the remainder of the Second New York, the general ordered them into the fray. Company K followed the turnpike out of town and then turned into the field against Boston's right flank. Maj. Samuel McIrvin led the remaining battalion, Companies F, I, D, and G, up the Snickersville Turnpike, before turning into the hayfield against the Confederate left flank. Kilpatrick also sent Lt. Col. William Stedman's Sixth Ohio to support the New Yorkers. As soon as the men emerged from town, they came under artillery fire from Captain Breathed's guns, firing over the Adam house and Boston's men.[11]

As quickly as the other regiments of his brigade arrived, Kilpatrick deployed them to secure the vital road network. He sent the Fourth New York and First Massachusetts up the Snickersville Turnpike, followed by Capt. Alanson Randol, commanding Battery

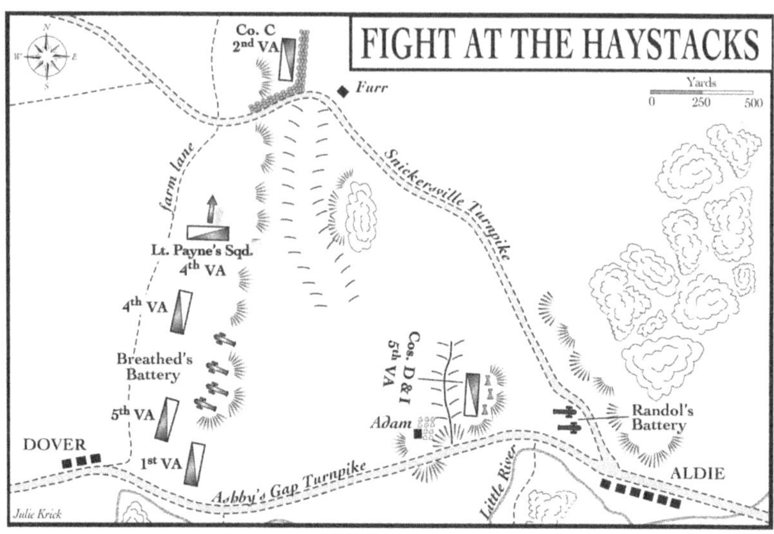

MAP 5. Fight at the haystacks. Created by Julie Krick.

E and G, First U.S. Artillery. The general ordered Randol to find a position on the high ground at the northwest end of town, from where he could defend both roads with two of his guns. "[We] went flying through the town, to the great bewilderment of the people who were gathered around the doors and windows of the houses," one gunner recalled. Randol hurried his guns into position on a narrow piece of high ground near the Snickersville pike. The long hot march had taken a toll on his horses, and one of them died shortly after reaching the top of the hill. As soon as his men rolled the guns into battery, Randol engaged Breathed's guns, almost a mile to the west.[12]

Until the Union guns took them under fire, Breathed's men concentrated their fire against the New Yorkers and Ohioans attacking the Virginians on the Adam farm knoll. "We ran a gauntlet of their fire for half a mile," recalled Capt. Norman Barrett, Sixth Ohio. "Shots struck, and shells burst to the right, the left, before and behind, but none struck our column." Henry Pepper would have disagreed, however, as a shell exploded just behind him, and a piece of shrapnel sliced through his back and lodged in his hip. Once the Buckeyes reached the protection of the knoll, the men caught their breath and moved from column into line, before making the final charge up the slope.[13]

Lieutenant Colonel Stedman held his men in place until Major McIrvin entered the hayfield from the Snickersville pike. Then, "with a wild hurrah we went like a whirlwind over the hill," Captain Barrett recalled. Cresting the knoll, "into the teeth of their fire," the Buckeyes saw the deep ravine for the first time. "A line of fire streamed from it as we came on, but most of our horses went over it at one brave bound, and the rebels soon felt our steel." Just as Maj. Benjamin Stanhope's horse leapt the ditch, a Southerner shot him in the elbow. Another bullet killed his horse, causing Stanhope to be thrown "violently against a tree." Stunned by the impact and with his arm shattered, Stanhope rolled "into the ditch among the Rebs and our men jumped their horses over him," one of his troopers affirmed. At least two other horses went down near the ditch or hesitated at the edge and threw their riders to the ground. Private William Warriner may have already been dismounted when a Virginian in the ditch saw Warriner standing above him and shot him in the groin.[14]

With the New Yorkers now sweeping in from their flanks and the Buckeyes already among them, many of Captain Boston's men surrendered in and around the ditch. The remainder ran back and joined their comrades sheltered behind the fence or in the orchard. Leaving a detail with the prisoners, the Yankees reformed their lines "and pushed on to the orchard," driving the last of Boston's men into the trees. Dismounting, some of the Federals tore down the fence "under a withering fire; then charged up through the orchard." Enraged by the fury of the fight and the loss of so many friends, the Yankees were ready for a brawl. Even with some of the Virginians surrendering, others continued to fight. As one New Yorker recalled, "some pistols went off while the surrender was in progress," and some "fancy saber work," became necessary before the last of the Southern stalwarts threw down their weapons.[15]

Errant artillery rounds from Breathed's guns added to the danger and confusion in the final moments of the fight. From their position on the hill several hundred yards behind the

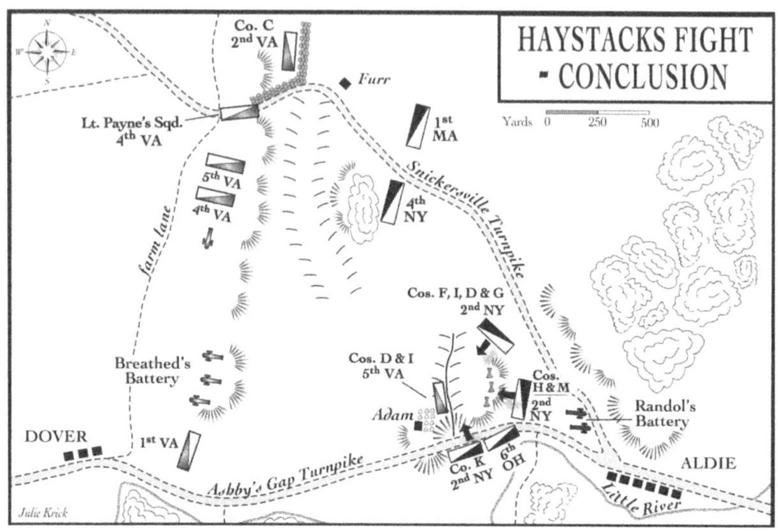

MAP 6. Haystacks fight—conclusion. Created by Julie Krick.

Adam house, the Southern gunners had been splitting their fire between the Union artillery near town and the fighting taking place around the orchard below them. But the house and farm buildings partially obscured their view of events in the orchard. Unaware their men had surrendered, the gunners continued to fire case shot toward the farm. When a shell shattered a nearby tree, one of the prisoners exclaimed, "Great heaven! Are we now to be killed by our own men?"[16]

Colonel Rosser boldly claimed that he had "ordered Boston to hold his position at all hazards, and nobly and faithfully did he obey. Onset after onset of the enemy he gallantly repulsed, until the enemy had killed one of his lieutenants, wounded another and his junior captain, and killed and wounded a third of his men—then he surrendered to overwhelming odds." In later years, Rosser described leading a couple of counterattacks against the Union's "weak-kneed cavalry," in a vain attempt to relieve the threat to Boston's men before being compelled by the Union artillery to retire to "a position from which I could not support [them] as well as before." But in a letter to his wife written the day after the battle, Rosser never mentioned Boston, or the valiant stand made by his squadron. Rather, he took credit for personally having saved the day. "Had it not been for me," he told his wife, with a total lack of humility, "there would have been another *surprise*," referring to the continuing controversy regarding Stuart's alleged surprise at Brandy Station.[17]

Captain Boston may have taken forty-five men into the fight at Aldie. Of these at least thirty-seven surrendered or were wounded and captured, including six officers. Rather than the heavy casualties described by Rosser, only five men, including Boston, had been wounded and no one had been killed. Captain Boston reportedly fought until he had fired his last round, and his determination in the final moments of the fight might have resulted in his death but for a Union officer who intervened between the captain and his antagonist. Lt. Fontaine Boston, Reuben's younger brother, surrendered with him and went with him to the prison camp at Johnson's Island, Ohio.[18]

Capt. Obediah Downing, Second New York, termed the fight at the haystacks "one of the most gallant charges ever made by our cavalry." Pvt. James Herrold, who never recovered the full use of his left arm after a Southern bullet struck him in the elbow, remembered the fight as "The Aldie Haystack Charge." In a fight lasting less than thirty minutes the Second New York and Sixth Ohio incurred about fifty-five casualties. The Buckeyes held their position and maintained a harassing fire against Breathed's gunners throughout the fighting along the Snickersville Turnpike. The New Yorkers escorted the prisoners from the field. As the weary men filed past Kilpatrick, a wag from Company M reportedly asked, "General, are you satisfied?" "Yes, yes, you did splendidly, and I'll have you for my escort the rest of the day," Kilpatrick replied. Another trooper in the squadron thought little of the "honor" of escorting the general, especially as Kilpatrick headed toward the fight developing on the Snickersville pike, but the soldier was relieved "to know that the alleged stain on the regiment had been wiped out."[19]

TEN

The Fiery Ordeal, June 17

When elected governor of Massachusetts, John Andrew believed himself to be "distrusted" by the upper crust of Boston society. Seeking to overcome such concerns, Andrew convinced several well-educated men from the elite families of the state to accept positions in his administration. When war came in April 1861, several of these advisors, including Horace Sargent, who had been educated at Harvard, persuaded Andrew to seek officers for the state's regiments from the same educated class. As one confidant told Andrew, to have a good army, "it is of the highest importance to have the best officers—Not the most popular men—Not the best Christians—but the *best* officers." Andrew sought, as his biographer explained, men who "had been trained to learn." He may also have sought young men with, as another colonel recalled, "the impulsive ardor of the morning of life."[1]

Horace Sargent had not attended West Point, but he was, as historian Richard Miller explains, a "gentleman from Harvard." So too was his brother, Lucius, as well as young officers like Henry L. Higginson and Charles Francis Adams. All traced their lineage to the Puritan bedrock of the nation, while Adams's pedigree placed him on the cusp of what might be termed American royalty, as his grandfather and great-grandfather had both served as president of the United States. Not wishing to live "upon his ancestry," however,

Adams entered the military only after much soul-searching. A morose, temperamental man, Adams had "few close friends" and often found himself at odds with his superiors. Though inclined to independent thought, Adams seemed to feed on an endless simmering anger, fueled by his abiding prejudices. His oft-quoted descriptions of life in the First Massachusetts Cavalry reflect his biases but when filtered and placed in context remain insightful and instructive.[2]

The events of June 17, 1863, remained etched in Adams's soul long after the smoke had cleared. In a moment of quiet reflection after the campaign he let his mind wander back and recall the march to Aldie. "Ah, what a squadron I had on the morning of the 17th of June!! Any man might have been proud of it." Adams rode at the head of Companies C and D, followed by four buglers on white horses. Behind the buglers rode the senior lieutenant and a sergeant, followed by the troopers "in closed up ranks of fours." The junior captain or senior lieutenant rode at the rear of the squadron, tasked with preventing men from dropping from the ranks. Adams counted ninety-three men in his squadron when he reached Aldie. In the December of his life, Adams still remembered his men with pride, terming them "young, athletic, ingenious, surprisingly alert and very adaptive."[3]

The men of the regiment were veterans now, tough, lean, and shabby. "We all need new clothes, for we are curiously ragged and dirty," Adams told his father on June 14. "My blue trousers are ragged from contact with the saddle and so covered with grease and dust that they would fry well. From frequent washing my flannel shirts are so shrunk about the throat that they utterly refuse to button . . . my waistcoat, once dark blue, is now a dusty brown. I have no gloves and those boots . . . hang together by doubtful threads. These, with hair cropped close to my head, a beard white with dust and such a dirty face, constitute my usual apparel." Though the men may have looked like tatterdemalions, they formed a proud regiment ever eager for battle. An hour after riding into Aldie, "but a remnant" remained.[4]

The sharp crack of pistols and carbines alerted the Bay Staters to the sudden skirmish erupting along the turnpike ahead of them. After the initial clash in and around the town, and before sending the Second New York and Sixth Ohio to drive the Virginians from the haystacks, General Kilpatrick made a hasty reconnaissance. Worried the enemy could attack his flank by way of the Snickersville Turnpike, he ordered Lt. Col. Greely Curtis, commanding the First Massachusetts in Horace Sargent's absence, to take his regiment, along with the Fourth New York, and secure the road. After watering their horses and filling their canteens, many for the last time, the men stepped back into their saddles and headed up the hill out of town along the Snickersville pike.[5]

Nearing a large woodlot about three-quarters of a mile west of town, Curtis deployed the regiments to either side of the road, the Fourth New York into a field on the south side and the First Massachusetts to the north. Maj. Henry Higginson and Capt. Lucius Sargent, possibly accompanied by Curtis, then rode ahead searching for a better vantage point along the hilly, winding road. As Higginson squinted into the late-afternoon sun, the enemy suddenly appeared cresting a hill. As the major shouted his warning, Curtis ordered Sargent to move his squadron into the road "and meet them as quick as possible."[6]

Before the men had ever seen combat, a trooper had promised the readers of his hometown newspaper, "The day may come when the First Mass. Cavalry must pass the fiery ordeal. A second Balaclava may be enacted," he warned, referring to the infamous charge of the Light Brigade during the Crimean War in 1854. He then assured his readers, "The regiment will not be found wanting." Now, even as they sat up in their saddles, wiped the sweat from their faces, and regripped their reins, the men could not have known that their "fiery ordeal" had arrived; their Balaclava lay just up the road.[7]

Like Kilpatrick, Colonel Munford knew the road network around Aldie and understood the threat posed by the Snickersville Turnpike. As the battle developed around the haystacks, he sent a courier to recall the Second and Third Virginia from Mountville. He also posted a reserve force, led by Lt. William Walton, Second Virginia, behind a stone wall along the crest of a ridge immediately west of a tight bend in the pike that commanded

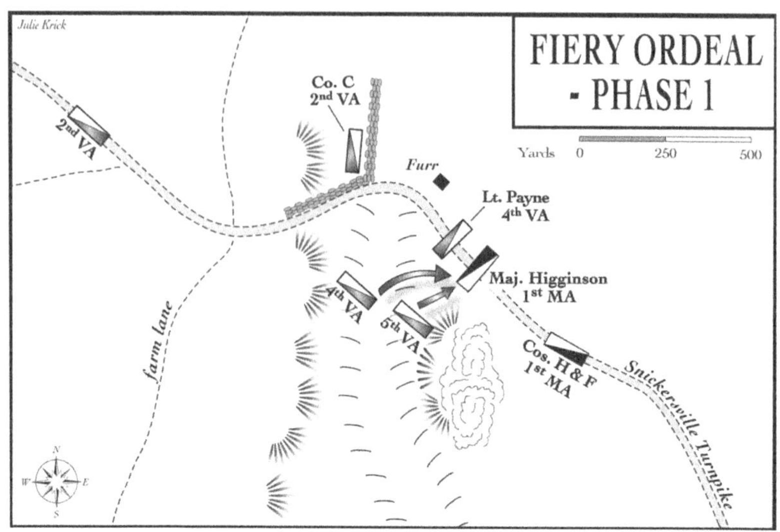

MAP 7. Fiery ordeal—phase 1. Created by Julie Krick.

the approach from Aldie. Munford then headed south across the wide western base of the triangular field formed by the two turnpikes and a sunken farm lane. Coming upon Capt. William Newton, commanding the Fourth Virginia, Munford ordered him to send a squadron to support Lieutenant Walton. Newton sent Lt. Alexander Dixon Payne's squadron. With the regiment still recovering from the pummeling received at Brandy Station, Payne's two companies numbered just twenty men. Reaching the Snickersville pike, Payne met briefly with Walton and then headed east, scouting the road toward Aldie. After passing the home of William Furr, the Virginians crested a hill and saw the group of Union officers in the road ahead.[8]

Responding to Lt. Colonel Curtis's order and chafing for a fight, Captain Sargent moved his squadron into the road. At the same time, Curtis sent a platoon of skirmishers into the field just north of the road, to protect Sargent's men when they advanced up the road. Surprised and outnumbered, Lieutenant Payne's Virginians unleashed a flurry of shots toward the Union skirmishers, before Payne ordered a hasty retreat. The combatants, blue and gray, raced past the Furr house with pistols barking and wounded men tumbling into the gullies along the road, until Payne's men reached the stone wall. There, they turned on the Bay Staters.[9]

Just as Captain Sargent seized a Southern laggard, another Virginian engaged him in a saber duel. Then a third Confederate rode up and stunned Sargent with a heavy blow from his saber. Struggling to clear his head, Sargent ordered his men to retire. But with the New Englanders scattered across the road and Furr farm, many were beyond the point of hearing the order. Watching from nearby, Lt. Colonel Curtis saw his men in trouble. He also saw another detachment of cavalry coming across the triangular field at a gallop. Looking to pull his men to safety, Curtis sent Major Higginson to assist Sargent in getting his men reformed and out of danger.[10]

After sending Lieutenant Payne's squadron over to the Snickersville Turnpike, Colonel Munford pulled together the remainder of the Fourth and Fifth Virginia and one gun from Captain Breathed's Battery. These troops were nearing the turnpike, with Colonel Rosser's Fifth Virginia in the lead, as Higginson and Sargent herded their men past the Furr house. Rosser aimed to cut them off and capture the entire squadron. Just then a skittish horse at the rear of the Union column threw its rider. Unwilling to abandon the field and possibly seeking to give the trooper time to remount his horse, Sargent turned his horse around and began taunting the onrushing Southerners. With the trooper back in his saddle, Sargent, Higginson, and a handful of other men spurred their horses toward the safety of their own lines. Moments later, Higginson realized they could not outrun the Confederates. Rosser was right behind them, and Higginson's horse had now been shot several times. Before the small group of New Englanders could unite for a common defense, Rosser's men dashed in and cut them off.[11]

Colonel Rosser killed one of the men and then shot Captain Sargent through the lungs. Then a lieutenant went down with a bullet through his pelvis, and Major Higginson found himself fighting three men, including Rosser. The major had just unhorsed one assailant when a bullet hit him in the lower back. As he fell from his horse the dismounted Southern trooper slashed him in the face with his saber. Moments later the last of Higginson's men fell into the road bleeding from sabers wounds to his head. Bodies of dead and wounded men now lay strewn across the ground and horses thrashed about in death throes.[12]

Lieutenant Charles Parsons took command of Sargent's squadron and led it toward the melee. The sight of the Yankees racing toward him convinced Rosser to withdraw, but only momentarily, as Captain Newton arrived with the remainder of the Fourth Virginia and quickly blunted the Yankee counterattack. Almost immediately, Parsons and his men found themselves nearly surrounded. His only avenue of escape lay to the north, across William Furr's farm fields. The long race to safety carried the squadron away from the battlefield for crucial minutes. The brief but furious combat cost the Federals sixteen men, including two senior officers, and an entire squadron had been driven from the field. Only the platoon of skirmishers remained. From a position east of the of the Furr house, they maintained a harassing fire against the Confederate force building west of the house.[13]

By now, Lt. Philip P. Johnston had his cannon in position on a slight rise behind the stone wall at the bend in the road. With all the Yankees having been driven from the field, Johnston began dueling with Captain Randol's two guns on the high ground west of Aldie. As the Southerners caught their breath, a group of them gathered to peer up at Randol's guns on the horizon, certain the gunners would not waste a round on them. Moments later two shots cut the air around them. By the third shot the gunners had the range, the round landing at the Southerners' feet and injuring one of the men before they could scatter.[14]

A few hundred yards east of Lieutenant Johnston's position, the battered survivors of Higginson's melee with Rosser struggled to reach safety and medical attention. Only two of the men were ambulatory, the sergeant, bleeding from head wounds, and the lieutenant with a bullet in his pelvis. Leading their horses, the sergeant aided the officer on an agonizing walk to safety. Major Higginson crawled over to Sargent and convinced him to get out of the road and take shelter near a small outbuilding. The major then crawled to a small stream where he quenched his

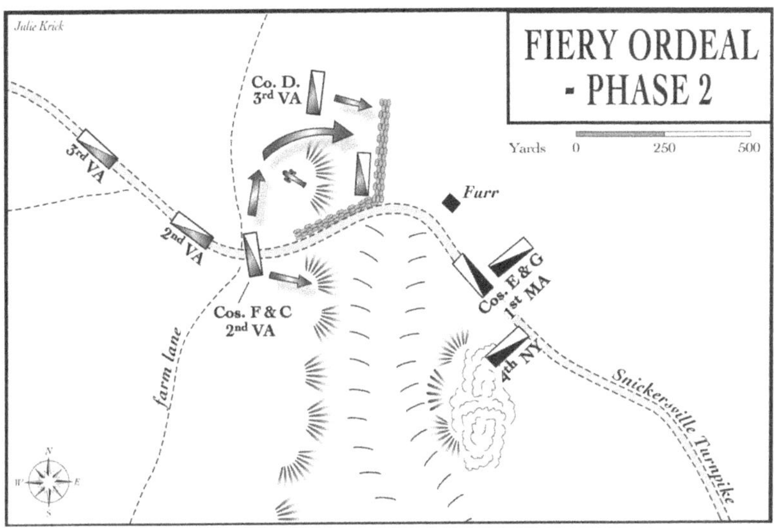

MAP 8. Fiery ordeal—phase 2. Created by Julie Krick.

thirst and washed the blood from his face. Hoping to find safety in the nearby woodlot, Higginson continued until a fence ended his journey. Unable to go on, Higginson penned a brief note to his father as he contemplated his own death. Near the end of the battle and having recovered some strength he stumbled to a nearby home. There some Federals placed him on a horse and led him back to Aldie.[15]

The lull lasted mere moments before Lt. Colonel Curtis ordered Capt. John Tewksbury, commanding Companies E and G, to clear the enemy from the road. Tewksbury attacked with his companies abreast, one company sweeping across the Furr farm while the second company attacked up the turnpike. Curtis supported his New Englanders with the Fourth New York, advancing across the triangular field just south of the pike, on Tewksbury's left flank. As soon as the men entered the bend in the road, they came under fire from Southerners posted behind the stone wall, including artillery fire from Lieutenant Johnston's gun. Then the Yankees noticed a fresh column of enemy cavalry coming toward them on the turnpike.[16]

Lt. Col. James Watts had arrived from Mountville with his

Second Virginia. By chance, the regiment's carbineers rode at the head of the column, and Watts dispersed them to either side of the road. Capt. William Graves ordered his company to fall in alongside the Virginians already holding the stone wall, with every fourth man leading the horses of his comrades away from the firing line. Capt. James Breckinridge turned his company into the field south of the road and onto a commanding ridge.[17]

After dispersing his carbineers, Watts led the following squadron against the oncoming Federals. According to Watts, "The enemy advanced in good style under a withering fire from front and flank." Spurring their horses and raising a Rebel Yell, Watts's Virginians crashed into the head of the Union column. The impact forced the Yankees to turn into the field south of the road. Raked by fire from Captain Breckinridge's men, the Yankees turned and fled back toward the woodlot across from the Furr house.[18]

Having met and repulsed the Union column in the road, Watts sent the remainder of the regiment into the fields to either side of the turnpike in time to meet the New Yorkers advancing south of the road and the remainder of Captain Tewksbury's men to the north. Spurring his horse over a fence, Watts "landed among the enemy" charging toward the stone wall. "Standing in his stirrups," Watts knocked the first Yankee he confronted "off his horse with his sabre." Again, the weight of Southern numbers carried the fight and forced the remainder of the Federals from thc field.[19]

Colonel Thomas Owen reached the battlefield just as this phase of the fight concluded. Munford directed him to deploy his carbineers along the stone wall, by extending the Southern line to the north, where a high-banked stream anchored the position. With Lieutenant Johnston's cannon firing over the head of his carbineers from the flat knoll behind the men, Munford had every reason to believe he could hold the position against any attack the Yankees could throw at him. "I doubt if there was a stronger position in 50 miles," he later declared. The stone wall runs along the north side of the turnpike to a point just east of the crest of a low ridge. There, the wall makes a ninety-degree turn to the north for about 650 feet. During the summer, the wall is often concealed behind a thick growth of vines, deceiving casual observers into believing they are looking at a low hedgerow rather than a stout, nearly impassable, wall. A rail fence ran along the turnpike between the wall and the Furr house. Another stone and rail fence lined the south side of the road, limiting movement into and out of the triangular field. During the brief lull in the fight, Colonel Watts ordered gaps pulled open in all the fences and walls. Abreast of the house, about seventy yards in front of the carbineers, the road makes a near ninety-degree turn from the northwest to southwest. Riders approaching from the east would be completely unaware of the ambush awaiting them at the stone wall until they entered the turn, at which point they were within point-blank cannon and carbine range. Munford had created a perfect killing ground.[20]

With half of the First Massachusetts driven from the field, Lt. Colonel Curtis directed Capt. Charles Adams to move his squadron into the triangular field south of the turnpike. Curtis, who had participated in the previous attack, now realized the strength of the Southern position, as well as the increasing number of enemy troops moving onto the high ground at the western end of the field. To meet the Southern threat, Curtis sought to coordinate his next effort, sending Captain Adams, supported by the Fourth New York, to clear the Virginians from the triangular field, while Lt. Charles Davis led the remaining two companies of the First Massachusetts in another attack along the turnpike. None of the ground favored the Federals. While Davis confronted the roadblock at the stone wall, Adams and the New Yorkers faced a ravine between them and the enemy. The ravine, wide and deep, would challenge the horses in the sweltering heat as they struggled up the steep sides. A large woodlot crowned the eastern slope across from the Furr house and provided some cover but would inhibit the ability of the cavalry to reform quickly. The western slope, however, leveled off onto a wide flat crest which favored the Virginians gathered there and would allow them to reform easily. The four companies of Bay Staters moved into position just as the New Yorkers fell back behind the woods following their last attack in support of Tewksbury. Curtis's hopes for a coordinated effort fell apart immediately.[21]

Col. Luigi di Cesnola's tenure in command of the Fourth New York had been marked by near constant turmoil. The regiment contained an especially wide diversity of foreigners, but it was not a "foreign regiment." Still, many critics in the Cavalry Corps had developed an abiding animosity toward the New Yorkers, and none more so than the deeply prejudiced Adams. The New Yorkers would never measure up to the bluebloods from Massachusetts and the attitudes of men like Adams, who looked down his nose at most anyone not of his social stratum, tainted their opinions of the men from New York. For Adams, the New Yorkers soon provided a ready excuse for his own failures and those of his superiors.[22]

Fighting for respect against the prejudice prevailing in the army, the enlisted men of the Fourth New York, especially the foreigners, viewed di Cesnola as their inspirational leader; they fought for their colonel rather than for the army. On June 16 Kilpatrick, now commanding the brigade led by di Cesnola at Brandy Station, ordered the colonel to report with his regiment to Union Mills at daybreak the following morning. Contrary to his orders, di Cesnola had bivouacked his men at Centreville, rather than Manassas Junction. When Kilpatrick challenged his authority to do so, the colonel, probably unaware Kilpatrick had taken command of the brigade, angrily replied, "By reason that no order or orderlies were sent to me." Both men, the new brigadier and the unhappy colonel, may have been seeking to establish or retain authority and the colonel's insubordinate tone led Kilpatrick to show the message to Pleasonton. The corps commander ordered di Cesnola's arrest. The colonel surrendered his sidearms and rode at the rear of his men as the regiment went into battle.[23]

With the fighting along the Ashby's Gap Turnpike ended, General Kilpatrick arrived and took control of the fight for the Snickersville Turnpike. With Curtis just then preparing to launch his attack, Kilpatrick's arrival may have caused some momentary confusion as he assumed command from Curtis. Neither Curtis nor Kilpatrick appreciated the severity of the fight the New Yorkers had just endured. If they had, neither informed either Captain Adams or Lieutenant Davis. Thus, when Adams moved his men into position for the attack, he was dismayed to see the "foreigners" falling back behind the woods to reform rather than moving into position on Adams's right flank. In fact, one of the dramatic moments of the battle was about to play out behind the woods and out of Adams's view.

The New Yorkers had attacked twice in support of Tewksbury. Colonel di Cesnola, still under arrest, had watched his men make the first charge and saw them repulsed. Then, without his weapons and unable to defend himself, the colonel rode to the head of his men and led a second attack that drove a company of the Second Virginia off the ridge and into the farm lane below. As Lt. Colonel Watts later described, after clearing the Yankees from the turnpike and the fields near the Furr house, he noticed "another Federal regiment which had attacked the single Company K on the right and was rapidly gaining our rear." Turning his men about, Watts caught the New Yorkers near the intersection of the farm lane and the turnpike, capturing many of them. Outnumbered and dispirited, the New Yorkers fell back across the ravine and behind the woods to reform.[24]

As the New Yorkers reined their lathered horses to a halt behind the woodlot, Lt. Llewellyn Estes, an aide on Kilpatrick's staff, rode up to di Cesnola and instructed him to make another attack, in conjunction with Adams and Davis. As they spoke, Estes learned the colonel "had just returned from a charge . . . without arms and while under arrest." Relaying the information to Kilpatrick, the general told Estes to ask Pleasonton to rescind his arrest order. When Pleasonton consented, Estes rode back and generously loaned di Cesnola his own sword. During the considerable delay necessitated by these events, Adams and Davis endured their own trial by fire, alone and unsupported.[25]

As soon as Adams brought his men out of the woodlot, they came under heavy fire from the Southern carbineers to their right front. Lieutenant Johnston's gun also unleashed a murderous fusillade of canister against Adams. One gunner later claimed, "That gun used more canister on that occasion than was ever used by the entire section in any previous engagement." Captain Randol's Union gunners countered by pouring in a heavy

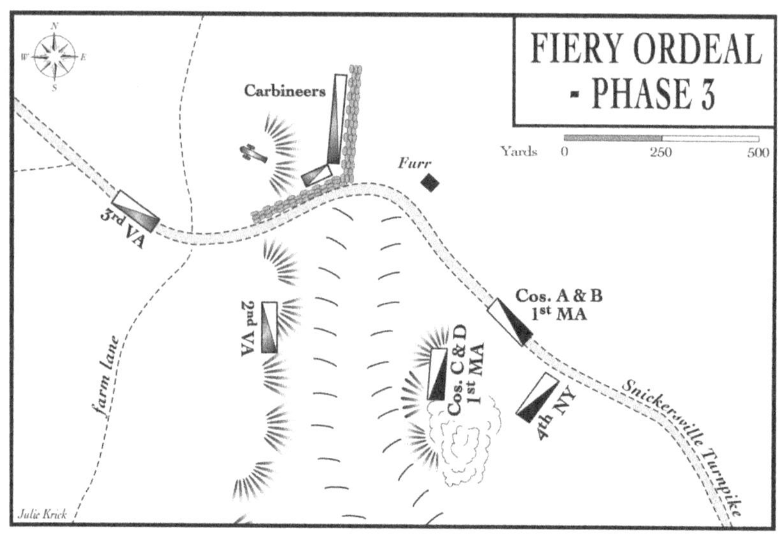

MAP 9. Fiery ordeal—phase 3. Created by Julie Krick.

counterbattery fire, which forced Johnston's men to seek cover on several occasions.[26]

Adams deployed his two companies in squadron front, two ranks deep. On the right of the line, nearest the road, Company D sustained all the fatalities in the squadron. "My poor men were just slaughtered and all we could do was to stand still and be shot down," a still shocked Adams told his father two days later. "The men fell right and left and the horses were shot through and through, and no man turned his back, but they only called on me to charge," he explained. "I [could not] charge, except across a ditch, up a hill and over two high stone walls, from behind which the enemy were slaying us; so I held my men there until, what with men shot down and horses wounded and plunging, my ranks were disordered and then I fell slowly back to some woods." The captain who so easily criticized others never accepted responsibility for his own inaction. Rather, he suggests his superiors, namely Curtis, forced him to stand and endure the lethal hail of lead. And, true to form, he blamed di Cesnola for giving "way without a fight or an instant's resistance." In truth, the New Yorkers had yet to reenter the fight.[27]

Shortly after Adams moved his men into the field, Lt. Charles Davis brought his squadron, seventy-five officers and men, into the road. Just twenty-three years old, Davis had returned from a staff assignment two days earlier and been placed in command of Companies A and B. Now, without realizing the Fourth New York had not moved into position and unable to see Adams's men being shot to pieces in front of the woods, Davis ordered his troopers to draw their sabers and started them forward. Nearing the Furr house, Davis probably ordered a charge, "unaware," as he later wrote, "of the peril that lurked but a short distance [ahead]."[28]

Mounted cavalry relied upon speed, shock or surprise, and momentum to break an enemy formation. To maintain unit cohesion and not exhaust the horses too early, cavalry rarely went straight to a gallop. Rather, the officers brought their men up from a walk to a trot, gaining speed and maintaining their ranks before hitting a canter over the last sixty yards or so, to gain the crucial advantage of shock and momentum. Davis's seventy-five men, moving in a column of fours, would have formed a mass of men and animals about 12 feet wide and nineteen ranks deep or about 220 feet in length. The spacing of officers, buglers, and noncommissioned officers would have further extended the column. Likewise, maneuvering distance between the two companies might also have extended the column, though the fences along the road prevented maneuver. But as the men approached the Furr house they entered a debris field of dead and wounded men and animals. Rather than accelerating, the men almost certainly slowed down, surrendering their momentum as they picked their way through the carnage littering the road.[29]

The Southerners, alerted to Davis's approach by the blare of bugles, the ominous sound of three hundred iron horseshoes striking the stones in the road, and the shouts of the men, delivered a crushing volley as soon as the Bay Staters came into view. As the solid mass of men and animals followed the curve of the road around to the left, the men exposed their right flank, which absorbed the full weight of the Southern volley. The Yankees immediately found themselves helpless under the devastating fire. Davis may have been the first to fall, one bullet glancing off his belt buckle and another punching through his upper right arm. Other bullets killed his horse, which collapsed on Davis, pinning him in the road. There, as he later described, he watched his "hapless [men] defenseless as unarmed children" quickly pile up behind him like a closing accordion. Within seconds, as Davis later recalled, "dead and dying men were heaped high." A Southern officer remembered "piling up" the Yankee horses in the road.[30]

Hit several times during the unequal contest, Pvt. John Weston thought the fight "the most desperate . . . on both sides that has been fought by cavalry." Resting in a hospital bed a few days later, Weston described the "perfect hail of bullets" that engulfed his men. "The road was narrow here and before we could get out of it[,] it was all blocked up with horses dead and wounded horses with their legs broken kicking and floundering amongst the men." Weston wondered how any of the men had survived the leaden hail. Men were shot, trampled, crushed, and dragged through the wreckage. Others struggled to control their frantic or injured mounts. Weston was shot as he fired his carbine. Seconds later his horse "was riddled with pistol shots." Hoping to guide his wounded animal out of the mayhem before it collapsed, Weston had traveled only a short distance when another shot dropped his horse "so quick that he struck on his head and turned a complete [somersault]." As Weston fell forward, the horse's hind legs knocked him down. Staggering to his feet, he saw another man killed nearby. Grabbing the reins of the man's horse, Weston mounted and fled to safety. Recounting his brush with death, Weston sardonically concluded, "Cavalry fighting against Cav. is exciting I can tell you."[31]

St. George Tucker Brooke, Second Virginia, watched from behind the stone wall as the Yankees approached. When the New Englanders entered the curve, he could see "the dust fly from their blue jackets as the bullets from our revolvers" struck them. During the fight, Brooke's horse "was shot and instantly killed under him." But with no shortage of riderless animals running around, Brooke secured one he believed a Union officer had been riding moments earlier.[32]

"If [Lieutenant] Davis is the officer who led the charges that were made against my [company] behind the rock wall he was certainly a brave man," Capt. William Graves, Second Virginia, asserted. "Each time they came we piled Yankees and horses in the road until it was blockaded, and if they had continued to charge we would have piled up more." Still, a few Federals, including Thomas McDevitt, made their way through the carnage and past the roadblock only to find themselves surrounded by Virginians near the farm lane. In a brief but furious fight near the intersection, a Southerner knocked McDevitt from his horse with a heavy saber stroke to his left arm. Before McDevitt could get out of the road, several horses ran over him and dislocated his hip. Sgt. James Hart fell mortally wounded. Cpl. August Schroder took a bullet through his groin. Pvt. Daniel Sherman died of wounds to his neck and chest, while George Smith survived five bullet wounds. Of the seventy-five men who followed Lieutenant Davis past the Furr house, sixty were killed, wounded, or captured.[33]

After helping to crush Lieutenant Davis's attack, Lt. Colonel Watts turned his attention back to Captain Adams's squadron in front of the woods. With no other Yankees in their immediate front, the carbineers behind the wall, along with Lieutenant Johnston's gunners, directed their fire against Adams, even as Watts and his Virginians spurred their horses down into the ravine and up the far slope toward the Bay Staters. Adams eventually received orders to dismount his men and move back into the woods, but he had waited too long. The Virginians slammed into his men and routed them. "In a second," Adams recalled, "the rebs were riding yelling and slashing among us. . . . resistance was impossible and I had just dismounted my squadron and given it to the enemy." Moments later, Adams joined his men "in a stampede to the rear." Two days later, a still bewildered Adams told his father, "How and why I escaped I can't say, for my men fell all around me; but neither I nor my horse was touched, nor were any of my officers or their horses." The fight had lasted but twenty minutes, according to Adams, during which time he lost sixty-one men. But for the arrival of the Fourth New York, a far greater number of his men would have made the long trek to a Southern prison.[34]

Released from arrest and carrying a borrowed sword, Colonel di Cesnola led his men back into the fray just as Adams and his survivors fled through the woods and as Watts and his Virginians retired to the far ridge crest. Over the course of the next few minutes, di Cesnola led several spirited attacks (he later claimed five), before being shot in the left arm and sabered across the head. Another bullet killed his horse. Concussed by the saber slash, he could not extricate himself before the animal toppled over and died, pinning him to the ground. Before the colonel could be rescued, Pvt. James Wade, Second Virginia, seized the hapless officer. Wade may already have been injured himself after having just "whipped three Yankees" with his saber. Overwhelmed by superior numbers and again leaderless, the New Yorkers retired across the ravine and through the woodlot.[35]

Colonel Munford had defeated every Union force thrown at him. Now, seeking a decisive victory, he ordered Col. Thomas Owen to lead his Third Virginia in a counterattack straight up the Snickersville Turnpike toward Aldie. While Owen formed his companies amid the wreckage of battle, other men pulled the wounded from the road. As the Virginians aligned their ranks, troopers from other regiments, including Colonel Rosser and his Fifth Virginia, rushed up to support Owen.[36]

The last stragglers from the First Massachusetts and Fourth New York, many of them wounded and some riding injured or exhausted animals, slowly made their way off the battlefield toward town and safety. Soon, however, they heard shouts, cheers, and the haunting Rebel Yell rising in the distance behind them. Glancing over their shoulders, the men, including Sgt. Albert Sherman, First Massachusetts, saw Confederates racing toward them and spurred their horses into a race for their own lines. Sergeant Sherman carried the guidon for Company G, but during the struggle with the Second Virginia, Company E's guidon-bearer had been wounded and Sherman's horse had been disabled. Now riding a horse picked up on the field, Sherman rescued Company E's guidon, after the color-sergeant went down with a wound. Then, while managing his horse and the two guidons, attached to their nine-foot lances, Sherman led as many as thirty-five men to safety, under a hail of fire from the onrushing Virginians.[37]

Nearing town, the Federals met General Kilpatrick. The young general knew his battered command was in trouble, and he needed his men to buy him time while he went for reinforcements. Most immediately, he needed them to protect Captain Randol's guns from almost certain capture. Lt. Charles Parsons, who had led Captain Sargent's squadron off the field in the opening moments of the fight, returned at the opportune time. Seeing Parsons and his troopers, Kilpatrick, the gifted orator of his West Point days, shouted, "Men of the 1st Massachusetts, you have done your duty, but I must ask you to do something more. If you will hold this ground [a few] minutes longer I will have the 1st Maine here to relieve you." At Kilpatrick's urging, the men threw a hasty barricade of fence rails across the road.[38]

Years later, one of the Bay Staters recalled the decisive moment with his own embellished eloquence. "After such an address, at such a time, soldiers worthy of the name would hold the ground if they knew a thousand bullets would whistle through their worthless bodies. At such supreme moments the cheek may blanch and the knees tremble but the immortal soul of man, rising on the mountain tops of inspiration commands its quaking tenement to do its will."[39]

ELEVEN

Men of Maine, June 17

Colonel Calvin Douty's First Maine had reached the outskirts of Aldie by 5 p.m. Fifty-one years old in 1863, Douty had been toughened by a life spent outdoors, working as a surveyor, an engineer, and the sheriff of Piscataquis County, in Northern Maine. Admirers believed Douty to be "a perfect soldier." Just after the fight at Brandy Station, one of his officers had remarked, "The Colonel of a regiment gives character to it, and our regiment has a good character." Like Douty, the men of the First Maine had gained a hard-earned reputation as some "of the most effective" troopers in the Cavalry Corps.[1]

Douty's division commander, General Gregg, had reached Aldie shortly after the opening skirmish between the Second New York and Fifth Virginia along the turnpike through town. Reacting quickly to the unexpected presence of enemy cavalry, Gregg sent a courier to Douty, ordering him to head south with his regiment as a hedge against another surprise by Southern troopers coming up from Thoroughfare Gap. Before the courier arrived, Douty's men had hastily filled their canteens, adjusted their saddle girths, and discharged their weapons to ensure they had fresh ammunition and fresh percussion caps seated. The colonel then wheeled his men out of line and headed south. The regiment had not gone far, however, before a galloper arrived bearing fresh orders; Gregg wanted the First Maine back in Aldie immediately. As a precaution, Douty left Lt. Col. Charles Smith behind with one battalion to watch the approaches from the gap. The men would have soon heard a steady booming of artillery once they reached the turnpike and turned west toward Aldie.[2]

Having decisively defeated every Union effort along the Snickersville Turnpike, Colonel Munford ordered the Second, Third, and Fifth Virginia regiments to follow up their success with a countercharge along the turnpike toward Aldie. Though he eagerly sought to further punish General Kilpatrick's brigade, Munford warned his commanders against chasing the Union fugitives too far. As the Southerners, led by Col. Thomas Owen, Third Virginia, carefully picked their way through the detritus of battle, Munford ordered Capt. William Newton to hold his Fourth Virginia behind as a reserve.[3]

In the excitement of the pursuit, some of the Southern horses became unmanageable, just as Colonel Owen and the lead riders overtook the blue-clad laggards. Glancing to his right, Owen might have seen men from other regiments overtaking the last fugitives from the Fourth New York in the triangular field. Then, with their horses tiring as they neared the town, Owen yelled for his men to halt. Heedless of the command, the eager troopers pressed their pursuit, until they saw a fresh detachment of Yankees pouring down the road from Aldie.[4]

After imploring the survivors of the First Massachusetts to brace themselves for the Confederate counterattack, Kilpatrick rode over to Captain Randol and told him to "load with canister." The beleaguered general then galloped into town in a desperate search for help. General Gregg had recalled the First Maine for just such an emergency. Riding back to where Colonel Douty's men waited in the road, Kilpatrick stood in his stirrups and shouted, "Men of Maine, you saved the day at Brandy Station, save it again at Aldie." With the still-searing sun slipping toward the crest of the mountains, one of Douty's men noted the time: 5:30 p.m.[5]

A New Yorker recalled seeing a group of generals and staff officers, including Lt. George Custer, clustered within the town shortly after the fighting had erupted. Custer, a member of General Pleasonton's staff, served as a liaison between Pleasonton and

Gregg during the day. The officers had stopped at Little River to water their horses and fill canteens. Contrary to the other men who walked their horses down the east bank of the river, Custer had crossed the stream to reach the undisturbed water on the west side. Moments later, as Custer headed back up the riverbank, his horse slipped, and horse and rider slid into the river. Chagrined and soaking wet, Custer sheepishly rejoined the other officers. Now, as the column headed up the Snickersville pike, a trooper would later recall "the storm of dust" that engulfed the men. Nearing the Union guns, the soldier could no longer distinguish individual men and soon could not distinguish "friends from foes." Riding near the head of the column with Douty, Custer's blue tunic and pants quickly took on the color of the road as dust clung to his wet uniform like iron shavings to a magnet.[6]

With the passage of time many versions of the First Maine's charge appeared in print. General Kilpatrick thrilled aging veterans at raucous reunions when he claimed the Rebels were "within ten feet of Randol's battery," when the regiment arrived and saved the day. In his diary, Pvt. Nathan Webb described arriving "just in time [as] the Rebs were swarming down the road." The urgency of the situation forced Colonel Douty to counterattack with only two companies, H and D. The squadron had barely formed "when the Rebels swarmed out of the woods almost upon us." Hearing Capt. Andrew Spurling order the men to draw sabers, Webb "felt a thrill go all through. We saw desperate work and we each one nerved himself to the task." No man could have been happier to see the New Englanders arrive than Alanson Randol, as almost exactly one year earlier (June 30, 1862) Confederate infantry had overrun his position and captured his guns at Glendale. Describing Randol's predicament at Aldie, one of his men explained, "Our guns were rendered utterly useless to fire on them by being up on a hill [as] we could not get the elevation in the position we were in and besides we would have killed some of our own men had we been able to fire." Randol had just called for his limbers to pull his guns to safety when Spurling's men came into sight. As the Yankees raced past the guns, other men from the First Massachusetts and Fourth New York fell in behind them.[7]

The men of Maine could hear the enemy before they could see them through the dust. Now, as they surged past the guns, Nathan Webb found his senses overwhelmed, as "clouds of dust filled the air . . . the quick sharp 'y-i-i-i, y-i-i-i' of the Rebels could be heard right in front of us." He heard Kilpatrick yelling for the men to attack, and then his comrades raised a shout of their own. A sergeant agreed, noting, "Such a yell mortal men never before heard as went up from our men as they charged." The Yankees swept along "like fiends incarnate, plowing the dust, yelling, cutting and slashing." Private James Hurd may have been the first man killed, when a bullet punched through his bridle hand. Unable to control his horse, Hurd fell into the road and died from a broken neck.[8]

Riding on the outside of the last set of fours, Nathan Webb threw his arm up just in time to block a saber blow before thrusting his own saber into his antagonist's chest. As the Southerner fell from his horse, Webb realized he had lost his company, which had turned into the fields to his right. Luckily, as he explained, "the dust was so thick I might as well have been half a mile away." Forming up with three comrades, the four Federals suddenly found themselves amid the enemy. They then saw their lieutenant rallying a platoon of men nearby. Before they could make their way to him, however, the Virginians unleashed a volley that wounded three horses and killed two of the four men. Only Webb escaped unhurt but having lost his bearings in the murk he mistakenly turned back toward the Southern position. Before he realized his error, a Southerner ran him down, using his horse like a battering ram. "The concussion grounded both of us," Webb explained. Struggling to free himself from under his horse, Webb saw two revolvers pointed at him and realized his fight was over. Beginning the long walk to Libby Prison, Webb took some solace as he glanced back at his adversary, a lieutenant grimacing from a broken leg suffered in the collision.[9]

Having stopped the threat to the Union guns and pushed the Confederates back to the Furr farm, Captain Spurling now found himself outnumbered and far from his own supports. Wisely, he ordered his men to retire and regroup. As Spurling turned his men out of the road, Lieutenant Custer, like Private Webb, found himself on the wrong side of the field. But, unlike the unfortunate Webb, Custer's luck held, owing to his dust covered uniform and his wide-brimmed straw hat. As he told a family member shortly thereafter, "I was surrounded by rebels, and cut off from my own men, but I made my way out safely, and all owing to my *hat*, which is . . . exactly like that worn by the rebels." Only one Virginian saw beyond the hat and dirty uniform, but Custer struck the onrushing trooper "across the face with [his] saber, knocking him off his horse." With his identity now revealed, Custer spurred his horse across the field and out of harm's way.[10]

As Colonel Owens's Virginians fell back to the Furr farm, they found the obstructions in the road more of a hazard than they had moments earlier. Lt. Robert Hubard's horse went down, and Hubard, with one foot caught in the stirrup, landed headfirst between the rear legs of another horse, "scuffling and kicking" in its death struggles. No sooner had he disentangled himself and stood up than he was knocked flat by a soldier jumping his horse over him. Leaping over a fence to escape the mayhem in the road, Hubard lost his saber and his revolver.[11]

By now, the men were nearing exhaustion, especially the Virginians, some of whom had been fighting for nearly an hour under the scorching sun. Colonel Rosser and the men of his Fifth Virginia had been especially busy, as they participated in all phases of the battle. Though a rugged, powerful man, the heat and near constant saber fighting had taken a toll on Rosser, who told his wife the next day, "I am almost completely exhausted. At one time yesterday I could scarcely lift my hand and now I find it difficult to write." At some point during the battle, Rosser's horse had been shot from under him, but he had escaped with only the loss of his hat.[12]

Beyond saving Randol's guns, the ferocity and speed of Captain Spurling's attack had freed numerous men of the First Massachusetts and Fourth New York, who, moments earlier, had been prisoners bound for Libby Prison. Cornelius Keating, First Massachusetts, was among the men freed. Though badly bruised by a bullet striking the buckle of his carbine sling, Keating had

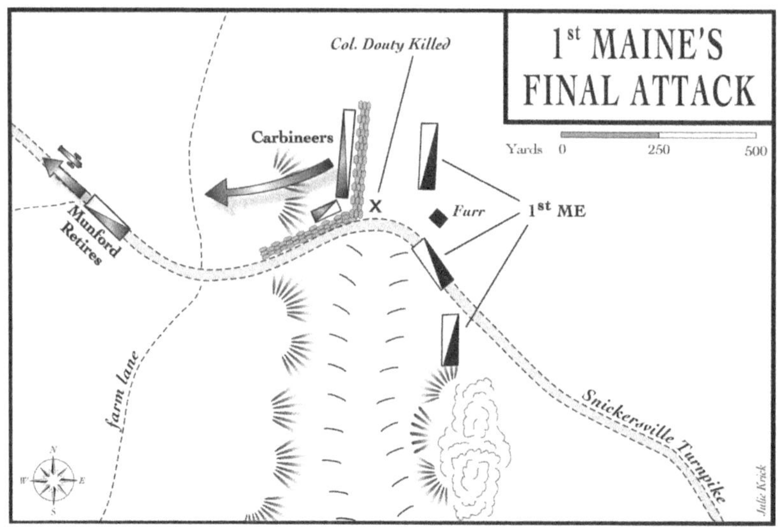

MAP 10. First Maine's final attack. Created by Julie Krick.

not suffered a debilitating wound, though the shock of the impact may have knocked him from his saddle. Exhausted, after being forced to run back toward the Southern lines, Keating had to be helped onto his savior's horse and carried back to Union lines.[13]

When Captain Spurling's men rejoined the regiment near the Union guns, General Kilpatrick ordered another attack. Leaving one squadron as a reserve, Colonel Douty formed his men, even as eager survivors from the First Massachusetts and Fourth New York again fell in behind the Mainers. Sending one column up the pike, Douty deployed the remainder of his men in a line to sweep across the Furr property. Like the Confederates, the men and horses were exhausted. They had been marching or fighting under a blazing sun since the first hours of daylight. They had had little to eat, and the water they found was, as one man described, "yellow stuff." As the weary stalwarts moved haltingly into formation, Kilpatrick, along with Douty and Custer, moved to the head of the formation. As a correspondent noted, "There was no hesitancy then. The Maine boys gave three cheers for Gen. Kilpatrick, and the whole column made a dash up the road."[14]

Inspired by the loud cheers, William Howe, First Maine, wondered if any of the officers could have impacted the outcome of the fight beyond this moment of inspiration. He also recalled feelings of "confusion and bewilderment," created by the "blinding" dust and "the storm of shot and shell which came pouring down into the road and spreading devastation to our troopers." Once the men moved forward, Howe felt the officers lost all control "over the infuriated old 1st [Maine] who at that . . . moment, knew no officers and who like a wild horse with the furor of a tornado plunged onward" across the fields and up the turnpike. "We had," Howe remembered, "but one object . . . to reach the heights or die."[15]

General Kilpatrick rode at the head of the men in the turnpike, accompanied by his bugler and his orderly. Charging into the teeth of the storm, the bugler's horse went down, throwing him from the saddle. Kilpatrick's horse took a bullet through the neck and staggered to a halt. As Capt. Henry Hall dashed by the general, he wondered if "Old Kil" may have been "deliberating whether to urge the bleeding brute further." Moments later the animal dropped dead.[16]

Captain Hall found the increasing darkness exacerbated his loss of spatial awareness. Thinking as he passed the general that he had now reached the head of the column, he raised his saber to strike at the first man coming toward him, only to find he had almost sabered Pvt. Isaiah Mosher. The hapless trooper had just been shot through his bridle arm and could not control his horse. Carrying an empty revolver, Mosher found himself surrounded by several Confederates who hacked at him with their sabers, while the man who had just shot him looked for an opportunity to finish him. Recovering from his near fatal mistake, Captain Hall sabered the revolver-wielding Virginian over the head, but when he tried to stab the man his dull blade would not penetrate the enemy's clothing. As Hall swung his saber toward another trooper, the Southerner fled. And, when Hall looked for Mosher, he had disappeared as well. Turning back toward the stone wall, Hall's horse stumbled and fell, pitching the captain from the saddle. As he watched the animal run toward the enemy line,

Hall saw one of his men bringing off a prisoner. Relieving the Southerner of his horse, Hall reentered the fray.[17]

With Kilpatrick leading the column in the turnpike, Colonel Douty rode with the men sweeping across the fields around the Furr home. William Howe had begun the second charge near the turnpike but had then chased an enemy trooper into the farm field. After emptying his revolver at the man and seeing him reeling in the saddle, Howe turned to rejoin his comrades. Heading for the turnpike, Howe saw Douty through the dust clouds. Falling in behind his colonel, Howe followed him toward the stone wall. Discerning Howe nearby, Douty yelled, "Where is the head of the regiment?" Howe pointed toward the bend in the road but as they neared the wall the murk became thicker as the dust merged with gun smoke. Disoriented, Douty turned toward the road and an opening in the fences. As he did so, Confederates behind the wall fired a volley, killing Douty and wounding Howe. Hit in the ankle, Howe crossed the road and spurred his horse over a fence and into the ravine south of the road. When his horse regained its feet, Howe raced for the safety of the woods where Captain Adams and his squadron had made their futile stand moments earlier.[18]

Capt. William Graves, Second Virginia, identified Pvt. Creed Hubbard as having fired the shot that killed Douty. Graves described Douty riding through an opening into the Confederate position and calling on Hubbard to surrender. "We killed him and his horse as soon as he came through," Graves acknowledged. Colonel Munford also saw Douty fall. "I was within forty steps of him. He could not have expected anything but death," as he called on one of the Virginians to surrender. "But he had unfortunately mistaken his man. [Hubbard] shot him as deliberately as he would have shot a deer."[19]

With the Southerners still stubbornly holding their position along the wall, the Union attack began to falter. Watching from near the woods, Maj. Stephen Boothby elected to send the reserve squadron into the fight. When Boothby asked Capt. Isaac Virgin if his men could drive the attack home, Virgin replied, "I have had all I could do to hold them back." Heading down into the ravine, a trooper shouted, "Come on, Boys; Here is for the honor of Old Maine." At the same time, Lt. Colonel Smith reached the field with his battalion and filed into the fields around the Furr house. As the men moved into formation, they scanned the field ahead. Noting the dead and wounded, they also observed the Confederates withdrawing.[20]

The Federals credited Major Boothby's final attack with driving the Virginians from their position. Lt. Colonel Smith thought the enemy had suddenly been routed. Or so it appeared. Colonel Munford had indeed ordered a hasty withdrawal. Yet none of the Federals had seen a lone rider gallop into the Southern position from the west and pull his lathered horse to a halt near Munford.[21]

TWELVE

Cut All to Pieces, June 17–18

Though his men loved him, Col. Alfred N. Duffié's superiors found him thin-skinned, emotional, insubordinate, and incompetent. Born in France on May 1, 1835, Napoleon Alexander Duffié enlisted in the French army and rose through the ranks to receive a commission in the cavalry. Shortly after reenlisting, Duffié fell in love with an American nurse. Following his heart, Duffié deserted, sailed for America, married, and then created a carefully crafted story of aristocratic lineage, military education, and battlefield prowess to escape being identified and arrested for desertion and taken back to France in chains. Presenting himself as Alfred N. Duffié, he accepted a commission as a captain in the Second New York. His quarrelsome nature soon prevailed, however, and his superiors arrested him twice within a matter of weeks. Then, in July 1862, with Duffié still at odds with his colonel and demanding a court-martial to clear his name, the governor of Rhode Island interceded and offered Duffié the colonelcy of the First Rhode Island.[1]

In April 1863 a friend spoke of Duffié's "military sagacity," but the Frenchman continued to run afoul of his superiors. Assigning Duffié to take command of the remount facility in Dumfries, General Hooker ordered him to relieve the infantry brigade securing the town. But only one tenth of the cavalrymen arrived armed for the task, forcing Hooker to leave the infantry in place. Two months later, and on the eve of the battle at Brandy Station, Duffié sheepishly reported one of his regiments in need of more than five hundred saddles. Then he admitted he needed thousands of percussion caps for his men's weapons. Duffié's inefficiency infuriated Pleasonton. A couple of days later, on the battlefield near Stevensburg, Duffié allowed a couple of hundred Southerners to hold his division at bay for critical hours, squandering a chance for victory. Consolidating his corps after the battle, Pleasonton eliminated a division and Duffié reverted to brigade command. Days later, Judson Kilpatrick, newly promoted to brigadier, took command of the brigade and the Frenchman returned to his regiment.[2]

At 3 a.m., June 17, Lt. Col. Andrew Alexander, Pleasonton's chief of staff, ordered General Gregg to have his division on the road within two hours. Alexander also told Gregg to send "one regiment of your command . . . through Thoroughfare Gap as far as Middleburg tonight scouting the country well in that vicinity." The following morning, June 18, the regiment was to follow a specified route through northern Loudoun County before rejoining the corps at Nolands Ferry. Duffié believed he had received the assignment as a malicious attempt by his superiors to end his career, but his lieutenant colonel, John Thompson, claimed Duffié succumbed to his ambition and requested the "independent command."[3]

The First Rhode Island, 275 men strong, departed Manassas Junction around 5 a.m. Duffié soon turned his men west toward Thoroughfare Gap, while the remainder of the brigade continued north. About 9:30 a.m. men of the advance guard encountered enemy pickets at the entrance to the gap. A few hasty shots triggered a fusillade of return fire from Confederates scattered among the trees and shrubs along the slopes. When the lead squadron arrived, one of the Federals excitedly exclaimed, "There are at least twice as many as there are of us." Pushing through the gap, the Rhode Islanders came under more concentrated fire from an organized force of Southerners drawn up in the open country west of the mountains.[4]

At the outset of the day's march, General Stuart sent Col. John Chambliss and his brigade to watch the road from Thoroughfare

Gap. Entering the service of the Confederacy in 1861, Chambliss received a commission as colonel of the Thirteenth Virginia Cavalry. Now, just a month shy of his thirtieth birthday, Chambliss had temporary command of General W. H. F. Lee's brigade, following Lee's wounding at Brandy Station.[5]

Passing through White Plains, Chambliss sent Col. Richard Beale and his Ninth Virginia ahead to scout the gap, "but not to engage in any fighting." Nearing the mountains, Beale sent a squad of men to examine the narrow passage. Finding no sign of the enemy, Beale set out a picket force and then allowed the remainder of the regiment to relax. Just as the last of the pickets reached the crest of the mountain, shots rang out within the pass below. As Beale and his officers reformed their men, Maj. Thomas Waller deployed a company to cover the retreat of the regiment.[6]

Like Beale, Colonel Duffié also sought to avoid a fight. And, like Beale, Duffié sent one company ahead to hold off Major Waller's men while the remainder of the Rhode Islanders turned north toward Middleburg and away from the Virginians. The long-range sniping lasted nearly two hours. The physical toll of the engagement had been light, with only a few horses killed or wounded, but the unexpected encounter, so early in the day and so far from help, shook the morale of the Yankees. Men who had been singing and joking before the skirmish now grew pensive. Determined to follow his orders, however, Duffié pressed ahead, leaving an enemy force behind him and Bull Run Mountain between him and help. With the enemy continuing to harass the Union rear guard, at least one of Duffié's men believed "someone had blundered" by sending a lone regiment so far away from the remainder of the corps.[7]

• • •

Having posted his three brigades to Aldie, Thoroughfare Gap, and Rectortown, Stuart made his headquarters at Middleburg. The town provided a central point from where he could easily communicate with or reinforce the brigades holding the gaps in Bull Run Mountain. After deploying Capt. William Wooldridge's two squadrons from the Fourth Virginia as a picket force around

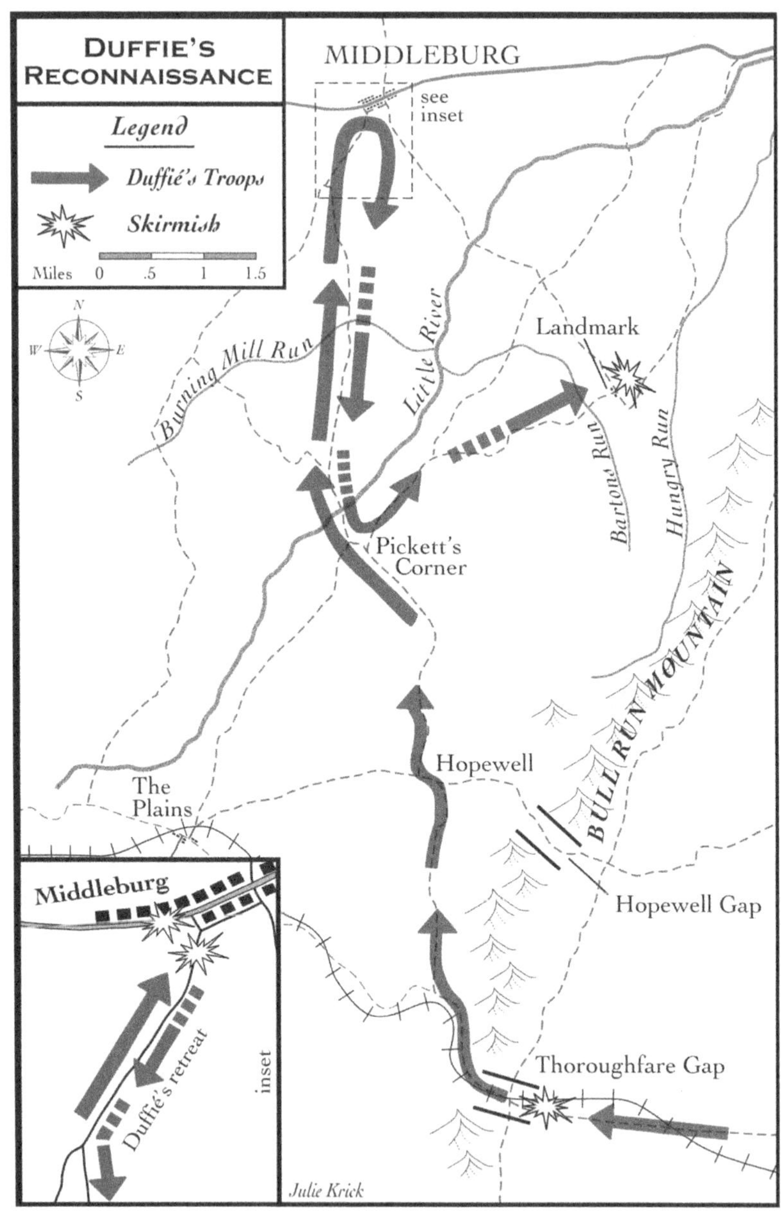

MAP 11. Duffie's reconnaissance. Created by Julie Krick

the town, Stuart and his staff relaxed, enjoyed a midday meal, and regaled "a circle of pretty young ladies" with thrilling tales of cavalry life. Then, around four o'clock, "the streets suddenly resounded with the cry of 'The Yankees are coming!'"[8]

The warning shattered the frivolity in an instant. Running for their horses, the officers dodged nervous citizens racing for the shelter of their homes and shops. Moments later, Stuart and his aides raced out of town, before halting atop a ridge known today as Mount Defiance. Calling Lt. Frank Robertson forward, Stuart ordered him to ride back through town and on to Aldie, to warn Colonel Munford that the enemy, in unknown strength, had arrived behind him. The general wanted Munford to retire along back roads to meet Stuart at Rector's Cross Roads. Believing Middleburg now teemed with Yankees, Robertson's fellow aides bade him goodbye, unsure if they would see him again.[9]

• • •

Colonel Duffié turned north on the road to Middleburg about 11 a.m. Though Confederates continued to harass his rear guard, Duffié, unlike some of his men, claimed to have been unconcerned. Guided by an escaped slave, the Federals followed a series of narrow, hilly roads through the crossroad settlements of Hopewell, Pickett's Corner, and Halfway. Seeking to conserve their horses, the men moved slowly, especially over a horse-killing six-mile stretch between Thoroughfare Gap and Picket's Corner.[10]

Entering Middleburg, Duffié sent scouts to examine the other roads into and out of town. Returning, they reported Colonel Munford's brigade to the east, in addition to the enemy force to the south. With two of their escape routes blocked by enemy cavalry, and an unknown force having just fled to the west, the New Englanders began to feel "a sense of impending disaster." Still, Duffié intended to hold the town as he had been directed, but with less than one hundred carbines in the command, his task would be nearly impossible. Leaving several companies to barricade the streets, he moved the remainder of the regiment into a large field on the southern outskirts of town. The field allowed him to feed and rest his horses, while nearby woods offered shelter in the event of trouble. Stone walls around the field afforded him a ready means of defense.[11]

Having made his arrangements, Duffié, in further adherence to his orders, sent Capt. Frank Allen and two men to try and break through the Southern lines to the east and notify General Kilpatrick of his predicament. Struggling to find their way through unfamiliar country in the dark, the three men dodged and deceived several groups of enemy pickets before reaching Kilpatrick's headquarters around 9 p.m. Kilpatrick notified his superiors of Duffié's situation, but at night, and with an enemy force of unknown size between them and Duffié, Pleasonton could do nothing until daylight.[12]

• • •

After sending his aide to warn Colonel Munford, Stuart continued to Rector's Cross Roads. From there he sent couriers to Colonel Chambliss and Brig. Gen. Beverly Robertson "to march without delay for Middleburg." Robertson arrived first, and Stuart sent him to drive the enemy out of the town immediately. Heading east with his Fourth and Fifth North Carolina, Robertson knew he would not reach the town before dark and had no sense of either the size of the enemy force or the nature of the defense the Yankees had established. And, like Duffié, Robertson's relationship with his superior was tenuous. Stuart had no faith in Robertson's tenacity or tactical ability on a battlefield, and so he sent Maj. Heros von Borcke to accompany him. Not only did the towering Prussian know the town and surrounding road network but Stuart may have charged him with holding Robertson's feet to the fire.[13]

Approaching Middleburg, Robertson encountered Captain Wooldridge's Virginians. Like Stuart, Wooldridge was eager to punish the Yankees who had driven him from town, and he asked to lead the assault against the barricades. Robertson assented and the Virginians led the North Carolinians forward "with a cheer."[14]

The scene, as viewed by the New Englanders, must have been dramatic as the last vestiges of sunlight silhouetted the onrushing Confederates. The Union defense of the barricades was brief, however, and not the "sanguinary struggle" described by von

Borcke. With only a small force left to defend the town and hold the fallback position south of town along the Plains Road, the Yankees simply did not have the men necessary to hold the barricades for long. The main Southern attack came from the west, but Robertson had wisely sent a second force to attack from the north. Compelled to defend two points, the Federals gave way quickly.[15]

Major von Borcke relished being one of the first through the barricades. The Prussian's description of "utter confusion" rings true, as panicked Yankees fled from the Southern horsemen and sought to gain their bearings in the dark, narrow streets. Pistol shots, shouted commands, the clatter of sabers, canteens, and horseshoes striking the hard road surface all created a cacophony of noise along streets dimly lit by candlelight escaping through shuttered windows. Minutes after crashing through the western barricades, von Borcke led a follow-up assault to the east, while Robertson led another column south along the Plains Road.[16]

Most of the Rhode Islanders fled south toward the fallback position. There, the men had dropped a tree across the road and now waited for the Southerners from behind a stone wall on the east side of the road. In the darkness, the tree remained nearly invisible across the twisting, undulating road. Lying in wait, the Federals could hear Southern officers barking commands. Moments later, the lead files of the Fifth North Carolina crashed into the tree and the entire column came to a sudden, tangled stop. Waiting silently, the Yankees held their fire until the Carolinians were well occupied with the barricade, and then, as one of the New Englanders described, "eighty carbines hurled death into the rebel ranks." Trapped in a deadly cul-de-sac between the tree and the stone walls, the Carolinians struggled to escape.[17]

Unable to move the tree, the Tar Heels retreated to town, but the Yankees had only moments to catch a breath before bugles and barked commands announced another attack. Again, the Carolinians crashed into the tree, drawing carbine and revolver fire from the men behind the wall. Men and horses going down in the road added to the confusion, as the Southerners again struggled to escape the ambush. Seeking an alternative, Robertson sent a smaller force to attack the Union position on foot. Stumbling and cursing their way through fields and brambles, and clattering as they climbed the walls, the Southerners achieved no surprise. At the last second, the Federals unleashed another volley and sent them back on the run.[18]

In the brief lull that followed, a courier arrived from Duffié with orders for the men to rejoin the main body of the regiment farther south. As the officers quietly called their men away from the wall, they could hear their Southern counterparts preparing to make another attack on foot. The Carolinians stormed the wall again just as the Yankees slipped away into the darkness. A final shot killed Pvt. Guilford Taylor, Fifth North Carolina. Taylor, who now rests in a quiet shaded cemetery within sight of where he fell, may have been the last man to die that day on the bloody fields around the once peaceful towns of Aldie and Middleburg.[19]

Confused, tired, and disoriented, the Federals groped their way through the near moonless night, unable to distinguish friend from foe. At least one group mistakenly stumbled into a pursuing group of Tar Heels. Shouted curses, oaths, and demands for surrender alerted other New Englanders to seek other routes to safety. The darkness made staying together nearly impossible. Some men never located Duffié and the regiment. A lucky few eventually found their way over the mountain to Centreville. Others fell into enemy hands.[20]

Listening to the sounds of the fight and considering what he knew of the enemy forces arrayed around him, the Frenchman soon realized the futility of trying to hold through the night. Gathering the remainder of the regiment, Duffié headed toward Bull Run Mountain. After crossing Burnt Mill Run and Little River, Duffié turned east and crossed Bartons Run, as he continued toward the mountain. Finding a large field near the hamlet of Landmark, Duffié allowed his men to bed down for the night. Tired and dejected, the New Englanders spent a cheerless night without cook fires, coffee, or food. Instead, they got what sleep they could while holding the reins of their horses. Like the men, the horses were tired, hungry, and thirsty. One trooper described them as so "jaded" as to be nearly useless. When the men awoke in the morning, they learned, to their dismay, that the enemy had slept in an adjoining field. As Capt. George Bliss later explained, they had spent the night "shut up among the mountains in a regular trap entirely surrounded by rebel cavalry."[21]

In the inky darkness, with just a sliver of a moon to guide them, Colonel Richard Beale and his Ninth Virginia had, indeed, gone into camp nearby, little dreaming the enemy was, as one of the Virginians said, within "the same field." As the first hints of dawn lightened the sky over Bull Run Mountain, Beale's quartermaster set out with a squadron of troopers in search of corn and hay for the animals. Nearby, and at the same hour, a group of hungry Yankees set out on a similar foraging mission. Then Duffié sent Captain Bliss with a second detachment to reconnoiter the area for "signs of the enemy." Just as Bliss returned and reported the road to Thoroughfare Gap appeared to be open, Southerners rode up on the Yankee foragers.[22]

Spurring their horses, the Confederates surprised the unwary Yankees, routing or capturing the entire group. With gunshots now echoing across the fields, Duffié ordered his men to mount and form by fours in the road. Just as they wheeled toward the sound of the gunfire, they saw a squadron of enemy troopers bearing down on them. As Captain Bliss turned toward the new threat, a bullet ricocheted off his upraised saber and struck his arm. Stunned, Bliss heard Duffié shout, "Go ahead boys, charge!" But rather than passion or zeal in his commander, Bliss saw only defeat.[23]

Nearly surrounded, the dispirited men jumped their horses over a stone wall into a lush wheat field. One trooper believed they would have escaped if they had immediately abandoned any further resistance and set out on their own accord. Instead, Duffié ordered them to turn and wait for the oncoming enemy. By doing so, they surrendered all the advantage and momentum of the charge to their foe. As the Virginians closed, the Federal line began to waver, and then the men broke and ran. Only a handful, led by Lt. Joseph Chedell, stayed behind, providing covering fire in a vain attempt to aid their comrades. When Chedell went down, Bugler Albert Tasker fired the last shots in his revolver and smashed his bugle just as the Virginians surrounded the small band. As the Southerners spurred their horses over the wall and into the field, an unknown officer stood by and protected Lieutenant Chedell, lying mortally wounded nearby.[24]

As Tasker and his dejected comrades headed for captivity, they may have heard their officers trying to rally the fleeing men behind them. Captain Bliss credited the New Englanders with forming for a last desperate attack. But then the remainder of the Ninth Virginia appeared. With the enemy advancing on them in three columns, the Rhode Islanders abandoned any pretense of resistance and broke for the mountain. As one Southern trooper explained, "each man, true to the Yankee instinct, sought safety for No. 1 in flight."[25]

Seeking to clear a path to safety, Duffié ordered Capt. Augustus Bixby to attack the Virginians nearest the mountain. But then a bullet punched through Bixby's leg and injured his horse. As Bixby's horse began to falter, Duffié abandoned the effort, shouting, "Cavalry in our rear, boys. Let us go." And go the men did, until their horses could go no farther. The Virginians chased them, like they might have chased their hounds on the scent of a fox in pleasanter days. They gathered up prisoners at nearly every step. "Our boys rushed on gallantly, dashing right into their midst with drawn sabers, cutting right and left, discharging the pistols of the captured into the ranks of their flying comrades, with deadly effect," a Southerner recalled gleefully. In the rough, wooded terrain, horses stumbled and fell from wounds, exhaustion, holes, and tree roots. Captain Bliss turned into the woods, only to be swept from the saddle by a low-hanging branch.[26]

As Captain Bixby's horse continued to struggle, another officer stayed with him. But then their frantic horses got tangled. As they fought to free themselves, one horse took a bullet in the neck. Somehow the men freed their mounts and made their way to safety. When Color Sgt. George Robbins's horse went down, Robbins tore the colors from the staff and stuffed them in his shirt. Lawrence Cronan carried his company guidon. Called upon to surrender, Cronan refused and was shot in the chest and arm. Just before falling from his horse, he handed the standard to a comrade. When his captors asked why he had not surrendered the guidon, Cronan replied, "It was not given to me for that purpose."[27]

Colonel Duffié and the First Rhode Island suffered a near catastrophic defeat. In addition to the dead and wounded, more than two hundred men had been captured. Survivors, including Duffié, Bixby, and Bliss, made their way into Union lines near Centreville over the next few days. After being knocked from his saddle, Captain Bliss hid in the woods before setting out for Union lines. Waiting, along with several comrades for the enemy to clear the area, Bliss penned a letter. "I haven't read [James Fenimore Cooper] for nothing," he told a friend, "and I intend to pilot this crowd safely out of the woods."[28]

Colonel Duffié reached the Union lines around 1:30 p.m., with what he termed "the gallant *débris* of my much-loved regiment—4 officers and 27 men," of the 275 he had taken into the Loudoun Valley. Other survivors trickled in over the next couple days, but the men spent the remainder of the campaign in Alexandria reorganizing and reequipping. Though his regiment had, as one officer asserted, been "cut all to pieces," Duffié's career rebounded within days. The man who had reinvented himself after deserting the French army was about to rise from the ashes a second time like the mythical phoenix.[29]

On May 13 General Hooker had published a stunningly harsh rebuttal to Gen. William Averell's report of his fight at Kelly's Ford two months earlier. Though Hooker denounced Averell's effort as a disappointing failure, the army commander had been impressed by the actions of several subordinates, most especially Duffié's dash across the Rappahannock River. Hooker asked the army to promote Duffié to brigadier to date from March 17, 1863. Sending in a second request the same day, Hooker again placed the Frenchman's name at the top of the list. Then, on June 20, two days after the disaster near Middleburg, Brig. Gen. Marsena Patrick, the army's provost marshal, sent a note to Senator Ira Harris, a powerful advocate for the cavalry, calling his "attention to the claims for promotion of an officer you already know, Col. Duffié." Citing the colonel's "intrepid bravery and dash," Patrick told Harris that "if promotion be the reward of gallantry in the field, Col. Duffié has certainly earned it and although recommended, heretofore, for increased rank, it has not yet been granted." Two days later, someone, most likely Duffié or Harris, discussed the matter with President Lincoln. Then, at Lincoln's request, Secretary of War Edwin Stanton met with Duffié. Stanton approved his promotion the following day. Though possibly apocryphal, the Frenchman is said to have innocently responded in his fractured English, "when I do well, they take no notice of me. When I go make one bad business, make one fool of myself, they promote me, make me General."[30]

Alfred Duffié's promotion enraged Alfred Pleasonton, who asked that he be court-martialed or have his appointment revoked, "in justice to the many gallant officers of the cavalry who have really distinguished themselves." Referring to Brandy Station, Pleasonton reminded his superior, that the Frenchman's "conduct is condemned by everyone, who knows of the affair," and he referred specifically to Duffié's negligence "in not seeing that [his men] were supplied with ammunition before they went into the fight as he was ordered." As to the disaster in the Loudoun Valley, Pleasonton termed Duffié as "totally unfitted to command a regiment." He also submitted a written statement from Lt. Col. Meriwether Lewis, Ninth Virginia. Lewis, who had been wounded and captured on June 21, described the fight on the morning of June 18, stating, "Col. Duffié's troops at once broke in confusion and ran without fighting at all." Having promoted Duffié at Lincoln's request, Stanton could not honor Pleasonton's plea. He did, however, ignore Duffié's preferred assignments, and sent him to West Virginia.[31]

Following Duffié's transfer, Lt. Col. John Thompson took command of the regiment. He later told Captain Bliss, "We can all say what we might have done in view of what we know now, but [Duffié] was embarrassed by his relations to the cavalry officers. He could not go back to them. . . . He did not want to go back to them at all, and his sagacity and shrewdness was shown by the fact that he went directly to General Hooker, to whom he told such a story as induced the General to send him at once to Washington endorsed for a Brigadier-General. Duffié had no idea of returning to [Pleasonton] with his command gone." Reflecting on the events around Middleburg, Thompson continued, "Duffié was in many respects an excellent soldier . . . but everything was subordinate to his personal ambition." Thompson, like Bliss, Lt. Colonel Lewis, and others, thought the regiment would have escaped if Duffié had kept moving rather than stopping near Landmark for the night. "It demoralizes a command to skulk and hide," Thompson admitted. But he also confessed, "The truth is, we disgraced ourselves by fleeing from a comparatively small force as we emerged from our hiding place."[32]

THIRTEEN

I Have Never Seen as Many Yankees Killed

When he received General Stuart's order to disengage at Aldie and retire toward Rectors Cross Roads, Colonel Munford reacted angrily and his tenuous relationship with Stuart may never have recovered. In his report of the fight, Munford proudly declared, "I do not hesitate to say that I have never seen as many Yankees killed in the same space of ground in any fight I have ever seen, or any battle-field in Virginia that I have been over. We held our ground until ordered by the major-general commanding to retire, and the Yankees had been so severely punished that they did not follow." Munford's dismay at his orders continued after the war. "I was ordered to retire," he told a former Union officer. Refusing to let the long-dead Stuart rest, Munford groused, "Gen. Stuart had been held in check and kept out of Middleburg by an inferior force compared to his command and we never had the credit from our side for what was done by us." The colonel had every reason to be proud of his accomplishments at Aldie, but his continuing antagonism toward Stuart was unfair, reflecting the degree to which their relationship had deteriorated rather than an accurate understanding of the military situation when Stuart sent the order.[1]

General Stuart had no alternative but to retreat westward when Colonel Duffié drove in the pickets around Middleburg. In the moment, Stuart could not have known the size of the enemy force entering the town. He could, however, safely assume the Yankees had forced a passage of Thoroughfare Gap, shoving Colonel Chambliss's brigade aside in the process. Stuart could not be faulted for assuming the enemy had arrived in at least brigade strength. Only by retiring westward could he maintain his communication with Chambliss and Robertson. To have allowed Munford to continue his battle with enemy forces of unknown strength in his front and rear would have been reckless. In the face of an unexpected attack on two fronts, Stuart needed to regroup and concentrate his command.

General Stuart's order reached Munford during a lull in the fighting. The pause afforded the Confederates the perfect opportunity to disengage. And, as ordered, Munford followed "a circuitous route," reaching the Ashby's Gap Turnpike west of Middleburg too late to assist in retaking the town. The fight at Aldie, "one of the most sanguinary cavalry battles of the war," in Stuart's opinion, as well as "most creditable to our arms and glorious to the veteran brigade of Brig. Gen. Fitz Lee," was over. Yet, in referring to Lee, the absent brigade commander, Stuart had pointedly ignored Munford, a snub which must have rankled the colonel as much as the order to retire. Tasked with preventing the Federals from locating Lee's army, Stuart had employed defensible terrain in the Loudoun Valley to trade distance for time. Time gained versus ground lost became his measuring stick for victory, and he had just gained a full day, while nearly wrecking an enemy brigade in the process.[2]

General Kilpatrick could not have been unhappy to see the Southerners leave. Shouldering the burden of the fight throughout the afternoon, the men and officers of the brigade had paid a steep price for the young general's aggressive nature, as well as their own, losing at least 310 men killed, wounded, and captured, compared to Munford's loss of about 137 men. The Federals believed they had driven their opponent from the field and gained a tactical victory. By defying General Hooker, Pleasonton had gained a foothold in the Loudoun Valley along both turnpikes. He now had two avenues to the Shenandoah Valley.[3]

The remainder of the Cavalry Corps had been on the move

throughout the day, with most of the command reaching Aldie while the fight progressed west of town. Col. Thomas Devin's brigade remained near Thoroughfare Gap, while Col. John Taylor's brigade brought up the rear of the corps. Tasked with riding herd on the supply wagons, Taylor's men stopped and started throughout the day as the wagons lurched along the narrow roads. In the evening, Taylor put his men into camp near Mount Zion Church. Col. William Gamble's brigade provided picket details around the battlefield during the night.[4]

Col. William Doster's Fourth Pennsylvania drew the unenviable task of policing the battlefield. Walking the ground by lantern light, the men gathered up weapons and debris of every description, as well as a damaged artillery caisson abandoned by the Confederates. Other men searched for missing comrades, buried the dead, and carried the wounded to buildings converted into hospitals. The bodies of several officers, including Colonel Douty and Lieutenant Whittaker, lay in town, awaiting the construction of rough-hewn caskets before being sent home. By the end of the following day, only the carcasses of the dead horses remained above ground, lying near mounds of freshly turned dirt. Yet with all the activity and the thousands of men moving about within and around Aldie, one strategically important event played out nearby unseen by any of Pleasonton's troopers.[5]

FOURTEEN

He Goes Where He Pleases, June 17

On the morning of June 17, Maj. John S. Mosby called for his men, Company A, Forty-Third Battalion, Virginia Cavalry, to rendezvous later in the day near Middleburg. Mosby then rode west to Piedmont Station, where he met with Jeb Stuart. Mosby had been scouting the positions of the advancing Union army for several days and relayed his information to Stuart during the meeting. Before departing, the two men agreed to meet in Middleburg later in the day. During the afternoon meeting, Mosby gained Stuart's approval to raid a Union cavalry camp at Seneca, Maryland, near Rowser's Ford on the Potomac River. Leaving Middleburg, Mosby led his men east, before turning north and pausing at a home north of Aldie. There the men enjoyed cool buttermilk and refreshing shade during a brief respite from the scorching heat. Moments later, the crack of cannon fire to the south shattered their quiet interlude.[1]

Ordering his men back into their saddles, Mosby turned them south toward the guns rather than north toward the river. He had determined that he could now be more useful by striking the enemy's line of communication and supply along the Little River Turnpike. Nearing the road in the dark, and after the fighting had concluded, Mosby secreted his partisans in a wooded area, before continuing with three men. Approaching the home of Almond Birch, near the hamlet of Lenah, east of Mount Zion Church,

Mosby saw a lone Yankee orderly tending to several horses at the home. Aided by darkness, Mosby approached the soldier and asked who owned the horses. When the soldier named the two officers inside enjoying Mr. Birch's hospitality, Mosby identified himself and took the man prisoner. Along with his three cohorts, Mosby then waited outside and seized the officers as they walked toward their horses. And, having learned from the cooperative orderly that the men carried an order from Hooker to Pleasonton, Mosby demanded the communication. Once safely away from the turnpike, the men rode to a local farm where Mosby read the captured document. Astonished at the information, Mosby termed the document the "'open sesame' to Hooker's army."[2]

• • •

As he had advised earlier, Hooker, along with his aide, Daniel Butterfield, had drafted detailed instructions for General Pleasonton, telling him not to "advance the main body of your cavalry beyond Aldie [under any circumstance] until further information is received of the movements of the enemy." Instead, Butterfield told the cavalry chief to hold his ground east of the town and to graze his horses "until your scouts can furnish us further information." And rather than the heavy reconnaissance through the Loudoun Valley planned for the eighteenth, Butterfield told Pleasonton to send only patrols to Leesburg, and Snicker's Gap. Hooker's aide also reminded Pleasonton of the importance of Thoroughfare Gap. Butterfield alerted the cavalry chief to a brigade-sized detachment of remounts waiting for him north of the Potomac and told him that General Stahel's cavalry would be reconnoitering the area of Warrenton and Sulphur Springs. Finally, he confirmed Hooker's continuing ignorance of Lee's intent. "They must have come for an object," said Butterfield, referring to Longstreet and Ewell, "and until we know where they are we cannot divine it." Hooker hoped the scouts sent into Snicker's Gap could uncover Lee's plan, but he had again determined to not risk the main body of his cavalry for the same purpose.[3]

• • •

Recognizing the importance of the captured order, Mosby tasked one of his men to carry the document through Union lines to Stuart, who then sent the message on to General Lee at Berryville. Both Lee and Stuart now knew Hooker's intentions and made their plans to counter the Union efforts. Stuart warned Brig. Gen. Wade Hampton to remain near Warrenton to turn back the Union reconnaissance headed his way. Stuart also sent Colonel Munford to Snicker's Gap to prevent any Federal scouting parties from penetrating the pass. Butterfield's passing mention of Union infantry may also have convinced Stuart to remain on the defensive, screening his own infantry but "continually threatening attack." When word of Mosby's exploit reached the Southern press, one editor opined, "It seems as if he can go where he pleases, and do what he chooses."[4]

FIFTEEN

Find Out Where the Enemy Is, June 18

On the night of June 17, Lt. Col. Elijah V. White led his Thirty-Fifth Battalion, Virginia Cavalry, across the Potomac River and struck the Union garrison at Point of Rocks, Maryland. White's Virginians overwhelmed several Union detachments, captured supply wagons, and destroyed a train. His foray, coupled with the engagements at Thoroughfare Gap, Middleburg, and Aldie, as well as General Richard Ewell's success at Winchester, confounded Union commanders as to Lee's intentions. With Confederate troops moving into Northern territory on such a wide front, the Federals needed to divine Lee's objectives: did he plan to invade Maryland and Pennsylvania, or had he sent troops across the Potomac as a means of masking an attack through the gaps in Bull Run Mountain? General Halleck found the rumors pouring in from Maryland and Pennsylvania "too confusing and contradictory to be relied upon." Not wishing to act upon "mere conjecture," Halleck needed "positive information" from Hooker's cavalry.[1]

Though he had gained a tactical victory at Aldie, General Pleasonton had not secured the intelligence Hooker sought regarding Lee's army. Rather than enjoying an intelligence triumph similar to the information seized by John Mosby, Pleasonton struggled to make sense of what little he had learned. He had gained a foothold into the Loudoun Valley but what was he to make of the heavy presence of Southern cavalry at the gaps in Bull Run Mountain? What did Stuart's presence in Middleburg rather than Pennsylvania mean for the long suspected Southern cavalry raid? Though he put up a bold front, expressing his certainty that no Southern infantry occupied the Loudoun Valley, as well as asserting his intention to punch through the gaps in the Blue Ridge, Pleasonton may have experienced his own doubts as to his next course of action. Having already defied Hooker by proceeding through Aldie Gap, Pleasonton had not received the new instructions Hooker had promised. On his own, and continuing to defy the orders he had received, Pleasonton determined to push ahead on June 18.[2]

Meanwhile, Hooker continued to play his game of semantics with Halleck in Washington. "All my cavalry are out," Hooker told his superior on the evening of June 17. Then, after passing along the details he had received of the fight at Aldie, Hooker repeated his assertion, "All my cavalry are out." Halleck could not be blamed if he believed Hooker to mean Pleasonton's entire corps was actively searching for Lee, when, in fact, Hooker had told Pleasonton (in the captured order) to send out only small details while allowing his main force to graze their horses.[3]

For all his bluster, Hooker struggled to sift facts from the rumors and conjectures landing on his desk. He had sought to establish a signal tower at Snicker's Gap overlooking the lower Shenandoah Valley, from where his scouts might observe Confederate troop movements. His plan had failed, however, when Mosby captured the officer Hooker sent to oversee the operation, and enemy cavalry now blocked his own horse soldiers from gaining access. The army commander also needed to establish and defend a point along the Potomac River where he could cross his army into Maryland. Most of all, he needed more cavalry. With Pleasonton's corps primarily employed as protection against a surprise attack through the gaps in Bull Run Mountain, Hooker increasingly relied upon General Julius Stahel's cavalry division for other scouting duty, including the reconnaissance to Warrenton in a final effort to locate General A. P. Hill's corps.[4]

In order to meet his need for more cavalry, Hooker redirected a brigade-sized force of remounted cavalry away from Pleasonton, holding them along the north side of the Potomac to secure the points where he expected to construct pontoon bridges and cross his army. To support the cavalrymen on the north bank of the river, Hooker sent the XI and XII Corps toward Leesburg to secure the south bank. When they arrived, both corps commanders joined Hooker in pleading for more cavalry. But with the heavy losses already sustained by General Kilpatrick, Pleasonton desperately needed the remounted men to bolster his own ranks. Hooker saw the cavalry shortage as another opportunity to pry additional troops, especially Stahel's division, away from General Heintzelman and the Department of Washington. Heintzelman, however, had no intention of surrendering his cavalry. Seeking to break the impasse, Hooker asked Halleck for authority to issue orders directly to Heintzelman's commanders without first gaining Heintzelman's approval. Over the next ten days, Hooker prodded and provoked, Heintzelman resisted, and Halleck dithered. Halleck's failure to provide a satisfactory resolution further poisoned his relationship with his army commander and ultimately led to Hooker submitting his resignation.[5]

With Stahel's cavalry operating along the northern and southern fringes of the army, Pleasonton continued to hold center stage along the western flank. Hooker still intended to hold Pleasonton close to the army and on a short tether, though his cautionary orders had not reached the cavalry chief. In the absence of the information contained in the captured order, but aware that enemy cavalry blocked his path into the valley, Pleasonton left two brigades to hold Thoroughfare Gap. Then, choosing to again defy Hooker, he sent two heavy columns into the Loudoun Valley along the Ashby's Gap and Snickersville pikes. Walking a bit of a tight rope, however, Pleasonton almost certainly urged his commanders to proceed with caution.[6]

General John Buford accompanied Col. William Gamble's brigade up the Snickersville Turnpike toward Snicker's Gap. Leaving Aldie at 10 a.m., June 18, the troopers picked their way through and around the many dead horses littering the road from the previous day's fighting. The stark evidence of the previous day's ambush would have kept Gamble's men wary. Nearing Goose Creek, east of Mountville, the troopers came under fire from Colonel Munford's pickets. Driving off the Southerners and leaving two guns from Lt. John Calef's Battery A, Second U.S. Artillery, to secure the crossing, Buford and Gamble pushed on toward the gap in the face of stiffening resistance. The Union effort came as no surprise to Stuart, who, with Hooker's captured orders in hand, had told his commanders to resist the Union probes but not to become heavily engaged. Thus, Munford fought a determined delaying action while slowly yielding before the Union advance. Colonel Gamble left pickets at every crossroads to provide warning of enemy troops moving against his flanks, and by early afternoon these sentinels had alerted him to the arrival of Southern reinforcements. With the animals tiring as they carried their riders up and down the rolling hills, with a growing enemy force in their front, and with Pleasonton's and Hooker's words of caution in their ears, Buford and Gamble pushed their advance to near Philomont before returning to Aldie.[7]

Like Gamble, Col. John Gregg had his brigade on the road from Aldie by 10 a.m., heading west along the Ashby's Gap Turnpike. Gregg had two missions: scout the road to Middleburg and search for Colonel Duffié and his First Rhode Island. Leaving the First Maine at Aldie, Gregg advanced with three regiments, and Lt. James Lancaster's two guns from Battery C, Third U.S. Artillery.[8]

General Stuart claimed to have withdrawn his North Carolinians from Middleburg to prevent a fight within the town, but he left his pickets intact and these Tar Heels put up a stiff fight before withdrawing. As the men of the Sixteenth Pennsylvania reached Wancopin Creek, east of town, fighting flared and lasted for several hours before the Pennsylvanians pulled back to replenish their ammunition. Unwilling to yield, Gregg brought up Lt. Col. William Doster's Fourth Pennsylvania and continued the duel. Tiring of the fruitless sniping, and supported by Lancaster's two guns, Doster sent his men thundering across the bridge and cleared the town.[9]

After overwhelming the First Rhode Island earlier in the morning, Colonel Chambliss approached Middleburg around 2 p.m. Reaching the turnpike, Chambliss directed some of his men to support the Tar Heels on the skirmish line. He then led the remainder to a high ridge west of town, where he established a strong defensive position. Once Chambliss had his men posted to block the pike, Stuart ordered the last of his skirmishers to retire from the bridge to the ridgeline, now known as Mount Defiance.[10]

Entering Middleburg, the Yankees located and released several Rhode Islanders who had been locked in stores since the previous evening. Once he had the town secured, Colonel Gregg pushed west and soon observed the two Southern brigades along the ridge. Considering the tenacious Southern stand east of town, Gregg found the idea of attacking the ridge unappealing. Having complied with his orders, Gregg held his ground until about six o'clock, when Pleasonton ordered him to retire. Leaving strong detachments to hold the roads from the gaps south of town, Gregg abandoned Middleburg and returned to Aldie.[11]

Going into bivouac, the soldiers, blue and gray, noted a change in the weather as clouds and a strengthening breeze heralded rain. By nightfall, men who had been sweltering during the day, sought cover from the first storm in weeks. Before long, the "rain, hail, thunder and lightning had become terrific," and the night became so dark that, according to one soldier, "bats ran into each other." The rain soon turned the suffocating dust to thick mud and by morning small streams overflowed their banks. Pelted by wind, rain, and hail, the men endured the storm "with a soldier's grace," one Southerner explained, "because we could not do otherwise."[12]

Pleasonton had again exceeded his orders, but his efforts had been thwarted by stiff Southern resistance and careful planning based upon information gleaned from the order captured by John Mosby. Receiving confirmation of Colonel Duffié's demise, and finally learning of the order captured the previous night, Pleasonton became more wary of proceeding too aggressively. Desperate to offer some scrap of information, however, Pleasonton forwarded rumors from slaves, who thought Lee might be falling back on Culpeper. He also offered to press the fight in the morning if he could take his entire corps into the Loudoun

Valley. "If the general will send Meade's corps to hold [Aldie Gap] . . . I will . . . compel the enemy to show his hand." Ignoring his request for assistance, Hooker retorted bluntly, "Your orders are to find out where the enemy is, if you have to lose men to do it." Hooker's continuing efforts to conceal his real intentions from his superiors must have left Pleasonton confused and limited his ability "to find out where the enemy is."[13]

With Pleasonton concentrating his efforts along the two turnpikes, Stuart retained Chambliss's regiments along the Ashby's Gap pike to bolster General Robertson's Tar Heels. When Brig. Gen. William Jones arrived with his brigade later in the day, Stuart sent him north to support Munford at Snicker's Gap. To the south, Brig. Gen. Wade Hampton held his position near Warrenton long enough to turn back General Stahel's reconnaissance. By nightfall, Stuart had thwarted all three Union efforts and he had four of his five brigades posted across the center of the Loudoun Valley, blocking the approaches to the Shenandoah Valley.[14]

Throughout the day, Lee had his men on the move. General Longstreet's I Corps bivouacked at midday between Upperville, Piedmont Station, and the hamlet of Paris, at the entrance to Ashby's Gap. Watching Union prisoners being herded through the gap, one Southerner opined, "Their horses and equipment will do much to make our cavalry more efficient." Learning of the fighting at Aldie and Middleburg, Longstreet tasked his artillery officers and engineers with selecting a strong defensive position near Paris. By evening, several battalions of artillery secured the approaches to Ashby's and Snickers Gaps. Watching the artillerymen toil though the evening storm, one Southern reporter told his readers, "We are now encamped among the clouds, drenched to the skin with rain, and nearly swept away by the wind which rushes through [Ashby's] Gap with great force."[15]

From their farm, Catherine Broun and her family had watched some of the fighting around Middleburg during the day. "No one spoke a word," she noted in her diary, but each "inwardly prayed that our men might whip them and that our friends might be protected." She could not yet know that before too many more hours had passed the fighting would resume nearly on her doorstep.[16]

SIXTEEN

The Engagement Was Resumed with Spirit, June 19

Brig. Gen. Marsena Patrick, Hooker's crusty Provost Marshal, had been out of sorts on the eighteenth due, in part, to the debilitating heat. But watching Hooker berate his aides who disagreed with his assessments of the military situation did nothing to improve Patrick's mood. "We get accurate information," Patrick explained, "but Hooker will not use it . . . his only salvation [is] to make it appear that the enemy's forces are larger than our own, which is false & he knows it." Frustrated with the army commander's lack of direction or plan, Patrick concluded, "He knows that Lee is his master and is afraid to meet him in fair battle."[1]

If Patrick thought the intelligence Hooker received to be accurate, others disagreed. Hooker's own intelligence officers, from his Bureau of Military Information, had grown increasingly frustrated by their lack of access to prisoners captured by Pleasonton's troopers during the recent fighting. Capt. John McEntee had accompanied the cavalry into the Loudoun Valley for the express purpose of gathering and compiling information from prisoners and residents. But, to his disgust, Pleasonton's aides refused to let McEntee examine captured documents or speak with prisoners. Convinced that Pleasonton had no intention of sharing information or credit, McEntee asked to be relieved of the onerous duty. Already limited by the strictures placed upon him by Hooker, Pleasonton should have leaned on McEntee for advice. Instead, he ignored him and drew his own, often erroneous conclusions.[2]

Though Pleasonton may have created some of his own problems, he also found himself the victim of poor intelligence. Based on several reports, including one from the much-respected John Buford, Pleasonton believed Stuart had incorporated mounted infantry into his cavalry division. Colonel Munford's stout defense at Aldie reinforced Pleasonton's belief and led to his request for assistance from General Meade's foot soldiers. Stuart had no mounted infantry, but repeated reports to the contrary left Pleasonton on the horns of a dilemma: just how aggressive should he be? In his published orders, Hooker continued to urge aggression, telling Pleasonton to "lose men" if necessary, to find Lee. But Pleasonton well knew the army commander's personal fears, as well as his unpublished demands for caution. By evening on June 18, Pleasonton had more cause for his own doubts; he knew the strength of the enemy position on Mount Defiance, and he had no infantry of his own in direct support. Thus, rather than reconnoitering along both turnpikes on the nineteenth, as he had the previous day, he concentrated his efforts along the Ashby's Gap Turnpike. He chose to send three brigades against Stuart's position, hoping to drive him off Mount Defiance or force him to retire by turning his flank.[3]

The men from both armies endured a long night and a storm of ever-increasing intensity. Pleasonton's men stood to horse nearly all night, with sentinels rotating on and off picket duty. The horses remained saddled, bridled, unfed, and unrested. The men dozed by their steeds, pelted by rain and hail, but few, if any slept before bugles roused them around 1 a.m. By two o'clock the troopers had watered and grained their horses, rolled, secured their waterproof ponchos, refilled their ammunition boxes, and cap pouches, and finished a hasty breakfast. Then they began the army tradition of hurry up and wait, standing for hours before Pleasonton, who may have waited for the roads to dry, finally gave the order to advance. General Gregg's two brigades, supported by two regiments from General Buford's Reserve Brigade, set out for Middleburg. Pleasonton then told Buford to send the remaining two regiments from the brigade around to the north, hoping to turn Stuart's left flank at Mount Defiance.[4]

The soldiers had initially welcomed the storm which brought relief from the heat and settled the dust, but the heavy rain and steady tread of men, horses, cannon, and wagons soon churned the fields to muck. Movement today across the soft ground would be slow, the men and animals pelted by clods of mud and splashed with water at every step, while the cloying mire would pull off horseshoes loosened the previous days on the hard, rocky roads. The relief from the heat proved fleeting. When the skies cleared, temperatures rose with the sun and the air became uncomfortable. By one estimate afternoon temperatures rose to ninety-eight degrees, though the heavy air portended more rain by nightfall.[5]

Jeb Stuart now had four of his five brigades in the Loudoun Valley: Jones and Munford blocking the roads to Snicker's Gap, and Robertson and Chambliss astride the Ashby's Gap Turnpike. Beverly Robertson's men had carried the previous day's fight until John Chambliss arrived in the afternoon. Once the brigades had united, Stuart retired to Mount Defiance, one mile west of Middleburg. There, the turnpike runs through a deep cut in the ridge, fronted on the south side by a cluster of structures, including a home and waystation or coach-stop, and a blacksmith's shop. Stone walls lined both sides of the road cut, as well as the east side of the ridge north of the pike. A narrow lane coursed south from the turnpike, past the home and shop and continuing into a large woodlot covering most of the southern end of the ridge. Open wheat fields, providing little cover, fronted the ridge to the east.

Following the fighting the previous day, Stuart had moved Robertson's Tar Heels into the woodlot. The Carolinians had fought well in the confusing night action through Middleburg on June 17, and again during the heavy skirmishing the next morning. Robertson's two regiments, the Fourth and Fifth North Carolina, carried the short-barreled version of the British Enfield Rifled Musket. Though shorter than the muskets carried by the infantry, the weapons had greater range than cavalry carbines but proved slower to reload than a breech-loading carbine. From the woods, the Carolinians could use their muskets with deadly effect against enemy troops crossing the open wheat fields, while benefitting from the protection of the trees during the reloading process. Their horses, secured by every fourth man, remained on the far side of the ridge, shielded from enemy fire.[6]

• • •

Jeb Stuart's relationship with Beverly Robertson was, in a word, strained. Stuart simply did not like Robertson nor respect him as a battlefield commander. Robertson had attended West Point from Amelia County, Virginia, and graduated in 1849. During his antebellum service with the Second Dragoons, Robertson earned a reputation as a proficient drillmaster. He had, according to biographer Patrick Bowmaster, also earned a reputation as "a dandy, a terrific dancer, and a real ladies' man." While assigned to Carlisle Barracks, Carlisle, Pennsylvania, Robertson may have met and begun courting Flora Cooke, daughter of Maj. Philip St. George Cooke. They may have resumed the courtship at Fort Leavenworth, though Jeb Stuart eventually won Flora's hand in marriage.[7]

The rivalry between the two young suitors may have sparked the tension between Stuart and Robertson, but the sectional crisis in the country may have also led to their mutual hostility. Stuart had been an early vocal supporter of the Southern cause and openly avowed his intentions to support the Confederacy. Robertson, on the other hand, had supported Virginia's secession but he hoped the state would remain neutral. He also openly blamed South Carolina for forcing the nation into war.[8]

Whatever the underlying cause of the friction between Stuart and Robertson, they were probably too dissimilar to have ever worked well together. While Stuart recognized Robertson's administrative talents, he saw him as lacking other abilities of a good cavalry commander, including a magnetic personality on the battlefield. One of Stuart's aides termed Robertson "perfectly unreliable" in battle. Stuart had openly rejoiced when Robertson had been sent to North Carolina in 1862, and he had been equally unhappy when Robertson returned in the spring of 1863. Robertson's lackluster performance at Brandy Station had done nothing to ease the tension between the two men.[9]

• • •

With Robertson holding the woods to the south, Stuart tasked John Chambliss's veterans, nearly fourteen hundred men from the Ninth, Tenth, and Thirteenth Virginia, as well as the Second North Carolina, with defending the road cut and northern end of Mount Defiance. Holding the Ninth Virginia, the largest of his regiments, as a mounted reserve on the reverse slope, Chambliss dismounted his other regiments. As every fourth man led the horses to the reverse side of the ridge, the other troopers took positions behind the stone walls overlooking the turnpike and crowning the eastern slope. Capt. William McGregor's Second Stuart Horse artillery supported Chambliss, with one of his guns blocking the turnpike near the blacksmith's shop. With his pickets posted well east of Middleburg and with his two brigades holding a strong position along the ridge, Stuart and his staff retired to his headquarters at Rector's Cross Roads, three miles to the west.[10]

The Fourth Pennsylvania led Colonel Gregg's brigade back to Middleburg. The stone walls lining the road, as well as the deep road cuts, impaired the ability of cavalry to quickly move from column into line once they met the enemy. Seeking to overcome the challenges created by these obstacles, commanders on both sides employed flanking columns moving through the fields alongside the roads. Such duty proved wearisome for man and beast as they covered greater distances over all manner of terrain, dodging trees, and low-hanging branches, crossing streams, maneuvering around and through steep-banked ravines, and jumping or making openings in fences and walls. The Tenth New York drew the onerous flank security duty on the nineteenth, with one battalion on each side of the road supporting the Pennsylvanians. The men from the Keystone State tried to take Middleburg in a quick dash but the Southerners, well posted along the main street, easily repulsed their first attempt. As the Fourth Pennsylvania fell back, Colonel Gregg brought up the

Sixteenth Pennsylvania and ordered them to support a second assault alongside the New Yorkers. Minutes later, with the New Yorkers sweeping around the town and through side streets, the Fourth Pennsylvania charged up the turnpike and drove the Southern pickets to Mount Defiance. Middleburg had just changed hands for the sixth time in three days.[11]

Riding into the open wheat fields west of town, Colonel Gregg gazed up at the Southern position, counting, with some trepidation, the cannon posted near the road cut and noting the walls and trees sheltering the enemy troopers. He directed the Fourth and Sixteenth Pennsylvania into the fields south of the pike. In sight of the Southerners, the Pennsylvanians probably entered the fields behind a line of mounted skirmishers with carbines "advanced," or braced against their right thigh. Splashing through the soggy fields for a mile, the men reached the farm then owned by William Benton and dismounted. Sending their horses back, the troopers unclipped their carbines from their slings, ensured they had a round in the breech, a percussion cap firmly seated, and then moved forward in skirmish order. Some of the men came under fire immediately from Carolinians sheltered behind the walls and headstones of the Cocke family cemetery.[12]

The First Maine and Tenth New York followed the Pennsylvanians into the fields, extending the skirmish line to the north across the turnpike. Finally, Lt. William Fuller brought his six guns of Battery C, Third U.S. Artillery, into position on high ground about one thousand yards east of Mount Defiance. The men brought the guns into action as quickly as the soggy fields allowed, seeking to drive Captain McGregor's battery off the ridge. The time was between 7 and 8 a.m.[13]

Not one of the young firebrands in the Cavalry Corps, Colonel Gregg is best described as steady and cautious rather than aggressive or daring, and the more he scanned the ridge the more the strength of the Southern position troubled him. Remembering the determined stand by the Tar Heels the previous day, as well as Pleasonton's reluctance to press the attack against the ridge during the afternoon, Gregg vacillated, content to let his artillery pound the Confederates. Prodded by his cousin, division commander David Gregg, John Irvin Gregg feared a slaughter as his men crossed the open fields. After several hours of ineffective sniping and skirmishing, the two officers met to discuss the daunting task before them. General Gregg finally agreed to bring up part of General Kilpatrick's brigade, along with the First and Fifth U.S., to strengthen the line north of the pike, allowing Colonel Gregg to consolidate and strengthen his line south of the road. Ordered to ignore any threats to his flanks and to concentrate his attack along the turnpike, the colonel pulled all but two companies of the First Maine off the skirmish line in anticipation of a mounted attack up the road. He then recalled eight companies of the Tenth New York to support the New Englanders. Finally, Gregg designated one squadron of the First Maine and several companies of the Fourth Pennsylvania to stand by on the Benton farm as a mounted reserve. With his plans in place, he ordered his cannoneers to redouble their efforts to silence the Southern guns.[14]

With the sun approaching its zenith, Gregg's skirmishers south of the pike began advancing with intervals of five paces between each man. The mounted detachments, with sabers drawn, remained 100 to 150 yards behind the skirmishers. But, despite all the planning, the advance of the Fourth Pennsylvania quickly ground to a halt around the Benton farm, due to the tenacious Carolinians clinging to their fortress in the small family cemetery. In time, however, the Yankee's quicker firing carbines drove the Southerners from the walled plot and sent them running for the woods. Having cleared their first obstacle, the Northerners paused to catch their breath before making the final dash to the trees. A few men ran into the Benton home and began sniping at the enemy from the upper windows. They enjoyed their perch only briefly, however, before Captain McGregor's gunners put a round through the house, driving the men out on the run. The Southern artillery began taking a toll up and down the skirmish line. Still, some of the men seemed exhilarated by, what one called, their "first carbine charge," even as they endured enemy fire in their dash across the field.[15]

Such excitement did not last long, however, as the attack soon

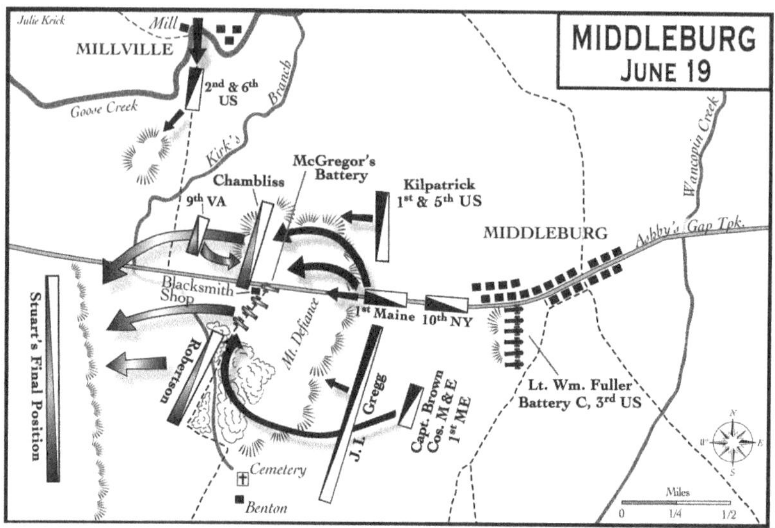

MAP 12. Middleburg, June 19. Created by Julie Krick.

ground to another halt. Not only could Gregg's cannoneers not silence the Southern guns, but the men had now entered the effective range of the Confederate Enfields. Casualties began to mount, and some of the skirmishers assumed a kneeling position or dropped to the ground to avoid the increasingly accurate fire. Casualties lay on the field for hours under a blistering sun, as the Union commanders needed everyman on the firing line.[16]

To the west, General Stuart had just laid down under the shade of an old tree when he heard Captain McGregor's guns open on the Union advance. Racing back toward the developing battle, Stuart rode up onto the ridge in time to observe the Yankees pushing into the wheat field and driving the Carolinians toward the woods. "The engagement," one Southern correspondent explained, had "resumed with spirit."[17]

Across the way, Union officers prodded their men back into action. Running into the woodlot, the Yankees sought to drive the Carolinians "from behind trees, stone walls and natural rifle-pits," according to a watching reporter. As the struggle continued among the trees, the correspondent thought the fight resembled "Indian warfare." Looking to break the stalemate, Capt. George Brown ordered his mounted squadron of the First Maine into action. As soon as the Union horsemen entered the wheat field, however, the Southern guns took them under fire. Though many of the rounds exploded behind the fast-moving troopers, one shell fragment killed a lieutenant. Urging their horses into the trees, Brown's men charged up to the main Confederate line behind a stone wall at the rear of the woodlot. Driven back by what Brown termed "murderous fire," the Federals fell back, regrouped, and attacked again.[18]

Lt. Ephraim Taylor's horse went down, just as a bullet knocked a sergeant from the saddle alongside Taylor. Bursting from the trees like a "swarm of bees," the Mainers fell back into the wheat field and prepared for a third assault. As they did so, Lieutenant Taylor emerged from the woods holding the wounded sergeant on his horse. With his men ready for another try at the Confederate line, Taylor mounted the sergeant's horse and took his position in the formation. Splitting his forty-man squadron by company, Brown ordered them to attack the wall from two directions. Plunging back into the trees, all could hear Taylor cheering them on. "There was something about that man that drew all towards him," an admiring trooper recalled. With the Yankees bearing down on them, the Carolinians seemed to concentrate their fire on Taylor and the young guidon-bearer riding by his side. Moments later, both men went down, fatally wounded. Then, at the last second, the Tar Heels abandoned the wall and ran for their horses. Shooting and slashing as they dashed among them, the Federals compelled nearly fifty men to surrender, including a lieutenant colonel. As the dismounted Pennsylvanians began herding the prisoners back to the Union lines, Captain Brown took stock of his position. He soon realized the Confederates had been defending the southern end of a small farm lane leading back toward the turnpike. And, with his own guns now silent, he could hear the roar of battle intensifying at the other end of the lane.[19]

After ordering his skirmishers to clear the woods, Colonel Gregg sent the remainder of the First Maine in a mounted charge up the turnpike against the heart of the enemy position. He supported the attack with carbineers from the Second and Tenth New York, the First and Fifth U.S., and two sections of Captain Graham's Battery. Like Kilpatrick, Gregg had learned to rely upon the New Englanders, now led by the much-respected Lt. Col. Charles Smith. With his options limited by the maze of stone walls and the deep road-cut, Smith sent one squadron in column up the road, several companies across the fields north of the pike, and two companies in a wider flanking attack around the northern end of the Confederate position.[20]

Captain George Kimball led the attack along the turnpike. With the Southern gunners furiously working their cannon against the Yankees crossing the wheat field to their right front, Kimball may have timed his surge up the ridge while the gunners reloaded, thereby avoiding a blast of canister against the head of his column. Still, the Yankees received a hail of fire from the Southern carbineers posted behind the walls about ten feet above the road. One of Kimball's officers recalled his own men firing their carbines as they drove into the Virginians "massed in the cut in the road." Emptying the cumbersome weapons, the men drew their sabers and began slashing at the gunners defending the cannon in the road. Knowing he could not allow his men to be caught "within the gauntlet of the stone walls," Kimball urged them forward into the open ground beyond. Then, as he rode over the crest, he saw the Ninth Virginia, nearly five hundred men strong, counterattacking from the north side of the road. Badly outnumbered, Kimball ordered his forty men to turn by "Fours—right about!" Easier said than done in the confined space, the turn created confusion as the enemy poured fire into their ranks from their positions above the road. Horses stumbled and fell, pitching their riders into the road. Gunfire took a toll, even as low-hanging branches swept other men from their saddles.[21]

Captain John Hungerford's squadron led the Ninth Virginia into the fray. Emptying their revolvers and then drawing their sabers, the Virginians crashed into the Yankees near the cannon. There, "a desperate encounter had begun between their leading files and our cannoneers," a Southern officer recalled. Closing on the Federals, Hungerford's bugler fatally shot Kimball in the chest. Moments later Hungerford fell to a Northern bullet. The counterattack, "sharp and bloody," lasted mere moments before the Virginians found themselves confronted by Lt. Colonel Smith and his contingent of the First Maine turning into the road from the north.[22]

The arrival of the Union reinforcements slowed the Southern counterattack, but only briefly. Lt. Charles Ford, 1st Maine, described the fighting along the hillcrest as brutal. Three of Ford's sergeants died at the head of the column, one of whom, Ford described as "the bravest of the brave." Their gallantry could not overcome superior numbers, however, and the Virginians forced Smith, Ford, and the other Federals to retire. As they fell back past the Southern cannon, one Union trooper lingered too long, emptying his carbine and his revolver into the enemy ranks before a saber blow knocked him unconscious. He awoke to find himself pinned under his dead horse. Extricated by the enemy, he soon began the march to a Southern prison.[23]

During the melee around the cannon, a Southern officer noticed an enemy trooper backed against a tree throwing rocks at several Confederates slashing him with their sabers. Fighting along the skirmish line near the turnpike, Sgt. Michael Logan, Sixteenth Pennsylvania, had exhausted his ammunition just as the Ninth Virginia came surging over the hillcrest. Unable to escape the enemy assault, Logan backed against a tree, swinging his carbine before resorting to throwing rocks in a vain attempt to ward off his assailants. In his one-sided ordeal, Logan received seven saber wounds. When a bullet knocked him off his feet, the enemy troopers left him to his fate.[24]

Speed, shock, and momentum are the keys to successful cavalry combat, and the vicious melee around the cannon had saved the gun but sapped the momentum from the Virginians' counterattack. Even as the Federals retired from the ridge, the Southerners were too spent and disorganized to pursue. Watching the ebb and flow of the fight, Colonel Gregg sought to take advantage of the confusion in the Southern ranks by sending Maj. Matthew Avery and his Tenth New York against them before they could reorganize. Neither Avery, a belligerent twenty-seven-year-old with a taste for the bottle and a reputation for becoming ill on the cusp of battle, nor his men enjoyed the sterling reputation of the First Maine. The New Yorkers had recently been embarrassed at Brandy Station, and only a timely attack by the First Maine had saved them from possible destruction. Now, Gregg presented Avery and his men with a chance to redeem their reputation.[25]

Maj. John Kemper led his squadron, about sixty-five men, up the narrow road in column of fours. Looking up at the ridge, the New Yorkers could see the cannon and the gray-clad troopers milling around, but Kemper gave his men little time to ponder their fate, as he ordered "Draw Sabre!" The Confederates saw the flash as the sun caught the steel and braced themselves for the attack. "Forward, March! Trot! Gallop! Charge!" The commands came quickly as Kemper sought to drive home his attack with as much speed and cohesion as possible. The Southern gunners delivered another volley as the carbineers from the Second North Carolina opened fire. Just as Kemper turned in his saddle to shout orders to lieutenants Edward Hawes and Horatio Boyd, a bullet struck Hawes in the chest. Mortally wounded, Hawes lost control of his horse and veered across the column, creating confusion as the men behind tried to avoid the dying officer. Seeking to restore order, Boyd, who had pulled abreast of Kemper, turned to encourage his men when a fatal bullet struck him, and he toppled over against Kemper. Other men and horses began falling. With his attack disintegrating, Kemper realized the terrible odds against him as the reorganized Virginians launched a second counterattack. Believing his position untenable, Kemper ordered his men to retreat. But in the din and confusion of battle, Kemper had misread the situation; Jeb Stuart had begun pulling his men off the ridge.[26]

The Ninth Virginia had turned back the First Maine just as the Pennsylvanians and Captain Brown's New Englanders finally drove the Tar Heels from their position in the woods. When Brown realized the Carolinians had been defending a farm lane that led back to the turnpike, he immediately reorganized his small band of men and led them toward the pike. At the same time, Jeb Stuart, along with Major von Borcke and two other aides, observed the Carolinians running from the woods toward their horses. The four officers raced over in a futile attempt to rally the men. Riding into the open field behind the woodlot, the small knot of officers presented an irresistible target for the Yankees pouring out of the trees. Festooned as they were with avian plumage and gold-braid, Stuart and von Borcke came under immediate fire and before they could escape; a bullet struck the towering Prussian in the neck. Catching von Borcke as he lurched in the saddle, Stuart's other aides led him to safety as Stuart spurred his horse back to the turnpike. With the Southern end of his line disintegrating, the general ordered the remainder of his men off the ridge, beginning with his horse artillery. Pulling their lanyards one last time as the New Yorkers began their attack, the gunners limbered the guns and headed for the next ridgeline less than a mile away. The Thirteenth Virginia and Second North Carolina slowly followed the guns, while Stuart and the Ninth Virginia held the crest and repulsed Major Kemper's attack.[27]

Coming down off the ridge, Kemper met Maj. Alvah Waters leading a second squadron numbering fewer than seventy men. Still believing the enemy intended to hold the ridge, Kemper warned Waters, "it's a slaughter pen" up there. Unwilling to disobey his orders, Waters continued up the slope, until a volley from the last carbineers holding the walls and the sight of the Ninth Virginia blocking the road convinced him otherwise. Outnumbered, he turned away even as Captain Brown arrived from the south and men from the Second and Fourth New York drove the last Confederate stalwarts from the wall north of the road. With Yankees sweeping into the road from their flanks, the last Southerners fell back from Mount Defiance.[28]

The Yankees had driven Stuart from his position but as they gazed westward, they realized the Southern cavalier had no intention of surrendering the field. Instead, he had stubbornly moved to another commanding position along the next ridge. For the Federals, their tactical victory brought little satisfaction. The terrain between the ridgelines mirrored the ground just gained; open fields to be traversed under enemy fire. With many of their men nearly out of ammunition, none of the Union commanders seemed anxious to resume the battle. Beyond Stuart's new position, Ashby's Gap and the Blue Ridge Mountains taunted the tired Yankees. As they scanned the horizon, the officers would have seen another storm fast approaching. Then, before they had fully considered their options, they heard gunfire to the northwest.[29]

• • •

In a late-morning dispatch, General Pleasonton told Hooker, "I directed . . . Gregg to move on Middleburg," and "one brigade" from Buford's division to move "by way of Union, to turn Middleburg and take the rebels in the rear." In fact, only two regiments, the Second and Sixth U.S., led by Maj. Charles Whiting and supported by one section of artillery, attempted the flanking maneuver.[30]

Major Whiting led his small force west along the Snickersville Turnpike, across Carter's bridge over Goose Creek and toward the small hamlet of Mountville, where he turned southwest toward Pot House and the road to Union. The Regulars may have been battling Southern pickets for several miles by the time they reached Pot House. Approaching the intersection, the Federals encountered a heavy picket reserve from Col. Thomas Rosser's Fifth Virginia. As the skirmishing escalated, Whiting ordered his artillery onto a hilltop commanding the road. Then, unsure of the size of the enemy force in his front, Whiting sent his men into a woodlot, where they found a stone wall which covered the roads and could be protected by the artillery. Watching the Yankees file off the road, one of Stuart's aides, who had been conversing with Rosser, raced off in search of help.[31]

Summoned by the staff officer, Lt. Col. Thomas Marshall soon reached Pot House with his Seventh Virginia, and the Sixth Virginia to support Rosser. Finding what he termed, "a good deal of confusion," Marshall sent the Seventh Virginia against Whiting's flank to drive the Regulars from the field. The effort quickly ground to a halt, however, as the Virginians encountered a stone wall blocking their path. After a short delay as men tore an opening in the wall, Marshall led the regiment "through the gap" only to encounter the Yankees well posted behind a second

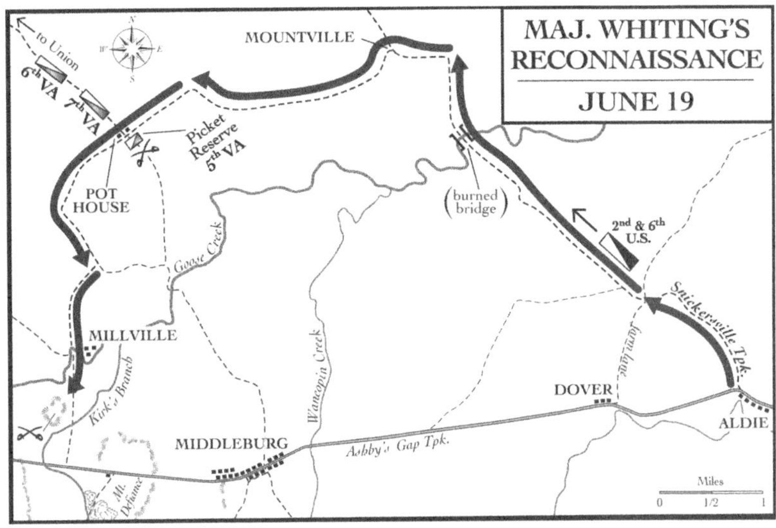

MAP 13. Maj. Whiting's reconnaissance, June 19. Created by Julie Krick.

wall. Determining the position to be too strong to overcome, Marshall ordered his men off the field and the entire force fell back to the village of Union.[32]

Having listened to the crash of cannon fire along the turnpike for several hours, and with the road to Union blocked, Whiting determined to continue south toward the turnpike and the ongoing battle at Mount Defiance. As the Yankees approached Millville, a small community two miles south of Pot House on the north bank of Goose Creek, the sounds of battle died away along the pike. Approaching the stream, Whiting's scouts reported enemy troopers on the far side of the crossing. Undeterred, Whiting sent his men splashing across the ford. Reaching the other side, the men entered a deep, narrow road cut, lined with fences and stone walls. Wary of being caught in the road, Whiting turned his two regiments into the fields west of the road and pointed them toward a small but dominating knoll. Spurring their horses up the grade, the Yankees saw Southerners racing toward the same knoll from the south. Unsure of the situation they had ridden into and with ominous thunderheads blocking the setting sun, the Regulars raced for the protection of a stone wall crowning the top of the hill.[33]

By chance, Whiting had arrived on the northern extension of the ridge along which Stuart had just established his new line of defense. With Yankees now on two sides of his position, and unsure of the size of Whiting's force, Stuart sent Col. John Chambliss, with two regiments, to try and hold Whiting at bay. Major Whiting faced the same uncertainties, and the sight of the onrushing Virginians brought the Regulars to a halt; should they dismount along the stone wall or meet the enemy on horseback? The "stone fence on the brow of the hill afforded a splendid position for dismounted men," one of Whiting's officers opined, and "should have been occupied at once. Had this been done & the men ordered to reserve their fire we might have gained a considerable advantage." Instead, the men opened an ineffective fire as they milled about on horseback waiting for Whiting to decide on a course of action. Having inflicted little injury on the Confederates, and with any advantage lost, the Federals finally dismounted and took position along the north side of the knoll. As the Virginians filtered into position along the southern portion of the wall, the combatants opened a desultory and generally harmless fire against each other. With bullets spattering and ricocheting off the rocks, Whiting brought his section of guns into action. The artillery tipped the balance and Chambliss pulled his men back out of range. Then, as the guns fell silent, the skies turned black, and the heavens opened.[34]

FIG. 1. Gen. Joseph Hooker. Courtesy Library of Congress, Civil War Collection, LC-DIG-ppmsca-19395.

FIG. 2. Gen. Alfred Pleasonton. Courtesy Library of Congress, Civil War Collection, LC-DIG-cwpb-06452.

FIG. 3. Gen. "Jeb" Stuart. Oil painting by Joe Umble. Author's collection.

FIG. 4. Gen. David M. Gregg. Courtesy Library of Congress, Civil War Collection, LC-DIG-cwpb-05643.

FIG. 5. *Cavalry Fight near Aldie,* the fight at the haystacks, by Edwin Forbes. Courtesy Library of Congress, Civil War Collection, LC-DIG-ppmsca-20544.

FIG. 6. Capt. Lucius Sargent, First Massachusetts. Courtesy Andrew German.

FIG. 7. Capt. Charles Francis Adams, First Massachusetts, *seated at left.* Courtesy Library of Congress, Civil War Collection, LC-USZC4-6732.

FIG. 8. Maj. Stephen Boothby, First Maine. Courtesy Digital Maine Repository, Maine State Archives, MacDonald Collection.

FIG. 9. Capt. Samuel Brown, Thirty-Ninth Virginia Battalion. Brown escorted Union prisoners to Winchester. Courtesy Dr. Ken Lawrence.

FIG. 10. Southern prisoners captured at Aldie. Courtesy Library of Congress, Civil War Collection, LC-DIG-ppmsca-33762.

FIG. 11. Col. Alfred Duffié, First Rhode Island Cavalry. Courtesy Library of Congress, Civil War Collection, LC-DIG-cwpb-01152.

FIG. 12. Gen. Beverly Robertson. Courtesy Library of Congress, Civil War Collection, LC-DIG-cwpb-06069.

FIG. 13. *1st Maine Cavalry Skirmishing*, possibly at Middleburg, by Alfred Waud. Courtesy Library of Congress, Civil War Collection, LC-DIG-ppmsca-21121.

FIG. 14. Maj. John Kemper, Tenth New York. Courtesy Kyle Stetz.

FIG. 15. Gen. Wade Hampton. Courtesy Library of Congress, Civil War Collection, LC-DIG-cwpb-07540.

FIG. 16. Col. Strong Vincent. Courtesy Library of Congress, Civil War Collection, LC-DIG-ppmsca-49621.

FIG. 17. *Explosion of a Rebel Limber at the Battle near Middleburg, June 21*, by Alfred Waud. Courtesy Library of Congress, Civil War Collection, LC-DIG-ppmsca-20895.

FIG. 18. Lt. William Fuller, Battery C, Third U.S. Artillery. Courtesy Britt Isenberg.

FIG. 19. Capt. William Houston, First North Carolina. Author photograph of painting in the Duplin County Court House, North Carolina. Courtesy Davis Brinson, county manager.

FIG. 20. Gen. John Buford. Courtesy Library of Congress, Civil War Collection, LC-DIG-ppmsca-39808.

FIG. 21. *Charge of Union Cavalry under Gen'l Pleasonton*, by Alfred Waud. The artist has probably depicted the fighting along the Trappe Road. Courtesy Library of Congress, Civil War Collection, LC-DIG-ppmsca-22555.

FIG. 22. *Battle near Upperville*, by Alfred Waud. The artist depicts the fighting at Vineyard Hill. Courtesy Library of Congress, Civil War Collection, LC-DIG-ppmsca-21082.

FIG. 23. Capt. Nehemiah Mann, Fourth New York, shown earlier in the war as a corporal in the First New York. Courtesy Library of Congress, Civil War Collection, LC-DIG-ppmsca-72264.

FIG. 24. Capt. Timothy Hanley, Ninth New York. Courtesy Britt Isenberg.

FIG. 25. *Your Men Bin Stealing My Hogs.* The artist describes the woman as an "F.F.V." or First Family Virginian, near Aldie. All local families would have waged a daily battle with troops from both sides to protect their crops and livestock. Courtesy Library of Congress, Civil War Collection, LC-DIG-ppmsca-20129.

SEVENTEEN

Enthusiastic Anticipation of an Exciting Time, June 20

Many of the troopers, blue and gray alike, spent a miserable night on picket duty, enduring the fury of the storm. Lashing winds tore tent pegs from the ground, scattering the flimsy shelters and leaving the men in camp as miserable as the sentinels. Pounding hail added to the chaos, as frightened horses broke free from their picket ropes and stampeded through the camps. Amanda Edmonds termed the storm "inglorious," as she watched and pitied "the poor rebs" battered by the elements. When the rain and wind finally abated, June 20 dawned cool, cloudy, and misty.[1]

During the day, Union infantrymen went into camp around Aldie by the thousands, leaving the local citizens to wonder if a terrible battle might soon consume their town. "The inhabitants, mostly women and children, looked sadly frightened at the terrible [preparations] being made in their midst," one of the foot soldiers observed. Helpless, the townsfolk watched as the soldiers trampled their crops, slaughtered their livestock, carried off milk, eggs, and other eatables, and seized horses and mules. Purloined fence rails fueled campfires upon which the Yankees cooked their meals, while the women and children, the old and infirm looked on, defiant and resolute in their certainty of final victory.[2]

Men on both sides stayed busy bringing in the last of the dead and wounded. Union surgeons established a field hospital in a store in Middleburg. From there, their patients rode in ambulances to Fairfax Station, where attendants placed them aboard trains for the trip into Alexandria or Washington. After being placed in rude coffins, several officers killed in the fighting began their final journeys home. Some enlisted men received hasty burials where they fell. Others, like Charles Marr, Sixteenth Pennsylvania, found a temporary resting place in Middleburg's Sharon Cemetery, alongside Southerners killed near the town in the earlier fighting. As his comrades laid Marr into the ground, one noted grimly, "Nothing new."[3]

Southern surgeons, led by Dr. Talcott Eliason, General Stuart's staff surgeon, established hospitals in or near Upperville. The doctor and his wife owned a home in Upperville, and Eliason ordered Major von Borcke taken there. The gravely wounded Prussian remained under Eliason's care until events on June 21 forced him to be evacuated to prevent his falling into enemy hands. Doctor Eliason may have also treated Pvt. Samuel Rice, Ninth Virginia. Prior to enlisting, Rice had resided in Northumberland County, Virginia, and his wife and children struggled to maintain their farm in his absence. He had just learned of an earlier Yankee raid through the county and in his last letter home had encouraged his wife to endure such trials, passed along his love, and assured her he would return home as soon as possible. Fate intervened, however. Felled by a Yankee bullet in the fighting around the blacksmith's shop, Rice died in a field hospital near Upperville on June 20 and rests today in the town's Ivy Hill Cemetery.[4]

The climactic fighting at Mount Defiance had lasted but a short time, though General Pleasonton had little to show for his efforts beyond an ever-growing butcher's bill. The loss of at least one hundred men killed, wounded, and captured, had gained only a mile of ground. When the guns fell silent, Southern campfires mocked him from another ridge a short distance away before flickering out under the pelting rain. Still, every man in the Cavalry Corps, from Pleasonton to the lowest private, took some solace from seeing the backs of the Southern cavaliers. "Such fighting has never been beaten," a jubilant trooper declared.

George Meade termed the fighting "brilliant," but Joseph Hooker needed more than small successes to divine Robert E. Lee's plans and objectives. By the end of the day, Hooker reluctantly began to loosen, though not release, the tether holding his cavalry to the gaps in Bull Run Mountain.[5]

Early on June 20, Pleasonton declared, with some conviction, that Lee would not attack through the gaps. By afternoon, however, he had begun to question his assumption as information gleaned from Southern infantrymen captured in the Loudoun Valley led him to conclude that the enemy "are moving this way." And, influenced by Hooker, he continued to focus on Thoroughfare Gap as the most likely point through which Lee would attack. He also advised the army commander to hold Aldie Gap, Leesburg, and the several fords along the Potomac River and near the town. With the gaps and Leesburg held in strength, "the mountain range will do the rest," he counseled.[6]

By nightfall, the several corps in the western wing of the Army of the Potomac had moved into positions from where they could defend the gaps and fords, with the XI and XII Corps near Leesburg, supported by the I Corps along the Loudoun-Fairfax County border. The V Corps had moved to Aldie, supported by the III Corps at Gum Spring and the II Corps near Centreville. With infantry now holding two of the three worrisome points, only Thoroughfare Gap remained an immediate concern. On the evening of June 19, Pleasonton had sent Col. John Taylor's brigade to relieve Colonel Devin's men at the gap, pending the arrival of the II Corps. With infantry holding Aldie and Devin back in the fold, John Buford could finally contribute his entire division to any future action. General Stahel had also assumed responsibility for smaller scouting missions, freeing additional men for Pleasonton's next effort. By Sunday, June 21, the cavalry chief would have five of his six brigades available for battle.[7]

But Jeb Stuart's dogged defense, combined with earlier reports of mounted infantry within the cavalier's ranks, as well as Longstreet's presence east of the Blue Ridge, continued to worry Pleasonton. "Our cavalry is really fighting infantry behind stone walls," he told Hooker on June 20. Doubtful that his troopers could force their way into Ashby's Gap through a cordon of both cavalry and infantry, Pleasonton reiterated his plea for infantry support and Hooker relented. Certain, however, that only four thousand troopers blocked Pleasonton's path to the gap, Hooker released just one division from Maj. Gen. George Meade's V Corps to cooperate with the cavalry. The army commander also suggested a plan wherein the infantry would fight a holding action along the Ashby's Gap Turnpike, while the cavalry swung around Stuart's left flank in overwhelming strength. Rather than four thousand men, however, Stuart now had his entire division blocking the roads to the Shenandoah Valley.[8]

• • •

Like Pleasonton, Stuart had lost at least one hundred men killed, wounded, or captured at Mount Defiance. Reinforcements bolstered his ranks, however, as Brig. Gen. Wade Hampton's brigade arrived, two thousand strong. After John Mosby had captured the Union officers and the orders they carried on June 17, Hampton, alerted by Stuart, had delayed his arrival to meet a Union reconnaissance to Warrenton and the Rappahannock River. Following a brief night action, the Yankees retired, and the Union commander reported that he had engaged "5,000 or 6,000" men. The exaggerated reports of Hampton's strength contributed to Pleasonton's unease on the nineteenth and continued to concern him as he made his plans for the twenty-first. The threat of such a large force coming against his flank from the south convinced Pleasonton to alter his plans. Rather than employing a small holding force along the turnpike and flanking Stuart, as Hooker had suggested, Pleasonton held his main force, including his infantry and two cavalry brigades, along the turnpike, while committing just one cavalry division to the turning movement.[9]

After rebuffing the Union probe on June 18, Hampton, accompanied by Capt. James Hart's Washington Artillery, joined Stuart on the twentieth. General Stuart now had his entire division of five brigades, more than eight thousand men, supported by five batteries, in the Loudoun Valley. After adjusting and strengthening his line, Stuart held Hampton's fresh command astride the Ashby's

Gap Turnpike, supported by Robertson and Chambliss on his left or northern flank. Farther north, Jones and Munford blocked the Snickersville Turnpike, as well as the roads by which the Federals had attempted to flank Stuart the previous day.[10]

And, like Pleasonton, Stuart expected to have infantry within supporting distance, but General Longstreet either misunderstood or deliberately exceeded his orders on June 20. As Longstreet sheepishly admitted later, Lee had told him to hold his corps "in readiness to move" toward the Potomac. But Longstreet pulled his infantry and artillery from their positions at Ashby's and Snicker's Gaps and sent them west across the Shenandoah River and into the Shenandoah Valley. The men found the river, swollen by the recent rain, treacherous; more importantly, the turbulent water now lay between Longstreet's foot soldiers and Stuart's cavalry. During the night and probably at Lee's insistence, Longstreet sent several batteries back across the river to their former positions along the eastern slope of the Blue Ridge.[11]

• • •

During the evening, Pleasonton called for his generals to meet him at Berkeley, the stately two-story home of William N. Berkeley. As the officers rode up the drive to the house, situated on a commanding hill at the west end of Aldie, they may have sensed another battle looming. General Meade had agreed to send his First Division to assist the cavalry, and several of the senior officers attended the meeting. Commanded by Brig. Gen. James Barnes, the division counted about thirty-four hundred men in three brigades. During the conference, Pleasonton explained his plan for a cooperative effort in which the infantry and Gregg's cavalry pinned down Stuart's dismounted carbineers while Buford's horsemen attempted to flank the Southern position. The gathering broke up about midnight, and bugles roused the soldiers two hours later.[12]

After a hasty breakfast, the infantrymen set out in light marching order. Meeting Pleasonton in Aldie, the men continued toward Middleburg at a rapid pace in, as a reporter accompanying the column noted, "enthusiastic anticipation of an exciting time."

Their best efforts aside, however, Pleasonton must have been disappointed. He had hoped to move the troops into position under cover of darkness, but the sun was already rising when the men reached Middleburg.[13]

General Gregg made his headquarters at the Beveridge House and Tavern in the center of Middleburg. Stepping down from his horse, Pleasonton met Gregg and entered the building. Climbing the stairs to the upper level, the officers stepped out onto the balcony. From there, they watched as their troops filed past on the street below, observed the enemy position to the west, and discussed any last-minute plans. Moments later, the officers left the building, mounted their horses, and followed the tail end of the column. With the prospect of battle looming, one of Gregg's troopers pleaded, "O Lord protect us by thy might."[14]

EIGHTEEN

Small but Important Riots, June 21

Having lost the opportunity to position his men under the cloak of darkness, General Pleasonton determined to use the cover provided by Mount Defiance to mask his deployment. Selecting Col. Strong Vincent's brigade, numbering about 1,360 men, to assist his cavalry with the early morning assault, Pleasonton left the other two brigades in reserve. Blessed with an instinctive eye for a battlefield, Vincent had earned an admirable reputation throughout the army as an officer who led with "ardor and energy." During the midnight meeting, Pleasonton had explained his desire to achieve a quick victory by enveloping the Southern position. He believed Stuart had deployed his mounted infantry south of the Ashby's Gap Turnpike and he tasked Vincent with driving them from the field, while the cavalry supported Vincent along the turnpike and through the fields north of the road. Pleasonton also sent John Buford, with his First Division, to flank Stuart from the north.[1]

As the infantry passed through Middleburg, Vincent ordered Lt. Col. Norval Welch to continue west along the turnpike with his Sixteenth Michigan Infantry, cross over Mount Defiance, and assault Stuart's position behind a heavy screen of skirmishers. About two hundred of the Wolverines had initially enlisted in the First Michigan Lancers, but the erstwhile regiment had been disbanded before any of the men saw duty as cavalry. Now, after a year of hard service, these men may have been especially eager to fight alongside veteran horse-soldiers. "The fracas commenced," one of the Michiganders explained, when the skirmishers exited the trees along Mount Defiance and entered the open fields fronting the Southern position. Colonel Welch selected two companies of sharpshooters as his skirmish companies. Each of the men had earned his position by placing ten consecutive shots within five inches of a target at 220 yards. Now, with one company to either side of the turnpike and a squadron of cavalry between them, the skirmishers advanced several hundred yards across open ground under increasingly heavy fire from artillery and cavalry posted behind stone walls.[2]

• • •

General Stuart had hoped to avoid battle on Sunday, and years later, an unrepentant Yankee wrote, "It was not easy to please Stuart on this occasion, and after falling under his censure for breaking the Sabbath, we aroused his indignation by bringing war to the doors of [the] peaceful" towns. If the soldiers balked at fighting on the Lord's Day, few said so. Instead, most remarked on the bright, sunny morning and the contrast between war and peace. "Never a brighter Sabbath dawned," a Mississippian declared. "It was one of those ideal June days that poets love and could truly be classed as *perfect*." And while a Southern artilleryman longed to hear the "silvery tones of the church bells" back home, a Yankee observed that "just about the time that the church bells at home commenced to call our friends to the house of God, our cannon were calling the rebels to His judgment bar." Miles away in Washington DC, poet Henry Wadsworth Longfellow pondered the contrast of "distant cannonading, mingling in with the sound of church bells and the chants of the choir in the church close by." Catherine Broun again found herself on the front line of battle as cannon discharges began rattling the glass in her windows. She prayed the enemy might "be driven as chaff before the wind," but on this Sunday her prayers went unanswered.[3]

• • •

General Wade Hampton's men bore the brunt of the opening attack along the turnpike. The burly South Carolinian had deployed the First North Carolina and the Mississippians of the Jeff Davis Legion along the open, broad ridge south of the road, with the end of their line anchored by a belt of woods. The Second South Carolina and the Georgians of Cobb's Legion held the northern end of Hampton's line. With about a mile of ground to defend, Hampton placed Col. Laurence Baker, First North Carolina, in command of his right wing and Col. Pierce M. B. Young, Cobb's Legion, in command of his left wing. General Robertson's North Carolinians held the ground between Hampton and the Goose Creek ford at Millville. Two of Capt. James Hart's guns supported the troopers from a position near the turnpike.[4]

Hampton and Robertson counted nearly three thousand men under their immediate command, though the number of troops along the skirmish line is difficult to estimate. Robertson's men, with their Enfield Rifled Muskets, were well equipped to fight on foot, and three-quarters of them would have manned the skirmish line, while their comrades held the horses. Hampton's men did not enjoy the same advantage, as many carried neither a carbine nor a rifle. Stuart's policy of distributing all the carbines in a regiment within two or three companies meant that only those few companies, minus the horse holders, faced Vincent's infantry. With Hampton at such a disadvantage he could not expect his troopers to hold their ground for long in the face of a determined assault. Still, the protection of the stone walls made up for a lack of numbers, and the Southerners gave the Union infantry more fight than they might otherwise have expected.

The Confederate artillery took the Michiganders under fire about 7 a.m. Moments later, two of Lt. William Fuller's 3-inch Ordnance Rifles, Battery C, Third U.S., responded from a position just south of the turnpike. With the Southern troopers mostly behind cover, the Union guns primarily engaged Hart in a counterbattery duel, while Hart split his fire, targeting the infantry with shell and case shot and Fuller's guns with solid shot. Colonel Vincent held his skirmishers out of range of the enemy's rifles and carbines for nearly an hour while Fuller tried to silence the

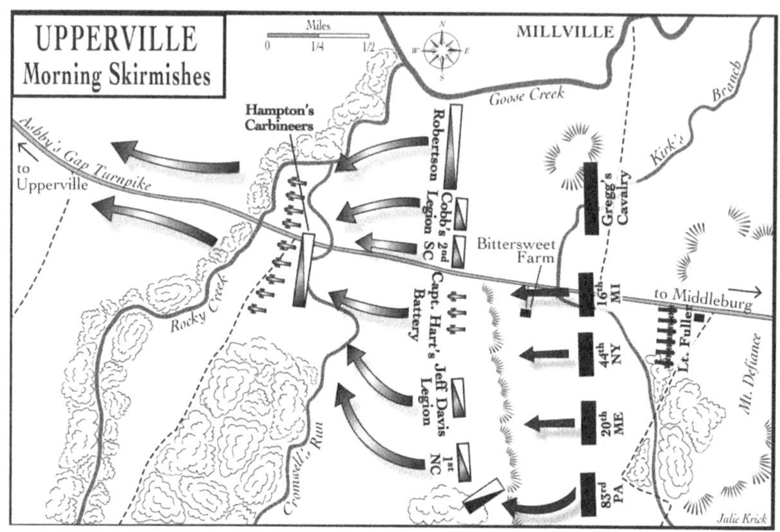

MAP 14. Upperville morning skirmishes. Created by Julie Krick

Southern guns. The delay also allowed the remainder of Vincent's brigade to move into position. The Forty-Fourth New York and Twentieth Maine extended the Union line to the south, while the Eighty-Third Pennsylvania made a longer march seeking to envelop the southern end of Hampton's line. General Pleasonton also hoped to hold the enemy in position until General Buford reached a point from where he could turn the northern end of the enemy line.[5]

With his men finally in position, Vincent sent them forward, ordering his sharpshooters to, "Stop that d——d battery hollering!" As the infantrymen resumed their advance and began targeting the Southern gunners, Lieutenant Fuller brought his other four guns into action. Moments later, the wooden axle supporting one of Hart's guns broke and the tube and carriage had to be carried off the field. With the rate of enemy fire now cut by half, the Yankees quickened their pace as they splashed across Kirk's Branch and started up the slope, driving the Southern troopers from the stone wall. The Wolverines may have paused momentarily behind the wall to catch their breath, as they realized another stone wall, already glistening with enemy rifle and carbine barrels, lay ahead of them.[6]

Along the turnpike, some of the Michiganders fought to clear stubborn Southerners from a farmhouse and several outbuildings. Resuming the advance moments later, the regiment took the double-quick toward the second wall, which protected Hampton's main position along the ridge. With his gunners now confronting Vincent's entire brigade, Captain Hart brought up his remaining two guns. Even with his entire battery in action, Hart found himself outnumbered six to three and forced to continue splitting his fire between the enemy skirmishers and the Union battery. Skirmish intervals of fifteen feet limited casualties in the Union ranks. Still, Hart's valiant gunners drew their share of Yankee blood. One of their rounds ripped the rifle from the hands of a New Yorker, splintering the weapon. The impact threw the unfortunate soldier into the air as shards of the shattered rifle tore through his body. Shrapnel knocked down a man from Maine with a chest wound. Across the field, a Yankee shell fragment struck a private from the Second South Carolina in the face. Then, with the enemy closing on his line, another one of Hart's guns broke under the strain of recoil from the heavy shells. With the pressure against his position increasing, and certain the cavalry supporting his battery could not withstand the Union assault much longer, Hart sent one of his two operable guns to the rear, from where it could cover the Southern retreat.[7]

Hart's lone remaining cannon now stood between the lines; the Southern cavalry having already begun falling back off the ridge. Then, with a tremendous gout of flame, the gun's ammunition chest exploded, even as the gunners were bringing up the horses to pull the weapon off the field. As he continued to concentrate the fire from his six guns against Hart's position, one of Fuller's rounds had scored a direct hit. One gunner described "a volcano of bursting shells" erupting from the limber as the ammunition exploded for several long seconds. Though the men survived shaken and singed, all but one of the horses had been killed or disabled. Unable to save the gun with one horse, the men reluctantly abandoned the weapon. Hart and his dejected gunners may have taken some solace from the earlier explosion of one of Lieutenant Fuller's ammunition chests. That explosion, which Fuller termed an accident, left three of his men with minor burns.[8]

Captain Judd Mott, who had raised one of the early Lancer companies and then brought the men over to the Sixteenth Michigan, fell mortally wounded in front of Hart's position. Months earlier, a friend had said of Mott, "He is one of those young men whose future, if he lives, will be useful and brilliant." Cpl. George Sidman, an undersized boyish-looking youth who had once brashly told Michigan's governor, "I love to fight and live on hard bread and pork," went down with a painful foot wound. As other men fell around him, Lt. George Cook reached Hart's abandoned cannon first. He shot the wounded horses still struggling in the traces and freed the lone uninjured animal. Then, as other men arrived, a bullet knocked Cook off his feet. With the men huddled around Cook and the gun, Lieutenant Fuller galloped up and demanded credit for capturing the trophy. Disgusted, Cook and his foot soldiers mistook the jubilant Fuller for a glory-seeking cavalryman who had taken no part in the action. But with the battle still underway, Fuller could not linger and quickly returned to his guns.[9]

According to Captain Hart, the loss of the gun "demoralized" Hampton's troopers and accelerated their retreat from the field. One Michigander, watching the Southern cavalry abandon the cannon, unfairly, termed their fight "an apology for a stand." But Stuart and Hampton had no intention of losing men needlessly in a slugfest with infantry. Rather, they simply wanted to buy as much time as possible while making the Federals pay a painful price for the ground they gained. And, unbeknown to the Wolverines, the final retreat had been triggered by events on the southern end of the field.[10]

After a long circuitous march, Vincent's Pennsylvanians struck the southern flank of Stuart's line just as the northern end began to crumble. With their flank turned, and the Forty-Fourth New York and Twentieth Maine Infantry bearing down on them from their front, the North Carolinians and Mississippians holding the end of Hampton's line finally gave way. The First North Carolina faced the heaviest pressure and, according to a Southern press account, "became nearly surrounded," as the enemy bore down on them from front and flank. Faced with capture or death, and with his horse-holders nowhere in sight, Capt. William Houston shouted for his men "to get away as fast as possible." Used to riding over difficult terrain, the troopers found running several hundred yards over "steep hills . . . very fatiguing," and some, including Houston, stopped briefly to catch their breath. Moments after resuming his sprint to safety, a bullet struck Houston in the head and killed him. Remembered as "the very soul of honor," the former state senator rests today in Middleburg's Sharon Cemetery.[11]

When the Tar Heels gave way, the remainder of the line became unhinged. Unable to hold against infantry attacking from two directions, the Mississippians of the Jeff Davis Legion fell back, followed by the South Carolinians. For a few harrowing minutes, only the Georgians of Cobb's Legion faced the Union assault. Maj. William Delony held his battalion on the line to the last moment, in what he described as "a terribly exposed position." The Georgians had retained their horses, and several had gone down to enemy fire. As his line gave way around him, Delony's scabbard absorbed the impact of a bullet, sparing his horse. Finally, a courier arrived from Hampton, ordering Delony "to fall back to the next crest," where Stuart had already begun preparing for another stand.[12]

About half a mile to the west, the Confederates reached the steep banks of Cromwell's Run. Finding enough open ground along a narrow ridge on the west side of the stream to make a stand, Stuart deployed his carbineers and artillery to defend the turnpike bridge. But with the rugged banks of Rocky Run just a few hundred yards to his rear, Stuart could not afford to be trapped here; his stand along Cromwell's Run would be brief. Starting most of his cavalry west toward Rector's Cross Roads and Goose Creek, Stuart deployed Hampton's carbineers to defend a stone wall overlooking the narrow span at Cromwell's Run. The men must have been heartened to see Capt. Marcellus Moorman's Battery unlimbering alongside Captain Hart's lone gun. Moments later, Capt. William McGregor pulled his four guns onto the ridge. The artillerymen had only moments to load and catch their breath before Lieutenant Fuller wheeled his six guns into battery across the stream and took them under fire. The battle resumed just as the Union infantry came trudging into view across the creek.[13]

Colonel Vincent kept his skirmishers well in advance of his main battle line as he pursued Stuart. Once the Southern guns opened, Vincent sent the men sprinting for the cover of a stone wall on the near side of the creek. With cavalry now taking a more active role north of the turnpike, the colonel concentrated his brigade south of the road. Then, with cannon fire crashing over their heads, the Union skirmishers vaulted the wall, scrambled down the banks to the stream and waded across. Stuart and Hampton had watched as Vincent organized his regiments for the attack. Certain they had already gained all the time they could defending the bridge, and not wanting to be trapped on the narrow ridge, the two officers again ordered their men to retire. Gaining the crest above the stream, the frustrated Yankees watched as their foe raced off to the west.[14]

One Michigander described the late-morning segment of the battle as "of a running nature," as Stuart fought and moved, and fought and moved again. Unlike a boxer, jabbing and moving, however, Stuart's men were on their heels, defending rather than attacking. A Buckeye, skirmishing north of the pike termed the "hills and hollows" as "entirely unsuited for cavalry operations," but he also recognized the "substantial character [of the] stone fences . . . which afforded the retreating foe most admirable positions for defense at almost every step." The high ground west of Goose Creek provided the next defensible position, and Stuart sent McGregor and Hart back to establish their guns on the ridge overlooking the creek. The Yankees would have to attack over another bridge and Stuart intended to make the narrow span a killing ground. Short of a pitched battle at the bridge, a show of force by his artillery, posted on the dominating ridge, would hold the Federals at bay and buy Stuart critical time. But the bridge lay nearly two miles away and Stuart could not be certain he could funnel two cavalry brigades and his artillery across the span before the Yankees forced him to reengage. He needed a delaying action, and Rector's Cross Roads, midway between Cromwell's Run and Goose Creek, provided the best opportunity.[15]

As Stuart and Hampton discussed their options, Col. John Black arrived with his First South Carolina. Having spent the night guarding the brigade supply train near Upperville, Black and his men rode up rested and ready for battle. "Here is Black with a fresh regiment. Get him in position," Stuart told Hampton. As Black recalled, Stuart had been "badly thumped and I was to take the brunt and cover the retreat." With Union infantry coming into view to the east, Hampton offered Black some words of encouragement "and ordered me to prepare." Surveying the ground, Black's grim visage must have brightened slightly as Captain Moorman wheeled his guns into battery nearby.[16]

Colonel Black selected Capt. Angus Brown to command the rear guard and support Moorman. Admired for his "stubborn coolness," Brown scattered his carbineers around the Rector home on the south side of the intersection, with Moorman's four guns to his front. The balance of the regiment remained mounted north of the turnpike. The Carolinians had only moments to ponder their future before Union horse artillery and cavalry rode into view.[17]

• • •

The men had been fighting for about five hours as the sun reached its apex. The gray cavalry had already yielded a couple miles of ground and lost three guns disabled or captured. Though his men may have been discouraged, Stuart needed to hold his position at Goose Creek for reasons more immediate than preventing the Yankees from reaching the gaps of the Blue Ridge. As Stuart fell back along the turnpike, he exposed his two brigades positioned just north of Goose Creek. Col. John Chambliss had posted his brigade as a blocking force along the Millville Road. A mile and a half north of and nearly parallel to the turnpike, the Millville Road ran west to the base of the Blue Ridge and provided an avenue by which the Yankees could turn Stuart's position on the pike. Brig. Gen. William "Grumble" Jones held his brigade along the road between Pot House and Union, about four miles north of Stuart's position. Stuart had charged Jones with denying the Yankees the roads through Union, which allowed access to Ashby's and Snicker's Gaps.

The sustained cannon fire throughout the morning had alerted Jones and Chambliss to the battle along the turnpike. Side roads and farm lanes also allowed Southern couriers to keep the two officers abreast of Stuart's plans. Likewise, Chambliss notified Stuart that a Union flanking force had engaged his men northwest of Middleburg. Stuart responded by ordering Jones and Chambliss to withdraw, link up, and meet him at Upperville. There, as he later explained, he planned to make a "determined stand." But, with Chambliss already engaged and Jones needing time to get his men on the road, Stuart had to hold his position at Goose Creek, or the brigades might be defeated in detail. With luck, the four brigades would unite at Upperville and meet Pleasonton on more even terms. In the best scenario, Jones and Chambliss would arrive on Pleasonton's flank in time to secure victory.[18]

Stuart had two other concerns necessitating a stand at Goose Creek. Major von Borcke still lay gravely wounded at Doctor Eliason's home in Upperville, and Stuart sought to ensure his safety. With little defensible terrain between Goose Creek and Upperville, Stuart needed time to arrange transport and locate a safe location where his aide could recover without fear of capture. Stuart also hoped to have infantry support waiting at Ashby's Gap, but with General Longstreet having pulled his corps across the Shenandoah River, the foot soldiers needed time to recross the river and move back into position along the mountain. Longstreet tasked Maj. Gen. Lafayette McLaws with supporting the cavalry, along with the artillery he had sent back the previous night. With his arrangements in place, Stuart turned his attention to the Yankees crowding onto the ridge on the east side of Goose Creek.[19]

• • •

Believing Stuart to be on the run and aware his infantry needed time to catch their breath and replenish their ammunition, Pleasonton urged his troopers to press the attack. The Union cavalry had been content to let the infantry carry the fight throughout

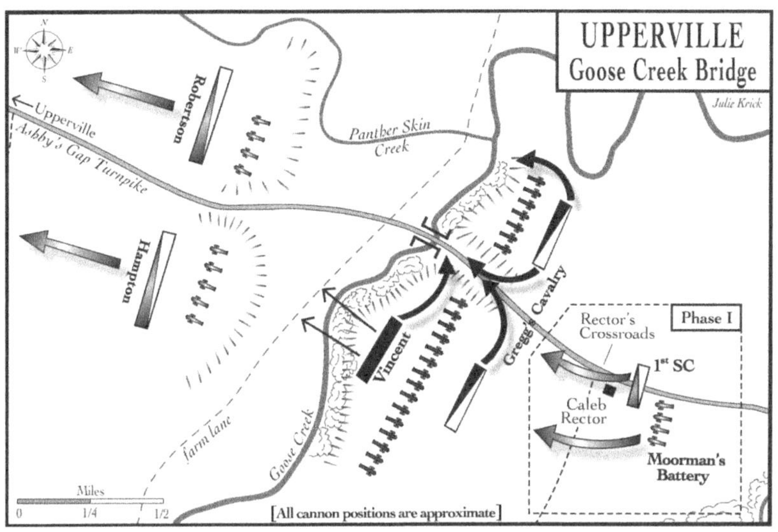

MAP 15. Upperville Goose Creek bridge. Created by Julie Krick.

the morning, but with the day advancing and Ashby's Gap still ten miles away, Pleasonton needed his men to keep the Confederates on the move. And, with Lieutenant Fuller having been outgunned at Cromwell's Run, Pleasonton brought up the remainder of his horse artillery, including the batteries commanded by Capt. Alanson Randol, Lt. John Calef, and four guns under Capt. William Graham. After refilling his ammunition chests, Fuller rejoined his comrades at Rector's Cross Roads. Throughout the remainder of the day, these officers leapfrogged their batteries back and forth across the turnpike, firing from one commanding position after another as they sought to suppress the fire from their stubborn counterparts.[20]

The South Carolinians at Rector's Cross Roads soon found themselves enduring a torrent of fire from the Union guns. With Colonel Black's mounted contingent presenting too great a target, Stuart ordered him to leave his carbineers in place and pull the remainder of the regiment across Goose Creek. Then, as Moorman began pulling his guns off the line, a shell from Fuller's Battery dismembered one of the Southern gunners. Another round tore a leg off a battery-mate. In the exchange of fire, one of Fuller's men had a leg torn off and died moments later. Once the last of the Southern guns had reached the far side of the bridge, Captain Brown began sending his men toward the crossing. In the process, several, including Brown, went down under a hail of carbine and artillery fire. Moments later, Union cavalry swarmed through the crossroads, taking Brown and other men prisoner. Then, believing Stuart to be on the run again, the Yankees spurred their animals in pursuit, only to learn otherwise as they crested the heights overlooking Goose Creek.[21]

Erected between 1801 and 1803, the stout four-arch stone bridge that carried the turnpike across Goose Creek in 1863 had already witnessed its share of American history. In just the last two years the bridge had borne thousands of troops crossing and recrossing the meandering stream, but it had yet to witness or endure sustained combat. Before the war, a tollhouse had stood east of the bridge. On June 21, not one of the thousands of men who crossed the span offered to pay the monetary toll.

Across the creek, and spanning both sides of the turnpike, Stuart already had five guns in position as Moorman's straining horses pulled his four guns up the slope and onto the ridge. As the last of the South Carolinians darted across the span, they saw Southern carbineers handing off their horses to comrades before running down toward stone walls and other cover in the scrub growth scattered across the wide flood plain on the west side of the creek. The horse-holders then led the animals to the reverse slope, seeking protection from the Union guns then coming into view across the creek. Scanning the Southern position, Colonel Black saw the other regiments moving into line. Seeking to facilitate rapid movement when the need arose, Black set some of his men to tearing gaps in the walls crisscrossing the fields. As he directed his men, he observed a woman standing outside a nearby home with her hands clasped "in calm despair." Admiring her fortitude, Black thought, "If God ever made a noble race of ladies they were Virginians." Then the cannon on both sides of the creek erupted as gunners yanked their lanyards and shattered his moment of reflection.[22]

The troopers of the Second and Fourth New York had been

skirmishing north of the turnpike throughout the morning. But now, with the day waning and the infantry beginning to tire, General Kilpatrick thought a quick cavalry charge might carry the bridge before Stuart established a strong defense. Kilpatrick had another concern as he assessed the battlefield; the steep, wooded slope around the bridge prevented his men from fording the stream in the immediate vicinity of the span. Should the Confederates destroy the structure, they would delay further pursuit. The aggressive young general wanted to seize the bridge before the enemy could damage or destroy it. Calling his New Yorkers into the road, Kilpatrick urged them forward, but his window of opportunity had already passed. As soon as the column came into view, the Southern horse artillery opened. With fire from as many as nine guns concentrated on the narrow crossing, the Yankees never had a chance, and the attempt ended almost before it began; to have continued would have been suicide.[23]

Even though the effort ended quickly, many of the infantry had reached the field in time to observe the futile attempt. Seeing an opportunity to upstage the horsemen, a captain in the Sixteenth Michigan Infantry asked for a chance to try his luck. "Give me horses to mount twenty-five men, and I'll take the bridge," Capt. Guy Fuller brazenly told a superior. Cooler heads prevailed, however, and Fuller returned to his men disappointed. As Pleasonton and his subordinates devised a plan to seize the crossing, their artillery, at least twenty-two guns, answered the belligerent challenge from Stuart's artillerymen.[24]

Almost immediately, a shell exploded within the ranks of Black's Carolinians, knocking down nine horses. Shrapnel from another shell struck Black in the head and nearly knocked him from his horse. With his orderly holding him in the saddle, Black reached an aid station just as another shell sent the doctor running for cover. One of Stuart's aides described the Union artillery as being arrayed "for a quarter mile along the opposite hills as regularly as on a parade ground." The unequal contest must have been nerve-racking, but the Southerners stood to their guns. One round killed six of Hart's horses, leading a man in the battery to term the Union shooting "superb." A flurry of shells burst in the ranks of Cobb's Legion, "killing one man, wounding several others and killing and wounding a number of horses." Union infantry also brought their guns to bear and killed several horses. For at least an hour, and maybe two, solid shot and explosive rounds arced over the creek.[25]

Along the ridge east of the stream, a young captain steadied his New Yorkers by coolly sitting on his horse as the shells rained down around him. The Sixth Ohio lost several men, including one killed during the shelling. "I bless God that he has seen fit to spare my unworthy life," one of the victims told his sister from a hospital bed the next day. "I tell you the balls of shell and grape flew," another Buckeye affirmed. Southern carbineers, probably the North Carolinians with their Enfield rifles, added their fire to the contest and drove the Federal troopers off the crest of the hill. Though sheltered behind stone walls, several of Vincent's infantry also fell victim to Confederate fire.[26]

The artillery cannonade did not match the more famous bombardment at Gettysburg thirteen days later for volume of fire or casualties inflicted, but the duel at Goose Creek was of the same duration. The guns stood just three-quarters of a mile from each other, firing over the deep chasm cut by nature. The noise of the discharges and explosions carried for miles and would have been deafening for the men and animals on the field. The bucolic scene that had first greeted the soldiers quickly disappeared as dirt and smoke from burnt powder created a heavy haze over the field. Soon, the fresh perfumes of summer vanished, replaced by the stench of sweat, blood, acrid gunpowder, and death. Regardless of the danger, dead and wounded artillery horses had to be unharnessed and spare horses brought up. Some horses had acclimated to the noise and chaos of battle, others had not. Holding and controlling one horse during the cannonade would have been difficult, holding and preventing four or more horses, several tons of nervous, plunging horseflesh from stampeding, must have been nearly impossible. The horse-holders could not move without orders, and though most had found locations sheltered from bullets they may not have been protected either from cannon fire or the resulting splinters from shattered trees; nor would they have been safe from rock fragments from walls struck by solid shot. Locked in place for an hour or more, the animals, several thousand on each side of the creek, added their own waste to the odors engulfing the men. The soldiers must have been eager to move when they finally observed the Union infantry preparing to advance.

A farm lane just west of the bridge allowed couriers to pass quickly between Stuart, at the bridge, and his two brigades retreating along the Millville Road to the north. During the cannonade, Union pressure against the men on the Millville Road increased and Stuart sent Lt. John Shoemaker's two-gun section from Moorman's Battery to bolster Colonel Chambliss's force. Watching Shoemaker pull his guns off the ridge may have convinced Union commanders to finally launch their assault on the bridge. Likewise, the sight of Union infantry moving off the hills and onto the turnpike prompted Stuart, who had managed a masterful effort so far, to abandon Goose Creek.[27]

Colonel Vincent preferred to attack on a wide front, sending the Sixteenth Michigan Infantry and several companies from the Second and Fourth New York Cavalry across the bridge, while his other regiments waded the stream. However, most of the foot soldiers found the slope too steep and too heavily wooded to descend. Others found the stream too deep to ford. Even as the hardiest of Vincent's men plunged into the creek, others struggled back up the bank and ran for the bridge, eventually crossing behind the Wolverines. Kilpatrick had also located a ford downstream and some of his troopers now splashed across the creek north of the bridge and turned Stuart's left flank.[28]

Once again, the combined arms assault proved anticlimactic as the Confederates waited until the last minute and then beat a hasty retreat, followed by frustrated Yankees, shouting, "Shoot them! Take them prisoners!" Though a few men had been killed or wounded, the assault proved largely bloodless. The final action at the bridge proved so precipitous that several wounded officers were left behind. Angered at being abandoned, the officers reportedly emptied their revolvers at the backs of their own men before falling into Union hands.[29]

With no defensible ground nearby, Stuart sent his men back to a low ridge, three miles away, on the eastern edge of Upperville, known as Vineyard Hill. Having been on the move, marching or fighting for twelve hours, Vincent's weary soldiers simply could not continue the running fight. Grateful for their assistance, Pleasonton left the infantry behind and sent his troopers in pursuit, seeking to push the enemy through Ashby's Gap. As the cavalrymen dashed off, the infantry found high ground on which to build cook fires, boil well-earned coffee, and hopefully catch a glimpse of the action to come. After fighting alongside the cavalry at Brandy Station a couple of weeks earlier, an infantryman had proclaimed his pride in the mounted arm and how "elated" he had been observing them in action. Now, Colonel Vincent echoed those thoughts, writing, "The charges of the cavalry, a sight I had never before witnessed, were truly inspiring, and . . . gave us a feeling of regret that we, too, were not mounted and could not join the chase."[30]

During the stand at Goose Creek, General Barnes had started a fresh brigade of infantry forward to assist or relieve Vincent's men as needed. These troops arrived after Stuart abandoned his position; they halted alongside Vincent's men. Marching through the area of the morning and early-afternoon fighting, a member of the 118th Pennsylvania found the fields "thickly strewn with the bodies of horses killed in action." The soldier counted eighteen dead horses in one yard. Some had been dead for several days and others mere hours. Weeks later, when the army passed through the battlefield again, an infantryman from Maine gazed at the bones "bleaching in the sun" and remembered the soldiers, friend, and foe alike, who now lay buried and forgotten in the fields "until Gabriel's horn shall call them up or until the elements shall absorb them."[31]

Soldiers and civilians had listened to the ebb and flow of battle for hours. The dull, ominous rumble of artillery fire had reached a peak at midday before the guns fell, briefly, silent. At her home near Vineyard Hill, Ida Dulany had listened to the throaty growl of the cannons, while keeping a wary eye on the clouds of smoke rising to the east. By 2 p.m. she knew the silence to be only fleeting as the combatants were on the move. Soon, she could see Stuart's cavalry spilling into the fields below her house, and her mind raced back to a Sunday the previous November, in which many of the same troops had battled over the same ground. "Could I think we were to go through the same ordeal of insolence and plunder and destruction, my heart would be heavy as lead," she observed in her diary, "but I must hope for the best and not make bad worse by anticipating evil." Walking up the hill near her home at Paris, Amanda Edmonds could also view the troops now moving dimly into view. Recoiling at the sight, she wondered, "did I ever dream of seeing and being in the midst of . . . two contending Cavalry forces[?]"[32]

Those beyond sight of the battle could only listen and ponder what the sounds portended. "We could hardly get anything concerning these riots even tho' so near us," a Union officer complained from near Aldie. Later, he learned, "it was cavalry fighting," what he described as "various small but important riots." The din of battle had died away but only briefly. The riot re-ignited in full fury when the two mounted forces finally came to grips around Upperville.[33]

NINETEEN

The Hottest Fighting I Ever Did, June 21

Few troopers in Brig. Gen. John Buford's First Cavalry Division had fired a shot or drawn a saber in the previous four days of fighting. His First Brigade, led by Col William Gamble, had scouted the road to Snicker's Gap on June 18 but other than light skirmishing the probe had been uneventful, and Gamble had turned back rather than confront the enemy posted in strength at the entrance to the gap. Buford had also been forced to leave his Second Brigade, led by Col. Thomas Devin, near Thoroughfare Gap for several days as a salve to ease General Hooker's continuing fears of a surprise attack by Southern infantry pouring through the gap. Only Maj. Charles Whiting's Reserve Brigade had seen combat at Middleburg, Pot House, and Millville on June 19. Buford and Gamble, meanwhile had spent the day marking time, guarding supply trains at Aldie, and securing the vital road junctions around the town.[1]

Born in 1826, John Buford was the oldest, most experienced, and most senior of Alfred Pleasonton's two division commanders. A Kentuckian by birth, Buford had received an appointment to West Point from Illinois. Upon graduating in 1848, he received a commission in the First U.S. Dragoons. The firing on Fort Sumter found Buford in Utah, serving as a captain in the Second Dragoons. After returning east in October 1861, he received an assignment with the army's Inspector General's Office, where he inspected horses and cavalry volunteers. Unencumbered by the towering ego of many of his contemporaries, Buford had watched through early 1862 as younger officers received commissions as colonels and brigadiers in the volunteers, while he remained a field-grade officer in the Regulars. Though he made his home in Illinois, his Kentucky lineage may have worked against him in Secretary of War Edwin Stanton's suspicious mind. Refusing to court favor, Buford did not receive the coveted single star of a brigadier until July 27, 1862.[2]

Taking command of a cavalry brigade in Maj. Gen. John Pope's Army of Virginia, Buford had an immediate impact on the success of the brigade. His tenure inspecting volunteers left him well versed in the many problems plaguing the cavalry, and he quickly set about correcting them. In short, he taught his men to be soldiers and his officers to lead. He led by example, sharing his men's trials and privations. He later served George McClellan and Ambrose Burnside as chief of cavalry, toiling behind the scenes to increase the efficiency of the mounted force. When Joseph Hooker formed the Cavalry Corps in February 1863, Buford asked to lead Western troops, but Regular Army blood coursed through his veins, so much so that he accepted a brigade command even though he had earned a division. "If the Regulars are to be put together—I believe they would prefer me to either of the other Cavalry Commanders," he offered. He wanted to lead "fighting" men, men with the experience and fortitude to stand and hold their ground in a desperate battle. General Stoneman obliged, assigning him to command the Reserve Brigade. Following the fight at Brandy Station, he took permanent command of the First Division, including his old Regulars and several proud Western regiments. The men revered and respected Buford. All gristle, grit, and quiet determination, the efficient, unassuming soldier must have been exasperated as he entered Pleasonton's headquarters on the evening of June 20. He had listened to the fighting for several days without participating. But now, relieved of responsibility for supply trains, road junctions, and mountain gaps, he could pitch into the coming fight with his entire division.[3]

Pleasonton's strategy meeting concluded after midnight, and

he expected Buford to have his men on the road to Middleburg by 2 a.m. Buford, however, soon found the timing to be "impracticable." Bugles began waking the men an hour before the planned departure, but with only a waxing crescent moon providing minimal light, couriers and quartermasters found their tasks nearly impossible in the darkness. Though food and forage had reached Aldie, Buford, considering the limited time available, ordered his officers to concentrate on the more vital task of drawing in their scattered pickets; the men and horses went hungry. Still, the division did not begin the six-mile march to Middleburg until after the other troops had passed.[4]

Once David Gregg and Strong Vincent had moved their commands through Middleburg, Buford entered the town and turned north and then west along a narrow, winding route to Millville. Pleasonton's plan called for Buford to make a quick dash across Goose Creek, turning Stuart's northern flank and then recrossing the stream at Millville to come up on Stuart's rear, while Vincent and Gregg held the Confederates in place at Kirk's Branch. The weight of five Union brigades would then fall upon Stuart's two brigades along the turnpike. Pleasonton appears to have presupposed that Stuart had left a gap in his line north of the road. Instead, as Buford soon learned, Stuart had posted the brigades of John Chambliss and "Grumble" Jones north of the road and near the waterway. These Southern veterans, Virginians, and North Carolinians, aided by narrow roads cut deep into rugged rocky terrain and watercourses flowing over their banks, began frustrating Buford as soon as he reached Goose Creek. Rather than trying to ford the flooded stream under fire, Buford turned north again, away from the developing fight along the turnpike, as he sought a gap in the Southern line. Quickly realizing the futility of his effort, he led Gamble and Maj. Samuel Starr, now commanding the Regulars, back to the ford, while Devin continued north, protecting their flank.[5]

By splitting his division, Buford broadened the front of the Union advance and fighting may have erupted along several roads as his brigades tried to punch through the Southern cordon. Stuart may have discussed options with Jones and Chambliss during the night, and now they began preparing to retreat by pulling in their supply wagons and some of their pickets, even as other men began contesting the Union advance. Should Buford force them to retire, Chambliss would do so along the Millville Road, while Jones would fall back through Union before eventually joining Chambliss.[6]

When Buford turned back to the ford, Colonel Devin with about 1,250 men from the Seventeenth Pennsylvania, Sixth and Ninth New York, and the Third West Virginia, continued north. Unlike Buford and Gamble, Devin was not a professional soldier but rather a house painter before the war. He had, however, recognized the gathering storm and had organized and led the First New York State Militia Cavalry. Yearning to learn the art of command and leadership, Devin drove himself and his men on the drill field. When he later faced an examination board during the war, his examining officer declared, "I can't teach Col. Devin anything about cavalry; he knows more about the tactics than I do." Devin mirrored Buford, tough, fearless, tender, and modest. Images reflect a ruddy-faced man with piercing almost ghostlike eyes. Having proven his worth throughout the war, Devin now found himself protecting the division while Buford and Gamble concentrated on the enemy in their front.[7]

The restrictive nature of the narrow, sunken roads, lined by stone walls and rail fences, continued to aid the defenders and forced Buford's brigade commanders, especially Gamble, to deploy strong flanking details. The main body of each brigade moved, at least initially, in column along the roads. In the event of contact with the enemy, the men would hold their positions hoping the strong skirmish lines and flanking parties could push the enemy aside. If not, the main body would redeploy, move up and out of the roads and through gaps in the walls before joining their comrades on the skirmish line.

The strength of Buford's advance may have forced the Southern pickets to initially give ground rather quickly. But by 10 a.m., both Chambliss and Jones had pulled in their pickets, and the skirmishing became more severe. Between noon and one o'clock, Stuart, knowing he would soon have to abandon his position at Goose

Creek, sent a courier telling Chambliss to retire. The colonel then passed the message to Jones at Union. The Southern retreat now became a race to Upperville and Ashby's Gap. With miles of ground to cover before they could rejoin Stuart at Upperville, the brigade commanders ordered their wagons and artillery to use the roads, while the troopers moved through the fields. Both officers also designated a rear guard, Chambliss selecting the Ninth Virginia, supported by Lieutenant Shoemaker's two guns, while Jones deployed carbineers from the Eleventh and Twelfth Virginia to hold Devin at bay.[8]

The heaviest skirmishing occurred on Col. William Gamble's front. He led Buford's western brigade, about sixteen hundred men from the Eighth and Twelfth Illinois, Third Indiana, and the oft-maligned easterners of the Eighth New York. A native of Ireland and a civil engineer by training, Gamble had entered the prewar army as a private in the First Dragoons and risen through the ranks to serve as sergeant major before returning to civilian life in 1843. Elected to serve as lieutenant colonel of the Eighth Illinois, his men soon termed him the "King of Terrors." Tough he may have been, but like Buford and Devin, Gamble was as unpretentious "as any old farmer." He "just suited us," a trooper recalled, and "a braver man never lived."[9]

Gamble had dismounted a squadron of the Third Indiana to seize the ford at Goose Creek, and the Hoosiers then continued to lead his advance beyond the creek, supported by a squadron from the Eighth Illinois. Gamble soon encountered Col. Richard Beale and his Ninth Virginia near Millville, where an open piece of ground near a sharp bend in the road provided the Southerners with the perfect opportunity to try and ambush Gamble's advance guard. The Irishman responded by deploying his column into a line of battle and ordering Lt. Theophile von Michalowski to unlimber his sections of guns, Battery K, First U.S. "A few well directed shells" convinced Beale to yield, and the Yankees soon resumed their advance. A mile down the road, the Virginians struck again, this time aided by a stone wall. A few more shells, however, and the Virginians, who sought only to buy time, gave way. Racing another mile and a half down the road, the Confederates made a final stand near Welbourne, the home of Richard H. Dulany, colonel of the Seventh Virginia.[10]

Posting his men east of Quaker Lane, the road on which Jones was now moving, Beale needed to hold his ground until Jones reached the intersection and turned onto the Millville Road. Outnumbered and with a difficult task before him, Beale deployed his men behind two stone walls and brought Shoemaker's guns into the fray. Gamble responded by shaking out another battle line and unlimbering his own guns. Under artillery fire, the Yankees advanced doggedly, eventually driving the enemy from the first wall. During the fight, Jones brought his men through the intersection at a gallop before ordering his rear guard to remain and assist Beale. Holding the Yankees at bay until the last minute, Beale finally ordered his men to retire. With the two brigades united, the final leg of the race to Upperville had just begun.[11]

The skirmishing had been heavy for several hours as the Yankees fought "to dislodge the enemy from behind the infernal stone fences which are five feet high and three thick, and form excellent breastworks," an exasperated trooper from Illinois explained. While Buford discussed his options with Gamble, troopers policed the field, bringing in the wounded and dead, including Pvt. Hanson Town, Eighth Illinois. Two days later, as his comrades rested near Aldie, a letter arrived for Town from his sister. His sergeant assumed the difficult task of informing her of his death. "Your letter . . . came too late to be read by . . . Hanson, whose heart on the 21st was pierced by a rifle ball aimed by the enemies of our country," the sergeant explained. "He fell facing the foe and in the cause . . . of reestablishing the respect and honor of our dear old flag." In closing, the sergeant assured her, "You and all his friends have the full sympathy of the whole company. We miss him [badly.]"[12]

Colonel Devin rejoined Buford soon after the guns went silent. With his division reunited, Buford had a decision to make. He had been charged with turning Stuart's northern flank and, try as he might, he had been unable to do so. Now, with the day waning and recognizing that Stuart might soon escape into Ashby's Gap, Buford pressed ahead, pursuing Jones and Chambliss. As he continued along the Millville Road, he soon heard Pleasonton's guns open again along the turnpike.[13]

Believing he had finally reached Stuart's flank, Buford elected to abandon his pursuit of the Southerners in his front. With Gamble in the van, Buford turned south on Greengarden Road and rode rapidly toward the sound of the guns. From hilltops, he could catch glimpses of troops moving ahead of him. Believing Pleasonton to be outnumbered, Buford called for his men to advance at "a brisk trot." But he soon ran "afoul of so many obstructions" along the narrow, hilly road that he could not maintain the pace. Then, a half-mile from the turnpike and a long carbine shot from the end of Stuart's line, Buford found his path blocked by Panther Skin Creek. Without a bridge and with the stream overflowing the steep, rocky banks, Buford anxiously looked for a point at which he might safely cross his command. Rather than seeing a ford, however, he saw what appeared to be unescorted Southern supply wagons on Trappe Road, a mile to his right across a level open field.

After uniting, Jones, and Chambliss, with eight regiments, six guns, and a train of wagons, had been in a race with Buford for several miles. As a trooper in the Twelfth Virginia recalled, the men moved in three columns at "double-quick time," through fields, ditches, and woodlots. Turning south onto Trappe Road, the horses began to tire and could no longer maintain the torrid pace. Soon the units became strung out. Jones wheeled his command into the fields on the west side of the road, Chambliss split his command along both sides of the road, and the rear guard maintained their positions behind the columns. Then, possibly sensing imminent danger, the Southern commanders ordered their men to begin bearing to the southwest, avoiding the extra distance to Upperville and the turnpike by cutting through the fields west of Trappe Road and directly toward Ashby's Gap. Doing so came at a cost, however, as the distance between regiments soon increased. Most critically, the fences, stone, and rail, which had aided the men throughout the previous several days, would, within minutes, become deadly obstacles, most especially the fences along both sides of Trappe Road.[14]

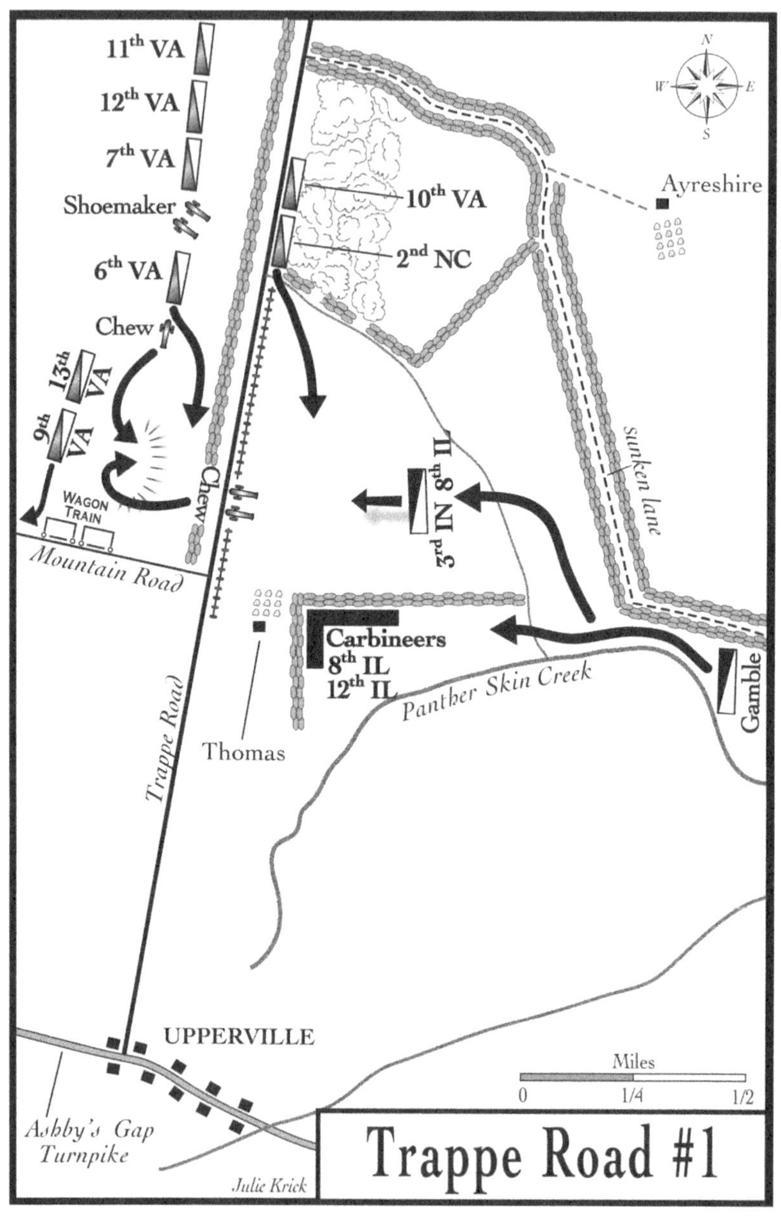

MAP 16. Trappe Road—phase 1. Created by Julie Krick.

The teamsters driving the wagons and the men of Capt. Roger Preston Chew's Ashby Artillery soon saw Yankees pouring into the far end of a large open field east of Trappe Road and just south of Ayrshire Farm. Mountain Road lay just ahead, and the teamsters urged their horses and mules into the lane, which would carry them into the foothills of the Blue Ridge and away from the Federals. The Second North Carolina, with fewer than two hundred men, followed Chew in the column but a large woodlot blocked their view of the field and the Yankee attack. Once they realized their predicament, the Carolinians had no chance to escape as they were on the east side of the road, corralled by the fences. The trees also prevented the men in the units following the Carolinians, including the Tenth Virginia and Lieutenant Shoemaker's section of artillery, from seeing the enemy. Jones had already moved his four regiments into the fields west of Trappe Road, followed by the rear guard.[15]

As soon as Buford determined to attack, Gamble sent several companies of carbineers toward Trappe Road to block the Confederates from escaping toward Upperville. Nearing the road, the troopers followed a stone wall west toward the home of Nathaniel Thomas. Just behind the home and Mr. Thomas's orchard, the wall turned south, forming an angle facing the Southern advance and within carbine range of the road. The carbineers dismounted as soon as they reached the corner of the wall and opened fire on the Confederates nearing the Mountain Road intersection. Gamble then sent the Third Indiana and Eighth Illinois into the open field, with the remainder of his force following behind. Nearing the Thomas house, Gamble brought the column into line, and with his eye on the Southern guns caught in the road ahead, ordered his buglers to blow "Charge!"[16]

Buford had finally gained a tactical advantage. "Never was the brigade taken at a greater disadvantage," one of the Southern officers later concluded. The sudden surprise, as the Union carbineers opened fire from the angle of the wall, caused "considerable confusion" in Chambliss's ranks. The men in the fields west of the road scattered temporarily. The troopers in the field east of the road had no option other than stand and fight. Caught in the road, Captain Chew determined to fight as well. One Southern cavalryman remembered Chew as "a most companionable, agreeable comrade in camp and as dashing a dare-devil in battle as ever drew a sword." Seeing the Yankees bearing down on Chew's lead section of two guns, a trooper from the Tenth Virginia quickly leaped his horse over the stone wall and raced up a nearby knoll to the west, certain he was about to witness a disaster. Instead, Chew calmly ordered some of his men to pull down fence rails on the east side of Trappe Road. As they did so, others loaded the guns with canister. Then, the Yankees at the angle began peppering the artillerists with carbine fire. A bullet killed one of the men dismantling the fence as Chew's horses dragged the guns through the gap and onto the edge of the field. Seconds later the men unhitched the guns and swung them toward the onrushing enemy.[17]

With no barrier protecting the guns, Lt. Col. David Clendenin, commanding the Eighth Illinois, yelled, "Boys, let's take the cannon." Within seconds the shout rang up and down the line, "Let's have those pieces." But as Gamble's line closed on the road, his formation began to lose integrity as stronger horses pulled ahead of weaker mounts and braver men spurred past the faint-hearted. And then the gunners yanked their lanyards. The first two rounds staggered the Yankees. A canister ball killed Gamble's horse, throwing the colonel to the ground. Hit in the face and chest, Clendenin's horse staggered out of line. Other horses went down, hurling their riders into the dirt or pinning them to the ground. The bodies now became obstructions, further breaking the momentum of the attack. The guns belched out eight more rounds as quickly as the men could sponge, load, and fire. As many as 240 iron balls may have torn through the Union ranks. The last rounds would have shredded the horses in front of the guns. Stunned by the shock of the artillery fire and the immediate loss of leadership, the Yankees fell back quickly. "We could see the fearful executions," one of Chew's men declared, as the canister rounds butchered the horses. When Chew retired moments later, forty-five dead horses lay in front of his position.[18]

With Gamble and Clendenin down, Maj. William Medill, Eighth

Illinois, took command of the brigade and immediately brought order out of chaos. After reforming the men, Medill led them forward into carbine range of Chew's guns. As one of the Illini described, "700 pieces blazed in the faces of the enemy," knocking down "men and horses." Medill's pressure convinced Chew to pull his guns across the road; no easy task with the "leaden hail . . . rattling on the smoking pieces." With the guns temporarily out of action and defenseless, the Yankees grew bolder, surging through Chew's abandoned position, into Trappe Road and up against the stone wall. Massed nearby, the men of the Sixth Virginia drew their revolvers and made a hasty countercharge to save the guns, but their horses refused to leap the stone wall on the west side of the road. Instead, the animals turned to the south along the wall, as the Virginians emptied their revolvers into the mass of blue. Seeing no quick access through the wall and with several Southern regiments arriving from the north, Medill pulled his men back across the road. Flush with adrenaline, one of the Federals quipped, "There is nothing like coming to close quarters with the butternuts." Medill had momentarily recovered the initiative but before he could reorganize his men and press his attack, the Second North Carolina charged from behind the woodlot and struck the Yankees in their right flank.[19]

Though badly outnumbered, the Carolinians had two advantages over their foe, five-shot Colt Revolving Rifles and Lt. Col. William H. F. "Billy" Payne. Though grievously wounded in the face thirteen months earlier, Payne, like Chew, excelled in the crucible of combat. The wound had not quenched his ardor for battle, and his enthusiasm now inspired his men as they plunged into the Union line. Aided only by a small detachment of the Tenth Virginia that had remained on the east side of the road, the Tar Heels drove the Yankees back to their dismounted carbineers at the Thomas house. Others fled across the field to the east, taking cover behind the walls of Sunken Lane. Surprise had aided Payne's attack, but the Carolinians soon needed help. When one of them went down, knocked from the saddle by a grazing shot to the head, he was immediately trampled by the horses behind him. Dragging himself to the shelter of the wall, and with dismounted Yankees firing from the other side and over his head, the injured Southerner had an unobstructed view for the remainder of the fight. Looking across the road, he would have seen other regiments milling about in the fields but no one coming to aid Payne. Years later the vision still hurt; the Carolinians, aided by a few Virginians, had saved the Southern guns but they lost at least twenty-one men in the process. A bitter soldier later complained, "I do not believe there was an engagement during the war in which a body of troops was more forsaken by comrades than the 'Second Horse' was on that occasion." Billy Payne, the eager warrior, had no choice but to fall back out of carbine range, covered by a few stalwart men and their revolving rifles.[20]

The fighting had been frantic and, briefly, hand-to-hand, before a momentary lull settled over the field. Captain Chew's quick, instinctive decisions, aided by the men of the Sixth Virginia and Second North Carolina, had saved his guns. With Medill's men preparing for another rush, Chew wheeled his two guns into battery alongside his other section, which had just arrived and gone into position on a knoll west of Trappe Road near Mountain Road. Though he knew his ammunition chests were dangerously depleted from the earlier skirmishing along Millville Road, Lieutenant Shoemaker also brought his two guns into battery nearby. As he did so, Jones urged his other regiments forward. Regardless of the lingering animosity felt by Payne and his men, the troopers caught on the west side of Trappe Road could do little to aid anyone during the first furious minutes of fighting until the several fences and walls along the road had been pulled open. The once friendly walls, had now, as a trooper in the Seventh Virginia described, become "pests," limiting the movement of the men. With Chew's guns now in battery on the knoll, some of the troopers pushed through the gaps opened earlier by his gunners. Other Virginians dismounted, handed their reins to comrades, and began tearing at the fences, throwing rocks and rails aside in a frantic effort to open additional gaps.[21]

After guiding their steeds through the openings, the men of the Seventh, Eleventh, and Twelfth Virginia spurred the animals across the road and into the field, while the Sixth Virginia remained behind, holding the ground on the west side of the road, and supporting the guns. As soon as the Virginians entered the road, they came under fire from the Union carbineers near the Thomas house. General Buford's two guns had now reached the field and opened on the Confederates. The appearance of the Union guns forced Chew and Shoemaker to split their fire between the cavalrymen in the field and the guns supporting them.[22]

Lieutenant Walter Buck, Seventh Virginia, and Capt. Charles O'Ferrall, Twelfth Virginia, had ridden together during the morning and early afternoon, bantering back and forth about their desire for a furlough. Thinking their only chance would be to suffer a wound, the two friends discussed the severity of the injury they were willing to incur. Now, with the battle in front of them, both men had returned to their regiments. Buck and the Seventh Virginia crossed the road near the Thomas house, while O'Ferrall and the Twelfth Virginia crossed to Buck's left, through the gap just vacated by Chew's gunners, and moved directly into the open field. The Union carbineers waiting behind the wall could not immediately turn their guns upon the Seventh Virginia, but they had a perfect field of fire toward the Twelfth Virginia. Under artillery and concentrated carbine fire, the Twelfth Virginia did not even have time to form before the withering Union volleys shattered their ranks and drove them back across the road. As O'Ferrall encouraged his men, a bullet struck him in the chest. Before he passed out, two comrades took hold of him and held him in the saddle as they sought to escape the fury around them. By then the Union cannon had the range and a shell exploded over the fence, killing Thomas Garber, the regimental color-bearer. Their comrades who had been with the rearguard, arrived just in time to see the regiment driven from the field. "It was the hardest fight that I ever saw it looked awful," one of them declared.[23]

Valor and zeal, regardless of whether the men wore blue or gray, drove the intensity of the fighting that engulfed the field. Few men fought harder than "Grumble" Jones, but he fought now because he had to, not because he wanted to. He ordered his men

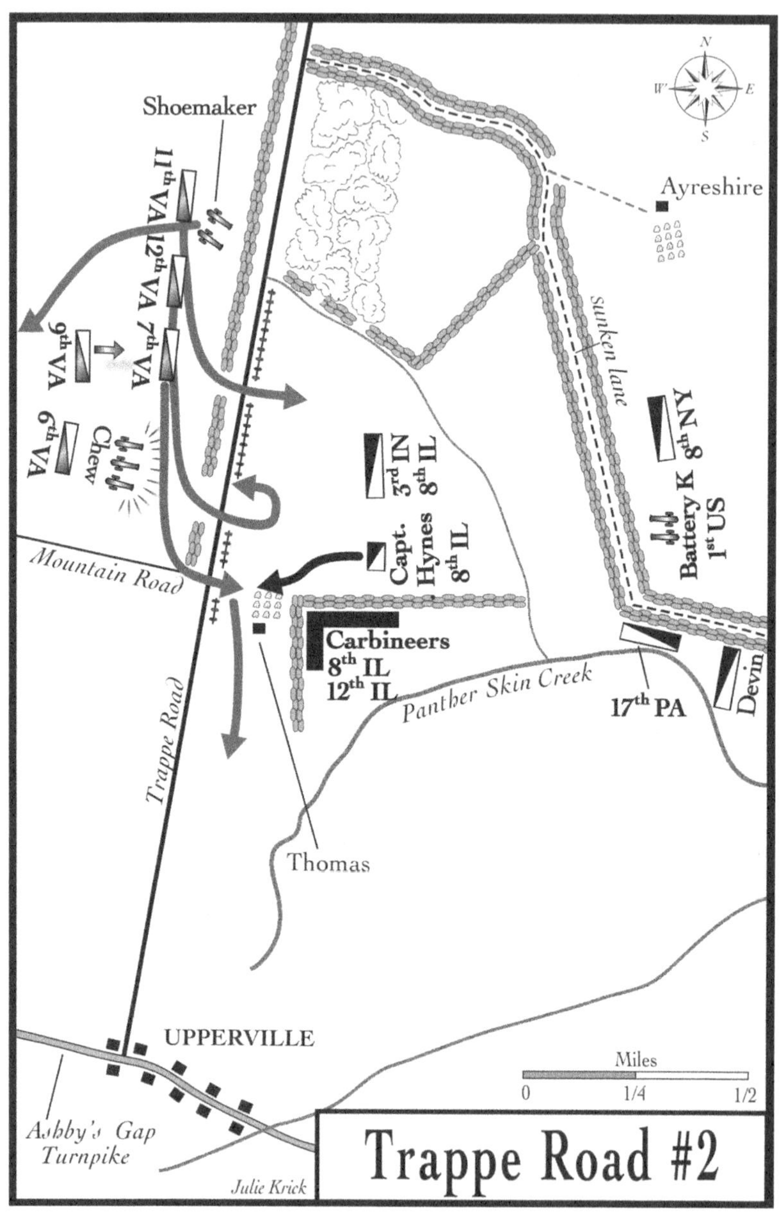

MAP 17. Trappe Road—phase 2. Created by Julie Krick.

into the breech to allow Chambliss to pull his men off the field and see them on their way to Ashby's Gap. Out of ammunition, Lieutenant Shoemaker also retired, following Chambliss onto Mountain Road and toward safety. Captain Chew stood by Jones, fighting his guns by sections, one covering the other as they slowly retired. With his men loading, sponging, and firing, Chew leapfrogged his two sections, retreating by recoil and manpower as he sought to keep his horses safely behind the guns. "This is undoubtedly the hardest place the battery has ever been in," a gunner declared hours later. "It seemed that the bullets flew at us from every direction, thick and fast," a battery-mate recalled. Chew maintained the fight to the very end, covering the withdrawal of each unit until the last man had reached safety.[24]

Buford and Gamble also enjoyed a good scrap, and they now looked to punish the Confederates before they could escape. The Eighth Illinois had earned a sterling reputation within the army, and few units fought with more determination or fervor. Now, with his men having caught their breath, Major Medill led the regiment, along with their comrades in the Twelfth Illinois and Third Indiana, back into the fray. As the men of the Seventh Virginia surged into Mr. Thomas's yard and orchard, seeking to drive the carbineers from the wall and open the road to Upperville, the troopers in the Eleventh Virginia spurred toward Medill and his oncoming Yankees. In seconds, the two lines collided with a tremendous shock.

For fifteen to twenty minutes the field, orchard, and yard rang with the crack of revolvers and carbines, the clash of steel against steel, the deep-throated roar of cannon, and the screams of angry and dying men. Clods of dirt pelted the combatants, adding to the stress and chaos each man must have experienced. Horses crashed together, crying in pain as they bit and kicked each other or fell from a shell burst or a bullet. To go down in the field meant grievous injury or death as hundreds of animals galloped back and forth, spurred on by their masters and their natural instincts to follow the herd. None of the combatants gave a thought to noting details for historians to glean decades later. Rather, each fought singular battles for survival. Shortly thereafter and with the fight still fresh in their minds, few could find words to describe the terrors and exhilaration of the hand-to-hand combat.[25]

One who tried, wrote, "Let your readers imagine if they can—[our] regiments . . . mingled promiscuously among [the] rebels, each fighting with the desperation of madmen. For fifteen minutes the roar of artillery, the whistling of shell, the buzz of grape and canister, the roar of small arms, and the fierce clash of the sabre, and the yells of the excited thousands—and then an idea of the excitement may be formed." Veterans believed the brief fight here to have been "far more severe and fierce than the fight at" Brandy Station.[26]

Charging ahead into the storm of fire, the Seventh Virginia, led by Lt. Col. Thomas Marshall, dashed into Mr. Thomas's front yard and orchard. Capt. Dennis Hynes, Eighth Illinois, alertly wheeled his squadron into the yard from the east and, after a sharp clash, parried Marshall's thrust and saved the Union position along the angle. Brothers William and Joseph Brent, Seventh Virginia, probably rode into the yard together. Within minutes, Joseph and his horse lay dead in the orchard. William's clothes and equipment had been pierced by several bullets. Three more struck his horse but the game mare brought him out of the maelstrom. Fighting nearby, Lieutenant Buck died from a bullet through the neck. One of the Virginians remembered the battle as "the hottest fighting I ever did, or ever expect to do," and he believed the slaughter of the horses was greater than in any battle of the kind during the war. Within minutes, Marshall and his men found themselves cut off from Trappe Road. Unable to rejoin the brigade, Marshall led his regiment off to the south, rejoining Stuart along the turnpike.[27]

The intense fighting in the open field was brief and disorganized. Units fought by squads and platoons rather than companies and squadrons. Bugles called the men to retreat, rally, and charge again. We relied upon "our revolvers and rebs on their swords," one of Medill's men recalled. "It was a tough fight" and "very exciting," he continued, "but a shot from a six-shooter, aimed by a Western man, is more than a match for a sword in the hands of the chivalry." To a Virginian watching from across Trappe Road, "the ground seemed to shake" as the lines crashed together. Then, as the "sabers flashed" and the revolvers cracked, the same observer noted, "they seemed to be killing each other very fast." A heavy slash from even a blunt saber could crush a bone, knock a weapon from an opponent's hand, or leave him concussed and reeling in the saddle. The power of the animals as they collided left the riders bruised and battered. Buford's men and horses had had little, if anything, to eat when they broke camp. Now the stress and adrenalin of battle, combined with the effort to control their frantic horses, wield their revolvers, seven-pound carbines, or heavy "wrist-breaker" sabers for minutes on end left the men exhausted. Adrenaline could only carry them so far. Constantly guiding their horses to one side and then the other as they dodged and parried with their opponents, the combatants soon became aware of a large body of gray-clad troopers entering the field from Trappe Road.[28]

Colonel John Chambliss had relied upon the Ninth Virginia throughout the day on June 19 at Middleburg, where their countercharges had repulsed every Union attack along the turnpike, and he had determined to hold them as a reserve again as the fighting developed along Trappe Road. Corralled by the fences as the fight had developed, the Southern commanders could not bring the full weight of their two brigades to bear as they would have wished, and so they had yielded the early advantages to their opponent. Still, as their men gained access through the fences, Chambliss and Jones continually brought fresh men into the fight while Colonel Gamble's men looked for help from Colonel Devin who had yet to reach the scene. Now, with most of the Southerners headed toward safety and with only the Eleventh Virginia and a small portion of the Seventh Virginia still fighting, Chambliss ordered the Ninth Virginia to close the affair.[29]

Colonel Beale's troopers had moved by detachments throughout the day, providing both advance and rearguard protection. Moments after the fighting erupted along Trappe Road, the main body of the regiment left the field, as Colonel Beale had, on his own accord, deemed "it useless to make a fight against such odds." Colonel Chambliss must have been furious as he sent a courier to recall the Virginians. Arriving with the fight still in the balance, Beale's men picked their way through the gaps along the road, and entered the fray "each man for himself," as one lieutenant recalled. Without taking time to reform, the men unsheathed their sabers, touched spurs to their horses' flanks and swept forward toward the melee in front of them.[30]

Exhausted, battered, and now outnumbered, the Yankees scattered as the Virginians sped toward them. Some of the blue-clad troopers fell back to the east, to the wall along Sunken Lane, others sought shelter with their comrades to the south, behind the wall near the Thomas house. A handful of men found themselves cut off from those positions and hastily retreated to a wall fronting the woods, near the northwest corner of the field. Rallying behind this wall, the men barely had time to catch their breath before some of the Virginians swarmed their barricade. The bravest Southerners spurred their horses over the wall and into the midst of the enemy, slashing their sabers left and right. Bleeding from gashes to his head and shoulder, one of the Yankees shot his assailant from his saddle before the Virginians retired.[31]

Some hand-to-hand fighting continued before concentrated Union fire and the arrival of fresh Union troops broke up the attack. Their countercharge lasted only moments, but the Virginians had gained time for their comrades to cross Trappe Road and join the caravan heading for Ashby's Gap. The assault had not been without a price, however, as nearly thirty men became casualties, including Lt. Col. Meriwether Lewis, who went down only a few feet from the angle with a bullet through a lung. Gazing at the bodies of men and animals scattered across the field, one of the Southerners wondered mournfully, "when shall this dreadful carnage cease?"[32]

The Yankees recovered the advantage when Colonel Devin arrived with his brigade and sent the Seventeenth Pennsylvania forward to aid Gamble's weary men. The Pennsylvanians swept through the Thomas orchard in a last effort to seize Chew's guns, but "the artillery fire was so hot" the Yankees quickly lost their enthusiasm and retired, having lost at least seven men to shell fire, including a lieutenant whose right leg was torn off below the knee.

Devin deployed the remainder of his brigade in the open field behind a heavy skirmish line from the Sixth New York. Moving slowly forward, but held at a distance by Chew's gunners, Devin settled for clearing the field and bringing in the wounded, rather than challenging Chew's heroic men. The Southern troopers had "in a measure retarded the federal advance," as one Confederate cavalryman explained, but "it was the well-served artillery that repulsed the enemy." As the guns fell silent along Trappe Road, the combatants would have heard the last shots of another desperate battle along the turnpike.[33]

TWENTY

In No Previous Collision Have They Manifested Such Implacable Hate, June 21

Crossing Goose Creek bridge, Gen. Alfred Pleasonton must have been vexed and frustrated. He had hoped to quickly overpower or drive the Southern cavalry from the Loudoun Valley, but even with all but one of his brigades at hand, and assisted by veteran infantry, he had been unsuccessful. Instead of a quick victory, his men had fought a series of tough skirmishes against a foe determined to hold them at bay for as long as possible. Riding up onto the ridge, which moments earlier had been crowned by Southern artillery, Pleasonton would have quickly grasped two critical points: his foe racing westward, and the sun dropping toward the crest of the Blue Ridge. He had been fighting for hours and had gained but six miles. With little daylight remaining, Ashby's Gap still taunted him ten miles to the west. At Pleasonton's urging, his men set off after the enemy at a run. One trooper said simply, "we just rushed them."[1]

The fighting along the turnpike throughout the morning and early afternoon reflected not the mobility and maneuver of traditional light cavalry but rather the tactical changes brought about by modern carbines and horse artillery. Cavalry could now fight as infantry to hold ground, and Gen. Jeb Stuart had directed his men to hold their ground as long as possible, while bloodying the enemy to the extent possible, before retreating and repeating the process from the next piece of advantageous terrain. But now, as Stuart's cavaliers fled westward with the Yankees in pursuit, horses, sabers, and revolvers in the hands of stouthearted men would determine the final clash of the day on the open plains around Upperville.

The long four mile run to the eastern edge of Upperville exhausted many horses, already worn down by the frenetic combat of the preceding hours and days. Regiments badly thinned during the fighting over the previous days now seemed to melt away as horses went lame or simply gave out at nearly every step along the rocky turnpike. Gen. Joseph Hooker's quartermaster had, the previous day, reported "huge" losses among Pleasonton's horses at Aldie and Middleburg. Then, alerting his superiors that Pleasonton planned to "engage Stuart's whole cavalry force" on the twenty-first, the officer had prophetically warned, "the loss of horses will be great." Aside from actual battle losses inflicted by bullets and shells, "the rough character of the roads . . . added to the casualties of every day's battle," as Stuart later explained. "In this way," he continued, "some regiments were reduced to less than 100 men."[2]

Remounts reached Washington almost daily, and quartermasters in Washington and Alexandria also began "stripping the teams and ambulances, putting mules and recuperating horses in their place" to make every healthy animal available for the cavalry. But the affected troopers had to go to Washington to obtain the remounts, and thus the ranks had grown ever thinner over the previous days. By the time Pleasonton's troopers approached the outskirts of Upperville, companies in some regiments resembled depleted platoons. In the morning, one squadron of the First Maine had but twenty-four men in the saddle. Another company, which numbered fifty men on the morning of June 17, counted a mere seven after today's fighting.[3]

Reining up along Vineyard Hill, a slight rise immediately east of town, Stuart's men had a few minutes to catch their breath and gulp some water from their canteens, while their lathered horses stood in formation heaving and quivering. Some of the riders almost certainly offered their horses water they had poured into their hats. Likewise, the blue-clad troopers halted once they came within sight of the Southern legions drawn up for battle.

From Oakley, her home nearly one mile southeast of Vineyard Hill, Ida Dulany soon heard the crack of carbines. Overcome by curiosity, she stepped out onto her balcony, noting the time as four o'clock. "I saw our men drawn up in line of battle . . . and the Yankees pouring in in every direction, up the turnpike, through our fields," and along the roads north of the pike. "Spell bound," she watched the battle unfold around her, while her family sheltered in the cellar. For the next half hour or so, she found herself in the cauldron of, arguably, the largest cavalry battle in Virginia to date. Across a field just two miles long, nine brigades of horsemen were about to clash in a brief but frenzied battle. As General Gregg later recalled, "The engagement at Upperville presented a very inspiring, spectacular effect. On two . . . roads, in view of each other, were two columns of our troops [John Buford's and his own] engaged in battle." A Georgian described the ground fronting Vineyard Hill as "admirably adapted for cavalry fighting," and no one had a better view than Mrs. Dulany.[4]

General Stuart still needed to hold the Federals out of Upperville until Colonel Chambliss and "Grumble" Jones safely extricated their men from the fighting along Trappe Road. Further, Stuart needed to ensure the safety of his own supply trains, which rumbled slowly toward Ashby's Gap. He also awaited word that General Longstreet's infantry had returned to their former positions along the Blue Ridge. But the men in the ranks knew little of these concerns. Rather, they knew they had been forced or ordered to retire from the battlefield at Mount Defiance on June 19, and from three successive positions this morning and early afternoon. These were men accustomed to seeing the backs of their enemies rather than showing their own backs to their blue-clad rivals. Tired, angry, and embarrassed, they may have understood they would soon retreat again, but they intended to exact a bloody toll first. Over the next few minutes, the fighting would be dramatic, mirroring the visually stunning paintings of mounted combat during the Napoleonic wars; boot-to-boot, saber-to-saber, and most importantly, man-to-man. For thirty minutes, the combatants cast chivalry aside and fought with a savagery seen on few other cavalry fields of the war.[5]

General Wade Hampton deployed his brigade along Vineyard Hill, the broad, flat ridge south of the turnpike. Sending a line of skirmishers forward, Hampton ordered the remainder of his men to take shelter in a woodlot on the southeast end of the ridge. A South Carolinian thought the general had looked "calm and composed" during the morning phase of the battle, but the fighting around Upperville brought forth the brawler in Hampton. His position included a high hedge of Osage Orange trees planted tightly together and enclosing an area of several acres immediately south of the pike, and with an opening on the eastern side.[6]

North Carolinians of General Beverly Robertson's brigade continued to defend the ground immediately north of the pike, with their left flank protected by Panther Skin Creek. Stuart's horse artillery, pounded throughout the day and with ammunition chests nearly empty, retired to Ashby's Gap. Stuart's troopers would continue this fight alone, which may have been just what they wanted.[7]

General Pleasonton had left his infantry behind but had no intention of leaving his artillery out of the coming fight. Four batteries, twenty-two guns, raced to keep up with Gregg's men in their hell-for-leather pursuit. As Hampton's men eagerly sought to close with their enemy and erase the stain of retreat, so Gregg's men sought to finish the job begun days earlier. They had their tormentors of the previous two years on the run, and they meant to keep them running.

General Judson Kilpatrick's battered brigade led the Union pursuit from Goose Creek. With two regiments, the First Massachusetts and First Rhode Island, out of the fight after their respective maulings at Aldie and Middleburg, Kilpatrick had only three understrength but game regiments in tow, the Second and Fourth New York and the Sixth Ohio. As his regimental commanders deployed their men, with the Sixth Ohio north of the turnpike, the Second New York along the road, and the Fourth New York south of the road, Kilpatrick may have met with Pleasonton and Gregg for a final hurried discussion. If so, they most likely did so near the intersection of the turnpike and the

Greengarden Road. The ridge crest just east of the intersection gave the men a clear view of the Southern line along Vineyard Hill, 750 yards to the west, and General Buford's men deploying for battle 1,250 yards to the north.

The three officers, Pleasonton, Gregg, and Kilpatrick, offered a striking contrast in appearance and personality. Always impeccably manicured and tailored, Pleasonton, like his two subordinates, was now bespattered with mud. Hard of hearing as the result of an exploding round at Antietam, the corps commander may have leaned from his saddle to hear the other two men over the growing tumult around them. With a wary eye cast toward the setting sun, Pleasonton may have slapped his ever-present riding whip against his hand or thrust it toward the mountains to emphasize his desire for speed. Gregg, tall, taciturn, and bearing a magnificent but now filthy beard, probably maintained his outwardly calm demeanor and may have puffed on his long-stemmed meerschaum pipe. By contrast, Kilpatrick may have been all nervous energy. He must have been especially weary but as the youngest of the three, he remained ever eager for battle. Remembered by one of his men for a "clarion voice" and his "indomitable will," as well as his "capacity for rallying his men and getting them into a charge," Kilpatrick may have been especially eager for the fight ahead. One can imagine one of his superiors reaching over and grabbing Kilpatrick's bridle or arm to keep him from bolting back into the fray before they finished issuing their instructions. He had already led at least one attack at Aldie and had a horse killed under him. In moments he would lead another.[8]

Kilpatrick moved his men off the ridge crest, across the Greengarden Road, and into the open fields. There, Maj. William Stedman deployed his Sixth Ohio, maybe 250 men strong, into "three columns with squadron front." The Second New York, advancing in the road and confined by walls on either side, presented a deep column of fours, while the twelve companies of the Fourth New York advanced in a single column of squadrons.[9]

Burdened by more than his share of critics during the war and today, Kilpatrick is often dismissed as a blundering fool: "Kill-Cavalry," rather than the "Old-Kil" fondly remembered by his men. But speaking of his tactical wisdom, one of his men said, "In preparation for, and during, a battle, none can excel him." Today, however, he had no time to examine the ground to his front. The young general knew Panther Skin Creek protected the right flank of his Buckeyes. His greatest concern lay with the Fourth New York. Battered at Aldie, the men had lost their inspirational leader, Colonel di Cesnola. They would also be presenting their left flank to General Hampton's veterans south of the road. Departing from his conference with Pleasonton and Gregg, Kilpatrick decided to lead the Fourth New York in person. But urged to move quickly by his superiors, he elected to attack before any of his supporting batteries had gone into position, and across a wide expanse of ground which appeared "favorable for a charge." He soon learned otherwise.[10]

As the officers finalized their plans, they saw help arriving. Earlier in the day, Gen. John Buford had detached Maj. Samuel Starr's Reserve Brigade, sending Starr across Goose Creek at Millville to aid Pleasonton. But Starr's regiments, the First, Second, Fifth, and Sixth U.S., were still in the fields north of the turnpike when Stuart elected to make his stand. Pleasonton sent a courier to hurry them along but, hemmed in by walls and fences, the brigade needed time to cross the pike and Pleasonton had run out of time. He would send Starr to assist Kilpatrick and hold Col. John Gregg's brigade in reserve, but for the moment, Kilpatrick was on his own.[11]

With only a few minutes to rest, Kilpatrick's horses may have just been recovering their wind after the long chase when he gave the order to advance. Writing three days later, the young general said simply, "I moved forward to the charge," but to have done so immediately across such a wide expanse of ground would have been foolhardy. Instead, he brought his men up from a walk to a trot, and then a canter or military gallop over the last fifty to sixty yards. As he closed the distance, he heard a loud cheer to his far right. Looking across the wide sweep of his brigade, he saw "Buford's people charging the enemy." Catching "the spirit that animated those brave men and with one wild hurrah!," Kilpatrick's Ohioans and New Yorkers "echoed back the shout and rushed upon the foe."[12]

The sight of two brigades of Union cavalry bearing down upon them unsettled General Robertson's Tar Heels. Tired and battered after several days of fighting, the Carolinians may not have recognized that Buford had not targeted them and could not reach them. Still, some of the Southerners began to break for the rear. Most of them held their positions behind a stone wall, however, and drove off at least one column of the Sixth Ohio with "murderous fire."[13]

Falling back, the Buckeyes on the right of the line reformed, sheathed their sabers, and loaded their carbines. Then, with the shouts of their officers carrying over the din of battle, they returned to the fight. On or near the turnpike, Capt. John Cryer pushed his squadron past the wall that had brought his comrades to a halt. Now, believing themselves flanked on both sides, the last of the Carolinians broke and ran for their horses. Watching them flee, Cryer pushed on, supporting the New Yorkers along the turnpike. Leaving the men on the far right to hold the wall as a rally point, Major Stedman allowed the Ohioans in the center column a few minutes to catch their breath.[14]

Realizing the fortunes of war might not favor his men this day, Stuart had previously told Hampton to fight his brigade as he saw fit, while he stayed with Robertson. If he had hoped to bolster the morale of the Carolinians, he had not succeeded. Hampton, who later disparaged Stuart's leadership, saying he "managed badly that day," credited his own men with salvaging "the blunders and disasters," for which he held Stuart responsible. Hampton would, in moments, lead a furious counterattack staving off a complete collapse but not before the men of his Second South Carolina found themselves caught up in Robertson's retreat.[15]

Thomas Jefferson Lipscomb, remembered as "a knightly and cultured gentleman," had served South Carolina in the opening days of the war as an infantryman, before raising a cavalry company and receiving a commission with the Second South Carolina. Promoted to lieutenant colonel for gallantry at Brandy Station, Lipscomb now found himself in a maelstrom as he anchored Hampton's left flank along the turnpike. Even as the men of the Second New York and Sixth Ohio rushed toward his line,

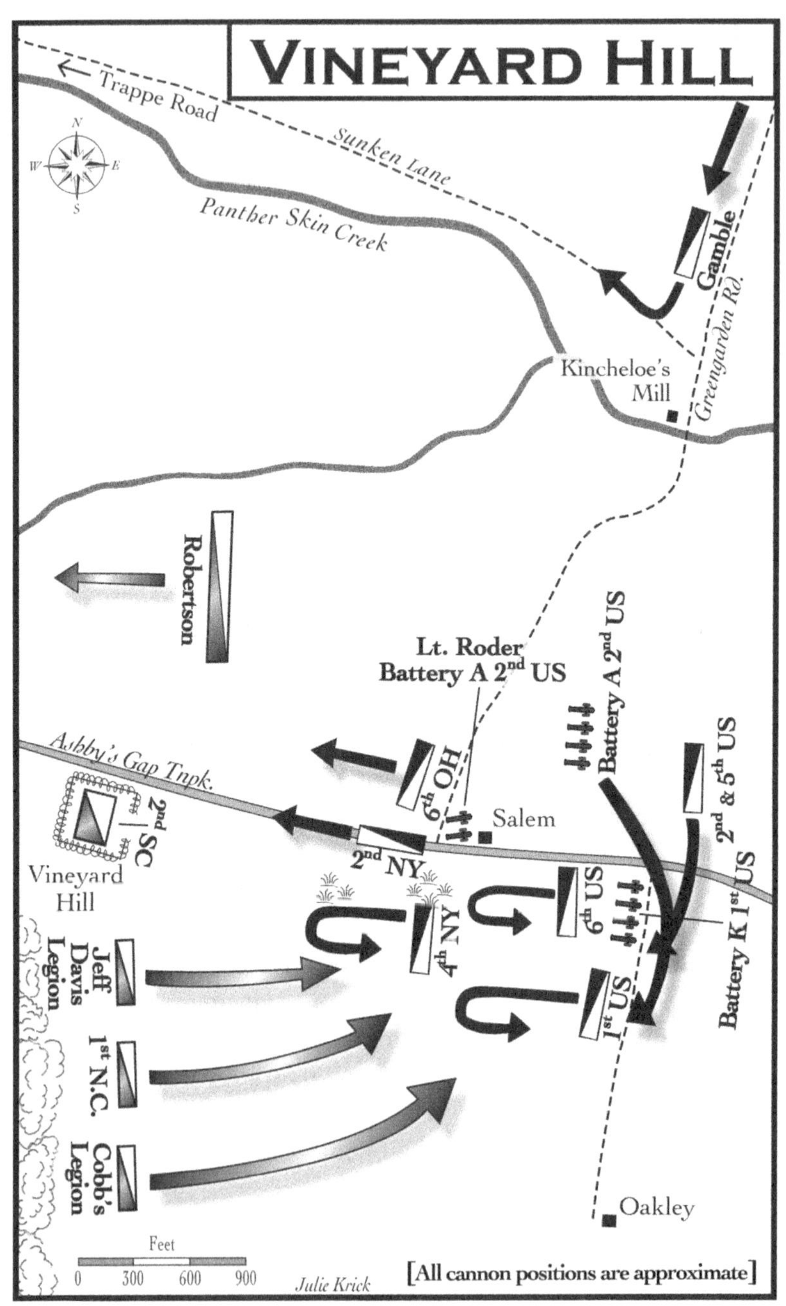

MAP 18. Vineyard Hill. Created by Julie Krick.

Robertson's horse-holders also ran toward his line with their horses in tow. As the remainder of the North Carolinians ran back from the skirmish line, many of the horses panicked, broke free, and bolted through Lipscomb's men.[16]

Pressing forward through the confused mass of men and horses, Lipscomb saw Stuart dashing about, gathering up several of the stray animals and saving them from capture. Stuart "sat his horse as if he were a part of him," an admiring trooper recalled. With the crisis of the day at hand, another observer thought the general "fought with the men like a common soldier." According to his adjutant, Maj. Henry B. McClellan, Stuart had "personally participated in [the battle] but little," until the fighting reached the outskirts of Upperville, though he had remained "in close observation of the field." When McClellan queried Stuart, the general replied, "that he had given all necessary instructions to his brigade commanders, and he wished them to feel the responsibility resting upon them, and to gain whatever honor the field might bring." But now, with success in the balance, Stuart again took command of his division.[17]

In the moment of crisis, Mother Nature came to Stuart's aid. The low ground in front of Vineyard Hill was especially soft and boggy. Likewise, the heavy rain of previous days had also turned the ground north of the road to mire. Just as the Federals drove home their attack, their horses, especially those near the pike, began sinking into the muck and lost momentum. Some horses panicked, throwing their riders as they struggled to free themselves. With the integrity of the Union attack disintegrating, and with the men near the road under fire from Lipscomb's men around the hedges on Vineyard Hill, the Second New York and elements of the Fourth New York retired. Only a couple companies from the Fourth New York on the extreme left of the line pressed the attack.[18]

Watching as the Union attacked broke down, Wade Hampton launched his counterattack from the nearby woods, sending Lt. Col. J. Fred Waring's Jeff Davis Legion against the New Yorkers. The legion, about three hundred strong, had been shifting positions along Hampton's line when he sent them into the fight.

Without taking time to reform, they turned and dashed forward. A stone wall, however, prevented some of them from coming to grips with the enemy. Sheathing their sabers, these men opened fire with their revolvers, even as their comrades sprinted around the wall and collided with the Federals. The Rebels quickly captured a handful of Yankees, while their comrades retired to reform and shake off the shock of the attack.[19]

Capt. Nehemiah Mann, a six-foot-tall Quaker, had deployed three platoons as skirmishers in front of his squadron. Just as Mann's fifty Federals approached the woods, Waring's Southerners bolted from the trees. The Southern charge, which carried across the Union line and toward the turnpike, swept Mann's skirmishers aside. One of the captain's subordinates recalled seeing Kilpatrick racing across the line to rally his men near the road. The general may have thought he could outrace the enemy, instead, the gray tide engulfed him.[20]

Watching as the Southerners hustled Kilpatrick off to captivity, Mann bellowed, "Men, are you heroes or are you cowards? Follow me—Charge!" Spurring his horse, Mann never doubted his men and never looked back. His troopers hesitated, however. Kilpatrick had precipitated their colonel's arrest four days earlier, and now a question must have flashed through their minds: did they want to risk their lives for the general? Seconds later, they responded. They admired and loved Captain Mann as they admired and loved Colonel di Cesnola. Spurring ahead with a shout, they raced after their captain.[21]

As Mann's counterattack unfolded, Hampton and Pleasonton continued to feed fresh regiments into the fight. Attacks and counterattacks rippled across the field, as regiments crashed into each other in a confusing fury. Horses stumbled in the mire and struggled to regain their feet; some crashed down from a bullet never to rise, others were bowled over in violent collisions. Men fell at every turn, stabbed, shot, or crushed under their steeds. Transfixed on her balcony, Ida Dulany's "blood turned cold" as she watched a horse "gallop by dragging a dead man behind him." Chronicling the events around her, she noted Yankees falling back and then advancing. Soon, even with her near–God's eye view, she lost track as the action unfolded too quickly. In fifteen minutes, the Jeff Davis Legion alone made at least four and possibly five charges against several enemy regiments, and it was into this frenzy of battle that Captain Mann now raced.[22]

The story of Captain Mann's courage soon spread across the country, one newspaper at a time. His men "could not hesitate at such a brave sight," an admiring reporter declared. "With but one impulse [they] shouted and followed their leader—too late to save him, for his ardor had given him a considerable start; but they broke through, rode over, and cut down the rebel ranks." The men succeeded in freeing Kilpatrick, but Mann had been sabered across his right cheek just as a bullet killed his horse. As he lay pinned on the ground, an enemy trooper rode by and shot him in the back. Days later, a reporter spoke with Mann in a hospital. The scribe sought to reconcile the officer's gentle Quaker faith with his ferocity on the battlefield. "No one would suppose, to hear them conversing in the soft 'thee and thou' language," the correspondent explained, "that there is underneath such a noble, fearless and resolute military spirit." Appalled that Mann had been shot in the back while helpless, another reporter declared, "in no previous collision have [the enemy] manifested such implacable hate." One of the captain's men later vowed, "I would give more for Captain Mann, commanding a brigade, than any general I have seen—except, perhaps, Kilpatrick, who frequently charges with the boys of our regiment."[23]

Major Samuel Starr's Reserve Brigade counted about 825 men in the saddle. Starr, a tyrannical officer, with three decades of service, had replaced Maj. Charles Whiting only hours earlier. The instability in command, as well as Starr's lack of experience in the cavalry, convinced General Pleasonton to take control of the brigade once the men reached the turnpike. As Kilpatrick had readied his men for their initial attack, Pleasonton sent Starr south of the road. Starr had held the men in column of squadrons north of the road. Passing through the narrow gaps in the walls forced the men back into column. Entering the fields south of the road, the regiments again sought to form column of squadrons, but with Kilpatrick's attack faltering, Pleasonton urged Starr to attack immediately. Seeking to comply, the First and Sixth U.S. formed "as well as time allowed . . . and the circumstances and ground would permit." The men of the Sixth U.S. attacked just south of the turnpike, even as the First U.S. moved behind them and to their left flank.[24]

The Regulars, backed by decades of tradition, discipline, and battlefield experience, had, for two years mocked and ridiculed the sloppy volunteers on the drill field. The disdain led to a rivalry between the veterans and volunteers. But now, only a scattering of grizzled old soldiers remained in the ranks, and but few officers. Captains, rather than colonels, headed the regiments, and a major, rather than a colonel or a brigadier, commanded the brigade. The Sixth U.S. had been raised in 1861 and had no more tradition or experience than any of the volunteer regiments. The men may have endured harsher discipline than volunteers, but a question lingered: could discipline compensate for a lack of leadership in the crucible of combat? The men were about to find out, and they would do so under the scrutiny of the volunteers.

Capt. George Cram had been an attorney at the outset of the war, before securing a captain's commission in the Sixth U.S. By December 1862 he found himself commanding the regiment as the senior officer present; a few months later, he was commanding the brigade, even though in the opinion of some of his men he could not "command a corporal's guard." In the short time they served together, Major Starr hounded and humiliated Cram at every turn. The captain, who seemed to wilt under Starr's gaze, now found himself leading his regiment into battle at the head of the brigade and under the eye of his tormentor.[25]

From a position just west of the entrance to Oakley farm, Cram ordered his men forward, but with Pleasonton and Gregg urging speed and Starr possibly shouting imprecations after him, Cram brought his men to the charge too soon. Almost before they started, the horses ran into the boggy ground that had disrupted Kilpatrick's attack. The men struggled to cross ditches and find their way through fences. Before they met the enemy, the horses had exhausted themselves and the men had lost the integrity of their formations. Now, standing nearly still, and with their animals heaving as they struggled to regain their wind and extricate themselves from the muck, the men saw the Confederates emerge from the hedge in front of them.[26]

One of the Yankees admitted firing just "two shots" before fleeing the Southern counterattack. Most of his comrades followed suit. On this day "of peculiar misfortunes," a dispirited trooper concluded, the regiment accomplished little. "With pistol and sabre," a lieutenant recalled, the enemy "drove us back probably in greater disorder than we charged them." Hemmed in by fences, the men had few choices as they sought to flee the "cloud of yelling gray wolves" rushing toward them. Cram ordered the men to wheel around to the south to escape the counterattack. In doing so they left the First U.S. entirely exposed to the enemy and may have disrupted the regiment's cohesion in the process.[27]

Moving forward a few moments after Cram, Capt. Richard Lord's First U.S. had not reached the slope when the Southern counterattack engulfed them. Neither Lord's years on the plain at West Point nor his experience in the antebellum army made any difference as he and his men immediately found themselves in a brutal fight for their lives. Lord may have tried to wheel his regiment to meet the Southern attack head on, but he had no time to complete the maneuver. Even if he had, the effort would have been for naught as Hampton threw the First North Carolina against Lord's left flank. And Hampton, never one to miss a brawl, went into the fight shouting "First North Carolina, follow me!" A trooper in the ranks recalled hearing the general yelling, "*Charge them my brave boys, charge them!*" Though slowed by the soft ground, the Tar Heels went at them with slashing sabers and screeching the Rebel Yell. The Yankees "met us briefly with his pistols popping like a fired canebreak," one explained, "but a few well plied surges of the keen blade soon told who were master of the field." Within moments, Yankees began rolling "from their horses, either from a blow inflicted or to save themselves of a descending one."[28]

Hitting Lord's ranks from several directions, the Southerners carved the Union regiment up like a pie, leaving the men in each slice fighting for their own survival and unable to aid others. The

Confederates swallowed up dozens of prisoners so quickly that the men remained unaccounted for days later. Even those who ended up in Union hospitals remained on the rolls as missing in action. For the next few minutes, experience meant nothing in the face of overwhelming numbers. A veteran, who bore a scar from an Indian arrow, took a bullet in his elbow just as another bullet sent his horse crashing to the ground. The violent fall broke two of the man's ribs. A recruit with just five months in the ranks found himself outmatched in a saber duel. Sustaining four wounds to his head, including one that opened his skull to his brain, the young man may have been nearly unconscious and struggling to stay in the saddle when another soldier punched his saber through his back and right lung. As he fell to the ground, his enemies left him, thinking his wounds must be fatal.[29]

A member of the Jeff Davis Legion watched two of his comrades run their sabers through their opponents. "In each instance," the soldier recalled, "the impetus of the men in swift charge drove their sabres *to the hilt* into and through his opponent, and as their steeds flashed past each other . . . each of these troopers was *hurled out of his saddle* upon the field." When another trooper appeared to be cut off by a sea of blue, he spurred his horse toward a narrow opening, defying cries to "Cut him down!" When a Yankee moved to block his path, the Southerner spurred his horse a final time, striking his opponent's horse on the shoulder and knocking horse and rider to the ground. Entangled in the same melee, a Union officer saw one of his men running his horse toward an enemy trooper. As they came together they fatally impaled each other with their sabers. He also recalled several gray-clad cavaliers rallying amid a sea of blue and noted wryly, "This shows how greatly excited men get in such a charge."[30]

Whereas all the wounds sustained by men of the Sixth U.S. had been from bullets, fired at a distance, the men of the First U.S. found themselves in a back-alley brawl, fighting with revolvers and sabers, up close and personal. As one Southerner concluded with a hint of pride, "There were more gory sabres on exhibition that afternoon in Hampton's brigade than [he] had seen before." A North Carolinian termed the combat "desperate."[31]

The men of the First U.S. found themselves fighting for their lives mere moments after General Kilpatrick launched his initial attack. The scope of the battlefield had grown and become ever more crowded. Kilpatrick's New Yorkers lingered on the field and Pleasonton started to send Cram's men back into the fight before changing his mind. The Union horse artillery had now entered the contest, with three batteries opening on the Southern lines from several locations near Greengarden Road. Deploying, in some cases, by two-gun sections, the battery commanders leap-frogged their guns ever nearer to the enemy positions. The Second and Fifth U.S. had also moved into the fields between Oakley and Vineyard Hill, protecting the guns and prepared to enter the fight, before Pleasonton decided to hold them back as a strong reserve.[32]

Before Captain Lord's men could extricate themselves, and as the First North Carolina fell back to reform, Lt. Col. William Deloney led Cobb's Legion into the fight. Doing so maintained the pressure on the wavering Yankees and persuaded the North Carolinians to launch another counterattack. With more Confederates pouring into the field, the Fourth New York also reentered the contest. Capt. William Parnell, an Irishman who had survived the Charge of the Light Brigade at Balaklava, led the New Yorkers against the men of the Jeff Davis and Cobb Legions. Moments later, Parnell took a bullet in his left hip, just before he received "several severe blows and cuts about the head, from sabres, and the butt of a carbine." Another bullet killed his horse and Parnell fell into Southern hands.[33]

Riding back and forth along Vineyard Hill, Stuart made a conspicuous target. He might have directed the battle from the relative safety of the Osage Orange hedge, but regardless of how one viewed his foppery, no one questioned his courage and magnetic personality. He had been the target of Yankee carbineers at Mount Defiance two days earlier and now found himself a target again. "The First Dragoons tried very hard to kill me," he later told his wife. "Four officers fired deliberately at me with their pistols several times while I was putting a Regiment at them which routed them." The nature and location of the fight involving the First U.S. militates against them being involved, but men from any of several regiments could have targeted Stuart.[34]

Once the Union guns began pounding his line, Stuart determined to leave. Upperville had been his last line of defense before he reached the mountains, but he knew now that Chambliss and Jones had escaped potential disaster on Trappe Road, that Major von Borcke had been moved to safety, and that Longstreet's infantry and artillery held Ashby's Gap. Hampton's brigade had bloodied two Union brigades but there was no longer a need to prolong the struggle. General Robertson had reformed his North Carolinians near Trappe Road to block any pursuit through the town, which allowed Hampton to disengage. As quickly as he could pull his men off the field, Hampton ordered them to retire by swinging around Upperville to the south and west. With the carbineers of the Second South Carolina serving as a rearguard, Hampton reformed his ranks and stubbornly retired at a walk. With Union artillery raking them "with a most galling fire," as one Southerner recalled, "our commands were withdrawn in good order." Attesting to the grim nature of the fight, another trooper concluded, "Old Father Time has been very industrious with his sickle." Even as Hampton retired, the guns did not fall silent, and Father Time continued to swing his sickle.[35]

Ashby's Gap still mocked Pleasonton. Though now just a few miles from the gap, the general saw his opportunity slipping away. He did not give up, however, and as soon as he saw Hampton withdrawing, he ordered his officers to redouble their efforts. General Kilpatrick immediately threw the men from the Second New York and Sixth Ohio into another attack along the turnpike, while the Fourth New York reformed in the bloody field to the south.[36]

With their ranks already thinned by the previous fighting, and with their horses hungry, thirsty, exhausted, and lame, "Old Kil's" men made another valiant, though ultimately futile effort. "Wild with enthusiasm," according to an Ohioan, the men surged ahead "not only in regiments and squadrons, but even in squads of eight or ten." The men of the Sixth Ohio had been watering their horses from a branch of Panther Skin Creek when Kilpatrick brought orders to clear the Southern rearguard from town. Capt. Delos

Northway immediately turned his squadron into the road and spurred toward the gray wall blocking the pike. The Southerners wavered briefly, before realizing Northway had only twenty men in his lead company. Regrouping, the Confederates "poured a perfect hail storm of bullets into my little band," Northway recalled. The men collided near today's Ivy Hill cemetery, where "there was the sharpest work it has ever been my fortune to know," the captain explained. Or, as another officer described tersely, "a good deal occurred in just a few seconds."[37]

At the head of his small column, Northway spurred his horse at the last second, opening a slight gap between himself and the sergeant to his right. Standing in his stirrups for added leverage, Northway delivered a backhand horizontal slash against the nearest Rebel in his path and nearly injured his sergeant in the process. The reprieve mattered little as the sergeant tumbled unconscious from his horse with a saber wound to his head seconds later. Then Northway received a slash across his face and chest. A man riding nearby cut down the captain's assailant but was shot in the process. Another man took a bullet in the face. Stunned and unable to see, the trooper lost his reins and called for a comrade to guide him from the melee. Unsupported and with his men falling all around him, Northway had no choice but to retire.[38]

Most of the Buckeyes fell back, convinced Kilpatrick had failed to provide the support he had promised. However, a sergeant later recalled Lt. George Custer riding up to his company commander and ordering him to support Northway's attack. A second veteran confirmed Custer's involvement and credited Custer with leading the effort but stated Northway had already retired. Custer may have led three charges into the town. The Buckeyes relied upon their sabers in their first assault but found themselves outmanned and outgunned. Reforming and drawing their revolvers, the men went back into the town. Before withdrawing the final time, both officers in one company had been shot and several other men had sustained saber wounds. The relentless tenacity and savagery of the Southern resistance continued to frustrate Pleasonton, but the gallantry and doggedness of the Buckeyes bought time for fresh regiments to arrive.[39]

Col. John Irvin Gregg's brigade had served as a ready reserve throughout the day and now waited near Greengarden Road. From here, the troopers supported Lt. John Roder's section of Lt. John Calef's Battery A, Second U.S. Artillery, firing from a position just north of the turnpike at Salem farm. The proximity of Gregg's brigade now brought them under Kilpatrick's eye as he looked for a fresh regiment to throw into the fight. As at Aldie, "Old-Kil's" brigade had fought to the point of exhaustion; a fresh regiment might just turn the tide of battle again. Talking with Pleasonton, Kilpatrick reportedly exclaimed, "If I had the First Maine, they would go through." Moments later, a courier carried a message to Col. Charles Smith, ordering him to bring his regiment forward.[40]

As his men filed into the road, Smith rode over to the cluster of senior officers. "Charge the town, drive out the enemy, and if possible get beyond," one of the generals instructed. Then, with his blood still up, and the excitement of battle etched across his face, Kilpatrick exclaimed, "That First Maine would charge straight into H-ll if they were ordered to." Examining the road ahead, lined by fences and walls, and now littered with the detritus of battle, Smith called for Capt. George Brown and ordered him to form his two companies into sections of eight. Kilpatrick then rode up, telling Brown "to go through this town and drive those fellows out." A musician before the war, Brown had earned a reputation as a singer of some ability, and Kilpatrick, recognizing the hard work ahead, asked the captain if he had a song to sing. Then, with his colonel riding alongside, the men moved forward at a trot. If Brown was of a mind to sing, the enemy never gave him a chance.[41]

When the Carolinians in Stuart's rearguard fell back deeper into the town, they lost their peripheral view of the battlefield. Moments later, the New Englanders entered the town and filled the Southerner's narrow field of vision. Still, the Confederates remained game and eager for battle, as they knew they had an ace up their sleeve. From a hiding spot somewhere in Upperville, the Rebels had wheeled a small howitzer into the middle of the road and rammed home a shell. As the Yankees bore down on them and the Southerners heard Smith call for his men to charge, the soldiers in front of the gun spurred their horses off to either side. The gunner yanked the lanyard just as the lucky Yankees cleared the muzzle. Unfortunately for the Confederates, the round sailed harmlessly over Smith's onrushing troopers.[42]

In the narrow road, at least one man could not avoid the gun and spurred his horse over the obstacle, as his comrades swept around the piece. Pushing deeper into the town, and with no room to maneuver, the blue column became ever more compact as they pursued the Carolinians. Emerging into the open country west of town brought no immediate relief, however, as high walls and fences continued to inhibit their ability to maneuver. And here, near Trappe Road, the Carolinians made their stand.[43]

General Stuart said little in his campaign report regarding the actions of Beverly Robertson and his Tar Heels at Upperville, and one can rightly wonder if words had passed between them after Robertson's hasty departure from the Vineyard Hill line moments earlier. But with Robertson's two regiments now serving as Stuart's rearguard, they needed to stand and fight until Hampton cleared the battlefield. In this moment, Stuart must have pushed aside his disdain for the man and offered some words of encouragement. Likewise, Robertson knew he would be fighting under Stuart's critical eye, and Robertson meant to keep his men to their task; they would stand and fight.[44]

A planter and an attorney in Camden County, North Carolina, before the war, Col. Dennis Ferebee organized the Fourth North Carolina Cavalry in August 1862. Remembered for his "prudence, coolness, and bravery," Ferebee, like Robertson, must have burned to redeem the honor of his regiment as he watched the Yankees pour through the western end of town. With some of his men deployed in the fields as carbineers, Ferebee sent his mounted contingent up the turnpike by squadrons to blunt the Union advance. According to one of his men, the Carolinians "made several desperate charges." Some of these attacks were made by men in the fields alongside the road, firing into the flanks of the Union column.[45]

In the narrow road, confined by the fences, the fighting became especially confusing. Both sides had trouble relieving their lead squadrons and moving up fresh troops. As the Northerners turned to retire, the men fired a volley from their revolvers to briefly hold the enemy at bay, allowing another squadron to move up and relieve them. Captain Brown had wisely ordered some of his men out of the road and into the fields as soon as they found an opening, and Maj. Stephen Boothby followed suit with the reserve. The battle continued in this manner for several minutes, with the men in the fields countercharging toward the road to strike their opponents in their flanks. Many men fell prisoner due to the inability of their jaded horses to maintain the punishing pace. Others were injured trying to leap their animals over the walls. A horse in Brown's company took a bullet in the neck just as his rider urged him over the wall. Rather than clearing the obstacle, the horse collapsed, crushing the trooper's shoulder and thigh.[46]

Within minutes the fighting spread across the road and the open fields and became another bloody melee in which there was no front or rear. When one of the Southerners punched his saber through the back of one the Mainers, the injured man turned and killed his assailant with his carbine. Another New Englander was leading several prisoners off the field when a Tar Heel sabered him through the back near the spine. Called upon to surrender, even as his opponent's saber protruded from his abdomen, the gravely wounded man knocked the Rebel from the saddle with his own sword. A Union captain, still recovering from wounds received at Brandy Station, found himself in a saber fight in which he sustained multiple wounds to his right arm and hand. Adrenaline only carried the men so far, however, and such fighting could not be maintained for long. As Colonel Smith ordered his men out of the fight, Pleasonton and Gregg fed in another fresh regiment.[47]

Moving through the town, Lt. Col. William Doster and the men of his Fourth Pennsylvania found the fight at a momentary standstill, with the Mainers glaring across the fields at the Tar Heels. Doster believed the enemy was preparing to make another attack and Robertson did not disappoint him. As Colonel Smith's men cleared the road, Doster brought up his lead battalion, spreading them across the road and nearby fields. Checking their carbines, the Pennsylvanians braced for the attack. Once Robertson unleashed his men, the Yankees from both regiments opened fire. The concentrated volleys broke the momentum of the attack and forced the Confederates to retire. Not wishing to allow the enemy to reform, Doster ordered an immediate countercharge, and again, the fighting became hand-to-hand. The combat carried the Pennsylvanians away from their supports, however, and Doster quickly pulled his men into the fields alongside the road. When a Southern squadron countercharged the men remaining in the road, the troopers in the fields wheeled and fired a devastating volley into their flanks.[48]

The Tar Heels now found themselves in a desperate position, caught between two enemy forces and cut off from their support. The bitter fighting continued as the Confederates tried to bull their way toward help. Without time to replace an empty carbine with a revolver or a saber, the men grappled with each other, trying to pull their opponent off their steeds. In some cases, the men fought across an intervening fence or wall. Lt. Colonel Doster remembered a moment of panic in his ranks as Southerners seemed to gain the upper hand. For a few seconds, the colonel found himself a prisoner before a quick saber thrust dropped his captor in the road and Doster raced back to his own men. As the two sides again separated, the colonel glanced behind him and saw one of his men standing defiantly in the road.[49]

Pvt. Wilson Vanatta enlisted in August 1861. Captured on the Peninsula almost exactly one year later, Vanatta rejoined his comrades in November 1862. Now, in the few moments the Fourth Pennsylvania had been engaged, Vanatta had "captured three prisoners and several horses, [and] helped to rally a small party of the First Maine," as well as men from his own regiment. Then, as his comrades fell back to regroup, Vanatta sat his horse in the road with his eyes toward the enemy. A few hundred yards to the west another man glared back just as defiantly.[50]

A wealthy plantation owner in Craven County, North Carolina, Peter Evans had paid to outfit his own cavalry company in October 1861. Six months later, enemy soldiers occupied his home and established a camp for escaped slaves on his property. Enraged,

Evans began terrorizing Union sympathizers across eastern North Carolina, before receiving a commission as colonel of the Fifth North Carolina. Now, as the fighting again settled into a momentary lull, Evans looked up the road toward the enemy he despised. He had run all day. Now he intended to fight.[51]

General Robertson must have known the fire that burned in Evans, but he also knew that Wade Hampton's brigade had now reached the turnpike. There was no longer a need to continue the bloodshed. Evans, however, looked at the situation as a regimental commander, whose home lay in Yankee hands. And, as Jeb Stuart's adjutant speculated, Evans may have sought to "atone for" the disgraceful retreat of his regiment from Vineyard Hill. Whatever his reason, Evans, on his own account, yelled, "Now, men, I want you to understand that I am going through!" Then, without hesitating or looking back, he spurred his horse up the turnpike toward the men from Pennsylvania and Maine. The troopers in Evans's lead company kicked their horses into a gallop behind him. Robertson yelled for the men to halt but if any of them heard, they ignored him. The remainder of the regiment obeyed the order and held their positions. Evans and the small group of men behind him were on their own.[52]

Across the way, the Yankees could see and hear Evans shout his intent but did not hear Robertson countermand the colonel. A lieutenant from the First Maine stood in the field north of the pike and watched as Evans "dashed for our line. His hat was blown off as he rushed down the pike, and his long gray locks were soon flying as he passed near where I was standing," the officer recalled. Misreading the situation, the lieutenant admired Evans's gallantry, while denigrating the "poltroons" who failed to support him. Admiration aside, Evans had reignited the battle and the Federals responded by pouring back into the road and surrounding the Tar Heels.[53]

One of the Pennsylvanians heard Evans shouting for his men to show no quarter. "Men never fought with more desperation than the rebels when they charged. They were fiends, not men," the soldier declared. Evans went down with a mortal bullet wound, and Doster credited Private Vanatta with firing the fatal shot.

According to Doster, Vanatta "charged the head of the advancing column, killing their leader and checking their furious assault." Then Vanatta, whom Doster later termed "the bravest of the brave," went down with a bullet in his right knee.[54]

The last half hour had seen near unrelenting combat, hand-to-hand like few infantrymen ever experienced. The guns fell silent only after the last of Evans's men became incapacitated or surrendered. The final struggle could not have lasted more than a few minutes. A few hundred yards to the west, General Robertson turned his men away from the bloody fields of Upperville and headed them to Ashby's Gap. The day had been trying. The fighting had lasted nearly ten hours and the Southern cavaliers had been driven ten miles. Few, if any, of the men had experienced such a day and it gnawed at them as they fell back to the infantry waiting along the mountains.

In time the Federals would remember the battle with pride but as they watched the Southerners retire, they were simply tired, hungry, and thirsty. Pleasonton ordered them to pursue but enemy artillery kept them at bay and convinced the general to turn back. Possession of the battlefield meant the victors had wounded men, blue and gray alike, to move to hospitals and dead to bury. They had a long night ahead. "Dead horses lay thick along the road," a Mainer observed, and solitary gunshots must have startled the men from time to time as a trooper put another wounded animal out of its misery. Riding back to camp, Lt. Colonel Doster surveyed the battlefield in the fading light and contemplated "the heaps of dead blue and gray." He watched as his surgeon examined the bodies in the fields west of town. The doctor found no one alive, as the constant charging through the fields "gave even the slightly wounded no chance for life." Pondering the events of the day, Doster's mind wandered back to the thrilling fictions and poems of his youth, of knights and chivalry, but now he saw only the grim reality. Years later, his memories of the day still haunted him. "How hard it seems for us strangers to kill these young men in sight of the cottages where some of them were raised," he wrote. He then concluded, "Thus passes a Sunday in war."[55]

TWENTY-ONE

A Horrid Looking Sight, June 21

General Gregg described the enemy's retreat from Upperville as "disorderly," and with Ashby's Gap now tantalizingly close, he and General Pleasonton urged their men to pursue. Hoping one final effort might push General Stuart through the gap, Pleasonton sent the Reserve Brigade forward alongside Gregg's troopers. They advanced gamely, until Southern guns began shelling them from the heights ahead. Reality took hold quickly as the shells began exploding overhead. "It now being very late in the evening," one officer explained, "and our object being accomplished, we halted under the fire of their guns . . . and made arrangements for the night." To stay in such a precarious position would have been foolish, however, and Pleasonton soon ordered his men back to Upperville.[1]

A certain euphoria must have seized the Yankees, as they had never seen Stuart's cavalry run in such a manner before. "The battle of Brandy Station had demonstrated to the men their superior strength," General Gregg asserted, but still, it had been the Federals who had eventually retired. Now, having pushed the Confederates all day, Pleasonton's men "felt they had but to encounter the enemy to defeat him." A correspondent spoke of the men as having delivered another of "Pleasonton's Poundings." Another termed the affair as "the greatest cavalry fight . . . that has yet taken place." But the thrill of victory could only carry the men so far. Tired, hungry, and riding horses ready to drop from exhaustion, the troopers found their elation soon vanished. Many of the men had endured "the most desperate fighting" they had ever experienced, and many had done so on empty stomachs. Once they had moved beyond the range of the Southern guns, the men wearily replenished their ammunition, watered and fed their horses, boiled coffee, and ate what remained in their haversacks. Others helped themselves to whatever food or livestock they could find on nearby farms.[2]

Writing of the day's events, some men boasted of personal exploits, while others sought meaning and solace as they mourned lost friends. "You ought to have seen us run them," one exclaimed. A trooper from the Twelfth Illinois concluded, "We can whip the Rebs anytime." A loyal Virginian bragged, "We scattered the rebels like sheep." Years later, a Pennsylvanian still remembered the "determined and persistent courage" displayed by his comrades.[3]

Even infantryman who had long denounced the contributions of the cavalry came away impressed. An officer in the Twentieth Maine regretted that he had not seen the fighting at Vineyard Hill, as those who did thought it "grand." One termed the cavalry charges "magnificent," another "glorious." An artilleryman who had witnessed the late-afternoon fighting explained, "They charge first by firing from the carbine, then out with the pistol and saber, and then comes the tug of war, but the Rebs can't stand cold steel . . . All honor to our cavalry."[4]

Along the slopes of the Blue Ridge, the troopers in gray and butternut spent a cool, wet night, as showers moved across the area. They had little to brag about, having, at least for the moment, lost their swagger. Some thought "Grumble" Jones had mismanaged his brigade along Trappe Road. North Carolinians thought they had been abandoned on Trappe Road by their brigade-mates from Virginia. Not only had Stuart lost his first artillery piece in battle but he had done so just days after an organized body of his men had surrendered. As an artilleryman admitted, "Our cavalry has done very badly today." A trooper confessed simply, "We were overpowered." Seeking to bolster morale back home, an editor opined, "This and the fight near

Brandy Station have been as hard as any during the war . . . The result in all the recent engagements has been, on our part, entire success." Soon, however, the rumblings within the cavalry division ignited another media frenzy.[5]

Along with the murmured complaints, the men tallied the loss of friends, horses, and equipment. "*Oh* Dear Comrade," a Tar Heel exclaimed, it was awful "to see how many of our boys were missing." Horses had become nearly as irreplaceable in the South as soldiers, and many men had lost their horses. Without a horse, a trooper faced a long trip home in search of another or the ignominy of walking until they located a replacement, or, even worse, a transfer to the infantry. Cavalry casualties could not be accurately tallied without considering lost horses.[6]

In the Union camps, the lucky men sat around warming campfires, while others spent the night on sentinel duty, policing the battlefield or burying the dead. Moments after fighting erupted in the fields along Trappe Road, Surgeon Abner Hard, Eighth Illinois, established a field hospital at Green Garden, the home of Jesse Richards. As night fell, the doctor looked to move his patients to better facilities near Aldie. Assessing the wounded, he noted a trooper with a bullet through the femoral artillery in his right leg. Only a tourniquet applied by his comrades had kept him alive. Certain the man would not survive the trip to Aldie, the doctor performed life-saving surgery by candlelight.[7]

Mortally wounded in the waning moments of the fight, Col. Peter Evans, Fifth North Carolina, had been taken by his captors to a nearby home for treatment. He later begged to be left where he could be cared for by Southerners but, according to an editor in North Carolina, "the brutes . . . refused, saying they had heard of him before, and would send him to Washington if certain death resulted." Evans died in Washington DC on July 24, 1863.[8]

A New Yorker termed the bodies of the dead "a horrid looking sight." John Buford believed his men, or local citizens, buried eighteen men along Trappe Road. Daylight revealed still more "scattered along the road." Three days after the battle, George Ayre, the owner of Ayrshire farm, found the body of a Southern trooper. He described the man as having "light hair, light mustache, no beard, had on gray jacket, light pants, boots, light brown shirt with red and blue stripes, red neck cloth made of a piece of sword sash; light felt hat," and wooden buttons. Ayre buried the young man "under an oak tree alongside a rail fence, running along a wheat field."[9]

The many civilians who had found themselves in the center of the fighting for the last few days still had trials to face. From her family's home near Front Royal, Lucy Buck had proudly watched Southern infantry march past her home on June 21. The next day, soldiers brought word of her brother's death along Trappe Road. Her father set out immediately, returning the next day with his son's body. Horrified at her brother's death, Lucy damned the Yankees who "had robbed him of everything." Once enamored with the cavalry, Walter's death quenched her interest.[10]

Catherine Broun and her family had been at the center of the storm for several days. On Sunday, rather than enjoying the reassuring peel of church bells, she had listened to artillery "booming from the hills around us" and could not but fear "that our beautiful country will be desolated." By evening her home again swarmed with voracious Federals looking for a meal. Likewise, Ida Dulany found her home "covered with Yankees, begging something to eat." Feisty and fiery as ever, Amanda Edmonds ignored the outcome of the battle. Rather, she looked about at the Southern soldiers and guns posted around Ashby's Gap and wished the enemy would attack, that they might be "[rendered] . . . immortal forever."[11]

Rebecca Williams resided in Waterford, a picturesque town in northern Loudoun County, where many residents had remained loyal to the Union. Like most of the townsfolk, Williams was a Quaker, and as she had listened to the rumble of guns over the previous days, she could not help but ponder "the great calamities sin had brought into our beautiful world."[12]

TWENTY-TWO

We Were after Them, June 22

At 5:30 on the afternoon of June 21, General Pleasonton told army commander Joseph Hooker, "I drove [Stuart] through Upperville into Ashby's Gap, and assured myself that the enemy had no infantry in Loudoun Valley." But he admitted that he had been unable to send scouts to the crest of the Blue Ridge, from where they could see into the Shenandoah Valley. Luckily, General Buford had sent a patrol from the Eighth New York to a point from where they could gaze into the valley. Buford probably did so as soon as the enemy had been driven from his front. The task would have been challenging and fraught with danger, as the men picked their way up narrow mountain trails in growing darkness. Reaching the crest, they observed an enemy encampment "about 2 miles long." Buford's initiative meant the Union efforts during the week had finally succeeded.[1]

The following morning, June 22, after interrogating prisoners and with Buford's information now in hand, Pleasonton sent Hooker another message, assuring him that Lee's entire army was either en route to or in the Shenandoah Valley. Pleasonton then advised, "Being satisfied I had accomplished all that the expedition designed, I returned to [Aldie.]" The cavalry chief's report, combined with information from other sources, convinced Hooker that Lee was not targeting the Army of the Potomac or Washington DC.[2]

General Pleasonton's return to Aldie had not been without some tense moments, however, as Stuart's horsemen pressed him closely. Col. John Taylor's brigade had missed the fighting over the previous days, and Pleasonton tasked Taylor with covering the corps on June 22. A Mexican War veteran, Taylor had earned a reputation as a "worthy commander." Trained by the lamented George Bayard, the men excelled at defensive fighting. With the infantry and cavalry departing in stages, to avoid clogging the roads, Taylor waited until everyone was well along their way before he began his slow retreat about 9 a.m.[3]

After a late start, General Stuart, who hoped to avoid another general engagement, began following the Yankees at a leisurely pace. However, he soon sensed an opportunity to punish the enemy as they reached the choke point at Goose Creek bridge. There, as one Virginian noted, "we were after them."[4]

Behind a strong skirmish line manned by men from the First Pennsylvania and First Maryland, and supported by two of Capt. Alanson Randol's guns, Colonel Taylor deployed the remainder of the First Pennsylvania, assisted by the Third Pennsylvania and First New Jersey. Several times, the Federals tried to goad the Southerners into renewing the previous day's contest. Instead, Stuart brought up his artillery, scattering the Yankees and nearly capturing Randol's guns with a quick charge. Like Stuart, Colonel Taylor did not want to precipitate another general engagement. Still, the Southerners grew bolder as they neared Middleburg, and Union casualties began to mount. Sensing Taylor's men tiring, General Gregg brought up his cousin's brigade as the men neared Aldie. Nearing the town, Stuart realized the Federals now had the advantage: they had reached their strength, including the entire Cavalry Corps along with infantry, while he had moved away from his support. With nothing further to be gained, he held his men around Middleburg.[5]

Moving east along the Snickersville Turnpike, Col. Thomas Munford had also pressed the Federals as they fell back. Munford's advance had been largely uncontested, but Col. Thomas Rosser loved a good fight. Nearing Goose Creek, Rosser determined to pitch into the Yankees one more time.

After establishing a picket line along the stream, near the bridge burned three days earlier, the men of the Ninth New York had already begun cooking dinner, when a squadron from Rosser's Fifth Virginia hit the pickets. Capt. Timothy Hanley, dubbed the "Fighting Captain" by his men, led his squadron in a counterattack and drove the Virginians back across the creek. Just as a third company arrived to reinforce Hanley, the Virginians attacked a second time. In the brief melee that resulted, the New Yorkers killed Maj. John Eells. His death convinced Rosser to abandon the effort and brought the fighting in the Loudoun Valley to an end.[6]

TWENTY-THREE

Continuing Controversy

When Jeb Stuart's cavaliers rode into Middleburg on June 22, the town changed hands for the seventh time in five days. Shortly thereafter the guns fell silent but as apprehensive residents began to venture from their homes, they must have wondered just how long their friends in butternut and gray would remain. "Oh, how it thrilled our hearts to see our own flag again and our men," Catherine Broun exclaimed, and she rejoiced having Southern soldiers to feed. Even with reduced stocks in her pantry, barns, and cribs, she fed dozens of famished Confederates and sent "baskets of provisions" to the sentinels standing watch on the hills around her farm. As they left her table, the grateful soldiers thanked her, avowing "they had never seen anything like the attention we paid" them.[1]

The residents of Middleburg had often reveled in the company of Stuart and his men, as they had on June 17. But if Stuart spent time in the town on June 22, he did not stay long and could not have been in the mood for celebrating. Dispersing his men to form a strong cordon around the Loudoun Valley, Stuart made his headquarters at Caleb Rector's home west of town.[2]

He had reason to be feeling rather glum, after the events of the previous few days, and he may have sought to avoid the distractions in town. Major von Borcke, the most gregarious member of his staff, was gone at a time when Stuart might have appreciated his kinship and laughter more than ever. The general must also have been feeling besieged, even as he tried to convince his wife otherwise. Flora had sent him several newspaper clippings in which editors continued to excoriate him regarding the fight at Brandy Station. During a quiet moment on June 20, he wrote her a brief letter. "The newspapers are false in *every statement* except to the victory," he assured her and mentioned von Borcke's wounding only as an afterthought.[3]

The long retreat and bitter fighting through Upperville the next day reignited the smoldering embers of the Brandy Station controversy. Peter Alexander, of the *Savannah Republican*, had been reporting from the front lines for much of the war. One editor termed him "the most reliable correspondent in the Confederacy." Marching with General Longstreet's corps, Alexander had reached Ashby's Gap on June 19, and he had remained with the infantry throughout the fighting on June 21. After listening to the grumbling and grousing within the cavalry division during the night, Alexander described Stuart's officers as "discouraged and mortified" and the men as "bordering on a state of demoralization." Alexander dismissed Stuart as "unequal to the duty of wielding and fighting so large a force as that now subject to his orders." He disparaged him for retreating thirteen miles and abandoning his dead and wounded.[4]

Alexander then called for a change of command, suggesting Richard Ewell or John Bell Hood as more qualified for Stuart's position. Though unwilling to term Stuart slow or stupid, Alexander believed the cavalry "requires a head that can conceive and combine as well as execute the orders of others." Rather than flowers, foppery, and frivolity, he thought Stuart's men need discipline and drill. The reporter's long epistle soon appeared in papers throughout the South, as well as several Northern dailies. In time, friends and supporters came to Stuart's defense, but their voices got lost in the clamor. Only General Lee could put the questions to rest, but he had a campaign to run and so the doubts lingered, sparked, in part, by Stuart's decisions in the coming weeks that further tainted his reputation in the eyes of his critics.[5]

The Southern populace had been spoiled by Stuart's success and the seeming ease with which his men had dominated their opponents time and again. Arrogance convinced his critics that the balance on the battlefield would never change, but it had. In their myopic view of events in the Loudoun Valley, Stuart's detractors failed to recognize that he had accomplished exactly what Lee had asked him to do. He had prevented the enemy from penetrating the gaps of the Blue Ridge for five critical days. Shunting aside his own thirst for victory in the wake of the Brandy Station controversy, Stuart had established a defense in depth by meeting his foe at the gaps in Bull Run Mountain. Doing so allowed him to trade distance for time. He had repeatedly yielded tactical battlefield success in return for achieving Lee's larger campaign objectives. Rather than risking his division at the outset of a crucial campaign in a personal quest for redemption, Stuart had inflicted higher casualties than he sustained by holding his men to an effective but unexciting defensive stratagem. Knowing his men would be at a disadvantage waging a defensive fight against his better armed opponent, Stuart had taken advantage of especially favorable terrain, including the hills, narrow roads, bridges, and the omnipresent stone walls. The tenacity of his men had convinced his opponent that he had encountered mounted infantry and forced him to employ infantry of his own.[6]

In targeting Stuart, Peter Alexander conveniently forgot Longstreet's unauthorized move across the Shenandoah River on June 20. Stuart had every reason to expect infantry support on June 21 if Longstreet had held his position at Ashby's Gap. Had he remained, Longstreet could have brought his brigades to Stuart's assistance much earlier in the day and well east of the mountains. Instead, the foot soldiers did not get back into position until the day had been lost. One of Stuart's supporters countered the critics, describing the retreat through Upperville as "one of the coolest and most deliberate of the war." He termed Stuart's leadership as "eminently skillful," but there was little glory in such victories.[7]

Though Stuart might have appreciated a few days to answer his detractors and rest his men and horses, Lee could not afford to extend him the luxury. At one o'clock on the morning of June

25, the cavalry chief rode away from the Rector home for the last time. He met three of his brigades near the town of Salem and then rode off into further controversy. But for the fighting in the Loudoun Valley, Stuart's Ride to Gettysburg might never have occurred. He had been tasked with screening the movement of Lee's army from Union eyes. Except for the Union advance on June 17, he might have continued to screen the Southern army, following the line of Bull Run—Catoctin Mountain, across the Potomac River and into Maryland and Pennsylvania. Union efforts to pierce his screen might have precipitated battle elsewhere or he might have reached Gettysburg with his division intact and in time to aid the army. General Pleasonton's decision to move through the gap at Aldie on June 17 forced Stuart and Lee to alter their plans and changed the course of the campaign.[8]

Without time to properly rest his horses prior to leaving Salem, Stuart's effectiveness over the next several days suffered. Aside from rest, his horses needed shoeing. Some of the first men into Aldie on June 17 had immediately gone looking for a blacksmith, but the arrival of Union troops ended their search. After the fighting concluded on June 22, Stuart dispersed his men, in part to allow them to have their animals shod as quickly as possible. Some troopers remained behind until they found a blacksmith. Others searched in vain. Those who drew picket duty never even unsaddled their horses.[9]

In a letter defending the cavalry, an anonymous soldier noted the need for horseshoes and nails in the command. He spoke of horses going "barefoot until their feet bled" and told how one man had paid "ten dollars for eight horse-shoe nails." He remembered the division receiving only three hundred new bridles when it needed three thousand. He described shoddy saddles falling apart in a day or ruining their horse's backs after four days. "Nothing but poverty makes a man take one," he explained. Dismissing such complaints as not "easily overcome," an editor countered by telling the soldiers, "Energy can accomplish miracles." Safely ensconced in Richmond, the scribe smugly told the soldiers to "do their duty, and we shall soon be more proud of the achievements of our cavalry than we have ever been." Indeed, the men did their duty, but none could have envisioned the trials ahead.[10]

TWENTY-FOUR

Continuing Success

Coming of age is a process, an evolution, and evolution takes time. The evolution of the young men in the Cavalry Corps, Army of the Potomac, from neophytes to hardened veterans had taken twenty-six months. Along the way, the troopers had surmounted many hurdles, including leaders who had no faith in them, misused or ignored them, and tried to disband them. They had learned that the boundless energy and enthusiasm of youth would take them only so far. They had, by June 1863, learned that they needed to be led and they had, reluctantly, accepted the need for military discipline. One question remained: Who would lead them?

Volunteer officers needed to learn how to drill, how and when to discipline, and most importantly, how to lead. They had to learn to be officers. In examining the evolution of the Union cavalry, historians tend to focus on the relatively small number of colonels and generals who led the cavalry through the critical year of 1863, while ignoring the maturation of the lieutenants, captains, and majors who rode in the ranks. Colonels and generals usually had a military background or had risen to positions of authority in their civilian pursuits. Lieutenants, captains, and, in many cases, majors, had little, if any experience leading men. Many were no more than boys themselves, and every one of them had to accept the meaning of words spoken by George Washington many years earlier: "It is the actions, and not the commission that makes the Officer." But, as cavalry historian Stephen Starr concluded, volunteer officers "had neither the habit of command, nor, with rare exceptions, the willingness to risk the unpopularity that went with the exercise of authority."[1]

The defining moment in the evolution of the Union cavalry came in early March 1863, following the embarrassing defeat the previous month at Hartwood Church. Enraged by the lack of leadership throughout the ranks of his mounted arm, Joseph Hooker exploded at one of his generals. "We *ought* to be invincible, and by God, sir, we *shall* be!" he thundered. "You have got to stop these disgraceful cavalry 'surprises.' I'll have no more of them," Hooker told the man. "I'll give you full power over your officers, to arrest, cashier, shoot—whatever you will—only you must stop these 'surprises.' And, sir, if you don't do it, I give you fair notice, I will relieve the whole of you and take the command of the cavalry myself!" General Hooker's emphatic threat took hold, and success followed. The men, who had finally accepted the need for accountability and obedience, had now learned to stick and stay in the fight; they had learned to trust their officers and each other. Likewise, their officers, who had also finally accepted the accountability demanded by Hooker, had learned how to lead them into and out of danger, all while gaining ever greater success.[2]

The mounted arm came of age in the Loudoun Valley in mid-June, leading one Southern officer to grudgingly admit, "The improvement in the cavalry of the enemy became painfully apparent in the fights around Upperville." In the days and weeks to follow, colonels and generals wrote their reports of the fighting, but few of these men appear to have played a truly decisive role in the combat. Rather, lieutenants, captains, and majors made most of the pivotal decisions, repeatedly seizing the initiative and inspiring their men by their words and deeds. Most all of them did their duty in relative anonymity, though three young captains gained a measure of enduring fame a week after the guns fell silent. In recommending George Custer, Elon Farnsworth, and Wesley Merritt for promotion to brigadier, Alfred Pleasonton, whether he meant to or not, acknowledged every young officer who led their men through the crucible in the Loudoun Valley.[3]

For the men and officers of the Cavalry Corps, success bred confidence and pride in themselves and their unit. The combination bred future success. The Federal troopers gained confidence and swagger in the Loudoun Valley. Flush with victory, a young officer spoke for many when he avowed, "I would not give up my commission as a Captain of Cavalry for anything an infantry regiment could offer me."[4]

Of the four generals in the Cavalry Corps, Alfred Pleasonton had the most impact on events in the Loudoun Valley. Historians assume, as Thomas Ryan has stated, that "Pleasonton floundered in his most important mission—to discover the location of Lee's army." But finding Lee's army did not become Pleasonton's primary mission until June 20/21. The cavalryman took his orders from Joseph Hooker, who took his orders from President Lincoln, Secretary of War Stanton, and General Henry Halleck. And while Hooker said one thing publicly, via telegraph, he said something entirely different in verbal orders or written orders delivered by courier. What Pleasonton knew of Hooker's scheme may never be fully known, but Hooker's orders to Pleasonton did not mirror his discussions with his superiors. In his published orders, Hooker told Pleasonton to find the enemy, even if doing so meant losing men. In private, the army commander told him to hold his corps together and to not venture into the Loudoun Valley. Hooker had been the victim of his own audacious plan for his spring campaign, in which he had sent all but one brigade of his Cavalry Corps away from his army. Without enough horsemen to screen his advance, he fell victim to an equally audacious flank attack and never recovered. Now, with his army again on the move in a campaign in which the enemy dictated the course of events, Hooker did not intend to lose his cavalry again.[5]

Once he placed his army in motion, Hooker envisioned a scenario where Lee attacked his divided army near the plains of Manassas. To do so, Lee would have to send his infantry through the gaps of Bull Run Mountain. Willing to accept battle on such terms, Hooker had no intention of sending his cavalry off on a reconnaissance mission into the Shenandoah Valley. Instead, he planned to hold his cavalry together east of Bull Run Mountain, from where his horsemen could screen and protect his infantry from another Chancellorsville-type surprise. Beginning on June 13, Pleasonton's primary mission, from both Hooker and wing commander John Reynolds, had been to protect the army from such an attack launched through the gaps of Bull Run Mountain. For eight critical days, at least one, and sometimes two of Pleasonton's brigades remained tied to Thoroughfare Gap.[6]

Though he comes down through history as a supremely ambitious man, Pleasonton risked his position by going against his commander's scheme on June 17, when he exceeded his orders and pushed through Aldie Gap into the Loudoun Valley. By doing so, he had precipitated, albeit unintentionally, the fight at Aldie, and the fighting to follow. Hooker had told him to graze his horses well east of Aldie, while risking only one regiment on a scout to the Blue Ridge gaps. Even after Pleasonton advised that he wanted to push through the gap (the militarily sound decision), Hooker reiterated his orders to stay well east of Bull Run Mountain. Some critics also fault Pleasonton for not pressing the retreating enemy on the evening of June 17, thereby squandering a chance to crush the Southern brigade between his pursuing troops and Colonel Duffié's lone regiment. Forgotten in such judgements is that the battle had ended at or near nightfall, and one of Pleasonton's brigades had sustained heavy casualties. To have pursued would have further violated Hooker's orders and hazarded more of the command. Likewise, Pleasonton and his subordinates are criticized for their caution on June 18, but Pleasonton had, again, exceeded his orders by pressing as far and as hard as he did in his search for enemy infantry.[7]

Finding Lee's army remained Pleasonton's secondary mission until June 20/21. Only then did Hooker allow him to pull his cavalry away from Thoroughfare Gap as infantry had arrived to assume the task, but Pleasonton's last brigade did not rejoin the corps in time to help him on June 21. Pleasonton had, prior to the fight at Aldie on June 17, sent numerous patrols across the Loudoun Valley to the gaps in the Blue Ridge Mountains, though none had caught sight of Lee's infantry. Much remains unknown regarding these scouting expeditions. What were the orders as actually given to the men who led the patrols? Did they understand the importance and urgency of locating the enemy? What risks were they to take? What risks did they take in their quest for information? Conversely, Pleasonton could only take their word for where they went, how long they stayed, what they saw, and how diligently they searched.

Once Pleasonton knew Stuart held the Loudoun Valley in strength, he could no longer send reconnoitering or scouting patrols into the valley without fighting or otherwise hazarding his men and further violating Hooker's orders. Not until June 21, and with Hooker's reluctant consent, did Pleasonton go after Stuart in an all-out effort to reach Ashby's Gap. But as hard as his men fought, Stuart's men fought just as hard. The elements also conspired against the Federals, as rocky terrain and high water, combined with stout Southern resistance, foiled General Buford's efforts to flank Stuart and possibly achieve a quick, decisive victory. Often criticized for not being a battlefield commander, Pleasonton directed the fight from the start. By late afternoon, however, as he peered up at Ashby's Gap, Pleasonton saw Southern guns and infantry blocking the pass. Even if he and his men had been willing and able, his horses simply did not have the legs to carry them farther.

By almost any measure, Pleasonton's victory at Upperville would have been remarkable, but Hooker had simply waited too long to unleash his cavalry. Even though Buford had sent a patrol to the crest of the Blue Ridge, Pleasonton had not punched through the pass, and so his victory rings hollow. The man who cared little for gathering and interpreting information was now forced to make guesses and his guesses always seemed to bring more questions than answers. Worse, he had, reportedly, prevented more qualified men from interrogating prisoners and reading captured documents.

On June 22, army headquarters distributed a circular trumpeting Pleasonton's victory at Upperville as "a disastrous day to the rebel cavalry." Hooker had already recommended his cavalry chief for promotion to major general and permanent command of the Cavalry Corps on June 18. The promotion came through as of June 22, though Pleasonton may not have learned of it for another day or so.[8]

On June 27 Pleasonton's troopers stepped into their saddles and splashed across the Potomac River. No one could know when or where the armies would clash, but as one prescient horseman told his wife, "I think it will be in Pennsylvania."[9]

APPENDIX A

Order of Battle

UNION

Cavalry Corps, Army of the Potomac —Brig. Gen. Alfred Pleasonton

FIRST DIVISION—Brig. Gen. John Buford

First Brigade—Col. William Gamble

Eighth Illinois—Lt. Col. David Clendenin
Twelfth Illinois (four companies)—Capt. George Shears[1]
Third Indiana (six companies)—Col. George Chapman
Eighth New York—Lt. Col. William Markell

Second Brigade—Col. Thomas Devin

Sixth New York (six companies)—Maj. William Beardsley
Ninth New York—Col. William Sackett
Seventeenth Pennsylvania (nine companies)—Col. Josiah Kellogg
Third West Virginia (two companies)—Capt. Seymour Conger

Reserve Brigade—Maj. Samuel Starr / Maj. Charles Whiting

First U.S. (ten companies)—Capt. Richard Lord
Second U.S.—Capt. Theophilus Rodenbough
Fifth U.S. (eleven companies)—Capt. Julius Mason
Sixth U.S. (ten companies)—Capt. George Cram

SECOND DIVISION—Brig. Gen. David M. Gregg

First Brigade—Col. John Taylor

First Maryland (eleven companies)—Lt. Col. James Deems
First New Jersey (nine companies)—Maj. Myron Beaumont
First Pennsylvania (seven companies)—Lt. Col. David Gardner
Third Pennsylvania—Lt. Col. Edward Jones

Second Brigade—Brig. Gen. Judson Kilpatrick

First Massachusetts (eight companies)—Lt. Col. Greeley Curtis
Second New York (ten companies)—Lt. Col. Otto Harhaus
Fourth New York—Col. Louis di Cesnola / Lt. Col. Augustus Pruyn
Sixth Ohio—(nine companies)—Maj. William Stedman
First Rhode Island—Col. Alfred Duffié

Third Brigade—Col. John Irvin Gregg

First Maine—(ten companies)—Col. Calvin Douty / Lt. Col. Charles Smith
Tenth New York—Maj. Matthew Avery
Fourth Pennsylvania—Lt. Col. William Doster
Sixteenth Pennsylvania—Lt. Col. John Robison

Second Brigade, Horse Artillery—Capt. John Tidball

Batteries E/G, First U.S.—Capt. Alanson Randol
Battery K, First U.S.—Capt. William Graham
Battery A, Second U.S.—Lt. John Calef
Battery C, Third U.S.—Lt. William Fuller

INFANTRY—Fifth Corps

Third Brigade—Col. Strong Vincent

Twentieth Maine—Lt. Col. Freeman Conner[2]
Sixteenth Michigan—Lt. Col. Norval Welch
Forty-Fourth New York—Col. James Rice
Eighty-Third Pennsylvania—Capt. Orpheus Woodward

CONFEDERATE

CAVALRY DIVISION, Army of Northern Virginia —Maj. Gen. James Ewell Brown "Jeb" Stuart

Brig. Gen. Fitzhugh Lee's Brigade —under temporary command of Col. Thomas Munford

First Virginia—Col. James Drake
Second Virginia—Lt. Col. James Watts / Maj. Cary Breckinridge
Third Virginia—Col. Thomas Owen
Fourth Virginia—Col. Williams Wickham / Capt. William Newton
Fifth Virginia—Col. Thomas Rosser

Brig. Gen. W. H. F. Lee's Brigade —under temporary command of Col. John Chambliss

Second North Carolina—Col. William Payne
Ninth Virginia—Col. Richard Beale
Tenth Virginia—Col. James Lucius Davis
Thirteenth Virginia—Maj. Joseph Gillette

Brig. Gen. Beverly Robertson's Brigade

Fourth North Carolina—Col. Dennis Ferebee
Fifth North Carolina—Col. Peter Evans

Brig. Gen. Wade Hampton's Brigade

First North Carolina—Col. Laurence Baker
First South Carolina—Col. John Black
Second South Carolina—Lt. Col. Thomas Lipscomb
Cobb's Legion—Col. Pierce Young
Jeff. Davis Legion—Lt. Col. J. Fred Waring
Phillips Legion—Lt. Col. William Rich

Brig. Gen. William E. Jones' Brigade

Sixth Virginia—Maj. Cabell Flournoy
Seventh Virginia—Lt. Col. Thomas Marshall
Eleventh Virginia—Col. Lunsford Lomax
Twelfth Virginia—Lt. Col. Thomas Massie

Horse Artillery Battalion—Major Robert Beckham

Ashby Horse Artillery—Capt. Roger Chew
First Stuart Horse Artillery—Capt. James Breathed
Second Stuart Horse Artillery—Capt. William McGregor
Washington Artillery—Capt. James Hart
Lynchburg Artillery—Capt. Marcellus Moorman

APPENDIX B

Casualties

These figures represent casualties identified by name and or date and location. As such they should be viewed as a minimum number of losses.

Abbreviations

KIA	Killed in Action
MIA	Missing in Action
MWIA	Mortally Wounded in Action
POW	Captured
WIA	Wounded in Action

ALDIE—JUNE 17, 1863

Brig. Gen. Judson Kilpatrick's Brigade

	KIA	MIA	MWIA	POW	POW/MIA	WIA	WIA/POW	Total
Second New York	10		4		5	20		39
Sixth Ohio	2		2			10		14
Fourth New York*	5				15	26	3	49
First Massachusetts	21		8	75		49	26	179

Col. John Irvin Gregg's Brigade

	KIA	MIA	MWIA	POW	POW/MIA	WIA	WIA/POW	Total
First Maine**	5		1			19	4	29

	KIA	MIA	MWIA	POW	POW/MIA	WIA	WIA/POW	Total
Col. Thomas Munford's Brigade								
First Virginia			1		1	4		6
Second Virginia	2			1		19		22
Third Virginia				15		7	2	24
Fourth Virginia	1				7	2		10
Fifth Virginia	1		2	49		8	9	69
First Stuart Horse Artillery	3					3		6

* Col. Luigi di Cesnola wounded and captured.

**Col. Calvin Douty killed.

TOTAL ALDIE CASUALTIES

Union	310
Confederate	137

COLONEL DUFFIÉ'S SCOUT TO MIDDLEBURG—JUNE 17 AND 18, 1863

Brig. Gen. Judson Kilpatrick's Brigade

	KIA	MWIA	POW	WIA	WIA/POW	Total
First Rhode Island	5	2	210	12		229
Brig. Gen. Beverly Robertson's Brigade						
Fourth North Carolina	1	1	3	6		11
Fifth North Carolina	3			6	3	12
Col. John Chambliss's Brigade						
Ninth Virginia					1	1

TOTAL CASUALTIES RELATED TO COL. DUFFIÉ'S SCOUT TO MIDDLEBURG JUNE 17 AND 18

Union	229
Confederate	24

MIDDLEBURG—JUNE 19, 1863

Col. John Irvin Gregg's Brigade

	KIA	MWIA	POW	POW/MIA	WIA	WIA/POW	Total
First Maine	10		2		20	4	36
Tenth New York	3	2	11		12	1	29
Sixteenth Pennsylvania	1		3		10		14
Fourth Pennsylvania*							
Brig. Gen. Judson Kilpatrick's Brigade							
Second New York	1				3		4
Fourth New York			7		4	1	12
Sixth Ohio		1			1		2
Maj. Charles Whiting's Reserve Brigade							
Second U.S.					1		1
Col. John Chambliss's Brigade							
Second North Carolina	1	2			1	1	5
Ninth Virginia	2	2			3	1	8
Thirteenth Virginia	4	2			14	1	21
Brig. Gen. Beverly Robertson's Brigade							
Fourth North Carolina	1		32		3	7	43
Fifth North Carolina	2	2	7		6	3	20
Brig. Gen. William Jones's Brigade							
Seventh Virginia					1		1

*Data unknown.

TOTAL CASUALTIES FOR THE JUNE 19 FIGHTING AROUND MIDDLEBURG AND MILLVILLE

Union	98
Confederate	98

UPPERVILLE — JUNE 21, 1863

	KIA	MWIA	MWIA/ POW	POW	POW/ MIA	WIA	WIA/ POW	Total
Col. Strong Vincent's Infantry Brigade								
Sixteenth Michigan		1				8		9
Twentieth Maine	1					7		8
Forty-Fourth New York	1					2		3
Eighty-Third Pennsylvania						1		1
Capt. William Fuller's Battery C								
Third U.S. Artillery	1					3		4
Brig. Gen. John Buford's First Cavalry Division								
Maj. Samuel Starr's Reserve Brigade								
First U.S.	1				38	10		49
Second U.S.*								
Fifth U.S.	1							1
Sixth U.S.					3	8		11
Col. William Gamble's Brigade								
Eighth Illinois	2					13		15
Twelfth Illinois	3					10		13
Third Indiana						5		5
Col. Thomas Devin's Brigade								
Seventeenth Pennsylvania						7		7
Brig. Gen. David Gregg's Second Cavalry Division								
Brig. Gen. Judson Kilpatrick's Brigade								
Second New York	1					2		3
Fourth New York		2			6	7	1	16
Sixth Ohio	1	3		2		13	6	25

	KIA	MWIA	MWIA/ POW	POW	POW/ MIA	WIA	WIA/ POW	Total
Col. John Irvin Gregg's Brigade								
First Maine				1		10		11
Fourth Pennsylvania						3		3
Sixteenth Pennsylvania*								
Tenth New York**								

Maj. Gen. Jeb Stuart's Cavalry Division

	KIA	MWIA	MWIA/ POW	POW	POW/ MIA	WIA	WIA/ POW	Total
Maj. Robert Beckham's Horse Artillery Battalion								
Capt. William McGregor's Second Stuart Horse Artillery						1		1
Capt. Marcellus Moorman's Lynchburg Battery	1	1		1		1		4
Capt. Roger Chew's Ashby Battery	1					1		2
Brig. Gen. Wade Hampton's Brigade								
First North Carolina	8	1		6		12	1	28
First South Carolina				10		2	1	13
Second South Carolina	2			2				4
Cobb's Legion				11		9		20
Jeff Davis Legion	4	2	1	10		13		30
Brig. Gen. Beverly Robertson's Brigade								
Fourth North Carolina	5	1		25		16	2	49
Fifth North Carolina	3	2	1			22	8	36
Col. John Chambliss's Brigade								
Second North Carolina	6	1		2		9	3	21
Ninth Virginia		1		3		10	2	16
Tenth Virginia	1					2		3
Thirteenth Virginia	1	1	1	4		2	1	10

	KIA	MWIA	MWIA/ POW	POW	POW/ MIA	WIA	WIA/ POW	Total
Brig. Gen. William Jones's Brigade								
Sixth Virginia	4			2		11		17
Seventh Virginia	5	5				10		20
Eleventh Virginia	2			1		15		18
Twelfth Virginia	2					16		18

*Data unknown.

**Probably not involved.

TOTAL UPPERVILLE CASUALTIES JUNE 21

Union	184
Confederate	300

JUNE 22 UNION RETREAT TO ALDIE

Col. John Taylor's Brigade

	KIA	MWIA	POW	WIA	Total
First Maryland				1*	1
First New Jersey	1				1
First Pennsylvania				1	1
Col. Thomas Devin's Brigade					
Sixth New York		1			1
Ninth New York	1		5	1	7
Col. Thomas Munford's Brigade					
Second Virginia			1		1
Fourth Virginia			2		2
Fifth Virginia	2		2		4

*Two other men may have been wounded but their names cannot be confirmed.

TOTAL CASUALTIES JUNE 22

Union	10
Confederate	7

TOTAL IDENTIFIED CASUALTIES JUNE 17–22

Union	831
Confederate	566

APPENDIX C

Horses, Ordnance, and Regimental Strength

In June 1864 the Union War Department published a lengthy circular specific to the care and use of horses in the cavalry service. Opening a section titled "Uses of Cavalry," the author states, "When cavalry is so managed that the men require remounting every two or three months, it is evidently improperly used, and most decided successes must be gained to at all justify such hard use of so expensive and important an arm of service." The minimum durability of cavalry horses "should be three years, if properly used," the author asserted. Published exactly one year after the all-day fight at Brandy Station, eleven months after the arduous Gettysburg Campaign, and one month into Gen. Ulysses Grant's army-wide campaign to end the war, such declarations seem, today, hopelessly optimistic, if not wildly unrealistic.[1]

In an expansive and heart-rending letter to his mother on May 12, 1863, Capt. Charles Adams, gave a more accurate picture of the way cavalry operated and the suffering the horses endured. "You are a slave to your horses," Adams declared, and when they break down, "you have two resources, one to send them to . . . the rear and so strip yourself of your command, and the other to force them on until they drop . . . The last course is the one I adopt." Seeking to help his mother understand his reasoning, Adams explained, "I do my best for my horses and am sorry for them; but all war is cruel and it is my business to bring every man

I can into the presence of the enemy, and so make war short. So I have but one rule, a horse must go until he can't be spurred any farther." Adams then lamented, "Poor brutes! How it would astonish and terrify you and all others at home with your sleek, well-fed animals, to see the weak, gaunt, rough animals, with each rib visible and the hip-bones starting through the flesh. . . . It would knock the romance out of you."[2]

Three weeks after Adams penned his letter, Gen. Robert E. Lee initiated his second invasion of the North. A week later, Adams and the First Massachusetts saw action at Brandy Station. He could not have envisioned the brutal horse-killing campaign that lay ahead, the grueling marches, searing heat, and near endless combat. The campaign marked a turning point, providing a new template for the war ahead, a template in which the cavalry continued a near daily grind of marching and fighting. Rather than lasting years, horses gave out in weeks or less. By one estimate, the Army of the Potomac's Cavalry Corps received thirty-five thousand horses between May and October 1863: an average of six thousand per month. As Gen. Henry Halleck noted, the army had remounted the Cavalry Corps every two months and he projected a need for 435,000 horses in 1864. Knowing the exigencies and realities of war, cavalry officers must have been dumbfounded as they read the June 1864 circular.[3]

When Gen. George Stoneman returned from his raid in early May 1863, he reported having "captured a sufficient number of horses to remount all that gave out or were broken down en route." According to Gen. Daniel Butterfield, the raiders "only complain of their horses being leg-weary and wanting shoes." Suspicious of such rosy reports, army commander Joseph Hooker demanded a more definitive accounting of the number of men ready "for immediate duty in the field." After a hasty appraisal of his corps, which numbered twelve thousand men and horses at the outset of the raid, Stoneman on May 12 counted but two thousand. One brigade numbered a mere 346 men and horses available for duty.[4]

Within two weeks, Stoneman had taken medical leave and been replaced by Gen. Alfred Pleasonton. Rumors of a Southern cavalry raid on Washington reached the War Department even as Pleasonton took command. The timing could not have been worse for Pleasonton's efforts, as almost all remounts went to Gen. Julius Stahel's cavalry division, tasked with protecting the capital. When Pleasonton asked for horses, the army had none to spare.[5]

On the eve of the great clash at Brandy Station, Pleasonton still needed two thousand horses to finish mounting his command. With no remounts forthcoming, Pleasonton crossed the Rappahannock River on June 9 with two infantry brigades in tow to bolster his ranks. When he surrendered the battlefield fourteen hours later, he left an unknown number of dead and wounded animals behind. Many others carried their riders back across the river only to fall victim to their injuries in coming days. Two regiments, the Fifth and Sixth U.S., lost more than one hundred horses between them. If their loss is an accurate measuring stick, the Cavalry Corps may have lost one thousand horses during or immediately after the battle.[6]

Still, with all the pressures on the supply chain, which included demands from every other army in the field, quartermasters expected to send eleven hundred horses to Pleasonton on June 10. But heavy demand led to other problems. Prices soared, increasing nearly 20 percent in one month, to $150 per head by the end of May. Seeking to take advantage of the crisis, farmers and other suppliers pressed quartermasters and inspectors to accept animals that did not meet army regulations.[7]

Army guidelines prohibited the purchase of mares, while stipulating the acceptable age, size, and color of animals to be purchased. Additional rules called for inspectors to measure each animal "by actual measurement," rather than estimating by eye. Examining an animal's mouth and teeth confirmed his age, while checking his eyes eliminated horses with cataracts or vision loss. Regulations called for inspectors to check each horse's legs and hooves for evidence of a series of ailments and required skin to be checked for mange. The horses were to be saddled and bridled to determine how easily they accepted the bit and to ensure "he is free from tricks such as rearing up and falling backwards." Finally, and most critically when one considers the large numbers of animals coming into the depots at a time, each horse was to be "violently exercised for fifteen or twenty minutes." Each animal was to be "ridden downhill to ascertain if his knees are weak, have him turned short around rapidly each way to ascertain if [he] has been injured in the shoulders." Jumping each animal over an obstacle or a ditch also allowed examiners to determine the strength of his legs. The entire process took at least twenty minutes per animal. Multiply by a few hundred animals at a time and one can envision how shortcuts and fraud took hold.[8]

General Montgomery Meigs repeatedly reminded his subordinates not to accept mares, but farmers and contractors only increased their pressure to do otherwise. As one officer complained, "farmers driving in their stock will not sell their horses unless the *mares* are taken also." Officers who broke the rules and showed higher numbers created morale problems for those who followed the rules but fell behind in obtaining sufficient stock. As the campaign season heated up, Meigs found himself exhorting his quartermasters to buy more animals while also counseling and encouraging those who wilted under the strain.[9]

Still, dedicated inspectors rejected hundreds of animals, including many which the army had already purchased. As one officer complained to Meigs after rejecting 50 percent of the animals in a lot, "At this rate I shall have my horse yards full of unserviceable stock in a very short time." In most cases the horses proved to be either too young, too old, blind, or partially so, or hampered by breathing problems or other ailments.[10]

Between the farm and the army, horses often traveled hundreds of miles by train, ship, barge, or road. Guidelines covered the care of the animals during transport, including feeding, watering and, if traveling by train, off-loading and exercise. The rules limited their time on the cars to twelve hours per day. Such orders must have proved entirely impracticable, however, when one considers the time needed to move them on and off the cars, as well as constructing or locating sidings alongside large plots of open ground or corrals large enough for hundreds of horses. Keeping enough men on hand to guard the horses and move them on and off the cars must have also proved prohibitive. Too often, the animals found themselves crammed into unventilated cars with inadequate food and water and no time off the cars. Under such conditions, many horses suffocated.[11]

Beyond the main depots, such as those around Washington DC and Alexandria, the army established temporary depots closer to the army as collection points for fresh remounts or for condemned or unserviceable animals. The short-term nature of these facilities or corrals usually meant a lack of security. In August an officer in charge of such a facility in the heart of John Mosby's Confederacy told a superior, "I have now 1,200 head of condemned horses. . . . I have tonight 2,200 loose animals . . . in this country devoid of fences. The care of them takes every man I have," but a continuing shortage of rolling stock, especially ventilated stock cars, often left the quartermasters and horses at the mercy of the elements and railroad personnel.[12]

Fresh remounts usually reached Washington stressed, aggressive, and hungry. Quickly herded into corrals, they often "lashed out, kicking and biting . . . inflicting cuts and broken bones, and giving every indication of their distress." Most arrived unbroken. Without any chance to rest or recover weight lost on their journey, the animals quickly made another trip out to the army. Soldiers who received them had no idea what they might expect when they rode into battle and their new mount experienced the terrors of combat for the first time. As one historian explained, "For a herd animal, with a strong preference for close social relationships, the camps, and corrals . . . may not only have been profoundly frightening places, they may . . . have been very lonely ones too."[13]

The army recognized the need to harden the horses for the exertions of cavalry service and to accustom them to the noise and chaos of battle. As explained in an army circular, "To take them from the farm or the stable immediately into service, and expect them to endure the fatigue and exposure, and to stand the firing of artillery and small arms, would be as unreasonable as to expect inexperienced militia to do as well as veteran troops." The document must have caused even battle-weary veterans to chuckle. The author called for three weeks of exercise, three to five hours per day, with nine months of preparatory training and exercise deemed to be ideal, before sending the horse into combat. Again, the exigencies and realities of the Gettysburg Campaign meant soldiers ignored such ideals entirely and horses went from the farm to the battlefield within weeks, if not days.[14]

By June Meigs could no longer meet the army requirement stipulating the minimum age of horses to be purchased while providing the thousands of horses needed by the men in the field. "I am sensible that a five-year-old horse is not as fit for cavalry service as one six years old," he told Pleasonton on June 1, "but it is a choice between five years old and a deficient supply." The younger horses reached the army within two weeks and saw their first action at Aldie on June 17, prompting Pleasonton to report, "A good many of the young and small horses, which have been sent for cavalry use, gave out yesterday, and I shall have many more dismounted men in a short time, from the hard service required of the horses and their unfitness to stand it."[15]

After the fight at Upperville, and probably at Pleasonton's urging, a correspondent reiterated the general's complaint, telling readers, "Such incessant and active service is very destructive to horse flesh, and I regret to say that fully half of some of our horse regiments are now ineffective for want of horses. The generally inferior class of horses heretofore furnished soon wears out, and not enough even [of such poor quality] have been supplied." Hundreds of other young horses had reached the army in the days just prior to the fighting in the Loudoun Valley but did not see action until after the cavalry crossed the Potomac River.[16]

Even as horses reached remount centers, other shortages prevented dismounted troopers from returning to their regiments quickly. Horses lost on the battlefield often meant the loss of all the equipment on the animal, including saddles, saddlebags, bridles, bits, blankets, brushes, curry combs, picket pins, feedbags, and spare ammunition, as well as the soldier's personal items and spare clothing. When a horse crashed to the ground from a bullet, collision, or shell wound, the impact could damage or destroy the trooper's carbine, which he carried on a sling across his shoulder. His saber might also be damaged, or his revolver lost. Each piece of lost or damaged equipment had to be replaced before the man returned to duty.

As the fighting in the Loudoun Valley began, militia units raised in Pennsylvania for the developing emergency competed with Pleasonton's command for needed equipment, weapons, and horses. Eastern arsenals soon found themselves stripped of all equipment and weapons. Fresh horses arrived but could not be forwarded to the army until saddles and other tack arrived. The Sixteenth Pennsylvania had missed the fight at Brandy Station because they needed five hundred saddles, which did not reach the men until after the fight at Aldie. Many of these saddles had been hastily assembled. Not only did they ruin the backs of the horses but they quickly fell apart and Pleasonton asked Meigs to accept no further shipments from the manufacturer.[17]

The day after Brandy Station, Pleasonton ordered his commanders to prepare requisitions to replace ammunition expended and to identify and replace equipment lost on the battlefield. General Buford needed five hundred carbines for his command alone. As replacements, he received the best "on hand." The commander of the Eighth New York received sixteen crates of "repaired arms," rather than the requested Sharps carbines. By June 22 the supply of carbines had been exhausted. I have "no carbines on hand," Gen. James Ripley, head of the Ordnance Department, told an officer, and "I cannot tell when there will be any."[18]

On June 21, 1863, one of Pleasonton's aides counted nearly one thousand men waiting at remount depots for horses and equipment. Hundreds more headed to the depots following the fight at Upperville. After a brief respite, the Cavalry Corps crossed the Potomac River and the near constant marching and fighting resumed and continued until mid-July. By one accounting, the corps received seventeen thousand remounts between early-May and the end of July, at an estimated price of $2.3 million or almost $80 million today. Rather than enjoying an endless supply of horses, equipment, and the newest weapons, the Cavalry Corps struggled to keep men equipped and in the field.[19]

General Stuart faced all the same problems, but with fewer alternatives. As his needs grew, so grew the length of his supply line. Weapons and equipment seized in battle and horses taken from prisoners and farmers proved to be his only salvation. Rather than resting in remount facilities, Southern troopers tried to keep up with their comrades on foot until they found a horse. Otherwise, they made a long journey home in search of a horse, or they transferred to the infantry.[20]

Seeking to keep as many of Stuart's men out of the saddle as possible, Gen. Henry Halleck told Hooker on June 25 to "impress every serviceable animal likely to fall into the hands of the enemy. There are many animals in Loudoun County and the adjacent parts of Maryland. These should be seized to save them from the enemy, as well as to supply yourself."[21]

Supply problems make determining the actual strength of a cavalry command more difficult than doing so for an infantry command, as effective or ready for duty strength includes men and horses. Men went on and off the sick list every day, deserted, or went home on furlough; alternatively, they transferred to duty as teamsters with the supply train, to hospitals as temporary staff, to artillery batteries as temporary replacements, to staff or escort duties, or to a myriad of other assignments. Men also went to dismount facilities when their horses broke down due to disease, overuse, or lack of proper care.

Horses, regardless of their size and strength, proved extremely fragile, especially under wartime conditions. The level of care and concern exhibited by their masters varied from man to man and from day to day based upon what duty a unit had been tasked with. Marching and fighting in the extreme heat of June 1863, under near constant battle conditions for six days exacted a toll we may never appreciate. During the critical six days in the Loudoun Valley, the horses may never have been unsaddled or received any of the daily care they received in camp. Many spent the day in battle and the night on picket duty, carrying the weight of the soldier the entire time. The availability of forage and grain, especially for the men on picket details, would have been inconsistent at best, while the long drought left the grass the animals might browse dry and of little nutritional value. Coated in dust, mud, and sweat, they may not have been groomed for the entire six days. The stone turnpikes quickly wore out or pulled off horseshoes, but the circumstances often meant keeping the animals in the ranks until they went lame or worse. Like their masters, horses went on and off the ready-for-duty list every day and if replacement animals could not be acquired quickly, the soldier went with his horse to a dismount facility. For these reasons and more, published figures regarding the strength of the Cavalry Corps on a given day represent little more than a fuzzy snapshot in time.

ABBREVIATIONS

ABP	Austin Blair Papers
ACPF	Appointment, Commissions and Personal File
AIHA	Albany Institute of History and Art, Albany NY
ALUVA	Alderman Library, University of Virginia, Charlottesville
BCDPL	Burton Collection, Detroit Public Library
BHLUV	Bailey-Howe Library, University of Vermont, Burlington
BLUM	Bentley Library, University of Michigan, Ann Arbor
BU	Brown University, Providence RI
CAP	Cadet Application Papers
CHLCMU	Clarke Historical Library, Central Michigan University, Mount Pleasant
CHS	Connecticut Historical Society, Hartford
CSR	Compiled Service Record
CWMC	Civil War Miscellaneous Collection
CWTIC	Civil War Times Illustrated Collection
DCCM	David Clendenin Court-Martial
DU	Duke University, Durham NC
FHLSC	Friends Historical Library, Swarthmore College, Swarthmore PA
GCC	Gregory Coco Collection
GO	General Order

HL	The Huntington Library, San Marino CA
HML	Hill Memorial Library, Louisiana State University
HRBML	Hargrett Rare Book and Manuscript Library
HSP	Historical Society of Pennsylvania
ISL	Indiana State Library, Indianapolis
JEBSC	James Ewell Brown Stuart Collection, Virginia Historical Society
LBHNM	Little Big Horn National Monument, Crow Agency MT
LC	Library of Congress, Manuscripts Division, Washington DC
LSU	Louisiana State University, Baton Rouge
LVA	Library of Virginia, Richmond
MBL	Mary Ball Library, Lancaster VA
MDAH	Mississippi Department of Archives and History, Jackson
MHS	Missouri Historical Society, St. Louis
MOC	Museum of the Confederacy, Richmond VA
MSA	Maine State Archives
MISLA	Michigan State Archives, Lansing
MJWC	Michael J. Winey Collection
MSUAHC	Michigan State University Archives and Historical Library, Lansing
NARA	National Archives and Records Administration, Washington DC
NCDAH	North Carolina Division of Archives and History, Raleigh
ND	No Date
NP	No Publisher
NPN	No Page Number
NYSAL	New York State Archives and Library, Albany
NYT	*New York Times*
OR	U.S. War Department, *The War of the Rebellion: A Compilation of the Official Records of the Union and Confederate Armies*, 128 vols. (Washington DC, 1890–1901). All references are to series 1 unless otherwise noted.

ORS Janet B. Hewett, Noah Andre Trudeau, and Bryce A. Suderow, eds., *Supplement of the Official Records of the Union and Confederate Armies* (Wilmington: Broadfoot Publishing, 1994). All cites refer to part 1 unless otherwise noted.
PCHS Peters Creek Historical Society, Venetia PA
PHMC Pennsylvania Historical and Museum Commission
PSA Pennsylvania State Archives
PWT *Philadelphia Weekly Times*
RG Record Group
RHS Rochester Historical Society, Rochester NY
RIHS Rhode Island Historical Society
RKKC Robert K. Krick Collection
RLOB Regimental Letter and Order Books
RMRMP Regimental Muster Rolls and Miscellaneous Papers
SHCUNC Southern Historical Collections, University of North Carolina, Chapel Hill
SO Special Order
UG University of Georgia, Athens
UM University of Michigan, Ann Arbor
UMSC University of Mississippi, Special Collections, University
USAHEC Army Heritage and Education Center, Carlisle PA
USMAWP United States Military Academy, West Point
VMHC Virginia Museum of History and Culture, Richmond
VSR Volunteer Service Record
VTHS Vermont Historical Society, Barre
WLCL William L. Clements Library, University of Michigan
WRHS Western Reserve Historical Society, Cleveland OH

NOTES

1. A Dashing Little Fellow

1. Lieutenant Kingsley to Stephen Pleasonton, November 22, 1839; Stephen Pleasonton to Joel Poinsett, November 27, 1839; and letter (author unreadable) to Stephen Pleasonton, November 29, 1839, CAP, M688, NARA. Alfred Pleasonton's birthdate has been confused over the years; Joseph Mills Hanson, in his "Artisan of a Cavalry Corps," 6, lists his birth month as June, while J. David Petruzzi gives his birth month as July in "Fleeting Fame," 22. In his letter, Stephen Pleasonton gives his birthday as January 7, 1824. See also Custer (now Donahue), "Knight of Romance."

2. Gen. Charles Gratiot to Stephen Pleasonton, Philadelphia, December 7, 1839; Alfred Pleasonton to Joel Poinsett, August 18, 1840, CAP, M688, NARA.

3. Alfred Pleasonton to Gen. Roger Jones, July 16, 1844; Alfred to the president, August 23, 1844; Alfred to General Jones, April 12, 1846, March 18, 1847, July 23, 1848, and April 7, 1850, and Stephen Pleasonton to George Crawford, April 16, 1850, RG 94, M567, NARA.

4. Alfred Pleasonton to Lt. John Trevitt, December 27, 1851, RG 94, Entry 159; Stephen Pleasonton to Jefferson Davis, March 7, 1853; Alfred Pleasonton to Col. Samuel Cooper, March 8, 1853, GO 4, July 1, 1854; Alfred Pleasonton to Colonel Cooper October 22, 1854; Augustus Pleasonton to Jefferson Davis, February 9, 1855; and Alfred Pleasonton to Davis, March 8, 1855, RG 94, M567, NARA; Rodenbough, *From Everglade to Canon*, 444. According to Augustus, Alfred returned from Mexico in poor health.

5. Col. William Harney to Col. Samuel Cooper, March 21, 1855; Alfred Pleasonton to Cooper, April 20, 1855, February 23, 1856, and September 23, 1856; and Lt. George Ihrie to Cooper, July 29, 1860, December 9 and 15, 1860, RG 93, M567, NARA; Adams, *General William S. Harney*, 32–33, 36, 47–51, 102–3, 139–40, 150, 159–73. In 1834 Harney beat a slave to death, fled from prosecution, and returned for trial only after the case had dropped from the headlines. His acquittal almost certainly reflected the societal attitudes and prejudices of the time. In 1847 during the battle of Chapultepec, Harney forced thirty Irish deserters to stand for hours under a broiling sun with a noose around their necks, before hanging them just as American troops gained the victory.

6. Adams, *General William S. Harney*, 212; William Harney to Secretary of War John Floyd, September 1860; Alfred Pleasonton to Maj. Gen. Robert Patterson, April 23, 1861; Patterson to Pleasonton, April 24, 1861; Pleasonton to Col. Edward Townsend, April 28, 1861; Lt. Col. Henry Scott to Pleasonton, May 2, 1861; and Pleasonton to Scott, May 4, 1861, RG 94, M567 and M619, NARA. Whether or not Pleasonton rejoined his regiment as ordered, prior to the command reaching Washington, is uncertain. Evidence, including post returns, suggests he did, while other evidence, including his own communications, suggests he did not.

7. Lambert, *Hundred Years*, 64–65; *OR* 12, pt. 3, 760–61; Alfred Pleasonton to AAG, Provost Marshall General, April 19, 1862, RG 94, M619; Pleasonton's Report of Civil War Service, RG 94, M1098; Pleasonton to Col. Rufus Ingalls and Asst. Sec. of War John Tucker to Gen. Montgomery Meigs, August 30, 1862, RG 107, M504, NARA; August Kautz Diary, June 30–July 8, August 13, 23, 26–27, 1862, LC; Sears, *Papers of George B. McClellan*, 396.

8. Styple, *Generals in Bronze*, 128; Hard, *History of the Eighth Cavalry Regiment*, 182; *Irish-American Weekly*, October 11, 1862; *New York Sun*, October 18, 1891.

9. Ford, *A Cycle of Adams Letters*, 1:8; Adams, *An Autobiography*, 153; Freiheit, *Boots and Saddles*, 404.

10. *OR* 19, pt. 1, 878, and pt. 2, 52.

11. Fordney, *George Stoneman*, 2; Ness, *Regular Army on the Eve of the Civil War*, 169; Waugh, *Class of 1846*, 46; Townsend, *Campaigns of a Non-Combatant*, 96. In a rather fawning sketch, the editors of the *Gallipolis Journal* [Ohio], May 21, 1863, refer to Stoneman as "dashing." Shortly after Chancellorsville, then–army commander Joseph Hooker, who repeatedly blamed Stoneman for his failed campaign, spoke of him as "a brave good man but [. . .] spoiled by McClellan and the piles," referring to Stoneman's debilitating battle with hemorrhoids; see Dennett, *Lincoln and the Civil War*, 85. Years later, Hooker referred to Stoneman as a "devil" and accused him of going to such an extreme to avoid the enemy that he "never accomplished anything," see *San Francisco Chronicle*, May 23, 1872.

12. *OR* 19, pt. 1, 73–74, and pt. 2, 50, 53, 77–78, 419.

13. *OR* 19, pt. 1, 73, and pt. 2, 39–40, 43–44. Historian Wilbur Nye termed Pleasonton's report "consistently mendacious"; see Nye, "How Stuart Got Back across the Potomac," 45.

14. *Louisville Daily Courier*, November 27, 1861; *Cattaraugus Freeman*, as quoted in *Fredonia Censor*, July 30, 1862; Laas, *Wartime Washington*, 194–95.

15. George Stoneman to Mrs. [Hardisty], September 30, 1862, and Capt. Richard Irwin to Stoneman, October 3, 1862, M504, NARA.

16. Basler, *The Collected Works of Abraham Lincoln*, 6:79–80, 93; *OR* 21, pt. 1, 815, and 25, pt. 2, 51; George Stoneman to Col. Robert Ramsay, January 1, 1866, RG 94, M1395, NARA; *San Francisco Chronicle*, May 23, 1872. Ever the politician, Lincoln may have been seeking to take advantage of Stoneman's connection to Maryland through his wife and her family as a means of further solidifying the state's place in the Union.

17. *OR* 25, pt. 2, 100–108; Gen. Alpheus Williams to Col. William Creighton, February 25, 1863, and Gen. Seth Williams to Gen. Daniel Butterfield, February 26, 1863, RG 393, Pt. 2, Entry 2193, NARA; Bigelow Jr., *Campaign of Chancellorsville*, 66. Hooker promised a major general's commission to Pleasonton if he prevented the Confederates from escaping. His promise hints at Pleasonton's ambition but the cavalryman did not respond. A full discussion of the fight at Hartwood Church is beyond the scope of this book.

Though Pleasonton appears dilatory, unpublished orders suggest a more complicated and confused situation than historians and critics portray. Many messages do not carry a time as to when sent or received making an accurate reconstruction of events nearly impossible. Had there been any credible evidence Pleasonton had knowingly sabotaged Stoneman's efforts to mount an effective response to the raid, Hooker would have called him to account for his actions.

18. *ORS*, 4, 537; Pickerill, *History of the Third Indiana Cavalry*, 69.

19. Lt. Frank W. Dickerson to Dear Father, May 23, 1863, CWMC, USAHEC; Urwin, *Custer Victorious*, 50; Lt. George Custer to Judge Christiancy, May 31, 1863, George Custer Papers, USMAWP. For other comments critical of Pleasonton during the same period see Col. John McIntosh to Gen. William Averell, May 8, 1863, William Averell Papers, NYSLA, and Walter Newhall to Dear Father, May 14, 1863, Walter Newhall Letters, HSP. See also Captain Adams to Mother, May 12, 1863, Ford, *A Cycle of Adams Letters*, 2:8. All three men had recently been in General Averell's division until Hooker relieved Averell and their comments, while all similar, need to be read within the context of Averell's being relieved from command.

20. *NYT*, May 5, 1863; *OR* 25, pt. 1, 773, 775. In his report and subsequent accounts, Pleasonton counted twenty-two guns on his line. In his letter of May 12, Captain Adams makes his oft-quoted comment describing Pleasonton as "a newspaper humbug. You always see his name in the papers." See Captain Adams to Mother, May 12, 1863, Ford, *Cycle of Adams Letters*, 2:8. The timing suggests Adams had read Swinton's account, but in an age of searchable digital newspaper databases no other evidence supports Adams's comment.

21. *OR* 25, pt. 1, 772–76, 787–88. See also Griffin, *Three Years a Soldier*, 97.

22. Pleasonton, "Successes and Failures," 180n; *NYT*, May 10, 1863. The statement referring to Pleasonton as having saved the army is credited to Maj. Clifford Thomson, one of Pleasonton's aides. Thomson, a former correspondent for the *New York Tribune*, was devoted to Pleasonton, referring to him once as the "Little Chief," see Thomson to Lincoln, May 21, 1864, Abraham Lincoln Papers, LC.

23. *OR* 25, pt. 1, 387, 394; Gen. Daniel Sickles to Edwin Stanton, May 17, 1863, RG 94, M1064, NARA (emphasis in original). Hooker may have offered or considered offering the command to Gen. Winfield S. Hancock and Gen. John Buford; see Hancock, *Reminiscences of Winfield Scott Hancock*, 182–83; *Brooklyn Eagle*, October 20, 1878. In his campaign report, dated May 20, 1863, the day Stoneman took medical leave, General Sickles enumerated the cannon collected by Pleasonton on May 2. As a matter of fact, or design, his total matched that given by Pleasonton in earlier accounts.

24. Gen. Alfred Pleasonton to Lt. Col. Andrew Alexander, May 20, 1863, Entry 1449, NARA; *OR* 25, pt. 2, 513. Seeking to prevent Stoneman's return, Hooker ordered him to report to the War Department for further orders once his medical leave expired; see Gen. Seth Williams, SO, June 5, 1863, RG 94, M1064, NARA. Hooker never forgave Stoneman, as well as General Oliver O. Howard, for, as Hooker said in 1878, "my failure at Chancellorsville." And, as Pleasonton may have done in October 1862, Hooker held Stoneman's Southern-born wife against him. As he wrote in a letter of March 24, 1879, Hooker deemed Stoneman to have been "emasculated" by his wife and his medical condition; see Hooker to Samuel P. Bates, December 24, 1878, and Hooker to Bates, March 24, 1879, Bates Collection, PHMC, PSA, courtesy of John Hennessy.

2. Rebuilding the Cavalry Corps

1. *OR* 25, pt. 1, 1067–71, and 25, pt. 2, 484; Col. Daniel Rucker to Col. Rufus Ingalls, May 12, 1863, M504, NARA.

2. *OR* 25, pt. 2, 469, 474–75, 480, 483, 493–94.

3. *OR* 25, pt. 2, 515–16; *ORS* 4, 474–75; Gen. Daniel Rucker to Capt. Colin Ferguson, May 23, 1863, M504; Unsigned Memorandum from General Meigs's Office, May 23, 1863, RG 92, Entry 225, NARA; *Boston Journal*, June 23, 1863. Though several Southern soldiers spoke of making a raid in letters home, no official Southern records confirming plans for such a raid have been found. However, the Federals could not ignore the threat, and attempts to thwart the raid governed their actions from May 20 until July 2, 1863. For a deeper discussion of the rumored raid see O'Neill, *Chasing Jeb Stuart and John Mosby*, 188–253.

4. *OR* 25, pt. 2, 516–17, 520. General Halleck badly overestimated the effective strength of the Cavalry Corps (that is the number of men and horses ready for duty in the field), when, on May 23, he counted nine thousand to ten thousand men ready for duty. On May 27 Pleasonton gave a more accurate estimate of fewer than five thousand men available for duty; see *OR* 25, pt. 2, 515, 533.

5. *OR* 25, pt. 2, 542–43; Gen. Daniel Rucker to Capt. George W. Meade, Capt. E. S. Allen to Capt. Perley Pitkin, Lt. John Spangler to Gen. David Gregg, and Spangler to Capt. W. H. Brown, all dated June 2, 1863, M504, SO 16 from Gen. Gregg, June 2, 1863, RG 393, Pt. 2, Entry 1534, and Pleasonton to Col. William Gamble, June 2, 1863, RG 393, Pt. 2, Entry 1464, NARA.

6. Capt. Andrew Cohen to Gen. John Buford, June 4, 1863, M504, NARA; *OR* 27, pt. 1, 31–33. Stahel did assist on June 9, but only by guarding Pleasonton's camps on the north bank of the Rappahannock River, at Pleasonton's request.

3. Reorganization

1. *OR* 27, pt. 1, 903, and 27, pt. 3, 45–46. On June 7, as Hooker and Pleasonton formulated their plans to attack Stuart, Col. George Sharpe offered his assessment of Stuart's strength. He believed Stuart's division numbered 12,900 men, while "observers" of Stuart's review thought he had twenty thousand men in the ranks. "I respectfully suggest," Sharpe told Hooker, "that a force of the enemy's cavalry, not less than 12,000 and possibly 15,000 men strong are on the eve of making the most important expedition ever attempted in this country." Hooker ordered Pleasonton "to disperse and destroy the rebel force assembled in the vicinity of Culpeper and to destroy his trains & supplies of all descriptions." Pleasonton had not done so, and he created a lasting controversy when he termed his mission a reconnaissance in force. Doing so allowed him to claim a significant victory, when, in fact, the battle resulted in a draw at best. Any detailed discussion about the battle of Brandy Station is beyond the scope of this book.

2. Mitchell, *Letters of Major General James E. B. Stuart*, 325; Frederick Newhall, "How Lee Lost the Use of His Cavalry," *PWT*, September 28, 1878. General Buford may have instigated the effort, seeking to learn the fate of his aide, Capt. Joseph O'Keeffe. Capt. Myles Keogh, another member of Buford's staff led the detail; see Lt. Col. Andrew Alexander to Gen. David Gregg, June 10, 1863, C. Ross Smith Papers, USAHEC.

3. *OR* 27, pt. 3, 37–39; Gen. Julius Stahel to John Devereux and Stahel to General Pleasonton, June 9, 1863, and Col. George Sharpe to Capt. John McEntee and Sharpe

to General Pleasonton, June 10, 1863, M504, NARA; Lt. Col. Andrew Alexander to Gen. John Buford, June 10, 1863, C. Ross Smith Papers, USAHEC.

4. Nathan Webb Diary, WLCL, UM; letter from an unidentified officer in the First Maine, June 11, 1863, *Bangor Daily Whig and Courier*, June 20, 1863; Tobie, *History of the First Maine Cavalry*, 156. The captured flag is often misidentified as belonging to the Fourth Virginia or Hampton Legion. Lt. J. Wade Wilson, Sixth Independent New York Battery, credited a man in his section with shooting the flag-bearer. But, according to Wilson, "a lame and skittish horse upon which he was mounted at the time," prevented the man from recovering the flag; see *OR* 27, pt. 1, 1027. Further confusing the matter, however, the soldier, identified by Wilson as Sylvanus Currant, does not appear on the battery roster. In fact Currant transferred to the battery in September 1862 from the First Massachusetts Infantry and served with the battery for the remainder of his enlistment.

5. General David Gregg's Circular, June 11, 1863, RG 393, Pt. 2, Entry 1534.

6. General Rufus Ingalls to Lt. Col. William LeDuc, June 8, 1863; Capt. E. S. Allen to Capt. Perley Pitkin, June 10, and June 11; Lt. Col. Charles Sawtelle to Capt. Samuel McKee, June 13, 1863, M504, NARA. By one account, the Federals lost more than fifteen hundred horses; see Baldino, *Family and Nation*, 161. The high demand for horses placed increased pressure on contractors to meet their contracts, which increased fraud. Inspectors soon began rejecting large numbers of horses as too old, too young, blind, wind-blown, spavined, and ring-boned, among other complaints; see for example, Gen. Montgomery Meigs to Maj. Stewart Van Vliet and Capt. H. B. Lacey to Capt. Charles Tompkins, June 13, 1863, RG 92, M745, NARA. Regarding Pleasonton still having to compete with Stahel for horses, see General Meigs to Gen. Daniel Rucker, June 8, 1863, RG 92, M745, NARA.

7. *OR* 27, pt. 3, 57, 64. Pleasonton made the changes after seeking Hooker's permission, though why he did so is unclear. He may have sought Hooker's okay, as Hooker seemed to admire Colonel Duffié and had recommended him for promotion on May 13. Duffie took command of di Cesnola's brigade, pending promotion of a permanent brigadier. Thus, di Cesnola resumed command of the Fourth New York. Col. Percy Wyndham had been wounded at Brandy Station and went to Washington to recover. Pleasonton did not remove him from brigade command.

8. Alfred Pleasonton to My Dear General, June 23, 1863, Alfred Pleasonton Papers, LC.

9. Judson Kilpatrick's Commission Branch File, RG 94, M1064, and Col. Judson Kilpatrick to Sen. Ira Harris, June 11, 1863, M504; General Alfred Pleasonton to Gen. Herman Haupt, June 11, 1863, C. Ross Smith Papers, USAHEC; *OR* 27, pt.3, 905.

4. Conflict and Controversy

1. J. H. Person to Dear Mother, June 10, 1863, Southgate-Jones Family Papers, DU; Bradshaw, *Diary of Charles William McVicar*, 13; *The Civil War Reminiscences of William Brent*, RKKC.

2. Hackley, *Little Fork Rangers*, 85; Wade Hampton's GO 24, June 11, 1863, RKKC; *OR* 27, pt. 2, 719–20.

3. Blackford, *War Years with Jeb Stuart*, 16; letter signed "Bohemian," October 5, 1861, *Richmond Dispatch*, October 8, 1861.

4. Wert, *Cavalryman of the Lost Cause*, 2, 7, 13, 17, 20–21; Charles Collins letter of November 19, 1849, and Thomas Averett to Sir, February 7, 1850, Stuart's West Point Application File, RG 94, M688, NARA.

5. Wert, *Cavalryman of the Lost Cause*, 25–29.

6. Wert, *Cavalryman of the Lost Cause*, 19, 29–30; Chalfant, *Cheyennes and Horse Soldiers*, 180–99, 203–4, 273–79.

7. Wert, *Cavalryman of the Lost Cause*, 36–39; Thomas, "'Greatest Service,'" 348, 352–55.

8. Thomas, "Greatest Service," 352, 355–57. Emphasis is Stuart's.

9. Wert, *Cavalryman of the Lost Cause*, 42–45, 64–65.

10. Letter signed "Bohemian," October 5, 1861, *Richmond Dispatch*, October 8, 1861; *Memphis Daily Appeal*, June 24, 1862.

11. Wert, *Cavalryman of the Lost Cause*, 221, 225–33; OR 25, pt. 2, 792. Disappointed at not receiving the corps, Stuart complained to Lee. Though his letter has been lost, Stuart's tenor may be surmised from Lee's cryptic response. Faced with a command crisis more critical than Stuart's bruised ego, Lee told his cavalry chief he hoped he did not "require bolstering by out-of-place expressions of my opinion."

12. *Richmond Sentinel*, June 11 and 12, 1863.

13. *Richmond Examiner*, June 13, 1863.

14. Jones, *Rebel War Clerk's Diary*, 223; James Foster to Dear Kate, June 13, 1863, James Foster and Family Collection, HML, LSU; Chiswell Dabney to Dear Father, June 14, 1863, Saunders Family Collection, VMHC.

15. Stuart to My Darling Wife, June 20, 1863, James Ewell Brown Stuart Collection, VHS; *Richmond Whig*, June 16, 1863.

5. An Army on the Move

1. OR 27, pt. 1, 34–35, 37–38, and pt. 3, 60, 72–73, 88–89; Sparks, *Inside Lincoln's Army*, 258. Hooker had advanced three corps on June 11, but he appears to have done so to counter the threat of the enemy crossing the river near Bealeton Station and cutting the Orange and Alexandria Railroad.

2. OR 27, pt. 1, 38, and pt. 3, 72–73, 82–83, 86–89; Ulric Dahlgren Memorandum Book, John Dahlgren Papers, LC.

3. OR 27, p.t 2, 185, and pt. 3, 92.

4. OR 27, pt. 2, 785; Col. Philip Figyelmesy to Gen. Samuel Heintzelman, June 8, 1863, RG 393, Pt. 1, Entry 5383, NARA; letter signed Q. M. S., First Michigan, Fairfax Court House, June 18, 1863, *Cass County Republican*, July 2, 1863. Major Brewer believed he had encountered 150 Southerners at Waterloo and another 300 at Front Royal, and trooper Q. M. S. believed these men belonged to Brig. Gen. Albert G. Jenkins's brigade and Brig. Gen. William E. Jones's brigade. That Brewer had just returned from the valley on June 12 may have convinced Hooker not to rush another reconnaissance to the valley.

5. OR 27, pt. 3, 81–82; Dahlgren Memorandum Book, LC. General Reynolds also ordered his infantry to concentrate at Manassas, possibly in view of receiving an attack through Thoroughfare Gap but also as a resupply point; see Reynolds to Gen. Seth Williams, June 13, 1863, M504, NARA. Following the meeting between Hooker and his commanders, Hooker's aide, Capt. Ulric Dahlgren, noted in his diary, "Quite evident that Bull Run will again be fought over." His statement almost certainly reflects the opinion expressed by Hooker during the meeting.

6. OR 27, pt. 3, 82, and 51, pt. 1, 1054; S. L. Gracey, *Annals of the Sixth Pennsylvania Cavalry* (Philadelphia PA, 1868), 176; Itinerary Sixth U.S. Cavalry, RG 94, M744, and General Reynolds to General Pleasonton, June 13, 1863, M504, NARA. Though a long

drought had prevailed for weeks, several accounts confirm rain during the evening, including Krick, *Civil War Weather*, 101.

7. *OR* 27, pt. 1, 973, and pt. 3, 82, 88; General Pleasonton to General Reynolds, June 13, 1863, C. Ross Smith Papers, USAHEC; John Barr Diary, HSP; Carlos Lyman Diary, WRHS; Neese, *Three Years in the Confederate Horse Artillery*, 180. At least one of Pleasonton's regiments remained detached from the corps for several weeks. After reconnoitering the Northern Neck, east of the Lower Rappahannock River, for evidence of a Southern column crossing the river below the army, the Eighth Pennsylvania received orders to assist Maj. Gen. Winfield Hancock and his II Corps covering the withdrawal of the army.

8. Lloyd, *History*, 56–57; Regimental Committee, *History*, 251; *NYT*, June 26, 1863; William Carter Diary, LVA; Col. Andrew Alexander to General Gregg, June 13, 1863, Entry 1449, and General Reynolds to General Williams, June 13, 1863, M504, NARA. When Beaumont's men tried to bluff their way past the pickets at Amissville, the Southerners identified themselves as General Ewell's men, but they probably belonged to Colonel Munford's cavalry brigade, as Ewell had already entered the Shenandoah Valley.

9. *OR* 27, pt. 1, 38, pt. 2, 185, and pt. 3, 84; Fishel, *Secret War*, 427; General Reynolds to General Williams, four messages of June 13, 1863, M504, NARA. Reynolds also found the telegraph line destroyed "for some distance," along the Warrenton or Marsh Road, which left him out of telegraphic communication with Hooker for several days. In response, Hooker told Pleasonton to detach a cavalry force to patrol the line; see Reynolds to Williams, June 13, 1863, M504, NARA.

10. Jonathan Hager Diary; Jones, *Under the Stars and Bars*, 110–11.

11. Samuel Gilpin Diary, LC; Charles Smith to Dear Parents, June 14, 1863, Smith Family Papers, CWMC, USAHEC. Emphasis is Gilpin's.

12. *OR* 27, pt. 3, 99; Gracey, *Annals*, 177. Hazeltine's account is written into his personal copy of Gracey's history at the HSP and provided by Clark Hall. Hazeltine's report may have influenced Pleasonton's inaccurate report to Hooker early on June 15; see *OR* 27, pt. 3, 114. As the Sixth U.S. passed through Thoroughfare Gap, guerrillas shot and killed Pvt. Nathaniel Owen. For more on Owen's death see Davis, *Common Soldier, Uncommon War*, 401–4; Tattnall Paulding Diary, courtesy of Dr. James Milgram; Caughey and Jones, *6th United States Cavalry*, 96.

13. General Reynolds to General Butterfield, June 14, 1863, M504, NARA; *OR* 27, pt. 3, 99, 104–6, and 51, pt. 1, 1054–55. Pleasonton replied to Reynolds's second message regarding Thoroughfare Gap after their meeting, suggesting the message reached Pleasonton's headquarters while he was with Reynolds. He replied at 11:15 a.m.

14. General Pleasonton to General Reynolds, June 14, 1863, C. Ross Smith Papers, USAHEC.

15. Col. John Taylor to General Gregg, June 14, 1863, Entry 1449, NARA. General Ewell began attacking the Union forces at Winchester on June 13, and the fighting continued through the fifteenth. Pleasonton and Reynolds may not have been aware of the crisis at Winchester, but officials in Washington would have known.

16. Gen. John Abercrombie to Lt. Col. Joseph Taylor, Lt. Col. T. A. Meysenberg to General Stahel, Maj. Harvey Baldwin to General Howard, and Stahel to Howard, all June 14, 1863, M504, NARA; Dexter Macomber Diary, CHLCMU. General Howard also asked Capt. Richard Dinsmore "to make observations in the direction of Thoroughfare Gap and Aldie," but Dinsmore found "the weather was such as to prevent me from

being of any service," see Dinsmore to Capt. Lemuel Norton, August 10, 1863, RG 393, Pt. I, Entry 4083, NARA, courtesy of the late Horace Mewborn. A third gap, Hopewell Gap, lay between Thoroughfare and Aldie Gaps.

17. Ulric Dahlgren Memorandum Book, LC; *OR* 27, pt. 1, 41–42. General Butterfield told Halleck on the fifteenth, "Two of our best scouts returned . . . yesterday. . . . Citizens say that the cavalry expedition was intended for Alexandria. . . . They believe that a great cavalry raid is now given up." However, in a letter the same day, a soldier in the Tenth Vermont Infantry, stationed along the Potomac River, noted, "Yesterday we heard that [Stuart] was coming this way with 12,000 Cavalry to make a raid through Maryland and PA." In fact, the idea of a raid against Washington lingered until July 2; see *OR* 27, pt. 1, 41, and William White to Dear Friend, June 14 & 15, 1863, William White Letters, VTHS.

18. *OR* 27, pt. 3, 114–15; General Reynolds to Gen. Daniel Butterfield, June 15, 1863, M504, NARA. Pleasonton based his conclusions regarding Longstreet upon information gathered June 14. Unfortunately, none of the reports from which he drew his conclusions have been found. Longstreet began departing Culpeper on the fifteenth and Stuart placed three of his brigades in motion on the same day to screen Longstreet's advance. Rather than lingering on the Rappahannock River, Ewell advised Lee at 5 a.m. on the fifteenth that he had taken Winchester, while Hill began moving toward Culpeper the same day. Hooker did not control the troops along the Monocacy River, but Pleasonton should have sent the message to Hooker to be forwarded to Stanton or Halleck. Whether angered by Pleasonton's subverting the chain of command or possibly at Stanton's or Halleck's direction, Hooker told Maj. Thomas Eckert, head of the military telegraph in Washington, "Have all Pleasonton's dispatches copied and sent to Asst. Sec. of War and Halleck." General Butterfield's message to Eckert is difficult to read but suggests a growing dissatisfaction with Pleasonton; see General Butterfield to Major Eckert, June 15, 1863, M504, NARA.

19. *OR* 27, pt. 3, 106, 116–17, 119. Pleasonton's location caused some confusion during the day. He had been ordered to concentrate at Centreville, but instead he directed his men to Manassas Junction. Though his decision violated his orders, kept his men behind the advance elements of the army, and may have further angered Hooker and Reynolds, Manassas Junction made more practical sense being along the railroad from where he could be more easily supplied. Pleasonton further confused his superiors when, at some point during the day, he made his headquarters at Union Mills, several miles east of Manassas Junction; see General Reynolds to General Butterfield, June 15, 1863, M504, NARA. Meade told Reynolds that morning, "Have not seen Pleasonton. An aide of his called at the telegraph office for his dispatches." In another message, Meade told Reynolds, "Lt. [George] Yates, ADC to Pleasonton, is here." See Meade to Reynolds, June 15, 1863, M504. Yates probably informed Meade of Pleasonton's conclusions regarding Ewell and Hill.

20. General Meade to General Reynolds, June 15, 1863, M504, NARA; Lt. Col. Andrew Alexander to General Gregg, and Alexander to General Buford, June 15, 1863, C. Ross Smith Papers, USAHEC; Norman Ball Diary, CHS; Carlos Lyman Diary; Regimental Committee, *History*, 251; Lloyd, *History*, 57; Hall, *History*, 129. Based upon diary and postwar accounts, most regiments followed the custom of hurry up and wait and left later than planned. Pleasonton also assigned batteries of horse artillery to move with

each brigade but did not specify the batteries by name or unit designation; see Lt. Colonel Alexander to Capt. John Tidball, C. Ross Smith Papers, USAHEC.

21. *OR* 27, pt. 3, 114; General Stahel to Lt. Col. Joseph Taylor, June 15, 1863, M504, NARA; Lt. Col. Andrew Alexander to General Buford, June 15, 1863, C. Ross Smith Papers, USAHEC; Paulding Diary; Rodenbough, *From Everglade to Canon*, 291. General Howard also sought to establish a signal station on Bull Run Mountain near Aldie and requested a cavalry escort from Stahel to assist his signal officers. Whether he set up the station is unknown; see Lt. Col. Meysenberg to Maj. Harvey Baldwin, June 15, 1863, M504, NARA. Major Starr may have ordered his regiments to withdraw from the area of Thoroughfare Gap by regiments, as historian Donald Caughey suggests; see Caughey and Jones, *6th United States Cavalry*, 96–97. Samuel Gracey states his regiment left the area of the gap at daylight on the fifteenth; see Gracey, *Annals*, 177. The Pennsylvanians, still recovering from their mauling at Brandy Station on June 9, retired to Fairfax Station and did not participate in any of the fighting in the Loudoun Valley; see *ORS* 3, 797.

22. Sparks, *Inside Lincoln's Army*, 259; *OR* 27, pt. 1, 34–35, 43–45, 47. Hooker and Halleck had been classmates at West Point, though the nature and cordiality of their relationship at the academy is unknown. Their outward hostility toward each other developed during their prewar service in California; see Marszalek, *Commander of All Lincoln's Armies*, 166.

23. *OR* 27, pt. 1, 45.

24. *OR* 27, pt. 1, 44–45.

25. *OR* 27, pt. 1, 47–48.

26. *OR* 27, pt. 1, 45–47.

27. *OR* 27, pt. 3, 146; General Pleasonton to Lt. Col. Andrew Alexander, June 16, 1863, M504, NARA. Southern accounts suggest some in the South believed Hooker blocked the gaps "to prevent a movement of Lee's army towards Manassas," see *Richmond Sentinel*, June 25, 1863.

28. General Pleasonton to General Ingalls, and General Butterfield to Pleasonton, June 16, 1863, M504; Colonel Gregg to General Gregg and Unknown to Pleasonton, June 16, 1863, Entry 1449, NARA; Pleasonton to Quartermaster at Alexandria, Lt. Col. Andrew Alexander to General Gregg and Pleasonton to Gen. Seth Williams, June 16, 1863, C. Ross Smith Papers, USAHEC. General Williams's message to Pleasonton on June 17, 1863 (*OR* 27, pt. 3, 171), confirms the meeting between Hooker and Pleasonton the previous day. They may have discussed what Hooker expected from his cavalry over the next several days and by doing so in person Hooker avoided a written record to be scrutinized by his superiors. Charles Sawtelle, Pleasonton's quartermaster, had been left to supervise the evacuation of the supply base at Aquia. He had not rejoined the Cavalry Corps on the sixteenth, and Pleasonton was handling all logistical matters in his absence; see Pleasonton to Butterfield and Alexander to General Gregg, June 16, 1863, C. Ross Smith Papers, USAHEC.

29. Gilpin Diary; Perry, *Life and Letters*, 194; Alfred Ryder to Dear Friends, June 16, 1863, Ryder Family Papers; Joseph King Letter, June 16, 1863, *Wolverine Citizen*, July 11, 1863 (emphasis in original).

30. *OR* 27, pt. 3, 151–52, and 51, pt. 1, 1060–61; *ORS* 5, 28.

6. Stuart Moves into Loudoun Valley

1. OR 27, pt. 3, 890, 896.

2. OR 27, pt. 2, 687; NYT, June 18, 1863; Thomason Jr., *JEB Stuart*, 412.

3. *Richmond Enquirer*, June 23, 1863; OR 27, pt. 2, 687.

4. OR 27, pt. 2, 687. Stuart may have left Hampton and Jones to bring up the rear of his division as they had suffered the heaviest casualties at Brandy Station and could use the extra rest; see Rod Andrew Jr., *Wade Hampton*, 155.

5. William Carter Diary; Longacre, *Cavalry at Gettysburg*, 28; Thomas Munford to John Batchelder, February 11, 1886, in Ladd and Ladd, *Batchelder Papers*, 2:1201. The date upon which Stuart's troopers began to move is uncertain. In his report, written in August, Stuart states that Munford moved on June 15, but Carter gives the date in his diary, presumably written at the time, as June 16. According to an 1886 letter from Munford, Fitz Lee was kicked by the horse either on the evening of June 16 or the morning of June 17 near Paris. Munford remembered being placed in command at Paris, while Lee accompanied the brigade in an ambulance. Thus, Lee may have briefly resumed command after Brandy Station, though other sources suggest Munford remained in command the entire time. The site of Stuart's main encampment on the night of June 16–17 is often referred to as Somerset or Somerset Mills. Local historian Lee Lawrence corrects the spelling in Lawrence, *Society of Rebels*, 184.

6. OR 27, pt. 2, 687; John Chowning Diary, MBL; Thomas W. B. Edwards's Diary, LVA; Clark, *Histories*, 3:559; Ephraim Bowman Diary, ALUVA.

7. Samuel S. Biddle to My Dear Rosa, June 16, 1863, Samuel S. Biddle Papers, DU; Bradshaw, Civil War Diary, typescript in author's possession; Theodore S. Garnett Jr., "Cavalry Service with Gen. Stuart," PWT, February 9, 1879.

8. Davis, "Cavalry in the Gettysburg Campaign," 326.

9. Scheel, *Loudoun Discovered*, 3:4–5, 14; John Kelly, "How Did Little River Get Its Name?" *Washington Post*, November 30, 2013; Snickersville Turnpike Association, "Driving Historic Snickersville Turnpike" (NP); Mosby Heritage Area Association, "Old Carolina Road" (NP).

10. Virginia Outdoors Foundation, "Aldie's Mills" (NP), 1; Scheel, *Loudoun Discovered*, 3:12–13.

11. Davis, "Cavalry in the Gettysburg Campaign," 326.

12. Nevins, *A Diary of Battle*, 119; letter signed Chaplain to Dear Union, June 23, 1863, *Rochester Daily Union & Advertiser*, June 29, 1863; Peter Alexander to Editor, June 19, 1863, *Savannah Republican*, July 6, 1863; Survivor's Association, *History of the Corn Exchange Regiment*, 225; McDonald, *A History of the Laurel Brigade*, 148.

13. Donker, *Diary of George S. Lockley*, 67; John Berry Diary, CWTIC, USAHEC; Survivor's Association, *History of the Corn Exchange Regiment*, 220; Theodore Case to Friend McKinstry, November 22, 1862, *Fredonia Censor*, December 3, 1862; Jonathan Hager Diary.

14. Survivor's Association, *History of the Corn Exchange Regiment*, 224; P. M. L. to Editor, April 6, 1863, *Grand Rapids Daily Eagle*, April 15, 1863; Brady, *Hurrah for the Artillery!*, 90, 100; Greenleaf, *Letters to Eliza*, 36; Acken, *Inside the Army of the Potomac*, 287; John Geary to Dear Wife, March 15, 1862, John Geary Letters, HSP.

15. Kimball Pearson, Letter of June 19, 1863, CWMC 2nd Series, USAHEC; Henry Smith to Dear Mother, Sisters and Brother, September 24, 1862, Henry A. Smith Letters, VTHS. For other examples of convalescents being paroled in the valley, see OR 19, pt.

2, 8; the Asa Story Diary, NYSAL, and accounts of Maj. Joseph Gilmer's expedition to Middleburg in February 1863.

16. Survivor's Association, *History of the Corn Exchange Regiment*, 227.

17. Meade, *Life and Letters of Meade*, 1:389; email from Lee Lawrence to author, July 5, 2017. Mrs. Lawrence recently published *Dark Days in Our Beloved Country* and *Society of Rebels*. Catherine Broun, who lived near Middleburg, and Amanda Edmonds, who lived near Paris, along with Ida Dulany, who lived near Upperville, and Susan Caldwell of Warrenton witnessed the war at their doorstep in mid-June 1863 and their letters and diaries help us to understand an often forgotten or ignored aspect of the conflict. Mrs. Lawrence has masterfully edited the Broun diary and reedited the Edmonds diary, and she kindly agreed to write a few comments for this study.

18. Welton, *"My Heart Is so Rebellious,"* 191.

19. Lawrence, *Dark Days in our Beloved Country*, I, v, 80; X to editor, April 1863, *Richmond Sentinel*, April 18, 1863.

20. Mackall, Meserve, and Sasscer, *Shadow of the Enemy*, xvii–xxviii, 159; Musick, *6th Virginia Cavalry*, 111. Prominent civilians often found themselves held as hostages by both sides as a means of assuring good treatment of other prisoners.

21. Lawrence, *Society of Rebels*, iv, 184.

7. Hooker's Ruse

1. *OR* 27, pt. 1, 46–48, pt. 3, 150–52. Neither Hooker's circular nor Pleasonton's brief order, as printed in the *OR*, include the time the orders were issued. Likewise, none of the unpublished dispatches regarding Pleasonton's meeting with Hooker at Fairfax Station include the time. Hooker probably gave Pleasonton his instructions in person during their meeting.

2. *OR* 27, pt. 1, 962, and pt. 3, 171–72, 178. The idea of sending a lone regiment on the most westerly circuit, and thus the most hazardous, probably originated with Hooker. Snickersville is modern Bluemont.

3. *OR* 27, pt. 3, 178. In his order, Pleasonton states (twice) his intention to make his headquarters at Aldie on the night of June 17, thus confirming he had always recognized the military importance of Aldie. Cardinal directions have been added to Pleasonton's order for clarity. Nolands Ferry dates to the colonial era and carried travelers on the Carolina Road across the Potomac River. Though Civil War maps show the name as Noland's, modern maps list the location as Nolands.

4. *OR* pt. 3, 171–72; U.S. Congress, *Report of the Joint Committee on the Conduct of the War*, 4:32–33.

5. *OR* pt. 3, 172.

6. Martin, *Kill-Cavalry*, 15–20. Kilpatrick preferred Judson and dropped his given first name while a young man.

7. Martin, *Kill-Cavalry*, 20–29; letter signed "A. D." to Dear father, June 11, 1861, *New York Tribune*, June 16, 1861; *Brooklyn Evening Star*, July 31, 1861; Venter, *Kill Jeff Davis*, 7–8; Heitman, *Historical Register and Dictionary*, 597. Samuel Martin takes a harshly negative view of Kilpatrick throughout his biography. The letter signed "A. D." offers a more positive assessment. Bruce Venter's study, though not a biography, offers a balanced appraisal of Kilpatrick.

8. Venter, *Kill Jeff Davis*, 3–4; Edwin Havens to Dear Father, October 12, 1863, Edwin Havens Letters and Diaries, MSUAHC. Some of the paperwork regarding his arrest may be found in his 1867 Commission Branch File at NARA or on Fold3. He was released and the charge dismissed after the owner of the property died suddenly.

9. Edwin Havens letter, the first page of which is missing but possibly dated to March 1864, MSUAHC; Greenwood, *Records of Five Years*, 177. Dr. Jack Welsh notes that "throughout 1863," Kilpatrick "complained frequently of pain in his back and kidney area, particularly after periods of exertion," and often traveled lying prone in an ambulance, see Welsh, *Medical Histories*, 193–94.

10. Angle, *Three Years*, 348; William Wells to Friend Anna, August 30, 1863, William Wells Papers, BHLUV; *OR* 27, pt. 1, 986; Martin, *Kill-Cavalry*, 89; Judson Kilpatrick's Commission Branch File, RG 94, M1064. The editors of the *OR* state, in a note at the bottom of 27, pt.1, 985, that Kilpatrick "was assigned" to the brigade on June 14. The order in which he announced taking command is dated June 16. Other evidence indicates he took command on June 15.

11. Capt. Andrew Cohen to Lt. Col. Andrew Alexander, June 14, 1863, Entry 1449, NARA; *OR* 27, pt. 3, 450; Crowninshield, *A History of the First Regiment Massachusetts Cavalry*, 68–69, 256–58. The missing battalion of the Second New York did not rejoin the regiment until late-July; see Capt. S. L. Brown to Gen. Daniel Rucker, July 17, 1863, M504, NARA. The missing battalion of the First Massachusetts never rejoined the regiment.

12. Capt. Ulric Dahlgren to General Butterfield, and Butterfield to Dahlgren, June 17, 1863, M504, NARA; U.S. Congress, *Report of the Joint Committee*, 4:32–33; Ulric Dahlgren Memorandum Book, LC. General Butterfield's message has been altered (words in brackets) for clarity, without changing Hooker's intent. The written instructions sent by courier rather than by telegraph at 4 p.m. never reached Pleasonton, as John Mosby captured the officer before he could deliver them. The first line of the order states, "Under no circumstances advance the main body of your cavalry beyond Aldie until further information is received of the movements of the enemy." See Gen. Seth Williams to Pleasonton, June 17, 1863, in the Charles Venable Papers, UNC. The entire order, as well as Mosby's role in capturing the order, is discussed in chapter 14.

8. Hard Work Lay Ahead

1. Jeffry Wert, "Colonel Tom Munford—A Man of Achievement, His Unhonored Service," *Civil War Times Illustrated*, June 1985, 29–30.

2. *OR* 12, pt. 1, 417, and pt. 2, 559, 737, 748; General Stuart to General, October 24, 1862, Stuart to General, February 4, 1863, and Stuart to General, September 10, 1863, in Mitchell, *Letters*, 271–75, 290–91, 340–41. See also Munford's Compiled Service Record for letters and petitions from friends and soldiers seeking his promotion. Evidence suggests he received an appointment as brigadier in the last days of the war, but the war ended before the appointment could be confirmed. Not everyone recognized Munford's gallantry, however, as evidenced by Col A. W. Harman's letter to Jedediah Hotchkiss, March 15, 1886, Jedediah Hotchkiss Papers, LC, courtesy of William Miller. "My experience with Col. Munford," Harman wrote, "is that his pen was more powerful than his sword."

3. *OR* 27, pt. 2, 682–83, 737–39; McClellan, *Life and Campaigns*, 283. Neither of the orders cited by Munford is signed by Stuart, but rather by aides. Though arriving late,

Munford incurred sixty-three casualties and lost twenty-nine horses. Munford believed, at least after the war, that Stuart had been surprised at Brandy Station. Whether he voiced his opinions to Stuart in the heated days after the battle is unknown.

4. OR 27, pt. 2, 687.

5. OR 27, pt. 2, 688.

6. OR 27, pt. 2, 739, 745. Stuart says nothing about dividing the command, but Munford and Wickham mention the division of responsibility in their reports. According to Munford, Stuart gave the order splitting the command at Upperville, but the brigade remained together until a point just east of Middleburg.

7. Warner, *Generals in Gray*, 335; Wallace, *Guide to Virginia Military Organizations*, 43; Stiles, *4th Virginia Cavalry*, 143; Williams Wickham's CSR, RG 94, NARA, Col. John Scott; "The Black Horse Cavalry," *PWT*, May 25, 1878; General Stuart to My Dear, Dear Wife, November 6, 1862, in Mitchell, *Letters*, 279.

8. McClellan, *Life and Campaigns*, 289; *Concord Register*, June 22, 1863; OR 27, pt. 2, 745.

9. OR 27, pt. 2, 739; Krick, *Civil War Weather*, 101. Munford said he sent his two regiments across to the Snickersville Turnpike from a point "three miles below Middleburg," or after the command reached Dover's Mill, but doing so would have entailed a rather roundabout route back to Mountville. A more direct route would have been for the men to turn north on the Sam Fred Road on the eastern edge of Middleburg. In an 1894 letter, Munford said he sent the First Virginia to Mountville along with the Second and Third Virginia, but this may be an error of memory, see the *Maine Bugle*, April 1894, 131–32.

9. The Aldie Haystack Charge

1. Nevins, *Diary of Battle*, 221; *New York Herald*, June 19, 1863; Meyer, *Civil War Experiences*, 34. The 2 p.m. temperature at Georgetown was 94 degrees, with the high temperature probably not reached until 3 or 4 p.m. Based upon fascinating new research, historian Jeff Harding believes the heat index for June 17 at 3 p.m. to have been 118 degrees, per phone discussion between author and Jeff Harding, March 22, 2022.

2. *NYT*, June 20, 1863.

3. Albert Wilson's Pension File, RG 94, NARA; Glazier, *Three Years in the Federal Cavalry*, 23. Originally organized as a regular army unit, the regiment contained men from Indiana, New Jersey, Connecticut, Vermont, and Pennsylvania. The Whitakers enlisted from Connecticut.

4. Henry C. Whitaker, "Carbine and Saber, The Fight at Aldie," *National Tribune*, June 9, 1887; *Hartford Daily Courant*. There is little agreement in the accounts as to where the first contact occurred. Kilpatrick reported his men were "less than one mile of [Aldie]," while a soldier writing after the war said the contact took place on the stone bridge over Little River in town. See Kilpatrick's Report in *ORS*, pt. 1, 5, 252; letter from Austin Jacobs, *National Tribune*, November 19, 1885. Henry Whitaker is not known to be related to Daniel and Edward.

5. OR 27, pt. 2, 747; Chaplain Edward Payson to the *New York Evangelist*, November 11, 1863.

6. Philip Neher to A. C. Hull, June 23, 1863, and Neher to My Dear Old Friend and Family, June 28, 1863, Neher Papers, AIHA; Albert Wilson and William Laing Pension Files, RG 94, NARA.

7. *OR* 27, pt. 1, 985–86, 996–97; Tobie, *History of the First Maine*, 156; *NYT*, June 20, 1863; Whitaker, "Carbine and Saber"; Edward Whitaker to My Dear Colonel, June 21, 1863, *First Maine Bugle*, July 1893, 94–95. Though several members of the Second New York reported the errant order that led to the near disaster at Fleetwood Hill, officers and men alike closed ranks to protect the identity of the officer who gave the command. Daniel Whitaker had served with Company D at Brandy Station. Edward Whitaker's letters confirm that Kilpatrick put Daniel Whitaker in command of the squadron. Henry Whitaker recalled eighteen men riding with Company M on June 17. Joseph Firth, Company M, later recalled only thirty-six men riding with the squadron at Aldie, see *National Tribune*, February 1, 1906. Well after the war, Willard Glazier, in *Battles for the Union*, 249, placed Samuel McIrvin in command of the squadron. Glazier was almost certainly not at Aldie as his company remained on the Peninsula until July 17, 1863; see Capt. S. L. Brown to Gen. Daniel Rucker, July 17, 1863, M504. James Moore places Major Samuel McIrvin in command of the attack in a very "dramatic" account; see Moore, *Kilpatrick and Our Cavalry*, 67.

8. *OR* 27, pt. 2, 745–47; Driver, *5th Virginia Cavalry*, 186; Col. Frank Loveland's account of the battle, *Forty-Seventh Annual Reunion*, 16; letter from John Divine to author, August 2, 1991. Placing Stuart's Horse Artillery on the fields at Aldie, Middleburg, and Upperville with any certainty is difficult. Breathed had five guns, including an English Whitworth, but that gun was damaged during the day, possibly while racing to the battlefield and probably saw no action. Wickham probably kept three guns along the Ashby's Gap Turnpike sending the fourth gun to the Snickersville Turnpike. The number of haystacks also remains uncertain. Henry Baldwin, Sixth Ohio, described a long low stack "forty feet long." See excerpt of letter dated August 2, 1863, provided by Ken Lawrence. Correspondent E. A. Paul counted six haystacks, while Henry Whitaker remembered just two. In his exaggerated description, Willard Glazier described rail barricades erected so high "the horses could not leap them." See *NYT*, June 20, 1863, Whitaker, "Carbine and Saber"; Glazier, *Three Years in the Federal Cavalry*, 228–29, and *Battles for the Union*, 248–49.

9. Whitaker, "Carbine and Saber"; Capt. Norman Barrett to Editor, June 24, 1863, *Cleveland Leader*, July 8, 1863.

10. J. E. Miller to Dear Sister, June 24, 1863, in William Dodge's Pension File, also Jasper Raymond's Pension File, RG 94, NARA. J. E. Miller, the bugler mentioned by Henry Whitaker is probably John E. Miller, Company M. Lt. Col. William Stedman, Sixth Ohio, described the ditch or ravine as "3 to 7 feet in depth and 6 to 8 feet in width"; see *OR* 27, pt. 1, 972.

11. *NYT*, June 20, 1863; Captain Barrett to Editor, *Cleveland Leader*, July 8, 1863.

12. *ORS* 5, 283; undated letter from Daniel Townsend, Randol's Battery, courtesy of Bradley Forbush.

13. Captain Barrett to Editor, *Cleveland Leader*, July 8, 1863; Henry Pepper Pension File, RG 94, NARA; *OR* 27, pt. 1, 972.

14. Captain Barrett to Editor, *Cleveland Leader*, July 8, 1863; Carlos Lyman to Dear Ones at Home, June 18, 1863, Carlos Lyman Papers, WRHS; *Newport Mercury*, July 4, 1863; Loveland, *Forty-Seventh Annual Reunion*, 16; Frank Moran's and William Warriner's Pension Files, RG 94, NARA. Doctor's amputated Major Stanhope's arm but he died about a week later, possibly from tetanus.

15. Loveland, *Forty-Seventh Annual Reunion,* 16; OR 27, pt. 2, 747; Austin Jacobs, "The Cavalry Charge at Aldie," *National Tribune,* November 19, 1885; Whitaker, "Carbine and Saber."

16. Whitaker, "Carbine and Saber"; OR 27, pt. 2, 747. Colonel Munford also spoke of the damage done to Boston's men by Breathed's artillery, attributing the problems to "bad ammunition"; see OR 27, pt. 2, 740.

17. OR 27, pt. 2, 747; Rosser, *The Cavalry, A.N.V.,* 30–31; Thomas Rosser to My Dear Wife, June 18, 1863, Thomas Rosser Correspondence, ALUVA. The emphasis is Rosser's. One of the difficulties trying to interpret and piece together the limited accounts of the fight at Aldie is determining how the fight at the haystacks overlapped the fighting along the Snickersville Turnpike. Few participants were involved in both phases of the battle, but Rosser was. He almost certainly led the first counterattack against the New Yorkers in the town, and he was engaged in the heavy fighting on the Snickersville pike, but no evidence confirms he led any attacks against either the Second New York or the Sixth Ohio at the haystacks. Rather, he led or participated in several charges against the First Massachusetts along the Snickersville pike and may have believed he was supporting Captain Boston and his men.

18. Driver, *5th Virginia Cavalry,* 135–270; Records of Confederate Prisoners, RG 94, Entry 179, NARA; Reuben Boston Entry, Volume 104, Roll of Honor Record, MOC, courtesy of Horace Mewborn; Peter White, "A Memoir of Col. R. B. Boston," Grand Camp Confederate Veterans, VMHC, courtesy of Horace Mewborn. Colonel Rosser may have preferred charges against Boston after he returned to the army in 1864, but no records survive; see Thomason, *Jeb Stuart,* 414. Thomason also believed Boston's surrender to be "the only formal surrender of an element of Stuart's cavalry" during the war. Rosser did court-martial Boston after the fight at Tom's Brook in 1864, and Boston was acquitted.

19. James Herrold's Pension File, RG 94, NARA; Captain Barrett to Editor, *Cleveland Leader,* July 8, 1863; OR 27, pt. 1, 972; Whitaker, "Carbine and Saber."

10. The Fiery Ordeal

1. Miller, "Brahmin Janissaries," 208, 212–13; Pearson, *Life of John A. Andrew,* 1:243; Gordon, *Brook Farm to Cedar Mountain,* 17.

2. Miller, "Brahmin Janissaries," 213; *Boston Herald,* November 18, 1915; *Springfield Republican,* March 21 and 23, 1915; Adams, *Autobiography,* 118, 121, 125–26.

3. Ford, *Cycle of Adams Letters,* 2:70; Adams, *Autobiography,* 137. Lt. Edward Flint may have commanded Company C on June 17, in the absence of the assigned captain, and as such he would have held the position at the rear of the squadron.

4. Crowninshield, *History of the First Regiment,* 152; Ford, *Cycle of Adams Letters,* 2:30; Adams, *Autobiography,* 153.

5. ORS, 5, 253.

6. *New Bedford Whaleman's Shipping List and Merchant's Transcript,* June 30, 1863. The news item credits Higginson with alerting the others to the arrival of the enemy and issuing the order to Sargent. The command structure of the regiment suggests Curtis, rather than Higginson, issued the order to Sargent.

7. "F" to Mr. Sentinel, December 14, 1861, *Waltham Sentinel,* December 20, 1861. The writer was George Parks, who spent the war in South Carolina. His reference to

Balaclava refers to the battle in the Crimean War in which the British Light Brigade made its famous charge.

8. *OR* 27, pt. 2, 740, 746; Alexander Dixon Payne Memorandum Book, Payne Family Papers, VMHC; *Staunton Spectator*, October 20, 1863. Lieutenant Walton and his men were part of Company C, Second Virginia. Regarding the Fourth Virginia; see also Scott, "The Black Horse Cavalry," *PWT*, May 25, 1878. Scott credits Payne with having thirty men. The legend of the Black Horse Cavalry persisted after the war and George Kilmer published an article in the *Logansport Pharos Tribune*, January 25, 1897, in which he refers to Payne's "30 men . . . as a forlorn hope." Kilmer took most of his story directly from Scott, and both accounts include an element of truth regarding Payne's men at Aldie, though Kilmer's is the more fanciful. The sunken farm lane is known today as Cobb House Road.

9. Crowninshield, *History of the First Regiment*, 144; *New Bedford Whaleman's Shipping List and Merchant's Transcript*, June 30, 1863; McClellan, *Life and Campaigns*, 299. Crowninshield states that Sargent ordered Lt. George Fillebrown to deploy a platoon as skirmishers, but as Fillebrown belonged to Company G, the order almost certainly came from Higginson or Curtis. In his report, written well after the battle, Col. Horace Sargent, who was not present, claimed that his brother drove Walton's pickets back one and a half miles before encountering the other Southerners. A shorter chase is more likely. Crowninshield, who was not present, described Curtis warning Sargent not to advance beyond an unidentified house, probably the Furr House. Once Curtis observed Sargent's men around the house, he ordered Major Higginson to bring them back. According to Crowninshield, Major Samuel Chamberlain, who had just returned to the regiment after recovering from wounds received at Kelly's Ford in March, but who had not officially resumed his duties, rode with Higginson to recall Sargent and Fillebrown.

10. Crowninshield, *History of the First Regiment*, 144; *New Bedford Whaleman's Shipping List and Merchant's Transcript*, June 30, 1863; McClellan, *Life and Campaigns*, 299.

11. *OR* 27, pt. 2, 740, 748; Henry Matthews, "On the Way to Gettysburg, Pa. Engagements at Aldie, Upperville and Middleburg," *Saint Mary's Beacon*, April 13, 1905; Trout, *Galloping Thunder*, 257; Crowninshield, *History of the First Regiment*, 144–45; Perry, *Life and Letters*, 196–97; *New Bedford Whaleman's Shipping List and Merchant's Transcript*, June 30, 1863. Only three squadrons of the Fourth Virginia fought at Aldie, the other two squadrons accompanied Stuart as his escort that day; see McClellan, *Life and Campaigns*, 298. Bob Trout has reprinted the entire series of articles by Henry Matthews in *Memoirs of the Stuart Horse Artillery Battalion*, vol. 2. The accounts of Higginson's group being cut off all vary in small details, but the basic facts are easily deduced, and the slight differences reconciled.

12. Perry, *Life and Letters*, 196–97; Crowninshield, *History of the First Regiment*, 145; *New Bedford Whaleman's Shipping List and Merchant's Transcript*, June 30, 1863; *Boston Traveler*, June 20, 1863, *Boston Evening Transcript*, June 22, 1863; Henry Higginson's CSR, and George Fillebrown's Pension Record, RG 94, NARA. Higginson and Rosser met after the war and Rosser asked to see "how good a job I did on your face that day at Aldie"; see Perry, *Life and Letters*, 196. Though Rosser's comment does not appear to match Higginson's recollection, it does confirm his involvement. However, Rosser had a horse killed during the battle, so he may have been the "trooper" referred to by Higginson.

13. Crowninshield, *History of the First Regiment*, 146; *Springfield Union*, June 18, 1913. Crowninshield credits the Second and Third Virginia with driving off Parsons, but the Fourth and Fifth Virginia may deserve the credit.

14. Cooke, "Fourth Virginia Cavalry," 104.

15. Crowninshield, *History of the First Regiment*, 146; Perry, *Life and Letters*, 195–96. All four of the men, Higginson, Sargent, Lt. George Fillebrown, and Sgt. John Martin, recovered, and all, except Higginson, returned to the regiment. Higginson returned to the army in 1864 and served as a staff officer for several months before receiving a medical discharge.

16. *OR* 27, pt. 1, 1052.

17. *OR* 27, pt. 2, 742; James Watts to T. T. Munford, September 1, 1897, Munford-Ellis Papers, DU; James Watts letter, August 31, 1891, in Irving Whitehead, *The Second Virginia Cavalry in the War, 1861–1865*, unpublished manuscript in the Irving Whitehead Papers, ALUVA; St. George Tucker Brooke Autobiography, VMHC. The two companies, C and F, numbered eighty men; see Moses Peter Rucker Reminiscences, Dr. James I. Robertson Jr., Civil War Sesquicentennial Legacy Collection, LVA.

18. *OR* 27, pt. 1, 1052, pt. 2, 742; James Watts to T. T. Munford, September 1, 1897, DU; James Watts letter, August 31, 1891, ALUVA; Brooke Autobiography, VMHC.

19. *OR* 27, pt. 1, 1052, pt. 2, 742; James Watts to T. T. Munford, September 1, 1897, DU; James Watts letter, August 31, 1891, ALUVA; Brooke Autobiography, VMHC.

20. *OR* 27, pt. 2, 740; *Maine Bugle*, 2, no. 4, October 1895, 342; Matthews, "On the Way to Gettysburg." Years later, Munford drew a map of the field with two guns supporting him from a position south of the road, rather than north. Copies of the map may be found in his papers at DU and in Lt. Charles Davis's Medal of Honor Application, RG 94, Entry 496, NARA. I have elected to rely upon his post-battle report, as well as the recollections of Henry Mathews, who served on Johnston's gun crew.

21. Crowninshield, *History of the First Regiment*, 148; Ford, *Cycle of Adams Letters*, 2:36–37.

22. Throughout the spring, the Fourth New York had been especially troubled by turmoil within the ranks of the officer corps. The turmoil, caused in part by di Cesnola's absence from the regiment early in the year, led to an acute shortage of officers, so much so that the regiment had been left behind guarding Kelly's Ford on June 9. The problem continued to hamper the regiment through the Loudoun Valley fighting. For a more detailed discussion, see my blog: O'Neill and Moran, "Turmoil in the 4th New York," parts 1 and 2.

23. General Kilpatrick to Colonel di Cesnola and di Cesnola to Kilpatrick, June 16, 1863, M504, NARA; Beyer and Keydel, *Deeds of Valor*, 1:212. The account in *Deeds of Valor* most closely matches the contemporary military evidence regarding the reason for di Cesnola's arrest. Other versions exist. In an account signed "Justice," the writer claims nepotism involving General Gregg and Colonel Gregg cost di Cesnola his brigade and led to an angry exchange between General Gregg and di Cesnola, leading the general to place di Cesnola under arrest; see *NYT*, July 6, 1863. However, Colonel Gregg never had command of di Cesnola's former brigade. John Anderson, who had served in the regiment under the name William Thorn, explained that the regiment had not been withdrawn from picket duty along the Rappahannock River until the evening of June 15. In the early hours of June 16, di Cesnola granted the men a two-hour rest break, which delayed their rejoining the brigade. Anderson believed Kilpatrick arrested di

Cesnola for granting the men the rest break; see John Anderson, "Cesnola's Arrest," *National Tribune*, March 28, 1901. Another account claimed that in rushing to rejoin the brigade, di Cesnola led his men through an infantry encampment, angering the commanding officer who placed him under arrest; see di Cesnola's Medal of Honor file, RG 94, Entry 496, NARA. Command of the regiment in his absence is unclear. Lt. Colonel Pruyn's name does not appear in any accounts, though he most likely took command on June 17.

24. *OR* 27, pt. 2, 740–41; James Watts to Thomas Munford, September 1, 1897, DU. The farm lane, known today as Cobb House Road, runs between the two turnpikes at the wide base of the triangular field.

25. L. L. Estes to Russell Alger, November 9, 1897, RG 94, Entry 496, NARA. In another account, possibly written by Kilpatrick, the general handed di Cesnola his own sword, telling him, "Colonel, you are a brave man; you are released from arrest . . . here is my sword; wear it in honor of this day." In another account, Kilpatrick told the colonel to bring the sword back "stained with blood." See Moore, *Kilpatrick and Our Cavalry*, 67–68; and "Di Cesnola's Arrest," *National Tribune*, March 28, 1901; also, *NYT*, June 20 and 22, 1863; and *Pittsburgh Evening Chronicle*, June 23, 1863.

26. Matthews, "On the Way to Gettysburg." Though Matthews provides a rare account from Breathed's Battery, horse artillery authority Robert Trout believes Matthews may not have been present during the fight, see Trout, *Galloping Thunder*, 700nn9–10. Daniel Townsend, a gunner with Randol's Battery, confirms Matthews's statement regarding driving Johnston's men from their gun on two occasions; see Townsend letter, courtesy of Bradley Forbush.

27. Ford, *Cycle of Adams Letters*, 2:36–36; Statement of Charles Flanders in Henry Crombie's Pension File, RG 94, NARA; emails from Andrew German, June 30, 2018, interpreting Flanders's brief description of the squadron's formation, and August 5, 2019, regarding the pace and speed of a charge.

28. Charles Davis to Thomas Munford, July 1, 1897, DU; "Major Davis Tells How Guidon Was Lost at Aldie," *Boston Journal*, April 19, 1905.

29. Andrew German helped develop my description of Davis's attack.

30. Charles Davis to Thomas Munford, July 1, 1897, DU; "Major Davis Tells How Guidon Was Lost at Aldie," *Boston Journal*, April 19, 1905; Charles Davis Pension File, RG 94, NARA; Dabney Ball to Dear Nettie, June 18, 63, Willard Family Papers, LC. In 1897 Davis unsuccessfully sought a Medal of Honor.

31. Frost and Frost, *Picket Pins and Sabers*, 49–51.

32. St. George Tucker Brooke Autobiography, VMHC.

33. Thomas McDevitt, August Schroder, Daniel Sherman, and George Smith Pension files, RG 94, NARA.

34. James Watts to Thomas Munford, September 1, 1897, DU; Ford, *Cycle of Adams Letters*, 2:37.

35. State of New York, *New York Monuments Commission*, 3:1122; *OR* 27, pt. 2, 742; Driver, *2nd Virginia Cavalry*, 279; James Watts to Thomas Munford, September 1, 1897, DU. Watts, who had been wounded at the woodlot, believed di Cesnola to have been killed. He survived and spent ten months in Libby Prison before being exchanged. In 1896 di Cesnola found himself entangled in a legal matter that became front page news for

months. Seeking to burnish his image, he engaged a former soldier to submit his name for the Medal of Honor. The War Department awarded the medal in December 1897.

36. *OR* 27, pt. 2, 741, 743, 746.

37. Robert Thruston Hubard Jr., *Reminiscences*, ALUVA; Crowninshield, *History of the First Regiment*, 151–52. Thomas P. Nanzig published Hubard's memoir as *The Civil War Memoirs of a Virginia Cavalryman.* The First Massachusetts lost at least one guidon at Aldie, see *Boston Journal*, April 19, 1905.

38. Oliver Downing Account, *Bivouac, an Independent Military Magazine*, 1883, 175–76, accessed September 25, 2020, http://13thmass.org/1863/aldie.html#mozTocId811171.

39. *Springfield Union*, June 18, 1913.

11. Men of Maine

1. *OR* 27, pt. 1, 975; Nathan Webb Diary; *Bangor Daily Whig and Courier*, June 20 and June 24, 1863.

2. *OR* 27, pt. 1, 952, 979; *Reunions of the First Maine Cavalry*, 7; *First Maine Bugle*, October 1891, 31–33.

3. *OR* 27, pt. 2, 741, 743, 746; William Carter Diary.

4. Hubard, *Reminiscences*.

5. *ORS*, 5, 253; *OR* 27, pt. 1, 952–53; Tobie, *History of the First Maine*, 152; *Reunions of the First Maine Cavalry*, 79; Nathan Webb Diary. Several versions of the incident survive. All differ in the details, but all agree that Kilpatrick made an impassioned plea to the First Maine.

6. Meyer, *Civil War Experiences*, 33–36; William Howe to Selden Connor, August 8, 1896, MSA; Ambrose, *Crazy Horse and Custer*, 187.

7. *ORS* 5, 253; *Reunions of the First Maine Cavalry*, 79; *Maine Bugle*, July 1894, 260–62; Nathan Webb Diary, Daniel Townsend Letter. An admiring editor said of Kilpatrick's skill as an orator, "There is an air about Gen. Kilpatrick that reaches out from him and surrounds his audience and enlists them under his banner as if by magic"; see *Kalamazoo Gazette*, February 18, 1876. Another saw him as "one of the windiest windbags in the United States," *Kalamazoo Gazette*, August 25, 1876.

8. Nathan Webb Diary; William Baker to My Dear Sister, June 21, 1863, William Baker Letters, SHCUNC; Tobie, *History of the First Maine*, 162.

9. Nathan Webb Diary.

10. George Custer to Lydia Reed, June 19, 1863, Elizabeth Custer Collection, LBHNM, as cited in Ambrose, *Crazy Horse and Custer*, 187; James C. Biddle to My Own Darling Little Wife, July 1, 1863, George Meade Papers, HSP, copy provided by Edward Longacre. As of 2017, the staff at the LBHNM could not locate the Custer letter cited by Ambrose.

11. Hubard, *Reminiscences*.

12. Thomas Rosser to My Dear Wife, June 18, 1863, ALUVA; Dabney Ball to Dear Nettie, June 18, 1863, Willard Family Papers, LC.

13. Cornelius Keating's Pension File, RG 94, NARA. During the countercharge, a Union trooper emerged from the fray with the regimental flag of the Fifth Virginia. In his regimental history, Crowninshield credits a man in Company E, First Massachusetts with capturing the flag, p. 151. Correspondent E. A. Paul credited a trooper from the First Massachusetts with capturing the flag of the Fourth Virginia. He then claimed a man from the Fourth New York killed the trooper and seized the flag before losing

it to another man from the First Massachusetts. Someone later clarified that the flag belonged to the Fifth Virginia. And even though regimental Color Sergeant William "Billy" Martin claimed he carried the flag from the field, the flag of the Fifth Virginia rests today in the MOC, labeled as having been captured at Aldie. See *OR* 27, pt. 2, 746; *NYT*, June 22, 1863; *Boston Journal*, April 19, 1905; *Richmond Whig*, August 3, 1863; Tobie, *History of the First Maine*, 162. Sergeant Martin is said to have carried the flag home after Appomattox, where his wife eventually used it "as aprons for the children"; see *Richmond Times Dispatch*, June 11, 1911. Further confusing the matter, an item in the *Boston Herald*, December 14, 1927, identified the flag then being returned to Virginia as belonging to the Fourth Virginia. In a news account published in 1864, an unnamed soldier correspondent from the Fourth New York wrote, "At Aldie . . . while a portion of our cavalry was driven back and nearly captured, the [Fourth New York] opportunely arrived, and by a spirited charge . . . [cut] off nearly one hundred men, with a battle-flag—all of whom surrendered and fell into the hands of the First Massachusetts," unidentified clipping in author's collection.

14. *ORS* 5, 253; *NYT*, June 20, 1863; *Reunions of the First Maine Cavalry*; *First Maine Bugle*, October 1891, 31.

15. William Howe Letter, August 8, 1896.

16. *NYT*, June 20, 1863; Tobie, *History of the First Maine*, 161; Charles Werkeiser's Pension File, RG 94, NARA. Werkeiser was the general's bugler and Dennis Murphy his orderly.

17. Tobie, *History of the First Maine*, 161–62.

18. Howe letter, August 8, 1896.

19. William Graves to Thomas Munford, August 25, 1897, DU; Driver, *2nd Virginia Cavalry*, 231; *First Maine Bugle*, October 1891, 39. Captain Graves said Douty rode into the Southern position, but Howe described Douty dying just in front of the wall, near a cul-de-sac created by the wall and a fence. Howe claimed Douty had been hit by two buckshot under the right arm pit.

20. *Reunions of the First Maine Cavalry*, 7, 35; Tobie, *History of the First Maine*, 164.

21. *Reunions of the First Maine Cavalry*, 7; Tobie, *History of the First Maine*, 164; *NYT*, June 20, 1863.

12. Cut All to Pieces

1. Tasker, "A Yankee Cavalryman Gets 'Gobble Up,'" 42; Wittenberg, *Union Cavalry Comes of Age*, 19–20; Blumberg, *Counterfeit Count in Blue*; Alfred Duffié's CSR and Second New York RLOB, RG 94, NARA. Though his date of birth is often given as 1833, other records record 1835, which corresponds more accurately with other facts.

2. Unsigned letter to Governor of Rhode Island, April 9, 1863, in Duffié's VSR file, RG 94, Entry 496; Col. Rufus Ingalls to Capt. Colin Ferguson, April 15, Gen. Daniel Butterfield to Colonel Duffié, April 16, General Pleasonton to Butterfield, April 17, Ingalls to Pleasonton, April 18, Duffié to Capt. William Price, June 4, Lt. Col. Andrew Alexander to Capt. Daniel Flagler, and Duffié to Price, June 7, Col. George Ramsey to Gen. James Ripley, Ripley to Maj. Theodore Laidley, June 8, 1863, M504, General Order of March 9, 1863, RG 393, Pt. 1, Entry 3986, NARA; Denison, *Sabres and Spurs*, 220; Slocum, *Life and Service*, 71–72; *National Tribune*, December 7, 1882. Denison claims Duffié went on leave, as opposed to being relieved. As he had earlier in the year, Duffié assumed command of the division based upon seniority after Hooker relieved Averell in May.

3. *OR* 27, pt. 1, 952–53, 962, pt. 3, 171, 178; *ORS* 5, 256; Bliss, *First Rhode Island*, 48–51. Exactly who selected Duffié for the mission remains unknown, as do the motives of the man who selected him, to include Duffié's own motives if he volunteered. Suggesting that Pleasonton, Gregg, or Kilpatrick would hazard the lives of 275 men as a means of eliminating a troublesome subordinate is a difficult charge to sustain. A less menacing possibility, aside from Duffié volunteering, is that his superiors saw the mission as a last opportunity for him to prove himself, or because they saw him as the best man for the job. He had spent a good amount of time in Loudoun County the previous fall and should have been familiar with the area he was to scout. Consider also that Duffié's superiors all thought the enemy to be in the Shenandoah Valley and Duffié's orders confined him to the Loudoun Valley. Accounts written by troopers with the benefit of hindsight confuse this point, suggesting his superiors knowingly sent him into a hive of Confederates. They did not. Hooker's own strictures upon Pleasonton not to risk his corps too far from the army must also be considered. Risking one regiment fit Hooker's orders to Pleasonton. Recall the plan conceived by Hooker and Pleasonton as described in chapter 7. Had Stuart moved into the Loudoun Valley one day later or Pleasonton advanced one day earlier, there may never have been any fighting in the valley. The lone regiment in the sweep through the valley would never have been more than a few miles from the support of the entire corps once the three columns set out on the second day. Fate, rather than animus or intrigue intervened, however. Finally, the daily rotation of brigades and regiments within a marching column as well as Duffié's seniority may have decided the matter.

4. *OR* 27, pt. 1, 963, 1055; Bliss, *First Rhode Island*, 7, 53; letter signed "Personne," August 26, 1862, *Charleston Daily Courier*, September 10, 1862; Tasker, "Yankee Cavalryman," 43. Some estimates of Duffié's force range as high as 400 men (see Bliss, 53) or 360 men (see *New York World*, June 23, 1863). I have relied upon statements from Duffié and Thompson.

5. Warner, *Generals in Gray*, 46–47. Chambliss had entered West Point from Hick's Ford (modern-day Emporia), Virginia, and had graduated with the class of 1853. Known as "Johnny" by his fellow cadets, Chambliss relished fine food and often skipped the bland academy fare in favor of oysters in the nearby town. See Houck, *Duty, Honor, Country*, 97, 151; Dr. Brown and Joseph Turner to Secretary of War, February 8, 1849, RG 94, M688, NARA.

6. Beale, *History of the Ninth Virginia Cavalry*, 70–71; Thomas Brown Edwards Diary.

7. *OR* 27, pt. 1, 973; *ORS*, Pt. 2, 69, 842; Tasker, "Yankee Cavalryman," 43.

8. *Maine Bugle*, April 1894, 126–28; *OR* 27, pt. 2, 685, 688; Reade and Trout, *In the Saddle*, 65; Garnett, "Cavalry Service with Gen. Stuart"; von Borcke, *Memoirs*, 415; Lawrence, *Dark Days in Our Beloved Country*, 84. Local lore places Stuart and his staff at either the Beveridge Hotel, currently the Red Fox Inn, or the Mansion House in the center of town at the intersection of Washington Street and Madison Street. However, Catherine Broun noted in her diary that "Stuart was at Dr. Powell's." Based upon her account, Stuart may have made his headquarters at the home of Dr. Francis Powell, at the SE corner of Washington Street and Pickney Street. Dr. Powell had been arrested by Yankee troops in April; see Lawrence, *Dark Days in Our Beloved Country*, 84, and the Turner-Baker Files, RG 94, M797, NARA. John Mosby described the frivolity as looking "like a dance around a Maypole"; see Mosby, *Stuart's Cavalry in the Gettysburg Campaign*, 62.

9. Reade, *In the Saddle*, 67. The name Mount Defiance reportedly stems from a property dispute between members of several local families; see Scheel, *Loudoun Discovered*, 3:1–4.

10. *OR* 27, pt. 1, 963; National Park Service, *Civil War in Loudoun Valley*, 10; *NYT*, June 22, 1863; *Newport Mercury*, January 5, 1889; Bliss, *First Rhode Island*, 8. In contrast to Duffié's casual assessment, Capt. George Bliss described "considerable skirmishing," and Sgt. William Gardiner remembered the rear guard charging the enemy before they finally broke contact. See George Bliss to Dear Gerald, June 18, 1863, George Bliss Papers, RIHS; William Gardiner, "Cavalry at Middleburg," *Philadelphia Weekly Times*, July 19, 1884. Capt. Frank Allen led the charge which drove the Southern pickets from the town.

11. Tasker, "Yankee Cavalryman," 43; *OR* 27, pt. 1, 963, 1056; *Providence Journal*, June 26, 1863; Gardiner, "Cavalry at Middleburg." Sorting out the companies left to hold the several positions is difficult, though Companies D, E, F, and G carried the carbines. Duffié may have pulled men from all four companies to man the barricades, as well as the secondary position south of town. John Mosby sharply criticized Duffié's decision to hold the town, writing "no man is fit to be an officer who has not the sense and courage to know when to disobey an order"; see Mosby, *Stuart's Cavalry*, 71. David Gregg defended Duffié as a product of the French army, "where an order must be obeyed to the letter"; see David M. Gregg Jr., *Brevet Major General David McMurtrie Gregg* (NP, 1934), David M. Gregg Papers, LC.

12. *OR* 27, pt. 1, 962–64; Green, *Incident in the Battle of Middleburg*, 9, 22. Green and Calvin Clafin accompanied Captain Allen on his ride. Green's account of finding Kilpatrick and other officers drinking and or drunk paints a salacious image and seems to provide further evidence that Kilpatrick and other senior officers abandoned or sacrificed Duffié and his men to their fate. However, few officers intentionally initiated combat operations after dark during the war. To have proceeded six miles in the dark with an exhausted command and against an enemy of unknown strength would have been foolhardy in the extreme. In addition to the reasons just stated, consider that the night would have been especially dark, as the moon was a waxing crescent, just one stage advanced from a new moon and provided only 1 percent illumination. Consider also, that many soldiers, due to poor diet, suffered night blindness. Though not well understood at the time, many doctors believed long exposure to intense sunlight led to night blindness, and June 17, one of the longest days of the year, had been very hot and sunny. For several examples of the criticism leveled against Pleasonton for not aiding Duffie see Coddington, *Gettysburg Campaign*, 78; Grandchamp, "'Ours Was a Desperate Position to Hold,'" 6, courtesy of Chris Army. See also "Moon Phase on: June 17, 1863," MoonGiant, www.moongiant.com/phase/06/17/1863; Lanska, "Vitamin A-Deficiency Eye Disease."

13. *OR* 27, pt. 2, 688; Edward Wooten, "Sketch of Company B, 5th North Carolina Cavalry," Confederate Veteran Papers, Box 4, DU; von Borcke, *Memoirs*, 415. Theodore Garnett claimed Stuart accompanied the men, but no other accounts confirm his account; see Garnett, "Cavalry Service." Rector's Cross Roads is modern-day Atoka.

14. Von Borcke, *Memoirs*, 415–16.

15. Von Borcke, *Memoirs*, 415–16; Gardiner, "Cavalry at Middleburg"; *Providence Evening Press*, June 26, 1863.

16. Von Borcke, *Memoirs*, 415–16; Gardiner, "Cavalry at Middleburg"; *Providence Evening Press*, June 26, 1863. Major von Borcke described a heavy fight east of town, with bullets flying and horses dying, and Robertson coming to his assistance, but no other accounts confirm his memory of events.

17. Gardiner, "Cavalry at Middleburg"; *Providence Evening Press*, June 26, 1863; Wooten, "Sketch of Company B." Wooten places his company at the head of the column.

18. Wooten, "Sketch of Company B"; Gardiner, "Cavalry at Middleburg"; *North Carolina Presbyterian*, July 4, 1863; *Wilmington Journal*, July 16, 1863.

19. *OR* 27, pt. 1, 1056; Gardiner, "Cavalry at Middleburg"; *Providence Evening Press*, June 26, 1863; *Providence Journal*, June 26, 1863; Wooten, "Sketch of Company B." Capt. Joshua Vose, First Rhode Island, mentioned, in a letter of June 22, 1863, withstanding five attacks but other accounts fail to support his claim; see the Vose letter in R. D. Madison's introduction to the 1994 Butternut and Blue edition of Denison's *Sabres and Spurs*, npn.

20. Gardiner, "Cavalry at Middleburg"; *Providence Journal*, June 26, 1863; *NYT*, June 22, 1863; *Charleston Mercury*, June 25, 1863.

21. Gardiner, "Cavalry at Middleburg"; *OR* 27, pt. 1, 963, 1056; George Bliss to Dear Gerald, June 18, 1863. Duffié's route has been a matter of debate for years, but a letter written by Chaplain Ethan R. Clarke provides the clues necessary to locate the area where the fight began the next morning; see the *Providence Evening Press*, August 29, 1863. About 10 p.m. Duffié sent about twenty men in a second attempt to contact General Kilpatrick, though none of the men is known to have reached Aldie.

22. Statement of Lt. Col. Meriwether Lewis, June 26, 1863, RG 393, Pt. 2, Entry 1439, NARA; Beale, *Lieutenant of Cavalry*, 100–101; John Towles Diary, LVA; John Chowning Diary; letter from Ninth Virginia, June 23, 1863, *Richmond Enquirer*, June 30, 1863; Bliss, *First Rhode Island Cavalry*, 15–16.

23. Bliss, *First Rhode Island Cavalry*, 15–16.

24. Bliss, *First Rhode Island Cavalry*, 16–18; Tasker, "Yankee Cavalryman," 43; *Providence Journal*, June 26, 1863; *NYT*, June 26, 1863; Beale, *History of the Ninth Virginia*, 71; letter from Ninth Virginia, June 23, 1863, *Richmond Enquirer*, June 30, 1863. Chedell and three comrades were buried where they fell. In August 1863 the regimental chaplain attempted to recover Chedell's remains at the request of his family. The chaplain found Chedell's body "too much decayed" to remove. The family recovered the remains in 1866. His three comrades probably remain on the field; see *Providence Evening Press*, August 29, 1863, and December 10, 1866.

25. Bliss, *First Rhode Island Cavalry*, 16–18; letter from Ninth Virginia, June 23, 1863, *Richmond Enquirer*, June 30, 1863.

26. *OR* 27, pt. 1, 963; Augustus Bixby's Pension File, RG 94, NARA; Bixby to his wife, June 18, 1863, *Manchester Daily Mirror*, June 22, 1863; George Bliss to Dear Gerald, June 18, 1863; Vose Letter in R. D. Madison's introduction to Denison's *Sabres and Spurs*; *NYT*, June 26, 1863.

27. *NYT*, June 26, 1863; *Providence Journal*, July 1, 1863; *ORS* 2, 69, 842; Denison, *Sabers and Spurs*, 278; Lawrence Cronin Pension File, RG 94, NARA; Grandchamp, "Our Regiment Has Just Been Cleaned Up," 11. The officer who assisted Bixby was Lt. Charles Sawyer, who took a bullet in his leg. As the wound healed the leg became permanently bent at an acute angle. Attempts to straighten the leg became too painful

and so Sawyer agreed to be anesthetized, allowing his doctors to put his leg in a splint. But he may have received too much chloroform, which triggered another ailment and Sawyer died on the table; see *Concord Independent Democrat*, November 26, 1863, and statement from his doctor in his widow's pension file on Fold3. After several days in captivity, George Robbins escaped still carrying the colors. On August 9, 1863, General Pleasonton recommended Robbins receive a commission for his actions. General Meade approved the request and Robbins mustered as a First Lieutenant on October 1, 1863. See Pleasonton to Gen. Lorenzo Thomas, August 9, 1863, RG 393, Pt. 2, Entry 1439, NARA; *Albany Evening Journal*, August 19, 1863; and Denison, *Sabres and Spurs*, 497. Robbins belonged to a battalion raised in New Hampshire, and the flag bore the coat of arms for New Hampshire on one side and Rhode Island on the other, see *Manchester Daily Mirror*, July 24, 1863. Jeb Stuart also credited Robertson's Tar Heels with capturing a flag. North Carolina restored and returned Company L's guidon to Rhode Island in 2008; email from Childs Burden to author, September 7, 2009.

28. Denison, *Sabres and Spurs*, 239; George Bliss to Dear Gerald, June 18, 1863.

29. *OR* 27, pt. 1, 964 (emphasis in original); George Bliss to Dear Gerald, June 18, 1863; Augustus Bixby to his wife, June 18, 1863, *Manchester Daily Mirror*, June 22, 1863. Bixby spoke of Duffié "crying like a child for 'his beloved regiment.'"

30. *OR* 25, pt. 1, 1073–74; General Hooker to Edwin Stanton, May 13, 1863, RG 393, Pt. 1, Entry 3986, and General Patrick to Senator Harris, Alfred Duffié's Commission Branch File, RG 94, M1064, NARA; Basler, *Collected Works of Abraham Lincoln*, 6:291–92; Warner, *Generals in Blue*, 131; Bliss, *First Rhode Island*, 27.

31. General Pleasonton to Adjutant General of the Army, June 29, 1863, RG 393, Pt. 2, Entry 1439, NARA; *ORS* 5, 299; Warner, *Generals in Blue*, 131. Lewis's statement is dated June 26, from a hospital in Aldie. His letter and Pleasonton's may also be found in the Commission Branch File.

32. Bliss, *First Rhode Island*, 50; Bliss to Dear Gerald, June 18, 1863; Statement of Lt. Col. Lewis, June 26, 1863, RG 393, Pt. 2, Entry 1439, NARA.

13. Many Yankees Killed

1. *OR* 27, pt. 2, 741; *Maine Bugle*, April 1894, 131–32. One soldier from the Second Virginia recalled some confusion as to who ordered the withdrawal and whether Munford should obey the order; see Moses Peter Rucker Reminiscences, LVA.

2. *OR* 27, pt. 2, 688. Stuart sent Munford back to watch the Snickersville Turnpike on June 18, where he saw little action throughout the remainder of the fighting in the Loudoun Valley.

3. As a result of losses sustained at Aldie and Middleburg on June 17 and 18, three regiments from the brigade, the First Massachusetts, First Rhode Island, and Fourth New York, did not participate in the three-day fight at Gettysburg.

4. Preston, *History of the Tenth Regiment*, 94; Mohr, *The Cormany Diaries*, 317; Cheney, *History of the Ninth Regiment*, 98; John Inglis Diary, NYSAL; Hall, *History of the 6th New York*, 129; *OR* 27, pt. 3, 193; Gilpin Diary; Charles Hampton Diary; Regimental Committee, *History of the Third Pennsylvania*, 252; Norton, *Deeds of Daring*, 67.

5. Meyer, *Civil War Experiences*, 36; *National Tribune*, November 19, 1885; Tobie, *History of the First Maine*, 162, 164; Edward Whittaker's CSR, RG 94, and Sketches showing Graves

of Union soldiers whose remains were Exhumed and Removed to National Cemetery at Arlington, Virginia, RG 92, Entry 225, NARA. Doctors established several hospitals, including at Mount Zion Church and the nearby barn of Unionist Alexander Davis.

14. He Goes Where He Pleases

1. Mosby, *Stuart's Cavalry*, 59–62. Piedmont Station is Delaplane today. A company of the Sixth Michigan Cavalry patrolled the river from their camp at Seneca. Mosby had raided the camp a week earlier, routing the Wolverines. Neither Mosby nor Stuart ever gave a reason for raiding the camp, however, the timing of the first raid, as well as the planned second raid, suggests that Stuart had always intended to cross the river at Rowser's Ford and Mosby timed his raids to drive out the Union security force ahead of Stuart's approach. In both instances, Union cavalry altered Stuart's plans by attacking him, first at Brandy Station and then at Aldie. The men had stopped at the home of James Gulick. He lived at "The Institute," an agricultural school known as the Loudoun Agricultural Mechanical Institute. Today the home is headquarters for the National Beagle Club of America. For a more detailed discussion of Mosby's activities, as well as the Federal response, see O'Neill, *Chasing Jeb Stuart and John Mosby*.

2. Mosby, *Stuart's Cavalry*, 63–65; Keen and Mewborn, *43rd Battalion Virginia Cavalry*, 68; Mosby, "Mosby's Ways," *PWT*, April 13, 1878; Mosby, "Mosby's Gobblers," *Boston Herald*, March 6, 1887.

3. Gen. Daniel Butterfield to Gen. Alfred Pleasonton, June 17, 1863, Charles S. Venable Papers, SHCUNC; Butterfield to Capt. Ulric Dahlgren, 3:30 p.m., June 17, 1863, M504, NARA. I am grateful to Horace Mewborn for sharing the document he first located. Hooker sent the order with Maj. William Sterling and Capt. Benjamin Fisher, the acting chief signal officer for the army. After delivering the message, Fisher had orders to erect a signal tower at Snicker's Gap. Early on June 18, Hooker told Halleck, "My instructions to [Pleasonton] were to find out what was behind" Munford's brigade at Aldie; see *OR* 27, pt. 1, 50. His directions to Pleasonton per the captured order say otherwise.

4. *OR* 27, pt. 2, 689; *Abingdon Virginian*, July 3, 1863. In his report, Stuart mentions several captured documents. In his postwar accounts, Mosby also refers to multiple orders but only the one document has been found.

15. Find Out Where the Enemy Is

1. *OR* 27, pt. 1, 50–55, pt. 2, 442, 770–71, and pt. 3, 200. Lt. Colonel White conducted the raid purely to satisfy his abiding dislike of Capt. Samuel Means and his Loudoun Rangers, a company of Union cavalry raised in and around Loudoun County. Still, his success served to further confuse Union authorities as to Lee's intentions.

2. *OR* 27, pt. 1, 907, and pt. 3, 173. Unaware that Mosby had captured the two officers just outside his picket lines, Pleasonton dismissed the rumored Southern raid as having been conducted by Mosby, Elijah White, and Brig. Gen. Albert Jenkins. Compounding his errors of interpretation, Pleasonton then inferred to Hooker that the raid had been concluded, see *OR* 27, pt. 1, 907.

3. *OR* 27, pt. 1, 50.

4. General Stahel sent the First Vermont and Eighteenth Pennsylvania to conduct the scout toward the Rappahannock River; see O'Neill, *Chasing Jeb Stuart and John Mosby*, 221–25.

5. *OR* 27, pt. 1, 51–52, pt. 3, 191, 193–95, 908, and 51, pt. 1, 1061–62; Capt. Samuel McKee to Gen. Seth Williams, Maj. Ira Spaulding to Gen. Henry Benham, Capt. Charles Turnbull to Williams, and Benham to Spaulding, June 18, 1863, M504; NARA; *ORS* 1, 5, 28–31. The engineer officers had doubts as to where to erect the bridge, but Benham said his orders specified Nolands Ferry. Early on the eighteenth, Hooker told Pleasonton to "hold Leesburg," to protect the bridge site. Doing so would have further limited his ability to scout toward the Shenandoah Valley. Hooker rescinded his order after the XII Corps reached the town, see *OR* 27, pt. 3, 178, 191, 195.

6. *OR* 27, pt. 1, 908–9; Hall, *History of the Sixth New York*, 129; John Inglis Diary; Thompson A. Snyder, *Recollections of Four Years with the Union Cavalry, 1861–1865* (NP, 1927), copy courtesy of the Fredericksburg and Spotsylvania National Military Park; Lloyd, *History of the First Reg't Pennsylvania Cavalry*, 57. Colonel Devin's and Colonel Taylor's brigades held Thoroughfare Gap.

7. *OR* 27, pt. 1, 908–10, 1029, and pt. 2, 689; Hard, *History of the Eighth Cavalry Regiment*, 250; Gilpin Diary; Abner Frank Diary, CWMC, USAHEC; William Redman to Editor, June 25, 1863, *Carroll County Weekly Mirror*, July 8, 1863; William Carter Diary; Glazier, *Three Years in the Federal Cavalry*, 231; Flavius Bellamy to Dear Parents, June 20, 1863, Flavius Bellamy Letters and Diary, ISL. The skirmishing resulted in no more than a handful of casualties. In his memoir, *Common Soldier, Uncommon War*, Sidney Davis, Sixth U.S., describes a skirmish involving his regiment. Other sources fail to confirm his account; instead, the Reserve Brigade remained in camp near Aldie. The events Davis describes probably took place on June 19. Davis also mentions one of the sergeants shooting a man for cowardice on the eighteenth, but historians Donald Caughey and Jimmy Jones could not confirm the story; see Caughey and Jones, *6th United States Cavalry in the Civil War.*

8. *OR* 27, pt. 1, 975, 1034; Mohr, *Cormany Diaries*, 319; Tobie, *History of the First Maine*, 165; Sixteenth Pennsylvania RLOB, NARA; Shultz, "From Aldie to Upperville," 22. At some unknown time after Mosby captured Hooker's order to Pleasonton and the afternoon of June 19, Pleasonton learned of the captured order from an orderly who escaped. What information the orderly might have known and passed on regarding the contents of the order is unknown but may have governed Pleasonton's actions on June 18 as well as June 19. Pleasonton received a copy of the order on June 19, see *OR* 27, pt. 3, 209–10.

9. *OR* 27, pt. 2, 689; Mohr, *Cormany Diaries*, 319; Isaac Ressler Diary, CWTIC, USAHEC; Shultz, "From Aldie to Upperville," 27; Doster, *Lincoln and Episodes of the Civil War*, 210; William A. Graham, "From Brandy Station to the Heights of Gettysburg," *Raleigh News and Observer*, February 7, 1904.

10. John Chowning Diary; Graham, "From Brandy Station to the Heights of Gettysburg"; Mohr, *The Cormany Diaries*, 319.

11. *NYT*, June 25, 1863; John Barr Diary; *OR* 27, pt. 1, 908–10, 975.

12. Glazier, *Three Years in the Federal Cavalry*, 231; Quaife, *From the Cannon's Mouth*, 215; Siliker, *Rebel Yell and Yankee Hurrah*, 93; Neese, *Three Years in the Confederate Horse Artillery*, 181.

13. *OR* 27, pt. 1, 908, and pt. 3, 193–95. Information provided by the orderly who escaped capture led Pleasonton to act "carefully," as he wrote on the nineteenth. Thus,

Pleasonton determined to retire from Mt. Defiance, as Stuart's actions, combined with the knowledge of the captured order, led him to believe Stuart was trying "to draw our troops onto their infantry"; see OR 27, pt. 1, 908, and pt. 2, 210.

14. OR 27, pt. 2, 689; Neese, *Three Years in the Confederate Horse Artillery*, 181.

15. OR 27, pt. 2, 357, 366, 387–88, 428–29, and 51, pt. 2, 724; Blackford and Blackford, *Letters from Lee's Army*, 178; *Savannah Republican*, July 6, 1863.

16. Lawrence, *Dark Days in Our Beloved Country*, 85.

16. Resumed with Spirit

1. Sparks, *Inside Lincoln's Army*, 261.

2. Fishel, *The Secret War for the Union*, 293; Capt. John McEntee to Col. George Sharpe, June 11, 1863, and June 19, 1863, RG 393, Pt. 1, Entry 3980, NARA. Specifically, McEntee disparaged Pleasonton's aides for reading captured mail and documents and then allowing the items "to blow away." See the *Springfield Republican* of June 18, 1863, regarding captured mail. On June 17, Hooker's adjutant general, Seth Williams, told Pleasonton to allow McEntee access to prisoners but McEntee's complaints suggest Pleasonton ignored the order, see OR 27, pt. 3, 172.

3. OR 27, pt. 1, 909, and pt. 3, 8, 173, 195; General Buford to General Gregg, June 19, 1863, Entry 1449, NARA; William Redman to Editor, June 25, 1863, *Carroll County Weekly Mirror*, July 8, 1863.

4. Hager Diary; Lloyd, *History*, 57; Cheney, *History of the Nineth Regiment*, 98; Isaac Ressler Diary; USAHEC; Carlos Lyman to Dear Sister Ednah, June 21, 1863; WRHS; Preston, *History of the Tenth Regiment*, 96; OR 27, pt. 1, 909–10, Paulding Diary. According to Pleasonton, Gregg advanced with three brigades. Close reading of the several accounts from troopers in the Reserve Brigade, however, confirms that Buford split the brigade, sending the First and Fifth U.S. with Gregg while employing the Second and Sixth U.S. as the flanking force.

5. Charles S. Wainwright Diary, HL, transcription courtesy of Bradley Forbush; State of New York, *Monuments Commission*, 3:1106. The high temperature recorded in Georgetown was eighty-one degrees; see Krick, *Civil War Weather*, 101.

6. Bliss, *First Rhode Island*, 34, 53; Busey and Martin, *Regimental Strengths and Losses*, 197. For more regarding the Enfields see Scarlata, "Enfield P53/61 Musketoon," 19–23, and Ray, "Musketoons and Rifle-Muskets."

7. Bowmaster, "Confederate Brig. Gen.," 1–4, courtesy of the author; Lowe, *Five Years a Dragoon*, 6.

8. B. H. Robertson to My Dear Brother, May 14, 1861, May 14, 1861, RG 94, M619, NARA; Bowmaster, "Confederate Brig. Gen.," 14–16.

9. Eggleston, *Rebel's Recollections*, 124; Blackford, *War Years with Jeb Stuart*, 229; Stuart to My Darling Wife, in Mitchell, *Letters*, 221; Bowmaster, "Confederate Brig. Gen.," 17.

10. Busey and Martin, *Regimental Strengths and Losses*, 197; Trout, *Memoirs of the Stuart Horse Artillery Battalion*, 2:301 and 1:51; Garnett, "Cavalry Service." The strength of Stuart's two brigades is difficult to determine, but Stuart later acknowledged their ranks had been "decimated for want of adequate shoeing facilities," with some regiments "reduced to less than 100 men"; see OR 27, pt. 2, 689, 709. Capt. Marcellus Moorman's Lynchburg Battery had spent the night prior to the fight along the ridge, but Stuart sent the battery to a reserve position at Rector's Cross Roads in the morning.

11. OR 27, pt. 1, 953; Preston, *History of the Tenth Regiment*, 96; Noble Preston to Col. Hugh Hastings, March 5, 1896, Grand Army of the Republic Files, NYSAL; Doster, *Lincoln and Episodes of the Civil War*, 210.

12. Meyer, *Civil War Experiences*, 36; Doster, *Lincoln and Episodes of the Civil War*, 210; OR 27, pt. 1, 975–76; Isaac Ressler Diary; Wynne C. Saffer, Compiler, *Fauquier County, Virginia 1861 Land Tax Maps, Silas Turner's District* (Study Presented to the Fauquier County Historical Society, 2015), Gott Library, Marshall VA, 4; Works Progress Administration, Fauquier County, Cocke Family Property, Fauquier County Library, Warrenton, Virginia; Sixteenth Pennsylvania RLOB, RG 94, NARA. George Washington Cocke had owned the property previously.

13. William Henry Forbush Diary, courtesy Bradley Forbush; Shultz, "From Aldie to Upperville," 32–33; Capt. Samuel McKee to Gen. Daniel Butterfield, June 19, 1863, M504, NARA. In his telegram of 8 a.m., Captain McKee reports hearing the distant sound of artillery for the previous two hours. Two hours may be a stretch considering Gregg's 6 a.m. departure time, though 7 or 8 a.m. seems reasonable. Col. Albert Jewett, also posted near the Potomac River, placed the opening of the artillery at 9 a.m.; see Colonel Jewett to Col. Joseph Taylor, June 19, 1863, M504, NARA. One or two sections of Capt. William Graham's Battery K, First U. S. Artillery probably accompanied Gregg's column and opened near Fuller's Battery; see OR 27, pt. 1, 1029, and Shultz, "From Aldie to Upperville," 32–33.

14. OR 27, pt. 1, 953–54, 972, 975–76; ORS 1, pt. 5, 254; Meyer, *Civil War Experiences*, 37–38; Whitman and True, *Maine in the War for the Union*, 362; C. W. Wiles, "On Horseback," *National Tribune*, October 7, 1886; letter from Captain George Brown, June 20, 1863, *Bangor Daily Whig and Courier*, June 25, 1863; *Record of Proceeding at the Fifth, Sixth and Seventh Annual Re-Union, 1876–78* (Augusta ME, 1879), 29; *First Maine Bugle*, October 1891, 25. The Second New York probably bore the brunt of the fight north of the pike, as most of the First Massachusetts and Sixth Ohio supported the artillery. Part of the Fourth Pennsylvania may have attacked on horseback but no definitive account has been found.

15. John Barr Diary; Poinsett, *Cavalry Tactics*, 274 75; Doster, *Lincoln and Episodes of the Civil War*, 210; Preston, *History of the Tenth Regiment*, 97; Isaac Ressler Diary. John Barr gives the time of the Union attack as "about noon." The Fourth and Sixteenth Pennsylvania counted about 740 men on June 19. With 185 men holding horses, the two regiments had about 555 men covering a mile of ground, or one man every ten feet. Both regiments may have also had a small, mounted reserve. If so, fewer men would have been on the skirmish line and the spacing increased.

16. John Ford to Dear Parents, July 5, 1863, John Ford Pension File, RG 94, NARA. John Ford had been riding in the same set of fours with his brother Reuben. Moving into the field, John moved off with the skirmishers while Reuben held their horses off the line. Just as John dropped to a prone position a bullet hit him in the shoulder. He remained on the field for two hours.

17. Von Borcke, *Memoirs*, 418; Garnett, "Cavalry Service"; *Richmond Enquirer*, June 23, 1863. Major von Borcke describes warning Stuart that he would be "forced to retreat," but William Blackford, another member of the general's staff who was present, described von Borcke's description as "fiction, pure and simple. Stuart never sought or allowed any such advice." See Blackford's annotated copy of von Borcke's *Memoirs* at ALUVA.

18. "From the Field," June 19, 1863, *NYT*, June 25, 1863; Brown letter, June 20, 1863, *Bangor Daily Whig and Courier*, June 25, 1863; Doster, *Lincoln and Episodes of the Civil War*, 211. Lt. Mark Neville was the officer killed.

19. "From the Field," June 19, 1863, *NYT*, June 25, 1863; George Brown letter, June 20, 1863, *Bangor Daily Whig and Courier*, June 25, 1863; George Brown letter, *Richmond Times Dispatch*, February 14, 1904; Doster, *Lincoln and Episodes of the Civil War*, 211; George Bartlett to Dear Father, June [20], 1863, *Bangor Daily Whig and Courier*, June 25, 1863; Tobie, *History of the First Maine*, 168; *Fourth Annual Re-Union of the First Maine Cavalry Association, 1875* (Augusta ME, 1876), 37; Charles Putnam Pension File, RG 94, NARA. Sgt. Charles Putnam carried the colors alongside Taylor.

20. *OR* 27, pt. 1, 976; Eugene Stocking to Dear Parents, October 4, 1863, MISA; Maine Adjutant General, *Annual Report of the Adjutant-General of the State of Maine, 1863* (Augusta ME, 1863), 55.

21. *First Maine Bugle*, October 1891, 25; *Records of Proceedings of the Eighth and Ninth Annual Re-Unions, 1879–1880* (Augusta ME, 1881), 52; Trout, *Galloping Thunder*, 264; Alvin Johnson Pension File, RG 94, NARA.

22. Beale, *Lieutenant of Cavalry*, 102; Beale, *History of the Ninth Virginia*, 72; *Augusta Maine Farmer*, July 2, 1863.

23. Lt. Charles Ford to Dear Sir, June 25, 1863, in Sgt. Justin Swett's Pension File, RG 94, NARA; Benjamin Knowles, "Pistol and Saber," *National Tribune*, September 13, 1900. Knowles based his account on a letter he wrote from Camp Parole, Annapolis, Maryland, July 26, 1863. The First Maine had about two hundred men fighting on the turnpike, while the Ninth Virginia counted about five hundred.

24. Beale, *Lieutenant of Cavalry*, 102; Nicholson, *Pennsylvania at Gettysburg*, 863; Tuten, "Remarkable Case," 558–60; Michael Logan's Pension File, RG 94, NARA. George Beale's description of this incident, suggests he was one of Logan's assailants.

25. Rea, *War Record and Personal Experiences*, 105. For a full discussion of the problems involving the Tenth New York, see O'Neill, "Col. John Lemmon." In a postwar account, Clifton Wiles placed the time of this attack at 4 p.m., "On Horseback," *National Tribune*, October 7, 1886.

26. Preston, *History of the Tenth Regiment*, 95; *First Maine Bugle*, April 1893, 70–71; Beale, *History of the Ninth Virginia*, 73; Henry Barker and Eleazer Collin's Pension Files, RG 94, NARA. Major Kemper led Companies F and I in the first charge and Major Alvah Waters followed with Companies B and D. Kemper wrote several accounts of his experience at Middleburg, including "A Cavalry Charge," *National Tribune*, July 10, 1890, and an unsuccessful application for a Medal of Honor in 1891, RG 94, Entry 496, NARA.

27. Von Borcke, *Memoirs*, 420–21; Blackford, *War Years*, 218–19; Garnett, "Cavalry Service"; Trout, *Memoirs of the Stuart Horse Artillery*, 2:301. In a letter to Flora on June 20, Stuart said the bullet "had passed me to hit" von Borcke. An April 26, 1864, article in the *Richmond Dispatch* also claimed the two officers were riding together when von Borcke was hit. The major repeated the claim in his *Memoirs*, but Blackford, in his annotated copy of the major's book disputed the claim, saying von Borcke was "at least 30 ft from the General when he was hit." Stuart's June 20, 1863, letter courtesy of Robert K. Krick.

28. *Bangor Daily Whig and Courier*, June 23, 1863; Preston, *History of the Tenth Regiment*, 96, 98.

29. *OR* 27, pt. 2, 689–90; James Gaston to Dear Wife, June 23, 1863, courtesy of Marilyn Palas, the PCHS, and Andrew German. At 11 a.m., Hooker resent a copy of the captured order to Pleasonton. Pleasonton may have received the copy during the battle. Combined with the tactical situation on the field, the order may have convinced Pleasonton to forgo any further action; see *OR* 27, pt. 3, 209.

30. *OR* 27, pt. 1, 909–10, and pt. 2, 759. Col. John Taylor's brigade relieved Colonel Devin at Thoroughfare Gap. Colonel Gamble's brigade remained near Aldie.

31. *OR* 27, pt. 1, 909–10, and pt. 2, 759; Rodenbough, *From Everglade to Canon*, 293; Paulding Diary; Chiswell Dabney to Dear father, June 20, 1863, Saunders Family Collection, VMHC. Pot House, also known as New Lisbon during the war, and known today as Leithtown, may have been named after a brick or pottery kiln though pot house was also English slang for a pub or tavern; see Scheel, *Loudoun Discovered*, 3:56–60. Thanks also to William Miller.

32. *OR* 27, pt. 2, 759; Memoir of Captain Samuel Brown Coyner, courtesy of Horace Mewborn; John Donahue Diary, LVA. After crossing Carter's bridge, Whiting left a squadron to secure the crossing. During Whiting's skirmish at Pot House, the officer commanding the force at the bridge, burned the structure as a precaution. General Buford termed the officer's actions as "mismanagement" in one communication and "stupidity" in another; see Buford to General Gregg, June 19, 1863, Entry 1449, NARA. Once Whiting advanced beyond Pot House, the Southern pickets retook the area, preventing Union couriers from reaching Whiting or Gregg via this route later in the day; see *OR* 27, pt. 3, 210, and *NYT*, June 25, 1863. The *NYT* correspondent identifies the security force as from the First U.S., which seems unlikely as the First operated with Gregg during the day. The reporter also claimed the officer burned the bridge after being attacked, but this also seems unlikely. Finally, Stuart incorrectly credits Rosser and Marshall with driving Whiting back across the creek.

33. Rodenbough, *From Everglade to Canon*, 293; Paulding Diary; *Bangor Daily Whig and Courier*, June 23, 1863; *Albany Evening Journal*, June 22, 1863. Millville, or Millsville, was a thriving community during the war. Except for foundations, the buildings have since disappeared, possibly as the result of a flood in 1936; see Scheel, *Loudoun Discovered*, 3:107–8. The road connecting Millville and the Ashby's Gap Turnpike is known today as Kirk's Branch Road. A landowner moved part of the road after the war, sparking a lawsuit in 1890. Most of the road remains on the original roadbed. Several accounts, including the *Albany Evening Journal*, place the time of this skirmish as 6 p.m.

34. Paulding Diary; *Bangor Daily Whig and Courier*, June 23, 1863; Rodenbough, *From Everglade to Canon*, 293. No Southern accounts of this action have been located.

17. Enthusiastic Anticipation

1. Barr Diary; Siliker, *Rebel Yell and Yankee Hurrah*, 93; Victor Comte to Dear Elise, June 21, 1863, BLUM; Daniel Townsend Diary, courtesy of Eric Wittenberg; Lawrence, *Society of Rebels*, 185; Gilpin Diary.

2. Berry Diary; Doster, *Lincoln and Episodes of the Civil War*, 211; Mohr, *Cormany Diaries*, 320.

3. Preston, *History of the Tenth Regiment*, 97; John Ford to Dear Parents, July 5, 1863, John Ford's Pension File, RG 94, NARA; Ball Diary; Ressler Diary. John Ford died August 10, 1863.

4. Driver, *1st Virginia Cavalry*, 171; von Borcke, *Memoirs*, 421–22; Northumberland County Historical Society, "Confederate Soldier," 39–41. On June 14, Surgeon Lafayette Guild, R. E. Lee's Medical Director, termed Doctor Eliason's "medical operation in the cavalry division" as "inefficient"; see Guild's Letter Book, RG 109, NARA.

5. *OR* 27, pt. 1, 193; George Bartlett to Dear Father, June 20, 1863, *Bangor Daily Whig and Courier*, June 25, 1863; Meade, *Life and Letters*, 1:386.

6. *OR* 27, pt. 1, 909–10, and pt. 3, 210.

7. *OR* 27, pt. 1, 54, and pt. 3, 224–25; Gen. Daniel Butterfield to Gen. George Meade, June 19, 1863, Entry 1449, and Butterfield to Gen. Oliver Howard, June 19, 1863, RG 393, Pt. 1, Entry 3964, NARA. Hooker also ordered his artillery commanders to "study positions for artillery" around Thoroughfare Gap; see *OR* 27, pt. 3, 212. Likewise, General Heintzelman alerted Hooker to the troops from his department stationed in Fairfax County, who could also respond should Lee attack through the gap. Heintzelman also told Stahel to comply with commands from Hooker to concentrate his cavalry in the event he might be needed to assist the army; see *OR* 27, pt. 3, 214. Once the II Corps arrived, Pleasonton ordered General Gregg to recall Colonel Taylor from the gap, but he would not arrive in time to participate in the June 21 fighting; see *OR* 27, pt. 3, 227. Finally, the Eighth Pennsylvania acted as an independent command attached to the II Corps (*OR* 27, pt. 3, 224), and the Sixth Pennsylvania remained near Fairfax Station; see Gracey, *Annals*, 177.

8. *OR* 27, pt. 1, 909, 911, and pt. 3, 223–24, 228.

9. *OR* 27, pt. 1, 910, and pt. 3, 208; Busey and Martin, *Regimental Strengths and Losses*, 195; Gen. John Buford to Gen. David Gregg, June 19, 1863, Entry 1449, NARA.

10. *OR* 27, pt. 1, 910, and pt. 2, 690; McSwain, *Crumbling Defenses*, 22–23. Pleasonton had received a more accurate estimate of Hampton's strength on June 19; see General Buford to General Gregg, June 19, 1863, Entry 1449, NARA.

11. *OR* 27, pt. 2, 357; Gallagher, *Fighting for the Confederacy*, 226; Haines, "Advance of Longstreet's First Corps," 23. One battery lost four hundred rounds of ammunition in the second crossing and one infantry regiment lost several thousand rounds of ammunition crossing back the following day; see *OR* 27, pt. 2, 428, and Haines, 23.

12. *OR* 27, pt. 1, 598, 911, 920; Judson, *History of the Eighty-Third*, 64; Busey and Martin, *Regimental Strengths and Losses*, 133; Berry Diary; letter from Leonard Hendricks, June 21, 1863, *New York Herald*, June 26, 1863. William Berkeley had been raised in the home, along with his three brothers. All four served as officers in the Eighth Virginia Infantry.

13. Letter from Leonard Hendricks, June 21, 1863, *New York Herald*, June 26, 1863. Several reporters were, in today's parlance, embedded with the cavalry, including a couple who also served as aides or couriers.

14. F. C. Newhall, "How Lee Lost the Use of His Cavalry," *PWT*, September 28, 1878; W. W. Williams to Edward Tobie, September 1, 1890, *Maine Bugle* (April 1891), 53; Lyman Diary. The Beveridge House and Tavern is the Red Fox Inn today.

18. Small but Important Riots

1. *New York Observer*, August 6, 1863; Judson, *History of the Eighty-Third*, 64; *OR* 27, pt. 1, 613. With an entire infantry division at his disposal, Pleasonton's use of only one brigade suggests caution urged by Hooker. Believing Southern infantry to be east of the Blue Ridge, Hooker may have agreed to provide infantry support with the stipulation that Pleasonton employed the men sparingly to avoid bringing on a larger contest.

2. Alfred Apted Diary, CWMC, USAHEC; Crawford, *16th Michigan Infantry*, 69, 81; Robertson, *Michigan in the Civil War*, 363. Both Company A and the Brady Sharpshooters may have been considered sharpshooter companies, but the Brady Sharpshooters had been raised as an independent sharpshooter unit with marksmanship requirements like Berdan's Sharpshooters. Company A advanced north of the turnpike and the Brady Sharpshooters to the south; see Giblem to Editor, June 23, 1863, *Detroit Advertiser and Tribune*, July 1, 1863. Colonel Vincent may have sent the Sixteenth Michigan into battle first to give his friend, Lt. Col. Welch, a chance to redeem his name following a court-martial in April, in which Vincent had served as Welch's attorney. Welch had been cleared, but questions lingered as to his patriotism.

3. *OR* 27, pt. 2, 690; Newhall, "How Lee Lost the Use of His Cavalry," *PWT*, September 28, 1878; Saussy, "Upperville's Cavalry Battle," 332; George Neese Diary, LVA; Capt. Norman Barrett letter, June 24, 1863, *Cleveland Leader*, July 8, 1863; Hilen, *Letters of Henry Wadsworth Longfellow*, 4:342–43; Lawrence, *Dark Days*, 86. Emphasis in original.

4. Brooks, *Butler and His Cavalry*, 174; Saussy, "Upperville's Cavalry Battle," 332; Trout, *Galloping Thunder*, 266. Two of Hampton's regiments, the First South Carolina and Phillips Legion, were not with the brigade. The First South Carolina joined the brigade later in the day, while Phillips Legion remained detached.

5. *OR* 27, pt. 1, 614–15. Col. Joshua Chamberlain had been struck by an illness, probably sunstroke on June 17. He remained near Gum Spring for several days; see Welsh, *Medical Histories*, 63. One of his men wrote on the morning of June 21, "Our Colonel is off duty and we dread to go into action without him"; see Nathan S. Clark Diary at https://digitalmaine.com/cgi/viewcontent.cgi?article=1000&context=hist_docs, accessed January 11, 2021.

6. *OR* 27, pt. 1, 53, 954, 1034–35; *Cleveland Leader*, July 28, 1863; Robertson, *Michigan in the Civil War*, 363; Saussy, "Upperville's Cavalry Battle," 332; letter from Alexander Wood in Saussy, "Campaigning with Stuart," 156–57. The battered remnant of the First Massachusetts supported Fuller's Battery throughout the day.

7. Robertson, *Michigan in the War*, 363; *New York Herald*, June 26, 1863; David Mapes, Forty-Fourth New York Infantry, and Samuel Gray, Twentieth Maine Infantry, Pension Files, RG 94, NARA; Brooks, *Butler and His Cavalry*, 177; Compiled Service Record for Frank Y. Salmons, Second South Carolina, Fold3.com; Trout, *Galloping Thunder*, 266–67; Trout, *Memoirs of the Stuart Horse Artillery Battalion*, 1:211.

8. *OR* 27, pt. 2, 690; Saussy, "Campaigning with Stuart," 156–57; Trout, *Galloping Thunder*, 266–67; Trout, *Memoirs of the Stuart Horse Artillery Battalion*, 1:211; Ladd, *The Batchelder Papers*, 2:1215; Robertson, *Michigan in the Civil War*, 363; *NYT*, June 25, 1863; *Richmond Dispatch*, April 26, 1864. Stuart acknowledged this gun to be the first one lost by his Horse Artillery Battalion in action with the enemy. The men injured in Fuller's Battery could not have been badly hurt as none of them mentions the incident in their pension claims.

9. William Howard to Gov. Austin Blair, November 28, 1862, and George Sidman to Blair, undated letter, ABP, BCDPL; Giblem to Editor, June 23, 1863, *Detroit Advertiser and Tribune*, July 1, 1863; George Sidman Pension File, RG 94, NARA; Robertson, *Michigan in the Civil War*, 363; Charles Salter to My Dear Friend, June 25, 1863, Divie Duffield Collection, BCDPL; Captain Mott had been dismissed as a result of regimental contretemps involving Lt. Colonel Welch, but he had retained his position pending an appeal.

In his report, Welch graciously said of Mott that he fell "cheering his men forward by word and deed, and doing his whole duty." Artillery expert David Shultz provided me with a copy of his unpublished manuscript, in which he points out Lieutenant Fuller's crucial wording regarding the capture of the gun.

10. Comments made by James Hart in a letter of December 12, 1885, courtesy of Clark B. Hall; Giblem to Editor, June 23, 1863, *Detroit Advertiser and Tribune*, July 1, 1863; Styple, *With a Flash of His Sword*, 33–34.

11. *Raleigh Daily State Journal*, July 8, 1863; undated letter signed "B," *Augusta Daily Chronicle and Sentinel*, August 20, 1863; McGowen and McGowen, *Flashes of Duplin's History and Government*, 409; letter from Chris Hartley to author, August 4, 1997. Though the Yankees held the ground for only a day, they may have buried the Confederate dead, including Houston; see Edwin Sloan to My Dear Wife, June 24, 1863, Edward R. Sloan Papers, Special Collections, DU. A note in Houston's service record reads, "Brave, kind and generous. His country and Friends mourn their irreparable loss."

12. Brooks, *Butler and His Cavalry*, 176–77; William Delony to My Dear Rose, June 20–23, 1863, William G. Delony Papers, HRBML, UG.

13. Trout, *Memoirs of the Stuart Horse Artillery Battalion*, 1:52, 211, and 2:301; *OR* 27, pt. 1, 614, 1035. Cromwell's Run is also termed Crummer's Run and Crummey's Run in contemporary accounts.

14. *OR* 27, pt. 1, 614, 616.

15. Giblem to Editor, June 23, 1863, *Detroit Advertiser and Tribune*, July 1, 1863; Capt. Norman Barrett to Editor, *Cleveland Leader*, July 8, 1863; McClellan, *Life and Campaigns*, 308.

16. McSwain, *Crumbling Defenses*, 25.

17. McSwain, *Crumbling Defenses*, 25–26. Black said he gave Captain Brown 200 men or about half the regiment, which would have meant about 150 men on the firing line. Black's estimate seems high, however. Stuart's policy of gathering his carbines within one or two companies, suggests Brown, of Company K, commanded a squadron at Rector's Cross Roads, numbering about 60 men.

18. *OR* 27, pt. 2, 690; *ORS* pt. 2, vol. 69, 842.

19. Scheibert, *Seven Months in the Rebel States*, 105–6; *OR* 27, pt. 2, 357, 374, 691. For von Borcke's dramatic account, see his own *Memoirs*, 423–25.

20. Robertson, *Michigan in the Civil War*, 363; *OR* 27, pt. 1, 1029–30, 1035; Townsend Diary; Shultz, "From Aldie to Upperville." Lt. Aaron Walcott's Battery C, Massachusetts Light Artillery, attached to Barnes's division supported the horse artillery but may not have been actively engaged.

21. *OR* 27, pt. 1, 1035; McSwain, *Crumbling Defenses*, 27; Shoemaker, *Shoemaker's Battery*, 41; Trout, *Memoirs of the Stuart Horse Artillery Battalion*, 1:52; *Richmond Whig*, July 1, 1863; Charles Kratka Pension File, RG 94, NARA; Turner Holley to Dear Eliza, July 12, 1863, Turner Holley Letters, Special Collections, DU. Union soldiers buried John Edmundson where he died. Later, his friends or the property owner placed a stone marker over his grave. The stone, which sits just south of Rte 50 and just east of the Atoka intersection, now bears a modern plaque bearing Edmundson's name; see Elizabeth Coe, "Middleburg Gravestone Mystery Solved," *Loudoun Times-Mirror* as cited at https://markerhunter.wordpress.com/2008/11/15/j-t-edmundson, accessed February 2, 2019. The other Southern gunner, Charles Saunders, died the following day.

22. McSwain, *Crumbling Defenses*, 27–28; Andy Lany, "Sixth Ohio Cavalry," *National Tribune*, September 27, 1883. The lady may have been Sarah Denham at Rose Hill Farm.

23. *ORS* pt. 1, 5, 254–55; Ferdinand Straub Pension File, RG 94, NARA.

24. *Detroit Free Press*, June 30, 1863. Captain Brown counted thirty-four Union guns. However, the Federals probably had no more than twenty-eight guns, if Lieutenant Walcott's battery moved onto the ridge.

25. McSwain, *Crumbling Defenses*, 27–29; John Esten Cooke, "The Hampton Legion," *PWT*, February 21, 1880; Brooks, *Stories of the Confederacy*, 260; Trout, *Memoirs of the Stuart Horse Artillery Battalion*, 1:52, 212; *Augusta Daily Chronicle & Sentinel*, August 20, 1863. When he wrote his memoirs, Black confused and commingled several events of the battle, but otherwise his description rings true.

26. Lt. John Ketchum to Dear Mother, June 23, 1863, in Duganne, *Fighting Quakers*, 72; Carlos Lyman to Dear Sister Ednah, June 22, 1863, Carlos Lyman Papers, WRHS; Thomas Covert to My Dear Wife, June 23, 1863, and July 23, 1863, Thomas Covert Letters CWMC, USAHEC; Spear et al., *Civil War Recollections of General Ellis Spear*, 30; George Hilton Pension File, RG 94, NARA.

27. Trout, *Memoirs of the Stuart Horse Artillery Battalion*, 1:52; Shoemaker, *Shoemaker's Battery*, 42. Several men from Chambliss's Thirteenth Virginia were captured at the bridge, suggesting that a squadron or more of the regiment had been guarding the bridge prior to Stuart's arrival.

28. *OR* 27, pt. 1, 614, 616; *ORS* 1, pt. 5, 254–55; Judson, *History of the Eighty-Third*, 64; Robertson, *Michigan in the Civil War*, 363; Spear et al., *Civil War Recollections of General Ellis Spear*, 30; Thomas Covert to My Dear Wife, June 23, 1863, and July 23, 1863, Thomas Covert Letters, USAHEC.

29. Judson, *History of the Eighty-Third*, 64; Robertson, *Michigan in the Civil War*, 363; Giblem to Editor, June 23, 1863, *Detroit Advertiser and Tribune*, July 1, 1863. Colonel Welch identified the wounded officers as Capt. John Jordan and Lt. Peter Thorp, Thirteenth Virginia. If the account of officers firing at their own men is accurate, Jordan and Thorp are the best candidates.

30. Giblem to Editor, June 23, 1863, *Detroit Advertiser and Tribune*, July 1, 1863; William Brown to Dear Brother, June 27, 1863, William Brown Collection, BU; Comey, *Legacy of Valor*, 124; *OR* 27, pt. 1, 615–16.

31. *OR* 27, pt. 1, 598; Smith, *History of the 118th Pennsylvania*, 224; Silliker, *Rebel Yell and the Yankee Hurrah*, 113.

32. Mackall, Meserve, and Sasscer, *In the Shadow of the Enemy*, 164–65; Lawrence, *Society of Rebels*, 185.

33. Capt. John Ames to Dear Mother, June 21, 1863, John Ames Letters, GCC, USAHEC.

19. The Hottest Fighting I Ever Did

1. Colonel Gamble had also sent Company H, Eighth Illinois, on a scout to the south on June 19. Lt. Edward Dowd led the company to near Markham, where he encountered enemy pickets; see letter signed "Cav" to Editor, June 24, 1863, *Woodstock Sentinel*, July 8, 1863.

2. Nolan, "Bold and Fearless Rider," 20, 35, 37; *Chicago Tribune*, October 16, 1861. Southern-born officers paid a price for their loyalty in Stanton's War Department, and

Stanton, reportedly, only agreed to promote Buford to major general when he had been assured Buford would not survive an illness later in the year.

3. Gen. John Buford to Gen. George Stoneman, February 9, 1863, Entry 1449, NARA.

4. *OR* 27, pt. 1, 902; "Moon Phase on: June 20, 1863," MoonGiant, https://www.moongiant.com/phase/6/20/1863, accessed March 14, 2019; Krick, *Civil War Weather*, 101. General Hooker may have dictated the late hour of Pleasonton's meeting, as the cavalryman could not draw up a plan until he knew if he would have infantry support. Buford's division was, in his words, "very much divided," referring to the long picket lines manned by his men. Also, the Reserve Brigade had remained near Middleburg after the June 19 fighting. See also "Genesee" to Dear Union, June 22, 1863, *Rochester Daily Union and Advertiser*, June 29, 1863.

5. *OR* 27, pt. 1, 920–21; Col. Thomas Devin to Captain, June 23, 1863, Entry 1449, NARA. Colonel Devin wrote two slightly different reports for the Upperville fight. I have relied upon his unpublished version in the archives. Through the month of June, command of the Reserve Brigade passed between Majors Charles Whiting and Samuel Starr. Whiting, the senior officer, led the brigade on June 9, but then went on sick leave and Starr took command. Whiting returned in time to lead the effort on June 19, but he was suddenly relieved prior to June 21 and replaced by Starr. On September 17, 1863, Maine's Republican senator, William Fessenden, accused Whiting of aligning himself with the Copperheads. President Lincoln then dismissed Whiting for "disloyalty and for using contemptuous and disrespectful words against the President of the United States." A newspaper editor attributed his dismissal to "some small potato civil influence," but Whiting had also been present when another officer had disparaged Lincoln. The ongoing case against that officer may have precipitated Whiting's removal on June 20 or 21. The War Department reinstated both officers after the war. Neither Whiting or Starr impressed Pleasonton and on June 22, he requested that Capt. Wesley Merritt be promoted to command the brigade. See *OR* 27, pt. 1, 913, and 29, pt. 2, 322; Senator William Fessenden to Edwin Stanton, September 17, 1863, RG 94, M797, NARA; *New York Herald* November 15, 1863; *Daily Milwaukee News*, December 3, 1863; Breshears, *Major Granville Haller*, 16. My thanks to Don Caughey for his assistance unraveling Whiting's status on June 21.

6. Coarse, solitary, and profane, William Jones earned the nickname "Grumble." He and Stuart disliked each other with the visceral intensity of a clan feud, and Jones refused to be cowed by Stuart's position and superior rank. Jones could and would fight, however, and he had gained a reputation as Stuart's "best outpost officer"; see McClellan, *Life and Campaigns*, 319, 321.

7. *NYT*, April 7, 1878. Only six companies of the Sixth New York and a couple companies of the Third West Virginia were present.

8. *ORS* pt. 2, 69, 842; *OR* 27, pt. 2, 750; Baylor, *Bull Run to Bull Run*, 148–49; Diary of W. H. Arehart, *Rockingham Recorder*, courtesy of Horace Mewborn; Beale, *History of the 9th Virginia*, 74; Ephraim Bowman to Dear Father, June 21–22, 1863, Ephraim Bowman Papers, ALUVA.

9. *OR* 27, pt. 1, 932; Heitman, *Historical Register and Dictionary*, 444; "G. C." to Editor, January 3, 1863; *Aurora Beacon*, January 15, 1863; J. M. Gardner, "Union versus Rebel Cavalry," *National Tribune*, May 24, 1888. Emphasis in original. Only six companies of the Third Indiana and five companies of the Twelfth Illinois were present.

10. OR 27, pt. 1, 932–33; Beale, *Lieutenant of Cavalry*, 104; Beale, *History of the 9th Virginia*, 74.

11. OR 27, pt. 1, 932–33; Beale, *Lieutenant of Cavalry*, 104; Beale, *History of the 9th Virginia*, 74; "Cav" to Editor, June 24, 1863, *Woodstock Sentinel*, July 8, 1863; William Redman to Editor, June 25, 1863; *Mount Carroll Mirror*, July 8, 1863.

12. "Sabre" to Editor, June 23, 1863, *Chicago Tribune*, June 30, 1863; Sgt. Henry Humphrey to Mrs. Jane Welch, June 23, 1863, *St. Albans Daily Messenger*, July 16, 1863.

13. OR 27, pt. 1, 921.

14. Ephraim Bowman to Dear Father, June 21–22, 1863, ALUVA; Edward Green Reminiscences and Letters, copy courtesy of Horace Mewborn; Beale, *Lieutenant of Cavalry*, 104; OR 27, pt. 2, 751. As the men turned toward Ashby's Gap, they used Fernow, home of Capt. Bruce Gibson, Sixth Virginia, as a landmark. See OR 27, pt. 2, 751; *Winchester Evening Star*, February 20, 1901, courtesy of Clark Hall; letter and maps provided by Claiborne Stokes, December 5, 1995.

15. Graham, "From Brandy Station to the Heights of Gettysburg"; John Z. Scott Memoir, VMHC; Beale, *History of the 9th Virginia*, 74; OR, 27, pt. 2, 751. Mountain Road is Llangollen Road today. Though the Thirteenth Virginia sustained at least eleven casualties, their involvement remains a mystery.

16. OR 27, pt. 1, 933; "Sabre" to Editor, June 23, 1863, *Chicago Tribune*, June 30, 1863. With the Southern artillery moving by sections throughout the caravan, the Federals never had a clear idea of the number of guns they faced. General Buford counted four, Gamble five, and a trooper counted only one; see OR 27, pt. 1, 921, 933, and the Hampton Diary. The Thomas home is known today as Kirkby.

17. McDonald, *History of the Laurel Brigade*, 150–51; Cauley, "Confederacy in the Lower Shenandoah Valley," 71; Bradshaw, *Civil War Diary*, 14; John Z. Scott Memoir, VMHC. Chew also credited Capt. Daniel Hatcher and his men of Company A, Seventh Virginia, with opening a part of the fence; see McDonald, 150. The exact number of guns, three or four, with Chew on June 21 is uncertain. One gun had been damaged at Brandy Station, but Chew may have received a captured Federal gun as a replacement. Still, the total number of guns in his battery remains unclear; see Trout, *Galloping Thunder*, 698n1. Also emails to author from Craig Swain, Leesburg VA, of February 21, 2017, and April 30, 2020.

18. John Z. Scott Memoir, VMHC; "Cav" to Editor, June 24, 1863, *Woodstock Sentinel*, July 8, 1863; "Sabre" to Editor, June 23, 1863, *Chicago Tribune*, June 30, 1863; DDCM, RG 153, NARA; Bradshaw, *Civil War Diary*, 16; McDonald, *History of the Laurel Brigade*, 151.

19. "Sabre" to Editor, June 23, 1863, *Chicago Tribune*, June 30, 1863; McDonald, *History of the Laurel Brigade*, 150; Opie, *Rebel Cavalryman*, 162.

20. Miller, *Decision at Tom's Brook*, xix; Graham, "From Brandy Station to the Heights of Gettysburg"; Graham, "Nineteenth Regiment (Second Cavalry)," 2:96; George Bryan to Dear Father, September 25, 1863, John Herritage Bryan Papers, NCDAH, copy courtesy of Roger Harrell, Hermosa Beach CA. Some of the stone walls which framed the battlefield survive, others have long since disappeared. Payne's men had to negotiate a section of woods and a stone wall.

21. OR 27, pt. 2, 751, 756, 759, 766; Shoemaker, *Shoemaker's Battery*, 42; Memoir of Captain Samuel Brown Coyner, 41; Edward Green Reminiscences and Letters; Bradshaw, *Civil War Diary*, 15; DDCM, RG 153, NARA.

22. *OR* 27, pt. 2, 751, 756.

23. O'Ferrall, *Forty Years of Active Service*, 71–72; Bradshaw, *Civil War Diary*, 15; Ephraim Bowman to Dear Father, June 21–22, 1863, ALUVA.

24. Bradshaw, *Civil War Diary*, 15; Neese, *Three Years*, 182.

25. Memoir of Captain Samuel Brown Coyner, 41; Gilpin Diary; William A. Curtis, Reminiscences of the War, copy provided by Horace Mewborn.

26. Letter signed Eques, Aldie, June 23, 1863, *Aurora Commercial*, July 2, 1863, copy courtesy of John Hennessy, Fredericksburg VA; Baldino, *Family and Nation under Fire*, 165.

27. "The Civil War Reminiscences of William Brent," partial typescript provided to the author by Claiborne Stokes, Mobile AL; "Lt. Walter Buck Furloughed Forever at Upperville," copy provided the author by the late John Divine; Memoir of Captain Samuel Brown Coyner, 41; *OR* 27, pt. 2, 759.

28. "Sabre" to Editor, June 23, 1863, *Chicago Tribune*, June 30, 1863; Ephraim Bowman to Dear Father, June 21–22, 1863, ALUVA.

29. Opie, *Rebel Cavalryman*, 162.

30. Beale, *History of the 9th Virginia*, 73–74; Beale, *Lieutenant of Cavalry*, 104; Edwards Diary.

31. DDCM, RG 153, and Franklin Schuster Pension File, RG 94, NARA.

32. Beale, *History of the 9th Virginia*, 75; Ann Meriwether Lewis Burrows to author, undated letter; Marshall E. Decker to My Ever Devoted Ella, June 22, 1863, copy provided by Mr. Decker Bristow, Hendersonville NC.

33. Beale, *History of the 9th Virginia*, 75; Col. Thomas Devin to Captain, June 23, 1863, Entry 1449, NARA; Moyer, *History of the Seventeenth Pennsylvania*, 47; Dr. Abner Hard's Casualty List, June 21, 1863, copy courtesy of Marshall Krolick, Weston FL; James Wood Pension File, RG 94, NARA; McDonald, *History of the Laurel Brigade*, 152.

20. Such Implacable Hate

1. *OR* 27, pt. 1, 954; Lt. C. W. Ford account, *Fourth Annual Re-Union of the First Maine Cavalry Association, 1875* (Augusta ME, 1875), 37, emphasis in original. The long run from Goose Creek galled Stuart for months, such that he felt the need to describe the retreat in some detail in his campaign report. "Nothing could exceed the coolness and self-possession of officers and men in these movements," he wrote. He described his men "performing evolutions with a precision . . . that must have wrung the tribute and admiration from the enemy." However, as one of his men admitted, "we retreated at a brisk pace." See *OR* 27, pt. 2, 690–91; undated letter signed "B," *Augusta Weekly Chronicle and Sentinel*, August 26, 1863.

2. Gen. Montgomery Meigs to Gen. Daniel Rucker, June 20, 1863, M745, NARA; *OR* 27, pt. 2, 709.

3. Gen. Montgomery Meigs to Gen. Daniel Rucker, June 20, 1863, M745, NARA; Aaron Stiles, "Reminiscences of the Charge of Company A, Sixth Ohio Volunteer Cavalry at Upperville, June 21, 1863," *Report of the Thirty-Fifth Annual Reunion, Sixth Ohio Volunteer Cavalry Association*, October 1900, 22–24, Dr. Ken Lawrence Collection; Reuel Porter to General Cilley, December 25, 1892, *Maine Bugle* 3, no. 12, 68.

4. Mackall, Meserve, and Sasscer, *In the Shadow of the Enemy*, 165; David M. Gregg, *The Second Cavalry Division of the Army of the Potomac in the Gettysburg Campaign*, 9, David McMurtrie Gregg Papers, LC; undated letter signed "B," *Augusta Weekly Chronicle and*

Sentinel, August 26, 1863. The June 9 battle at Brandy Station is unquestioned as the largest cavalry battle of the war, but for about thirty minutes, more cavalry engaged in combat at the same time on a smaller field at Upperville than at Brandy Station.

5. By some accounts, the fighting between Oakley and Vineyard Hill lasted but fifteen minutes, before continuing through the town and concluding near Trappe Road.

6. Brooks, *Butler and His Cavalry*, 177; Wade Hampton to H. B. McClellan, January 14, 1878, H. B. McClellan Papers, VMHC; Baylor, *Bull Run to Bull Run*, 149; letter from Paul Hasse and Paul Ziluca to author, March 14, 2007.

7. Trout, *Galloping Thunder*, 273.

8. Welsh, *Medical Histories*, 260; Loveland, "A Valued Paper from Col. Loveland," 18; Burgess, *David Gregg Pennsylvania Cavalryman*, 12; *Philadelphia Press*, June 25, 1863; Glazier, *Three Years in the Federal Cavalry*, 135; Meyer, *Civil War Experiences*, 97.

9. Capt. Norman Barrett to Editor, June 24, 1863, *Cleveland Leader*, July 8, 1863. Major Stedman sent out pioneers to tear down wooden fences in the path of his men between Greengarden Road and the enemy; see Wells Bushnell account in Staats, *History of the Sixth Ohio*, 1:312.

10. *ORS* 1, pt. 5, 255; Glazier, *Three Years in the Federal Cavalry*, 135. Regardless of how one feels about Judson Kilpatrick, cavalry officers had to think quickly in the moment of crisis, and he did. His personality and ambition created problems for him, and he could get into trouble given too much time to work a problem, but he never hesitated when his men and commanders needed him most. Still, Glazier may have gone overboard in complimenting his former commander. He may also have lifted the idea for this section of his work from Moore's *Kilpatrick and Our Cavalry*, 72–73. In a letter to the author of January 18, 2010, historian Bruce Venter, a Kilpatrick authority, explained why he thought James Moore may have served as Kilpatrick's ghostwriter on this work.

11. The Sixth Pennsylvania remained detached from Major Starr's brigade.

12. *ORS* 1, pt. 5, 255.

13. Capt. Norman Barrett to Editor, June 24, 1863, *Cleveland Leader*, July 8, 1863; Reminiscences of Media Evans, SHCUNC.

14. Capt. Norman Barrett to Editor, June 24, 1863, *Cleveland Leader*, July 8, 1863; *OR* 27, pt. 1, 973; *ORS* 1, pt. 5, 255.

15. Wade Hampton to H. B. McClellan, January 14, 1878, H. B. McClellan Papers, VMHC.

16. *Newberry Herald and News*, November 6, 1908; Brooks, *Butler and His Cavalry*, 179–80.

17. Brooks, *Butler and His Cavalry*, 179–80; Cooke, "The Hampton Legion," *PWT*, February 21, 1880; McClellan, *Life and Campaigns*, 314. Stuart's decision to remove himself from command to this point may reflect his other concerns, including seeing to Major von Borcke's safety, coordinating the retreat of Jones and Chambliss, and ensuring the security of Ashby's Gap. Even as he managed such other concerns, Stuart was, as another aide described, "in the very hottest of the press"; see Cooke, *Wearing of the Gray*, 238. Today, Hampton's criticism of Stuart seems unfair and may more accurately reflect Hampton's growing disdain for Stuart rather than actual field leadership.

18. *OR* 27, pt. 2, 690; *ORS* 1, pt. 5, 255; Charles Office Pension File, RG 94, NARA; Meyer, *Civil War Experiences*, 39.

19. Meyer, *Civil War Experiences*, 39; Wade Hampton to H. B. McClellan, January 14, 1878, H. B. McClellan Papers, VMHC; Capt. David Waldhauer Letters, June 23, 1863, *Savannah Republican*, July 2, 1863; Diary of Samuel A. J. Creekmore, Record Group 9, MDAH; Busey and Martin, *Regimental Strengths and Losses*, 195.

20. Lt. John Ketchum to Dear Mother, June 23, 1863, in Duganne, *Fighting Quakers*, 71–72.

21. *Detroit Free Press*, July 4, 1863.

22. Mackall, Meserve, and Sasscer, *In the Shadow of the Enemy*, 165; Jesse Sparkman Diary, USMC, copy courtesy of Clark Hall; Lt. William Gordon account, as quoted in Hopkins, *Little Jeff*, 142. All these participants time the fight at fifteen minutes duration.

23. *Detroit Free Press*, July 4, 1863; *New York Tribune*, July 3, 1863; Ketcham letter in Duganne, *Fighting Quakers*, 71–72.

24. *OR* 27, pt. 1, 921, 946–47, 954, and pt. 3, 258; Returns for Regular Army Cavalry Regiments, RG 94, M744, NARA; *National Tribune*, December 3, 1891; Benjamin Engel to Samuel Starr, August 7, 1891, Samuel H. Starr Papers, MHS, copy courtesy of Michael Miller, Fairfax VA; Paulding Diary. Several estimates of the brigade's strength are available, including the 825 given by Pleasonton on June 22, 1863; 1735 men cited by Don Caughey, "Reserve Brigade Attrition"; and 1922 men, cited by Busey and Martin, *Regimental Strengths and Losses*, 103. Charles Irving Wilson, surgeon-in-chief, Reserve Brigades gives a figure of 1,284 men on June 21, 1863, in a medical document provided by Marshall Krolick, Weston FL. Wilson credits the Sixth U.S. with 330 men while the regimental commander counted but 254 men. The Sixth Pennsylvania was not with the brigade on June 21, and hundreds of other men were either en route to a dismount camp or had not yet rejoined their units. Subtracting the men of the Sixth Pennsylvania from Don Caughey's figure of 1735 and then applying the difference between the official figure for the Sixth U.S. and Capt. George Cram's figure to the other regiments in the brigade, Pleasonton's count of 825 men appears accurate.

25. Caughey, "Reserve Brigade Attrition." Cram had been captured and paroled on May 12, 1863, and later admitted to serving during the summer campaign while awaiting exchange and in violation of his parole, see Cram to Lt. Col. A. J. Alexander, October 27, 1863, M619, NARA.

26. *OR* 27, pt. 1, 946; Davis, *Common Soldier, Uncommon War*, 414; Paulding Diary.

27. Davis, *Common Soldier, Uncommon War*, 415. Accounts ridiculing the regulars soon appeared in the press. An item in the *NYT*, June 23, 1863, stated, "The brigade of regulars . . . much to the amusement of all, wheeled and hurried out of range." See also James Gaston to Dear Wife, June 23, 1863, Gaston Letters, PCHS.

28. Eugene Stocking to Dear Parents, October 4, 1863, MISLA; McClellan, *Life and Campaigns*, 311–13; letter from David Rea, *Charlotte Daily Bulletin*, July 7, 1863, emphasis in original.

29. John Fogarty and James McCauley Pension Files, RG 94, NARA; U.S. Government, *Medical and Surgical History*, 8:466–67.

30. Saussy, "Upperville's Cavalry Battle," 334, emphasis in original; Isaac R. Dunkelberger Memoir, MJWC, USAHEC.

31. Saussy, "Upperville's Cavalry Battle," 335; letter from Lt. J. H. Fuller, June 23, 1863, *Wilmington Journal*, July 2, 1863.

32. *OR* 27, pt. 1, 946–47, 1029–30, 1035; Randol, "Horse-Artilleryman's Diary," 418; Townsend Diary.

33. *OR* 27, pt. 1, 732; William Delony to My Dear Rose, June 20–23, 1863, HRBML; *San Francisco Chronicle and San Francisco Call,* August 21, 1910; William Parnell to Adjutant General, January 14, 1871, RG 94, M1395, and Parnell's Compiled Service and Pension Files, RG 94, NARA. For a more detailed account of Parnell's life, see O'Neill, "William Parnell, a Forgotten Hero."

34. Wade Hampton to H. B. McClellan, January 14, 1878, H. B. McClellan Papers, VMHC; J. E. B. Stuart to My Darling Wife, June 23, 1863, as quoted in Mitchell, *Letters of Stuart,* 325–26. A New York correspondent, citing Southern prisoners, described a shell exploding over Stuart's head, "killing several persons in his immediate vicinity"; see *New York Herald,* June 25, 1863.

35. *OR* 27, pt. 2, 357; Wade Hampton to H. B. McClellan, January 14, 1878, H. B. McClellan Papers, VMHC; Rea Letter, *Charlotte Daily Bulletin,* July 7, 1863; D. M. Cress Memoir, with letter from Fred C. Foard to W. G. Means, March 6, 1917, courtesy of Horace Mewborn.

36. "WVB" to Parents, June 23, 1863, New York State Military Museum and Veterans Research Center, https://dmna.ny.gov/historic/reghist/civil/cavalry/2ndCav/2ndCavCWN.htm, accessed March 24, 2020.

37. *OR* 27, pt. 1, 973; Capt. Delos Northway to Dear Friends at Home, June 23, 1863, copy courtesy of Dr. Ken Lawrence; Capt. Norman Barrett to Editor, June 24, 1863, *Cleveland Leader,* July 8, 1863; Aaron Stiles, "Reminiscences," 22. Ivy Hill Cemetery was established in 1894, across the turnpike from Vineyard Hill.

38. Stiles, "Reminiscences," 22; Delos Northway to Dear Friends at Home, June 23, 1863; Thomas Covert to My Dear Wife, CWMC, USAHEC; Aaron Stiles and Francis Baker Pension Files, NARA.

39. George Wilson and John Roberts Pension Files, RG 94, NARA; Andrew Landers, "Sixth Ohio Cavalry and Their Brilliant Achievements—A Dash with Custer," *National Tribune,* September 27, 1883. The *National Tribune* story is attributed to Andy Lany, but the author's correct name is probably Andrew Landers, who rode in George Wilson's Company G. Landers claims that Custer tried to establish an ambush, sending Northway to draw the Confederates out of the town and into the fire of the remainder of the regiment.

40. *OR* 27, pt. 1, 983, 1030; Mohr, *Cormany Diaries,* 320; Merrill, *Campaigns of the First Maine,* 130.

41. Maine Adjutant General, *Annual Report,* 55; Merrill, *Campaigns of the First Maine,* 131; Tobie, *History of the First Maine,* 170–71.

42. Maine Adjutant General, *Annual Report,* 55; Merrill, *Campaigns of the First Maine,* 131; Tobie, *History of the First Maine,* 171.

43. Merrill, *Campaigns of the First Maine,* 131; *ORS* 1, pt. 5, 255; William Baker to My Dear Sister, June 21, 1863, William B. Baker Letters, SHCUNC.

44. *OR* 27, pt. 2, 691.

45. *Raleigh News and Observer,* May 10, 1884; *Greensborough Patriot,* August 6, 1863; Reuel Porter Pension File, RG 94, NARA. Ferebee complained in July 1864 that he had never received a colonel's commission, only an appointment as colonel; see letter in his Compiled Service File.

46. William Baker to My Dear Sister, June 21, 1863, SHCUNC; Reuel Porter Pension File, RG 94, NARA.

47. Charles Eastman, Simeon Holden, and Andrew Spurling's Pension Files, RG 94, NARA; Tobie, *History of the First Maine*, 174.

48. *OR* 27, pt. 1, 983–84.

49. Doster, *Lincoln and Episodes of the Civil War*, 212–13.

50. Regimental General Order, signed by Colonel Doster, Fourth Pennsylvania RLOB, and Wilson Vanatta Compiled Service and Pension Files, RG 94, NARA.

51. Dembickie and Klecker, "Where the Heck Is Evans Mill?"; Mobley, *James City*, 23–24, copy courtesy of Richard McAdoo, Oriental NC.

52. McClellan, *Life and Campaigns*, 312.

53. Horatio Libby, "Middleburg and Upperville," *Maine Bugle* (October 1891), Call 6, 26; *OR* 27, pt. 1, 984; letter signed "S. C. M.," June 24, 1863, *Daily Morning Chronicle*, June 29, 1863, copy provided by Horace Mewborn.

54. Letter signed "S. C. M.," June 24, 1863, *Daily Morning Chronicle*, June 29, 1863; Regimental General Order, August 2, 1863, Fourth Pennsylvania RLOB, and Wilson Vanatta's Compiled Service and Pension Files, RG 94, NARA. Edward A. Paul, the correspondent, who served Kilpatrick as an unofficial aide, credited the general with trying to save Evans's life at risk of his own. For more on Vanatta, see O'Neill, "Bravest of the Brave," parts 1 and 2.

55. Doster, *Lincoln and Episodes of the Civil War*, 212–14; William Baker to Dear Sister, June 21, 1863, SHCUNC.

21. A Horrid Looking Sight

1. *OR* 27, pt. 1, 947–48, 954; James Gaston to Dear Wife, June 23, 1863, Gaston Letters. The battle most likely ended between four-thirty and five o'clock. Correspondent Edward Paul timed his report at 5 p.m. and Pleasonton wrote his first telegram at 5:30.

2. *OR* 27, pt. 1, 954; *Philadelphia Press*, June 25, 1863; *Maine Cultivator and Hallowell Gazette*, June 27, 1863; Gilpin Diary; Daniel Pulis to Dear Parents, June 23, 1863, Daniel Pulis Letters, RHS; Townsend Diary.

3. William Redman to Editor, June 25, 1863, *Carroll County Weekly Mirror*, July 8, 1863; "W. S." to Editor, July 17, 1863, *Wheeling Daily Intelligencer*, July 27, 1863; *New York Tribune*, June 21, 1863; William Penn Lloyd, "The First Pennsylvania Cavalry in the Gettysburg Campaign," *Philadelphia Press*, May 26, 1886.

4. Styple, *With a Flash of His Sword*, 34; Acken, *Inside the Army of the Potomac*, 185; Parker, *Story of the Thirty-Second*, 164; David B. Boynton to Dear Sister, June 23, 1863, Museum Quality Americana, http://www.mqamericana.com/3rd_Mass_Bty_Lt_Art_Getthtml, accessed July 19, 2012.

5. Opie, *Rebel Cavalryman*, 162; Graham, "From Brandy Station to the Heights of Gettysburg"; Bradshaw, *Civil War Diary*; Edwin Sloan to My Dear Wife, June 24, 1863, Sloan Papers; *Fayetteville Presbyterian*, July 4, 1863.

6. *Reminiscences of Media Evans*, SHCUNC. Emphasis in original.

7. Hard, *History of the Eighth Cavalry*, 253–54; Jeremiah Pickett Pension File, RG 94, NARA. Adolphus Richards, whose parents owned Green Garden, served in the Seventh Virginia Cavalry before joining John Mosby's Forty-Third Battalion.

8. *Charlotte Western Democrat*, July 14, 1863; Peter Evans's Compiled Service Record, Fold3.

9. Inglis Diary; OR 27, pt. 1, 921; Williamson, *Mosby's Rangers*, 75; George Ayre Farm Ledger, History Broker, http://www.historybroker.com/collection/ayre/view/items/index2.htm, accessed in 2017, courtesy of Claiborne Stokes, Mobile AL.

10. Buck, *Sad Earth, Sweet Heaven*, 202–7.

11. Lawrence, *Dark Days in Our Beloved Country*, 86; Mackall, Meserve, and Sasscer, *In the Shadow of the Enemy*, 165–66; Lawrence, *Society of Rebels*, 185.

12. Rebecca Williams Diary, FHLSC, as quoted in Chamberlain and Souders, *Between Reb and Yank*, 185.

22. We Were after Them

1. OR 27, pt. 1, 911–13; ORS 1, pt. 5, 299; NYT, June 25, 1863; Daniel Pulis to Dear Parents, June 23, 1863, Pulis Letters. Daniel Pulis was a member of the patrol, but he says nothing of what the men saw from the mountain. Other accounts, including the NYT correspondent who termed the patrol "a bold reconnaissance," confirm that soldiers did gain the crest and confirm the location of Southern infantry in the valley. For a conflicting account, see "A Boy Spy in Dixie," *National Tribune*, June 28, 1888. The unknown author appears to identify himself as a soldier in Buford's command. In his rambling story, he claims to have been a member of the patrol but saw "nothing at all like an army below us."

2. OR 27, pt. 1, 912–13, and pt. 3, 248–50. Hooker had also received information from officers in Maryland, including Gen. Daniel Tyler on June 21, 1863, M504, NARA.

3. OR 27, pt. 1, 599, 969; "Pennsylvania's Cavalier, Gen. John P. Taylor," *National Tribune*, September 3, 1914; William Penn Lloyd, "The First Pennsylvania in the Gettysburg Campaign," *Philadelphia Press*, May 26, 1886; unsigned Letter of August 7, 1863, *Philadelphia Inquirer*, August 12, 1863; Reuel Porter to General Cilley, December 25, 1892, *Maine Bugle* (April 1893), Call 12, 68; Smith, *History of the 118th Pennsylvania Volunteers*, 227; Paulding Diary; Hall, *History of the 6th New York*, 131; Ressler Diary; James Gaston to Dear Wife, June 23, 1863, Gaston Letters.

4. Neese, *Three Years in the Horse Artillery*, 184; Garnett, "Cavalry Service"; OR 27, pt. 1, 969; Ephraim Bowman to Dear Father, June 28, 1863, Bowman Papers.

5. OR 27, pt. 1, 968–70; Regimental Committee, *History of the Third Pennsylvania Cavalry*, 252–53; James Gaston to Dear Wife, June 23, 1863, Gaston Letters; Lloyd, "The First Pennsylvania Cavalry in the Gettysburg Campaign"; Townsend Diary; unsigned letter, June 23, 1863, *National Tribune*, December 28, 1882; Memoirs of John Z. H. Scott; Pyne, *Ride to War*, 128; William Armbruster Pension, RG 94, NARA.

6. Inglis Diary; Cheney, *History of the Nineth New York*, 100; NYT, June 26, 1863; Theodore Case to Editors, June 8, 1863, *Fredonia Censor*, June 17, 1863; Carter Diary.

23. Continuing Controversy

1. Lawrence, *Dark Days in Our Beloved County*, 87.

2. McClellan, *Life and Campaigns*, 316.

3. General Stuart to My Dear Flora, June 20, 1863 (emphasis in original), copy courtesy of Robert K. Krick.

4. *Edgefield Advertiser*, August 12, 1863; *Savannah Republican*, July 6, 1863.

5. *Savannah Republican*, July 6, 1863. Members of Stuart's staff may have written some of the rebuttals and Stuart may have written one himself; see Thomason, *Jeb*

Stuart, 410. Criticism of Stuart's leadership at Upperville continued into September; see *Richmond Whig,* September 25, 1863.

6. *Richmond Sentinel,* June 25, 1863.

7. Unsigned letter of August 12, 1863, *Richmond Whig,* August 18, 1863. The *Whig,* which had been especially critical of Stuart and his men, printed an apology on September 29, 1863.

8. *OR* 27, pt. 2, 688, 692.

9. *OR* 27, pt. 2, 611, 709; *New York Herald,* June 19, 1863; Chowning Diary; Donahue Diary; and Carter Diary.

10. "Cavalry" to Editor, *Richmond Whig,* October 2, 1863; *Richmond Whig,* September 29, 1863.

24. Continuing Success

1. Lengel, *General George Washington,* 64; Starr, "Inner Life," 160.

2. *St. Albans Daily Messenger,* April 9, 1863; Moore, *Anecdotes, Poetry, and Incidents,* 305. See also George Stoneman's order of March 6, 1863, Twelfth Illinois RLOB, and General Averell's order of the same date, First Rhode Island RLOB, RG 94, NARA.

3. Blackford, *War Years with Jeb Stuart,* 221.

4. *New York Tribune,* June 24, 1863.

5. Ryan, *Spies, Scouts, and Secrets,* 214; O'Neill, *Cavalry Battles,* 160.

6. Ryan, *Spies, Scouts, and Secrets,* 214; O'Neill, *Cavalry Battles,* 160.

7. Ryan, *Spies, Scouts, and Secrets,* 194–95. Pleasonton certainly knew of Hooker's threat to Averell in March, a threat covering every officer in the corps. He had seen Averell relieved by Hooker following his less-than-aggressive performance in the Stoneman Raid, as well as the abuse Hooker had heaped upon Stoneman following the raid. Pleasonton had also been a party to the story fabricated as to his role at Chancellorsville, as a means of allaying any of President Lincoln's concerns regarding Hooker's relieving Stoneman. Pleasonton had then replaced Stoneman as corps commander, but only in a temporary capacity. Thus, he had taken a huge risk in disobeying his commander on June 17 and 18 and risking his position. Further, Hooker had, in the captured order written on the afternoon of June 17, revoked his approval of Pleasonton's plan to move the entire corps into the Loudoun Valley on June 18. Pleasonton had taken another risk, albeit unknowingly, by sending several brigades out toward the Shenandoah Valley on June 18. Pleasonton may have called these brigades back only after receiving a copy of the order on the afternoon on June 18.

8. *OR* 27, pt. 1, 51, 90, and pt. 3, 254. See also Gen. Rufus Ingalls to Lt. Col. Charles Sawtelle, June 22, 1863, M504, and Fifteenth Vermont Infantry RMRMP, NARA. Though promoted, Pleasonton may never have received permanent command of the corps. After the war, Hooker said of Pleasonton, "he is so much given to exaggeration I never dare to rely upon his statements too fully." Whether he felt so during the war is uncertain; see Hooker to Samuel Bates, July 12, 1878, Bates Collection, PSA, courtesy of John Hennessy.

9. Victor Comte to Dear Elise, June 28, 1863, Victor Comte Letters, BLUM.

Appendix A

1. The regiment remained widely scattered following the Stoneman Raid of late-April and early-May. Evidence suggests four companies had rejoined the army, while other

companies, along with Col. Arno Voss, finally reached Alexandria on or about June 18 to be remounted. A third detachment remained at Gloucester Point, near Yorktown, Virginia, awaiting horses; see Colonel Voss to Adjt. Gen. Lorenzo Thomas, June 18, 1863, RG 94, Entry 496, NARA.

2. Colonel Vincent placed Lt. Col. Conner, Forty-Fourth New York, in temporary command of the regiment during the absence of Lt. Col. Joshua Chamberlain and Maj. Charles Gilmore, both of whom were sick; see *OR* 27, pt. 1, 614.

Appendix C

1. Circular 44, June 9, 1864, published by Asst. Adjt. Gen. Edward Townsend, under the authority of Secretary of War Edwin Stanton, RG 94, Entry 181, NARA.

2. Ford, *Cycle of Adams Letters*, 2:3–5.

3. *Boston Congregationalist*, December 18, 1863; *Chicago Tribune*, August 28, 1863; *Springfield Republican*, December 15, 1863.

4. *OR* 25, pt. 1, 1069, and pt. 2, 469, 483–84, 487, 533; Col. Eugene von Kielmansegge to Gen. David Gregg, May 18, 1863, Entry 1449, NARA.

5. *OR* 25, pt. 2, 516, 533; *ORS* Series 1, pt. 4, 474–75; Gen. Rufus Ingalls to Gen. Daniel Rucker, May 24, 1863, and Rucker to Ingalls, May 25, 1863, M504, NARA. For a complete discussion of the Union response to the rumored raid on Washington, see O'Neill, *Chasing Jeb Stuart and John Mosby*, 187–253.

6. Gen. Rufus Ingalls to Gen. Daniel Rucker, June 7, 1863, and Ingalls to Lt. Col. William Le Duc, June 8, 1863, M504, and Gen. Montgomery Meigs to Gen. Daniel Rucker, June 8, 1863, RG 92, M745, NARA; *ORS* Series 1, pt. 5, 244, 247.

7. Capt. E. S. Allen to Capt. Perley Pitkin, June 10, 1863, M504, and Gen. Montgomery Meigs to Captain Fuller, May 30, 1863, RG 92, M745, NARA.

8. Court-martial of Capt. Richard C. M. Lord, RG 153, NARA.

9. Gen. Montgomery Meigs to Capt. G. W. Lee, August 30, 1862, and May 5, 1863, Meigs to Capt. W. Van Ness, May 26, 1863, and Meigs to Capt. Charles Fuller, June 15, 1863, RG 92, M745, and M504, and Unknown to Meigs, May 22, 1863 (emphasis in original), RG 92, Entry 225, NARA. On June 17, Meigs made an exception, allowing an officer to purchase mares if "they are the product of that debatable country and not bought there on speculation, and if they belong to loyal owners, it may be as well to take them at fair prices and thus prevent the rebels from getting possession of them in the next raid"; see Meigs to Col. J. Taylor, June 17, 1863, RG 92, M745, NARA.

10. Unknown officer to Meigs, June 10, 1863, RG 92, Entry 225, Meigs to Capt. D. Dickinson, May 29, 1863, Dickinson to Meigs, June 9, 1863, and Capt. H. Lacey to Captain Tompkins, June 8, 1863, RG 92, M745, NARA.

11. Circular 44, June 9, 1864, RG 94, Entry 181, Gen. Daniel Rucker to Gen. Rufus Ingalls, July 12, 1863, General Ingalls to Capt. John McHarg, July 12, 1863, General Rucker to Capt. Luther Peirce, August 2, 1863, M504, and Captain Boyd to General Meigs, July 24, 1863, RG 92, Entry 225, NARA.

12. Capt. Luther Peirce to Gen. Daniel Rucker, August 3, 1863, M504, NARA.

13. Phillips, "Writing Horses into American Civil War History," 167–68.

14. Circular 44, June 9, 1864, RG 94, Entry 181, NARA.

15. Gen. Montgomery Meigs to Gen. Alfred Pleasonton, June 1, 1863, RG 92, M745, NARA; *OR* 27, pt. 1, 907–8. In his letter of June 1, 1863, Meigs reported more than fourteen thousand disabled horses held in government corrals and pastures.

16. *NYT*, June 24, 1863. An officer in the Third Pennsylvania, whose regiment had seen little combat in the Loudoun Valley, estimated the regiment lost seventy-two horses to exhaustion or other ailments on the march between the Potomac River and Gettysburg. If each of the regiments in the corps had lost a like number, the corps would have lost nearly nineteen hundred horses during the same period. See Acken, *Blue-Blooded Cavalryman*, 272n60; Regimental Committee, *History of the Third Pennsylvania*, 266. In a letter written from Washington DC on July 2, a trooper from the Ninth New York estimated five thousand cavalrymen waited in the city to join the army or rejoin their regiments. Though he identified one new regiment, the Thirteenth New York, most of the men were veterans waiting for horses and or equipment before rejoining their units. The date of the letter precludes Gettysburg battle losses from inflating his estimate; see Theodore Case to Editor, July 2, 1863, *Fredonia Censor*, July 15, 1863.

17. *OR* 27, pt. 3, 134–35; Gen. Alfred Pleasonton to Gen. Seth Williams, June 16, 1863, C. Ross Smith Papers, USAHEC; Capt. Samuel McKee to Gen. Daniel Butterfield, June 16, 1863, Col. Alfred Duffié to Capt. William Price, June 4, 1863, Duffié to Capt. Andrew Cohen, June 5, 1863, Gen. James Ripley to Maj. Theodore Laidley, June 8, 1863, and Pleasonton to Gen. Montgomery Meigs, June 26, 1863, M504. The Seventeenth Pennsylvania may also have needed five hundred saddles on the eve of Brandy Station; see Lt. Col. Andrew Alexander to Capt. Daniel Flagler, and Flagler to Alexander, June 7, 1863, M504, NARA.

18. Cavalry Corps Circular, June 10, 1863, Entry 1449, Gen. James Ripley to Col. George Ramsey, Ripley to Lt. William Dean, and Ripley to Maj. Robert Wainwright, June 12, 1863, E. Stebbins to Maj. Edmund Pope, June 11, 1863, Capt. Daniel Flagler to Lieutenant Dean, and Flagler to Colonel Ramsay, June 11, 1863, Ramsay to General Ripley, June 18, 1863, E. Stebbins to Lt. William Perkins, June 19, 1863, and Ripley to William Wiley, June 22, 1863, M504, NARA. General Stuart counted 401 captured firearms, including 165 Sharps carbines; see *OR* 27, pt. 2, 719–20.

19. Capt. Andrew Cohen to Gen. Alfred Pleasonton, June 21, 1863, Entry 1449, NARA; *OR* 27, pt. 3, 258; *Boston Congregationalist*, December 18, 1863. Arguably, the most pernicious myth of the entire campaign concerns the Cavalry Corps having been issued Spencer seven-shot carbines prior to Gettysburg. In truth, the army did not sign the contract for the weapons until mid-July and did not receive the first weapons until October; see Marcot, *Spencer Repeating Firearms*, 63–66.

20. The amount of information available for the Union cavalry and the supply challenges faced by Montgomery Meigs, Rufus Ingalls, and Alfred Pleasonton is vast, the detail almost overwhelming. Unfortunately, the opposite holds true for Southern records, few of which survived the war.

21. *OR* 27, pt. 1, 57. Similar orders went to other units, including Capt. Samuel Means and his Loudoun Rangers, see Gen. Daniel Rucker to Capt. Henry Lacey, June 25, 1863, RG 92, Entry 225, NARA.

BIBLIOGRAPHY

Archives and Manuscript Materials

Ames, John. Letters. Gregory Coco Collection, United States Army and Education Center, Carlisle PA.

Apted, Alfred. Diary. Civil War Miscellaneous Collection, United States Army and Education Center, Carlisle PA.

Averell, William. Papers. New York State Library and Archives, Albany.

Baker, William. Letters. Southern Historical Collections, University of North Carolina, Chapel Hill.

Baldwin, Henry. Letter. Dr. Ken Lawrence Collection, Huntsburg OH.

Ball, Norman. Diary. Connecticut Historical Society, Hartford.

Barr, John. Diary. Historical Society of Pennsylvania, Philadelphia.

Bates, Samuel P. Papers. Pennsylvania State Archives, Harrisburg.

Bellamy, Flavius. Papers. Indiana State Library, Indianapolis.

Berry, John. Diary. Civil War Times Illustrated Collection, United States Army and Education Center, Carlisle PA.

Biddle, Samuel S. Papers. Duke University Library, Durham NC.

Blair, Austin. Papers. Burton Historical Collections, Detroit Public Library MI.

Bliss, George. Letters. Rhode Island Historical Society, Providence.

Blumberg, Arnold. Manuscript Copy of "Counterfeit Count in Blue: Brigadier General Alfred N. Duffié." Arnold Blumberg Collection, Baltimore MD.

Bowman, Ephraim. Papers. University of Virginia Library, Charlottesville.

Brent, William. Reminiscences. Robert K. Krick Collection, Fredericksburg VA.

Brooke, St. George Tucker. Autobiography. Virginia Museum of History & Culture, Richmond.

Brown, William. Papers. Brown University, Providence RI.

Bryan, John H. Papers. North Carolina Office of Archives and History, Raleigh.

Carter, William. Diary. Library of Virginia. Richmond.

Chowning, John. Diary. Mary Ball Library, Lancaster VA.

Clark, Nathan S. Diary. Digital Maine Repository, https://digitalmaine.com.
Comte, Victor. Letters. Bentley Library, University of Michigan, Ann Arbor.
Confederate Veteran Papers, Duke University Library, Durham NC.
Covert, Thomas. Letters. Civil War Miscellaneous Collection, United States Army and Education Center, Carlisle PA.
Coyner, Samuel Brown. Memoir. Horace Mewborn Collection, New Bern NC.
Creekmore, Samuel A. J. Diary. Mississippi Department of Archives and History, Jackson.
Cress, D. M. Memoir. Horace Mewborn Collection, New Bern NC.
Curtis, William A. Reminiscences. Horace Mewborn Collection, New Bern NC.
Custer, George A. Papers. U.S. Military Academy, West Point NY.
Dahlgren, John. Papers. Library of Congress, Washington DC.
Decker, Marshall E. Letters. Decker Bristow Collection, Hendersonville NC.
Delony, William G. Papers. Hargrett Rare Book and Manuscript Library, University of Georgia, Athens.
Donahue, John. Diary. Library of Virginia. Richmond.
Duffield, Diffie. Papers. Burton Historical Collections, Detroit Public Library MI.
Dunkelberger, Isaac R. Memoir. Michael J. Winey Collection, United States Army and Education Center, Carlisle PA.
Edwards, Thomas W. B. Diary. Library of Virginia, Richmond.
Evans, Media. Reminiscences. Southern Historical Collections, University of North Carolina, Chapel Hill.
Forbush, William Henry. Diary. Bradley Forbush Collection, Gordonsville VA.
Foster, James. James Foster and Family Collection, Louisiana State University, Baton Rouge.
Frank, Abner. Diary. Civil War Miscellaneous Collection, United States Army and Education Center, Carlisle PA.
Gaston, James. Letters. Peters Creek Historical Society, Venetia PA.
Geary, John. Letters. Historical Society of Pennsylvania, Philadelphia.
Gilpin, Samuel. Papers. Library of Congress, Washington DC.
Grand Army of the Republic Files. New York State Archives and Library, Albany.
Green, Edward. Papers. Horace Mewborn Collection, New Bern NC.
Gregg, David M. Papers. Library of Congress, Washington DC.
Guild, Lafayette. Letter Book. Richmond National Battlefield Park VA.
Hager, Jonathan. Diary. University of Virginia Library, Charlottesville.
Hall, Clark B. Miscellaneous Papers and Communications. Culpeper VA.
Hampton, Charles. Diary. Clark Historical Library, Central Michigan University, Mount Pleasant.
Hampton, Wade. General Order, June 11, 1863. Robert K. Krick Collection, Fredericksburg VA.
Hard, Abner. Casualty List, 1st Cavalry Division. Marshall Krolick Collection, Weston FL.
Havens, Edwin. Letters and Diaries. Archives and Historical Collections, Michigan State University, Lansing.
Holley, Turner. Letters. Duke University Library, Durham NC.
Hotchkiss, Jedediah. Papers. Library of Congress, Washington DC.
Howe, William. Papers. Maine State Archives, Augusta.
Hubard, Robert Thruston, Jr. Reminiscences. University of Virginia Library, Charlottesville.

Inglis, John. Diary. Albany Institute of History and Art, Albany NY.
Kautz, August S. Papers. Library of Congress, Washington DC.
Lincoln, Abraham. Papers. Library of Congress, Washington DC.
Lyman, Carlos. Collection. Western Reserve Historical Society, Cleveland OH.
Macomber, Dexter. Diary. Clark Historical Library, Central Michigan University, Mount Pleasant.
McClellan, H. B. Papers. Virginia Museum of History and Culture, Richmond.
Meade, George G. Papers. Historical Society of Pennsylvania, Philadelphia.
Military Order of the Loyal Legion. David Ramsey Clendenin Memoriam Bulletin. Marshall Krolick Collection, Weston FL.
Miscellaneous Papers, Clippings, and Communications. Robert F. O'Neill Collection, King George VA.
Munford-Ellis. Papers. Duke University Library, Durham NC.
Neese, George. Diary. Library of Virginia, Richmond.
Neher, Philip. Papers. Albany Institute of History and Art, Albany NY.
Newhall, Walter. Letters. Historical Society of Pennsylvania, Philadelphia.
Northway, Delos. Letters. Dr. Ken Lawrence Collection, Huntsburg OH.
Paulding, Tattnall. Diary. Dr. James Milgram Collection, Chicago.
Payne Family. Papers. Virginia Museum of History and Culture, Richmond.
Pearson, Kimball. Letters. Civil War Times Illustrated Collection, 2nd Series, United States Army and Education Center, Carlisle PA.
Pleasonton, Alfred. Papers. Library of Congress, Washington DC.
Pulis, Daniel. Letters. Rochester Historical Society, Rochester NY.
Record Group 92. Records of the Office of the Quartermaster General. National Archives, Washington DC.
Entry 225, Consolidated Correspondence.
Entry 1616, Telegrams Sent to Conductors and Engineers.
M745, Letters Sent by the Office of the Quartermaster General.
Record Group 94. Records of the Adjutant General's Office, Compiled Service Records of Volunteer Union Soldiers. National Archives, Washington DC.
Entry 179, Records of Confederate Prisoners.
Entry 181, Horse Books.
Entry 496, Volunteer Service Records.
M567, Letters Received by the Office of the Adjutant General (1822–1860).
M619, Letters Received by the Office of the Adjutant General (1861–1870).
M688, U.S. Military Academy Cadet Application Papers.
M744, Returns from Regular Army Cavalry Regiments.
M797, Case Files of Investigations of Levi C. Turner and Lafayette C. Baker.
M1064, Letters Received by the Commission Branch.
M1098, U.S. Army General's Reports of Civil War Service.
M1395, Appointment, Commission, and Personal Files.
Regimental Letter and Order Books.
Regimental Muster Rolls and Miscellaneous Papers.
Record Group 107. Records of the Office of the Secretary of War. M504, Telegrams Collected by the Secretary of War. National Archives, Washington DC.
Record Group 109. Confederate Records. M324, Compiled Service Records of Confederate Soldiers from Virginia. National Archives, Washington DC.

Record Group 153. Records of the Judge Advocate General. National Archives, Washington DC.
Record Group 393. Part 1, Records of the U.S. Army Continental Commands. National Archives, Washington DC.
Entry 3964, Letters Sent and Received.
Entry 3966, Letters Sent by General Casey at White House.
Entry 3980, Miscellaneous Letters, Reports, and Lists.
Entry 3986, Two or More Name File.
Entry 4083, Signal Officer Letters and Reports.
Entry 5383, Letters Received, Department of Washington.
Record Group 393. Part 2, Records of the U.S. Army Continental Commands. National Archives, Washington DC.
Entry 1439, Letters Sent.
Entry 1449, Letters, Telegrams, Reports, and Lists Received.
Entry 1464, Letters Sent by the Acting Inspector General.
Entry 1534, Letters and Telegrams Sent and General Orders Issued.
Entry 1588, Letters Sent.
Ressler, Isaac. Diary. Civil War Times Illustrated Collection, United States Army and Education Center, Carlisle, PA.
Roll of Honor Record. Museum of the Confederacy, Richmond VA.
Rosser, Thomas. Correspondence. University of Virginia Library, Charlottesville.
Rucker, Moses Peter. Reminiscences. Dr. James I. Robertson Civil War Sesquicentennial Collection, Library of Virginia, Richmond.
Ryder Family. Papers. Bentley Library, University of Michigan, Ann Arbor.
Saffer, Wynne C. Papers. The Gott Library, Marshall VA.
Saunders Family. Collection. Virginia Museum of History & Culture, Richmond.
Scott, John Z. Memoir. Virginia Museum of History & Culture, Richmond.
Shultz, David. "From Aldie to Upperville: Federal Horse Artillery, a Prelude to Gettysburg." Unpublished manuscript provided by the author.
Sloan, Edward R. Papers. Duke University Library, Durham NC.
Smith, Charles. Letter, Smith Family Papers. Civil War Miscellaneous Collection, United States Army Heritage and Education Center, Carlisle PA.
Smith, C. Ross. Papers. United States Army Heritage and Education Center, Carlisle PA.
Smith, Henry A. Letters. Vermont Historical Society, Vermont History Center, Barre.
Snyder, Thompson A. Papers. Fredericksburg and Spotsylvania National Military Park VA.
Southgate-Jones Family. Papers. Duke University Library, Durham NC.
Sparkman, Jesse. Diary. University of Mississippi, Special Collections, University.
Starr, Samuel H. Papers. Missouri Historical Society, St. Louis.
Stiles, Aaron. Papers. Dr. Ken Lawrence Collection, Huntsburg OH.
Stocking, Eugene. Letters. Michigan State Archives, Lansing.
Stokes, Claiborne. Miscellaneous Papers and Communications. Mobile AL.
Story, Asa. Diary. New York State Archives and Library, Albany.
Stuart, James Ewell Brown. Collection. Virginia Museum of History and Culture, Richmond.
Stuart, James Ewell Brown. Letter. Robert K. Krick Collection, Fredericksburg VA.
Taylor, Ephraim H. Letters and Diary. Dr. Charles W. Plummer Collection, Auburn ME.
Towles, John. Diary. Library of Virginia. Richmond.
Townsend, Daniel. Diary. Eric Wittenberg Collection, Columbus OH.

Townsend, Daniel. Letter. Bradley Forbush Collection, Gordonsville VA.
Venable, Charles S. Papers. Southern Historical Collections, University of North Carolina, Chapel Hill.
Von Koerber, Vincent. Collection. University of Virginia Library, Charlottesville.
Wainwright, Charles S. Diary. Henry E. Huntington Library, San Marino CA.
Webb, Nathan. Diary. William L. Clements Library, University of Michigan, Ann Arbor.
Wells, William. Letters. Bailey Howe Library, University of Vermont, Burlington.
White, Peter. Papers. Virginia Museum of History and Culture, Richmond.
White, William. Letters. Vermont Historical Society, Vermont History Center, Barre.
Whitehead, Irving. Papers. University of Virginia Library, Charlottesville.
Willard Family. Papers. Library of Congress, Washington DC.
Williams, Rebecca K. Diary. Friends Historical Library, Swarthmore College, Swarthmore PA.
Works Progress Administration Files. Fauquier Library, Warrenton VA.

Published Works

Acken, J. Gregory, ed. *Blue-Blooded Cavalryman: Captain William Brooke Rawle in the Army of the Potomac, May 1863–August 1865*. Kent OH: Kent State University Press, 2019.
———. *Inside the Army of the Potomac: The Civil War Experience of Captain Francis Adams Donaldson*. Mechanicsburg PA: Stackpole, 1998.
Adams, Charles Francis. *Charles Francis Adams 1835–1915: An Autobiography*. Boston: Houghton Mifflin, 1916.
Adams, George R. *General William S. Harney: Prince of Dragoons*. Lincoln: University of Nebraska Press, 2001.
Ambrose, Stephen E. *Crazy Horse and Custer: The Parallel Lives of Two American Warriors*. New York: Doubleday, 1975.
Andrew, Rod, Jr. *Wade Hampton: Confederate Warrior to Southern Redeemer*. Chapel Hill: University of North Carolina Press, 2008.
Angle, Paul M., ed. *Three Years in the Army of the Cumberland: The Letters and Diary of Major James Connelly*. Bloomington: University of Indiana Press, 1959.
Baldino, Georgiann, ed. *A Family and Nation under Fire: The Civil War Letters and Journals of William and Joseph Medill*. Kent OH: Kent State University Press, 2018.
Basler, Roy, ed. *The Collected Works of Abraham Lincoln*. 9 vols. New Brunswick NJ: Rutgers University Press, 1953.
Baylor, George. *Bull Run to Bull Run; or, Four Years in the Army of Northern Virginia*. Richmond VA: NP, 1900.
Beale, George W. *A Lieutenant of Cavalry in Lee's Army*. Reprint, Baltimore MD: Butternut and Blue, 1994.
Beale, Richard L. T. *History of the Ninth Virginia Cavalry in the War between the States*. Reprint, Amissville VA: American Fundamentalist, 1981.
Beyer, Walter F., and Oscar F. Keydel, eds. *Deeds of Valor: How American Heroes Won the Medal of Honor*. 2 vols. Detroit MI: Perrien-Keydel, 1907.
Bigelow, John, Jr. *The Campaign of Chancellorsville*. New Haven CN: 1910.
Blackford, Susan Leigh, and Charles Minor Blackford. *Letters from Lee's Army or Memoirs of Life in and out of the Army in Virginia during the War between the States*. New York: Scribner, 1947.
Blackford, William W. *War Years with Jeb Stuart*. Baton Rouge: Louisiana State University Press, 1993.

Bliss, George. *The First Rhode Island Cavalry at Middleburg, Va.* Providence: Rhode Island Soldiers and Sailors Historical Society, 1889.

Bowmaster, Patrick. "Confederate Brig. Gen. B. H. Robertson and the 1863 Gettysburg Campaign." MA thesis, Virginia Polytechnic Institute and State University, Blacksburg, 1995.

Bradshaw, Bruce, ed. *Civil War Diary of Charles William McVicar.* Washington DC: NP, 1977.

Brady, James P., compiler. *Hurrah for the Artillery! Knaps Independent Battery "E," Pennsylvania Light Artillery.* Gettysburg PA: Thomas Publications, 1992.

Breshears, Guy. *Major Granville Haller: Dismissed with Malice.* Westminster MD: Heritage Books, 2006.

Brooks, U. R. *Butler and His Cavalry in the War of Secession 1861–1865.* Reprint, Camden SC: Guild Bindery Press, 1989.

———. *Stories of the Confederacy.* Camden SC: Guild Bindery Press, 1991.

Buck, Lucy Rebecca. *Sad Earth, Sweet Heaven: The Diary of Lucy Rebecca Buck, during the War between the States, Front Royal, Virginia, December 25, 1861–April 15, 1865.* Edited by William Buck. Birmingham AL: Cornerstone, 1973.

Burgess, Milton V. *David Gregg Pennsylvania Cavalryman.* State College PA: Nittany Valley Offset, 1984.

Busey, John W., and David G. Martin. *Regimental Strengths and Losses at Gettysburg.* Hightstown NJ: Longstreet House, 1986.

Caughey, Donald C. "Fiddlers Green: George C. Cram." *Regular Cavalry in the Civil War* (blog), May 26, 2009. https://regularcavalryincivilwar.wordpress.com/2009/05/26/fiddlers-green-george-c-cram.

———. "Reserve Brigade Attrition in the Gettysburg Campaign." *Regular Cavalry in the Civil War* (blog), June 20, 2013. https://regularcavalryincivilwar.wordpress.com.

Caughey, Donald C., and Jimmy J. Jones. *The 6th United States Cavalry in the Civil War: A History and Roster.* Jefferson NC: McFarland, 2013.

Cauley, Avis Mary Curtis. "The Confederacy in the Lower Shenandoah Valley as Illustrated by the Career of Colonel Roger Preston Chew." MA thesis, University of Pittsburgh, 1937.

Chalfant, William. *Cheyennes and Horse Soldiers: The 1857 Expedition and the Battle of Solomon's Fork.* Norman: University of Oklahoma Press, 1989.

Chamberlain, Taylor M., and John M. Souders. *Between Reb and Yank: A Civil War History of Northern Loudoun County, Virginia.* Jefferson NC: McFarland, 2011.

Cheney, Newel. *History of the Ninth Regiment New York Volunteer Cavalry.* Jamestown NY: Martin Merz and Son, 1901.

Clark, Walter, ed. *Histories of the Several Regiments and Battalions from North Carolina in the Great War 1861–1865.* 5 vols. Goldsboro: North Carolina State University Print Shop, 1901.

Coddington, Edwin B. *The Gettysburg Campaign: A Study in Command.* Dayton OH: Morningside Bookshop, 1979.

Comey, Lyman Richard, ed. *A Legacy of Valor: The Memoirs and Letters of Captain Henry Newton Comey, 2nd Massachusetts Infantry.* Knoxville: University of Tennessee Press, 2004.

Cooke, J. Churchill. "With the Fourth Virginia Cavalry, C.S.A." *Confederate Veteran,* no. 36: (1928): 104.

Cooke, John Esten. *Wearing of the Gray; Personal Portraits, Scenes and Adventures of the War.* New York: E. B. Treat, 1867.

Crawford, Kim. *The 16th Michigan Infantry.* Dayton OH: Morningside House, 2002.

Crowninshield, Benjamin W. *A History of the First Regiment of Massachusetts Cavalry Volunteers.* Boston: Houghton, Mifflin, 1891. Reprint, Baltimore: Butternut and Blue, 1995.

Custer, Andie. "The Knight of Romance: General Alfred Pleasonton in the Gettysburg Campaign." *Blue and Gray,* no. 22 (Spring 2005): 6–20.

Davis, George B. "Cavalry in the Gettysburg Campaign." *Journal of the United States Cavalry Association* 1 (1888): 325–48.

Davis, Sidney Morris. *Common Soldier, Uncommon War: Life as a Cavalryman in the Civil War.* Edited by Charles Cooney. Bethesda MD: Port City Press, 1994.

Denison, Frederic. *Sabres and Spurs: The First Regiment Rhode Island Cavalry in the Civil War.* Reprint, Baltimore: Butternut and Blue, 1994.

Dennett, Tyler. *Lincoln and the Civil War in the Diaries and Letters of John Hay.* New York: Dodd, Mead, 1939.

Donker, Russell F., ed. *The Civil War Diary of George S. Lockley.* Grand Rapids MI: Ted Brink, 1962.

Doster, William. *Lincoln and Episodes of the Civil War.* New York: G. P. Putnam's Sons, 1915.

Driver, Robert J., Jr. *1st Virginia Cavalry.* Lynchburg VA: H. E. Howard, 1991.

———. *2nd Virginia Cavalry.* Lynchburg VA: H. E. Howard, 1995.

———. *5th Virginia Cavalry.* Lynchburg VA: H. E. Howard, 1997.

Duganne, A. J. H. *The Fighting Quakers: A True Story of the War for Our Union.* Reprint, Farmville VA: Farmville Printing, 1995.

Eggleston, George Cary. *A Rebel's Recollections.* New York: G. P. Putnam's Sons, 1878.

Fishel, Edwin C. *The Secret War for the Union: The Untold Story of Military Intelligence in the Civil War.* Boston: Houghton Mifflin, 1996.

Ford, Worthington Chauncey, ed. *A Cycle of Adams Letters 1861–1865.* 2 vols. Boston: Houghton Mifflin, 1920.

Fordney, Ben Fuller. *George Stoneman: A Biography of the Union General.* Jefferson NC: McFarland, 2008.

Freiheit, Laurence H. *Boots and Saddles: Cavalry during the Maryland Campaign of September 1862.* Iowa City: Camp Pope, 2012.

Frost, Robert, and Nancy Frost. *Picket Pins and Sabers.* Ashland KY: Economy Printers, 1971.

Gallagher, Gary W., ed. *Fighting for the Confederacy: The Personal Recollections of General Edward Porter Alexander.* Chapel Hill: University of North Carolina Press, 1989.

Glazier, Willard. *Battles for the Union.* Hartford CT: Gilman, 1878.

———. *Three Years in the Federal Cavalry.* New York: R. H. Ferguson, 1874.

Gordon, George H. *Brook Farm to Cedar Mountain in the War of the Great Rebellion 1861–1862.* Boston: NP, 1883.

Gracey, S. L. *Annals of the Sixth Pennsylvania Cavalry.* Philadelphia: E. H. Butler, 1868.

Graham, William A. "Nineteenth Regiment (Second Cavalry)." Vol. 2 of *Histories of the Several Regiments and Battalions from North Carolina in the Great War, 1861–'65,* edited by Walter Clark. Goldsboro NC: Nash Brothers, 1901.

Grandchamp, Robert. "'Our Regiment Has Just Been Cleaned Up': The 1st Rhode Island Cavalry at Middleburg." *Gettysburg Magazine,* no. 37 (2007): 7–15.

———. "'Ours Was a Desperate Position to Hold.'" *Gettysburg Magazine,* no. 64 (2021): 6.

Green, Charles O. *An Incident in the Battle of Middleburg, June 17, 1863.* Providence: Rhode Island Soldiers and Sailors Historical Society, 1911.

Greenleaf, Margery, ed. *Letters to Eliza from a Union Soldier, 1862–1865*. Chicago: Follett, 1970.

Greenwood, Grace. *Records of Five Years*. Boston: Ticknor and Fields, 1867.

Griffin, Richard N., ed. *Three Years a Soldier: The Diary and Newspaper Correspondence of Private George Perkins, Sixth New York Independent Battery, 1861–1864*. Knoxville: University of Tennessee Press, 2006.

Hackley, Woodford B. *The Little Fork Rangers: A Sketch of Company D, 4th Virginia Cavalry*. Richmond VA: Press of the Dietz Printing Co., 1927.

Haines, Douglas Craig. "The Advance of Longstreet's First Corps to Gettysburg." *Gettysburg Magazine*, no. 39 (2008): 7–44.

Hall, Hillman. *History of the 6th New York Cavalry*. Worcester MA: Blanchard Press, 1908.

Hancock, Almira R. *Reminiscences of Winfield Scott Hancock by His Wife*. New York: Charles L. Webster, 1887.

Hanson, Joseph Mills. "The Artisan of a Cavalry Corps, Alfred Pleasonton." *Cavalry Journal* 41, no. 172 (July–August 1932): 5–15.

Hard, Abner. *History of the Eighth Cavalry Regiment Illinois Volunteers: During the Great Rebellion*. Aurora IL: NP, 1868; reprint Dayton OH: Morningside Edition, 1984.

Heitman, Francis B. *Historical Register and Dictionary of the United States Army: From Its Organization, September 29, 1789, to March 2, 1903*. 2 vols. Reprint, Gaithersburg MD: Olde Soldier Books, 1988.

Hewett, Janet B., Noah Andre Trudeau, and Bryce A. Suderow, eds. *Supplement of the Official Records of the Union and Confederate Armies*. Wilmington NC: Broadfoot, 1994.

Hilen, Andrew, ed. *The Letters of Henry Wadsworth Longfellow, 1857–1865*. 6 vols. Cambridge MA: Belknap Press of Harvard University Press, 1972.

Hopkins, Donald A. *The Little Jeff: The Jeff Davis Legion, Cavalry, Army of Northern Virginia*. Shippensburg PA: White Mane Books, 1999.

Houck, Peter W. *Duty, Honor, Country: The Diary and Biography of General William P. Craighill, Cadet at West Point 1849–1853*. Lynchburg VA: Warwick House, 1993.

Hubard, Robert T., Jr. *The Civil War Memoirs of a Virginia Cavalryman*. Edited by Thomas P. Nanzig. Tuscaloosa: University of Alabama Press, 2007.

Jones, Benjamin W. *Under the Stars and Bars: A History of the Surry Light Artillery*. Richmond VA: Everett Waddey, 1901.

Jones, John B. *A Rebel War Clerk's Diary*. Edited by Ear Schenck Miers. New York: Sagamore Press, 1958.

Judson, A. M. *History of the Eighty-Third Regiment Pennsylvania Volunteers*. Erie PA: B. F. H. Lynn, 1865.

Keen, Hugh C., and Horace Mewborn. *43rd Battalion Virginia Cavalry: Mosby's Command*. Lynchburg VA: H. E. Howard, 1993.

Krick, Robert K. *Civil War Weather in Virginia*. Tuscaloosa: University of Alabama Press, 2007.

Laas, Virginia Jeans, ed. *Wartime Washington: The Civil War Letters of Elizabeth Blair Lee*. Urbana: University of Illinois Press, 1991.

Ladd, David L., and Audrey J. Ladd, eds. *The Batchelder Papers: Gettysburg in Their Own Words*. 3 vols. Dayton OH: Morningside, 1994.

Lambert, Joseph I. *One Hundred Years with the Second Cavalry*. Fort Riley KS: Press of the Capper Printing Company, 1939.

Lanska, Douglas J. "Vitamin A-Deficiency Eye Disease among Soldiers in the U.S. Civil War: Spectrum of Clinical Disease." *Military Medicine*, no. 180 (July 2015): 774–79.

Lawrence, Lee, ed. *Dark Days in Our Beloved Country: The Civil War Diary of Catherine Hopkins Broun.* Warrenton VA: Piedmont Press and Graphics, 2014.

———. *Society of Rebels: Diary of Amanda Edmonds, Northern Virginia 1857–1867.* Warrenton VA: Piedmont Press & Graphics, 2017.

Lengel, Edward G. *General George Washington: A Military Life.* New York City: Random House, 2005.

Libby, Horatio. "Middleburg and Upperville." *Maine Bugle*, October 1891, Call 6: 25–27.

Lloyd, William P. *History of the First Reg't Pennsylvania Reserve Cavalry.* Philadelphia: King and Baird, 1864.

Longacre, Edward G. *The Cavalry at Gettysburg: A Tactical Study of Mounted Operations during the Civil War's Pivotal Campaign 9 June–14 July 1863.* Rutherford NJ: Fairleigh Dickinson University Press, 1986.

Loveland, Frank. "A Valued Paper from Col. Loveland." *Report of the Forty-Seventh Annual Reunion, Sixth Ohio Veteran Volunteer Cavalry Association*, Warren OH, October 1912, 14–20.

Lowe, Percival G. *Five Years a Dragoon ('49–'54) and Other Adventures on the Great Plains.* Reprint, Norman: University of Oklahoma Press, 1965.

Mackall, Mary, Stevan Meserve, and Anne Mackall Sasscer, eds. *In the Shadow of the Enemy: The Civil War Journal of Ida Powell Dulany.* Reprint, Knoxville TN: University of Tennessee Press, 2010.

Maine Adjutant General. *Annual Report of the Adjutant-General of the State of Maine, 1863.* Augusta: Adjutant General's Office, 1863.

Marcot, Roy M. *Spencer Repeating Firearms.* Irvine CA: Northwood Heritage Press, 1983.

Marszalek, John F. *Commander of All Lincoln's Armies: A Life of General Henry W. Halleck.* Cambridge MA: Belknap Press of Harvard University Press, 2004.

Martin, Samuel J. *Kill-Cavalry: The Life of General Hugh Judson Kilpatrick.* Mechanicsburg PA: Stackpole Books, 2000.

McClellan, Henry B. *The Life and Campaigns of Major-General J. E. B. Stuart.* Reprint, Little Rock AR: Eagle Press of Little Rock, 1987.

McDonald, William N. *A History of the Laurel Brigade.* Reprint, Gaithersburg MD: Olde Soldier Books, 1987.

McGowen, Faison, and Pearl McGowen, eds. *Flashes of Duplin's History and Government.* Kenansville NC: Privately Printed, 1971.

McSwain, Eleanor D., ed. *Crumbling Defenses or Memoirs and Reminiscences of John Logan Black, Colonel C.S.A.* Macon GA: J. W. Burke, 1960.

Meade, George Gordon, ed. *The Life and Letters of George Gordon Meade.* 2 vols. Reprint, Baltimore MD: Butternut and Blue, 1994.

Merrill, Samuel H. *The Campaigns of the First Maine and First District of Columbia Cavalry.* Portland ME: B. Thursto, 1866.

Meyer, Henry C. *Civil War Experiences under Bayard, Gregg, Kilpatrick, Custer, Raulston, and Newberry 1862, 1863, 1864.* New York, NP, 1911.

Miller, Richard. "Brahmin Janissaries: John A. Andrew Mobilizes Massachusetts' Upper Class for the Civil War." *New England Quarterly* 75, no. 2 (June 2002): 204–34.

Miller, William J. *Decision at Tom's Brook: George Custer, Thomas Rosser, and the Joy of the Fight.* El Dorado CA: Savas Beatie, 2016. Accessed March 24, 2019. https://

decisionattomsbrook.com/2016/03/17/discoveries-among-the-dead-l-payne-the-patriot/.

———. "Discoveries among the Dead," March 3, 2016. https://decisionattomsbrook.com.

Mitchell, Adele H., ed. *The Letters of Major General James E. B. Stuart.* Fairfax VA: Stuart-Mosby Historical Society, 1990.

Mobley, Joe A. *James City: A Black Community in North Carolina 1863–1900.* Raleigh: North Carolina Division of Archives and History, 1981.

Mohr, James, ed. *The Cormany Diaries: A Northern Family in the Civil War.* Pittsburgh: University of Pittsburgh Press, 1982.

Moore, Frank, compiler. *Anecdotes, Poetry, and Incidents of the War: North and South, 1860–1865.* New York City: Arundel, 1882.

Moore, James. *Kilpatrick and Our Cavalry: Comprising a Sketch of the Life of General Kilpatrick.* New York: Hurst, 1865.

Mosby, John S. *Stuart's Cavalry in the Gettysburg Campaign.* Reprint, Gaithersburg MD: Olde Soldier Books, 1987.

Moyer, Henry P. *History of the Seventeenth Pennsylvania Volunteer Cavalry.* Lebanon PA: Sowers Printing, 1911.

Murphy, Daniel. *William Washington: American Light Dragoon.* Yardley PA: Westholme, 2014.

Murphy, Robert J. "'I Have No Faith in Foreigners': Pleasonton Clears the Way for His Boy Generals." *Gettysburg Magazine,* no. 45 (2011): 23–32.

Musick, Michael P. *6th Virginia Cavalry.* Lynchburg VA: H. E. Howard, 1990.

National Park Service. *The Civil War in Loudoun Valley: The Cavalry Battles of Aldie, Middleburg, and Upperville, June 1863.* Washington DC: NP, 2004.

Neese, George M. *Three Years in the Confederate Horse Artillery.* Reprint, Dayton OH: Morningside House, 1988.

Ness, George T., Jr. *The Regular Army on the Eve of the Civil War.* Baltimore: Toomey Press, 1990.

Nevins, Allan, ed. *A Diary of Battle: The Personal Journals of Colonel Charles S. Wainwright, 1861–1865.* Gettysburg PA: Stan Clark Military Books, n.d.

Nicholson, John Page, ed. *Pennsylvania at Gettysburg: Ceremonies at the Dedication of the Monuments.* Harrisburg PA: E. K. Meyers, State Printer, 1904.

Nolan, James D. "A Bold and Fearless Rider: The Life of Major General John Buford." MA thesis, St. John's University, New York, 1993.

Northumberland County Historical Society. "A Confederate Soldier Who Did Not Return." *Bulletin of the Northumberland County Historical Society,* no. 26 (1989): 39–41.

Norton, Henry. *Deeds of Daring or History of the Eighth N. Y. Volunteer Cavalry.* Norwich NY: Chenango Telegraph Printing House, 1889.

Nye, Wilbur S. "How Stuart Got Back across the Potomac." *Civil War Times Illustrated,* no. 4 (January 1966): 44–48.

O'Ferrall, Charles T. *Forty Years of Active Service.* New York: Neal, 1904.

O'Neill, Robert F. "Bravest of the Brave." *Small but Important Riots* (blog), February 10, 2016. https://smallbutimportantriots.com.

———. *The Cavalry Battles of Aldie, Middleburg and Upperville.* Lynchburg VA: H. E. Howard, 1993.

———. *Chasing Jeb Stuart and John Mosby: The Union Cavalry in Northern Virginia from Second Manassas to Gettysburg.* Jefferson NC: McFarland, 2012.

———. "Col. John Lemmon—A Colonel at War with His Men." *Small but Important Riots* (blog), September–November 2018, smallbutimportantriots.com

———. "William Parnell, a Forgotten Hero." *Small but Important Riots* (blog), August 15, 2016. https://smallbutimportantriots.com.

O'Neill, Robert F., and Robert Moran. "Turmoil in the 4th New York Volunteer Cavalry." *Small but Important Riots* (blog), April 18, 2021. https://smallbutimportantriots.com.

Opie, John N. *A Rebel Cavalryman with Lee Stuart and Jackson.* Reprint, Dayton OH: Morningside, 1997.

Parker, Francis J. *The Story of the Thirty-Second Regiment Massachusetts Infantry.* Boston: C. W. Calkins, 1880.

Pearson, Henry Greenleaf. *The Life of John A. Andrew, Governor of Massachusetts 1861–1865.* Vol. 1. Boston: Houghton, Mifflin, 1904.

Perry, Bliss. *Life and Letters of Henry Lee Higginson.* Boston: Atlantic Monthly Press, 1921.

Petruzzi, J. David. "The Fleeting Fame of Alfred Pleasonton." *America's Civil War,* March 2005, 22–28.

Phillips, Gervase. "Writing Horses into American Civil War History." *War in History,* no. 1 (April 2013): 160–81.

Pickerill, W. N. *History of the Third Indiana Cavalry.* Indianapolis IN: Aetna Printing, 1906.

Pleasonton, Alfred. "The Successes and Failures of Chancellorsville." In *Retreat from Gettysburg,* ed. Robert U. Johnson and Clarence C. Buel. Vol. 3 of *Battles and Leaders of the Civil War.* Reprint, New York: Castle Books, 1956: 172–82.

Poinsett, J. R. *Cavalry Tactics.* Washington DC: Government Printing Office, 1864.

Preston, Noble. *History of the Tenth Regiment of Cavalry New York State Volunteers.* New York: D. Appleton, 1892.

Price, George F. *Across the Continent with the Fifth Cavalry.* New York: D. Van Nostrand, 1883.

Pyne, Henry R. *Ride to War: The History of the First New Jersey Cavalry.* Edited by Earl Schenck Miers. New Brunswick NJ: Rutgers University Press, 1961.

Quaife, Milo M., ed. *From the Cannon's Mouth: The Civil War Letters of General Alpheus S. Williams.* Lincoln: University of Nebraska Press, 1995.

Randol, Alanson. "A Horse-Artilleryman's Diary." *Journal of the Military Service Institution,* no. 16 (December 1885): 418.

Ray, Fred. "Musketoons and Rifle-Muskets: What's in a Name?" May 18, 2020. Accessed May 23, 2020. http://www.brettschulte.net/CWBlog/2020/05/18/musketoons-and-rifle-muskets-whats-in-a-name/.

Rea, Lilian, ed. *War Record and Personal Experiences of Walter Raleigh Robbins, from April 22, 1861 to August 4, 1865.* Privately printed, 1923.

Reade, Frank Robertson, and Robert J. Trout, eds. *In the Saddle with Stuart: The Story of Frank Smith Robertson of Jeb Stuart's Staff.* Gettysburg PA: Thomas Publications, 1998.

Regimental Committee. *History of the Third Pennsylvania Cavalry.* Philadelphia: Franklin, 1905.

Report of the Forty-Seventh Annual Reunion of the Sixth Ohio Veteran Volunteer Cavalry Association. Warren: NP, 1912.

Reunions of the First Maine Cavalry, 1879–1880. Augusta ME, 1881.

Robertson, John, compiler. *Michigan in the Civil War.* Lansing MI: W. S. George, 1882.

Rodenbough, Theophilus F. *From Everglade to Canon with the Second United States Cavalry.* New York: D. Van Nostrand, 1875. Reprint, Norman: University of Oklahoma Press edition, 2000.

Rosser, Thomas. *The Cavalry, A.N.V. Address by Gen'l T. L. Rosser at the Seventh Annual Reunion of the Association of the Maryland Line.* Baltimore: Sun Book and Job Printing Office, 1889.

Ryan, Thomas J. *Spies, Scouts, and Secrets in the Gettysburg Campaign.* El Dorado Hills CA: Savas Beatie, 2015.

Saussy, G. N. "Campaigning with Stuart." *Watson's Magazine* 13, no. 2 (June 1911): 152–57.

———. "Upperville's Cavalry Battle." *Watson's Jeffersonian Magazine* 4 (April 1910): 332–336.

Scarlata, Paul. "Enfield P53/61 Musketoon." *Guns of the Old West,* Winter 2015.

Scheel, Eugene M. *Loudoun Discovered: Communities, Corners and Crossroads.* 5 vols. Leesburg VA: Friends of the Thomas Balch Library, 2002.

Scheibert, Justus. *Seven Months in the Rebel States during the North American War, 1863.* Edited by William S. Hoole. Tuscaloosa AL: Confederate, 1958.

Sears, Stephen W., ed. *The Civil War Papers of George B. McClellan: Selected Correspondence 1860–1865.* New York: Da Capo, 1992.

Shoemaker, John J. *Shoemaker's Battery, Stuart Horse Artillery.* Memphis TN: S. C. Toof, 1908.

Siliker, Ruth L., ed. *The Rebel Yell and Yankee Hurrah: The Civil War Journal of a Maine Volunteer.* Camden ME: Down East Books, 1985.

Slocum, Charles E. *The Life and Service of Major-General Henry Warner Slocum.* Toledo OH: Slocum, 1913.

Smith, John L., compiler. *History of the 118th Pennsylvania Volunteers, Corn Exchange Regiment.* Philadelphia: J. L. Smith, 1905.

Sparks, David S., ed. *Inside Lincoln's Army: The Diary of General Marsena Rudolph Patrick, Provost Marshal General, Army of the Potomac.* New York: Thomas Yoseloff, 1964.

Spear, Abbott, Andrea Hawkes, Marie McCosh, Craig Symonds, and Michael Alpert, eds. *The Civil War Recollections of General Ellis Spear.* Orono: University of Maine Press, 1997.

Staats, Richard J. *The History of the Sixth Ohio Volunteer Cavalry 1861–1865.* 2 vols. Westminster MD: Heritage Books, 2006.

Starr, Stephen Z. "The Inner Life of the First Vermont Volunteer Cavalry, 1861–1865." *Vermont History* 46 (Summer 1978): 157–74.

State of New York. *New York Monuments Commission for the Battlefields of Gettysburg and Chattanooga; Final Report on the Battle of Gettysburg.* 3 vols. Albany NY: J. B. Lyon, 1900.

Steffen, Randy. *The Horse Soldier 1776–1943.* 4 vols. Norman: University of Oklahoma Press, 1978.

Stiles, Kenneth L. *4th Virginia Cavalry.* Lynchburg: H. E. Howard, 1985.

Styple, William B., ed. *Generals in Bronze: Interviewing the Commanders of the Civil War.* Kearny NJ: Belle Grove, 2005.

———. *With a Flash of His Sword: The Writings of Major Holman S. Melcher, 20th Maine Infantry.* Kearny NJ: Belle Grove, 1994.

Survivor's Association. *History of the Corn Exchange Regiment, 118th Pennsylvania Volunteers.* Philadelphia: J. L. Smith, 1905.

Swain, Craig. "J. T. Edmundson." *To the Sound of Guns* (blog), November 11, 2015. Accessed February 2, 2019. https://markerhunter.wordpress.com.

Tasker, Albert. "A Yankee Cavalryman Gets 'Gobbled Up.'" *Civil War Times Illustrated* 62, (January 1968): 42–44.

Thomas, Emory M., ed. "'The Greatest Service I Rendered the State,' J. E. B. Stuart's Account of the Capture of John Brown." *Virginia Magazine of History and Biography* 94, no. 3 (July 1986): 345–57.

Thomason, John W., Jr. *JEB Stuart.* New York: Charles Scribner's Sons, 1930.

Tobie, Edward P. *History of the First Maine Cavalry, 1861–1865.* Reprint, Gaithersburg MD: Ron R. Van Sickle Military Books edition, 1987.

Townsend, George A. *Campaigns of a Non-Combatant and His Romaunt Abroad during the War.* New York: Blelock, 1866.

Trout, Robert J. *Galloping Thunder: The Stuart Horse Artillery Battalion.* Mechanicsburg PA: Stackpole Books, 2002.

———. *Memoirs of the Stuart Horse Artillery Battalion.* 2 vols. Knoxville: University of Tennessee Press, 2010.

Tuten, James. "A Remarkable Case: A Surgeon's Letter to the Huntington County Globe." *Pennsylvania Magazine of History and Biography* 135, no. 6 (October 2011): 558–60.

Urwin, Gregory J. W. *Custer Victorious: The Civil War Battles of General George Armstrong Custer.* Rutherford NJ: Fairleigh Dickinson University Press, 1983.

U.S. Congress. *Report of the Joint Committee on the Conduct of the War.* 9 vols. Reprint, Wilmington NC: Broadfoot, 1999.

U.S. Government Printing Office. *Medical and Surgical History of the Civil War.* 15 vols. Reprint, Wilmington NC: Broadfoot, 1990.

Venter, Bruce. *Kill Jeff Davis: The Union Raid on Richmond, 1864.* Norman: University of Oklahoma Press, 2016.

von Borcke, Heros. *Memoirs of the Confederate War for Independence.* Reprint, Gaithersburg MD: Butternut Press, 1985.

Wallace, Lee A., Jr. *A Guide to Virginia Military Organizations 1861–1865.* Lynchburg VA: H. E. Howard, 1986.

Warner, Ezra. *Generals in Blue: Lives of the Union Commanders.* Reprint, Baton Rouge: Louisiana State University Press, 1981.

———. *Generals in Gray: Lives of Confederate Commanders.* Reprint, Baton Rouge: Louisiana State University Press, 1981 ed.

Waugh, John C. *The Class of 1846, from West Point to Appomattox: Stonewall Jackson, George McClellan and Their Brothers.* New York: Grand Central, 1994.

Welsh, Jack D. *Medical Histories of Union Generals.* Kent OH: Kent State University Press, 1996.

Welton, J. Michael, ed. *"My Heart Is so Rebellious": The Caldwell Letters 1861–1865.* Warrenton VA: n.d.

Wert, Jeffry D. *Cavalryman of the Lost Cause: A Biography of J. E. B. Stuart.* New York: Simon and Schuster, 2008.

———. "Colonel Tom Munford—A Man of Achievement, His Unhonored Service." *Civil War Times Illustrated* 24 (June 1985): 28–34.

Whitman, William, and Charles True. *Maine in the War for the Union: A History of the Part Borne by Maine Troops in the Suppression of the American Rebellion.* Lewiston ME: Nelson Dingley Jr., 1865.

Williamson, James J. *Mosby's Rangers.* Reprint, Alexandria VA: Time-Life Books, 1982.

Wittenberg, Eric J. *The Union Cavalry Comes of Age: Hartwood Church to Brandy Station, 1863.* Washington DC: Brassey's, 2003.

INDEX